TOR DARKNET BUNDLE: MASTER THE ART OF INVISIBILITY

LANCE HENDERSON

COPYRIGHT

BURNERS & BLACK MARKETS

PREFACE

Hell hath no fury like a woman scorned.

Scorned might be the wrong word choice here, since it was I who invited the Homeland Security agents into my home.

"Come on in, the water's warm," I told them.

They strolled in like vampires. It felt a little queasy to walk behind them, like today was some kind of initiation day or something and I was the fresh white meat of the month. I also noticed one of them (the female) humming softly as she came in. Some death row harmonica tune as I recall. The one from Shawshank Redemption. Or was it The Green Mile?

To be honest neither resembled Mulder or Scully like I thought they would (nor had a gun that I could see), but it didn't really matter. Both agents sounded professional; suited up and as stone-faced as any statue on Easter Isle with little in the way of humor or human warmth that could be discerned. Automatons dressed to kill. In fact, the male agent looked every bit the consummate professional hitman Alberto the Shadow was in Scarface. You didn't turn your back on a guy like that.

Yet here I was contemplating asking them to leave after only inviting them in a nanosecond ago. Wasn't happening. Worse was the whiff of air my nostrils caught scent of as they passed me. It was the scent of something dead. Or maybe just the last guy that asked them to leave.

As I poured a drink I asked myself, were they real agents? I couldn't tell. I suppose I should have asked for ID but I was still feeling jet-lagged from the Rio trip. With two days to go before Mardi Gras, I'd raced home from the New Orleans airport to get some sleep so I could meet my brother to fast-paint an Endymion parade float at mom's house. Only this time I'd be late. Terribly late. Because vampires.

A fitting end I suppose, since my brother Stephen and I have PhDs in lateness. Like clockwork I had waited until the 11th hour to do what Mom tasked us with: paint the Endymion float fast and neat and all cool like something out of Willy Wonka. Only fast and *neat* where we were concerned was like asking the Marx brothers to do a rush job on a Mona Lisa forgery. I could paint well enough, but my brother, like Groucho, painted single-handedly with one hand holding a joint as the other brushed. Hustling was his specialty, not painting. He hustled everything. Even me.

He'd often give me a list of places where his friends lay in wait along Veterans Blvd near New Orleans, friends who dressed the part but none of whom were actually veterans. The mission? Bomb them with the best booty and beads when our float came around. Only knowing my brother like I do, he'd brag down at Igor's bar long and loud like some train in the night and take all the credit. I'd get nothing.

The man never gave credit for squat unless he was in trouble with the law. Even as far back as sixth grade, he'd scoff whenever I said to knock off the bar bragging in the school yard. It never helped. Sooner or later, I warned, a shark would come along and sink a mouthful of teeth into those lying teeth of his.

Then one scorcher of a day in August (middle school, as I recall), a thresher shark showed up when he caught the attention of the local police. It seemed one freckled boy told every other boy in the school yard that my brother had bragged he owned a shed containing every automatic weapon imaginable, even (I kid you not) a suitcase nuke straight out of Fallout. They all bought this lie, of course, only one of the ugly kids he'd teased had ratted him out. Shocker, right? Next thing you know our puritan principal summoned him and the cops and when the boys in blue arrived, they cuffed him like he'd pinched every girl's pink bum in the yard.

I sat there mumbling and trembling in Ms. Needles math class thinking I was next on the hit list. Had I overheard the words 'search warrant'? And that odd scent that one of the cops dragged with her. A dead animal? No not quite. It reeked of a dead human.

Truth be told I was more worried about my secret stash. They'd steal my porn stash and take Suzanne Somers away from me forever, I was sure of it. Asses would sting (mine) and if not by Dad than surely that sharkey cop with the razor-thin mustache whose last name sounded an awful lot like 'thresher'.

But my brother didn't rat. They suspended him and Dad hit the roof, but he didn't rat. Turned out that my father pulled some strings to keep him out of jail. The lucky loser.

Fast forward to now, in my living room, and that same shark cop from sixth grade eying me in perfect dark; her eyes filled with wet Texas crude looking to bury a dinosaur like me. She'd no doubt had eaten a few dinosaurs by now, slit a few throats on the way to the top, and now here she was staring me down like I was a fresh-born kitten meant for the Coyote grill. Come on in, the water's warm, I'd said. Stupid.

Speaking of, my brother was in trouble again. A deep sea of trouble.

It seemed that he had targeted hidden Tor sites scattered around the Darknet, playing his usual lame pranks, when in one instance he took it too far. The two agents came because, well, Stephen just didn't know when to leave on a high note. He had told two under-cover agents that he owned an underground storage bunker full of illegals that he sold off as sex slaves for a grand a pop. A side hustle, he called it. I knew this to be a prank, but they did not. How could they?

Only now the very shark I'd warned him about had come back to bite *me*. Oh irony. Teaching Tor when he didn't understand the risks posed by Google and all other social media tyrants was a colossal blunder of biblical proportions on my part. A terrible mistake and one I'd not likely recover from. It was like handing Frodo's Ring of Power to one of those guys down at the Bayou Swamp Tour that stick their heads into the mouths of crocs for a few dollars more. A lot of fat good it'd do.

Oh and he had used a cell phone. Brilliant, right?

It hadn't been hard to track the goober down. Google had helped them connect-the-dots. Now they were here for a side of beef off my backside, the only question being which side.

So I escorted the agents into my kitchen expecting to be butchered by my own knives. I politely I offered them a beer or a Coke or a steak. Hell even a three month old Twinkie, which they declined. I huffed and then straddled a bar stool and invited them to do the same. Once again they declined. They could not be bought, bribed or bamboozled for any price.

"This won't take long," the male agent said. It's what all agents said, everywhere. Even the census taker has said the same a year prior and as I recall it'd taken forever and a day. The next words he said cut like dry ice.

"We take every threat to this nation seriously, Lance. Your brother has made some serious threats," said the taller agent as he crossed his bulky arms. "He's in our custody now but whether he stays there depends on you. In this very instant."

Custody? I didn't believe him. "Do tell," I said as I folded my skinny arms.

"We'd like to see your phone."

My heart stopped as all color drained from my face, all monochrome.

"Ahem. Right now," added the female agent. It was then that I asked for ID. They showed it but it was too late. They were in like Flynn.

"Prostitution rings carry a hefty sentence as does issuing threats to federal law enforcement officers," the agent began to say, "... and even dumping manure on our department's front lawn."

He glanced around the kitchen, running his hand along the granite countertop.

"Asset forfeiture is a big industry these days." He knocked on granite.

No shit, I thought. Asset forfeiture, courtesy of the ATF and DEA, had been a very profitable industry for eons and all the more for the US government. I'd known guys with small basement grow-ops that lost their homes and land to the Feds both in Canada and the States. I took nothing for granted where those guys were concerned.

But I knew not to talk without a lawyer present... except I'd already invited them in and like true vampires it became apparent that they weren't keen on leaving without the item they came for. Why oh why me. With my voice quaking I let out a little protest that ended up sounding more like a mew instead of a roar. A cat going to the vet.

"I'm not giving you my phone," I squeaked. "I don't care what kooky story my idiot brother told you."

"Excuse me?" the lady asked. She giggled at this, a giggle that sounded like a cat chewing up a squishy mouse or toothpaste squeezed out of a tube. "You cannot win against the federal government. Hand it over."

"Hand what over?"

"THE PHONE."

" Oh, that. Err... No."

"No? Why not?" she asked.

I stabbed a finger at her just as I raised my voice. "Either make an arrest or leave! I'll not be bullied into submission without a warrant by a couple of federal thugs named Frick and Frack. My phone is encrypted so it'll do you no good anyway. But I've got a landline here and my lawyer on retainer so let me just call him up and get a recording going."

They both looked at each other. "We'll be back," the man said. As they closed the door I heard the lock slide into place like a jail cell slamming home. My cell phone was about to become my jail cell. Had I hammered the last nail into my own coffin?

Furiously I sped over to my brother's house, so fast I nearly hit a dog peeing on a fire hydrant and didn't stop to look back. I was livid. *Beyond* livid. I had no clue if Agent Frick would be back, warrant in one hand and a noose in the other, but I'd be damned if I was going to swing from the nearest tree without knowing what stupid thing my brother'd done to bring on this level of heat.

I found him parked outside his spooky old house in that fire-engine red truck I'd hated for years, AC-DC blaring Back in Black. He was twirling his pornstache, no worry in the world about his fate or mine. Typical. I wanted to smack him. Hard. Right upside his head the way Rick James did to a few tag-a-longs back in the 80s. But I stopped when I saw Facebook front and center. Not only *that* abomination but Twitter, Google Plus, Skype, Viber and Whatsapp, with Tor running in the background.

Tor! Sweet lawd almighty.

I grit my teeth and shouted "DUMMY!" into his ear and watched as his phone fell into his Bud Light glass under the hot pink fuzzy dice. He cursed me out.

"Azzzzhole," he yelled. He wiped it off, waterproof. Gangly and unshaven, he talked like that skinny gyro captain loser from Road Warrior who believed in the concept of shared wealth - as long as it belonged to someone else and was his for the taking.

"Couple of goons hassled me today," he mumbled. "Same here... *brother*." I replied. "Somethin' about you making threats? And... a manure dump on a federal building's front lawn?"

After a long sigh, a belch and a few coarse threats I finally dragged the intel out of him. How he'd not only issued threats over

Tor but that he'd put in an order for a dump truck to pile a ton of manure on the FBI and Homeland Security's front lawn using a credit card over Tor. *My* credit card. He pulled it from his wallet and frisbeed it into my face with the stupidest comment I'd ever heard.

"Tor didn't work with your card. You ain't paid up or somethin'?"

It was here that I went dark on him.

I pulled the knuckle-dragger out and inside the house kicking and screaming before letting loose with every curse I knew. He flailed like the swordfish we caught in the Gulf of Mexico, fins everywhere like a crazy person, swinging and sweating and stabbing.

When we finally simmered down I noticed the state of his living room. The place was ransacked more than usual. Beer cans piled high with a vacant space where the PC had been lie visible. Three guesses as to who took it. The FBI had come and let it slide but apparently they had friends in Homeland who needed a fresh piece of meat. Two slabs actually, order up.

When I pressed him on it he replied that Homeland carted it away while powered on using a portable power source of some kind. I knew about such things, but did he? Nope. This is the Gyro Captain guy. The fool who liked to say 'Don't play me the fool!' guy.

He tried to get up so I shoved him back down and yelled, "You stay in that spot and don't you move a muscle until I'm finished!"

I threw everything I'd said the week prior into his face again (opsec stuff mostly), and swore I'd take mom's house back in a New York minute if he didn't listen this time. It wasn't enough that his ass and ego stung. He needed a lobotomy.

"You're good at that nekkid Tor stuff. I ain't! 'Sides, you talk too fast how in hell can I keep up with that technical mojo?"

He was right. I always talked too fast even back in sixth grade and on a few sweaty occasions I could swear that I could literally see my words flying over and around his uncombed head; like if you shined a flashlight through those ears you'd see his eyes flash. So I went slow. Turtle slow. Talking with my hands like some Italian piano player before a grand performance.

"Look," I began. "If you're going to play the Riddler and prank alphabet agencies then the absolute least you can do is to muck it all up in your own name and do so with some residue of competence. It's embarrassing when my name comes into it. Why'd you use my card for it? Why bring me into it at all?"

Nothing but deadbeat excuses came back.

My voice went as low and deadly serious as a neurosurgeon when discussing a terminal patient. I wanted to take a red hot searing iron of opsec rules to his butt cheeks but knowing him he'd forget they were there. So instead I decided what he needed was a foundation of the basics, the why, the wherewithal, the way, the whole enchilada when it came to cell phones and anonymity. Why we do *this* instead of *that* and what happens if we *don't*.

"Why?" he'd ask.

"Because guys who never sweat the small stuff as long as the power button is greenlit get burned, that's why."

Then along comes some taffer with a badge and a gruff voice who hits him with one small threat and then another and another, and all in a friendly 'knock and talk' and at that point he might as well slap the cuffs on himself. He doesn't see the overall context, the trap being set, and ends up like Gulliver with the Lilliputians, pinned to the ground by a million tiny threads he can't even see.

I talked about the giants: Google. Twitter. Facebook. How the lying scumbags were little more than modern-day witch hunters who cooperated with cops to enforce a gazillion laws no one cared about but made them millions every year.

I droned on about encryption, explaining how it always worked it's wonders if it was automatic and running under the hood. I told him he had lazy man's opsec, a clown's, and that sooner or later someone would throw a grenade into that clown's wardrobe and it'd make all the papers with nice colorful photos of his private stash all laid bare. I told him of the types of encryption most used, HTTPS in the browser and cell to tower connections for his cellular calls, that they performed so well because he was *unaware of their presence.*

"Encrypt everything," I repeated. I hammered this over and over, especially on cell phones no matter if he had something to hide or not. "It should be there and working its magic under the hood without you having to hit the ON switch."

"Why?" he asked.

"Because if you're only going to flip that encryption switch when and only when you need to secure your data, you relay that data's significance as though you'd pulled a fire alarm."

We talked about Tor and it's brother Freenet and how both are used by Chinese dissidents but that since *every* Chinese dissident uses those apps that this has caused problems for anyone wanting real anonymity. If its only used for committing dissident-like things then China's ruling elite class can cherry-pick anyone off one by one and all by that one lone homing signal. The same that the FBI had done (with a little help from my credit card).

Then I said that the reverse is equally true.

"If everybody employs encryption *everywhere*, then instead of it being a signal to the fire department to come put out a fire, it becomes impossible to tell who is using it to chat about Leonardo DeCaprio's latest round of clubgirls from someone intent on sparking a revolution. Use encryption for every little thing you do and you'll save lives on the other side of the planet without even knowing it."

He shot me a dumbfounded look like encryption had nothing to do with cell phones or Tor.

"If you'd bothered to pay attention in sixth grade, you'd have learned all about state-sanctioned liars like the Gestapo in Nazi Germany and KGB in Soviet Russia, enough to see through that agent's lies." I pointed to the door. "Like Agent Frick. Didn't her name seem familiar to you?"

"You shut your mouth!" he snapped. "They had a no-knock warrant what was I supposed to do, tell em' to get lost?"

"You just answered your own question."

"Huh?"

"You shut your mouth. You said it brother. You don't say squat without an attorney."

He thought on this for a long while before I continued.

"Something else, too. You also failed on account of having an unencrypted phone and PC. If the encrypted data is in *your* hands and not *theirs* you're in less danger of being bullied around. You have more leeway. Do China dissidents? In China once they *take away* encryption and guns, they'll seize your property rights, birth rights, your progeny and what follows after that is a bloody mutiny or complete slavery where all legal rights are changed so that you cannot resist. You cannot fight back."

"And after that?" he asked.

"Who knows. The Stalinist regime may enact a murder campaign to eliminate anyone perceived as an enemy of the state. That's anyone with a gun or encrypted files. You saw what happened to all those screaming Muslims over there in Beijing a few years back. They rounded up all those fools and shot them at dawn and didn't look back."

"Probably didn't wait till dawn I reckon," he said. "They ain't used encryption though is what I heard."

I smiled. "Might not have helped anyway. But thank God for the 5th amendment in the United States."

A long silence. I needed one more example. Something modern.

"Look at Apple and the FBI. The Feds wanted to set a precedent in breaking that terrorist's phone."

"Precedent? Why's that?" he asked.

"Take any random shooter's phone. The FBI already has the chat logs, flash drives, and iCloud data from them. They just make those statements to get public support for backdoors since there's nothing the data on the iPhone can tell them that they don't know already."

"But if that happens..."

"Everyone's screwed a hundred ways from Sunday. Apple gave the them access to everything that exists and still gave them additional forensic advice on top of that. That fact alone proved it was a backdoor fishing expedition."

"Yeah. Yeah yer right I figger."

"And it's impossible for a backdoor to target just one phone. Any new backdoor will target everyone's phone, every class, at a minimum, such as one iPhone 5c affecting all the others. The FBI wants Apple to code in a backdoor that's signed by Apple without messing up the decryption keys. Do that and it would almost certainly escalate international tensions about European privacy too, not just the US."

He nodded slowly.

"They'd blot out any hope of Safe Harbor for good by proving that safe harbor is anything but 'safe'."

Underneath his long-sleeved shirt I could see he was wearing a that hideous Lord of the Rings tee, still grey and ragged and reeking of the same cheap Bud Light Lime he'd swigged on opening night. At the tip I could see it was either Gandalf or Saruman peeking over the mountaintops. I couldn't tell which.

"This isn't Saruman tinkering around. This is global Sauron, creating his Ring."

"But I'm just *one* guy. *One* peon."

"You only need *one* guy, *one* peon."

I pointed out the window, up at the clouds. "See that? Picture yourself way up there in a grand hall with your great-grandfather and several generations of your lineage going back eons when they're all telling their brave tales. Imagine telling them with a straight face that you left it up to some other peon because you weren't up to learning how to evade not only Google but the NSA and the FBI because it's easier to just focus on you and your late nights blowing money on anti-freeze daiquiris and Angry Birds or Facebook updates and pranking the FBI building with a truckload of bullshit."

"Now imagine them shaking their heads in disgust at this over-grown kid too proud to build out a fortress of doom - a guy whose only concerns were for his own hide and to hell with what his forefathers fought for. They'd view you as lacking courage and any sense of ethics. They'd look upon you as a lesser human being. A joke to humanity. A sheep. Can you imagine Frodo doing that to Elrond, Gandalf, Legolas and the rest of the crew and giving them a three-fingered salute as he slid that ring down his finger and snuck off into the night?

"Hale no."

"Me neither. When push comes to shove it's our *nonactions* and not our actions that bury us. We dig our own graves far too often enough, brother, so let's not pay others to do it while we're still breathing. In the meantime I'll show you how to smooth that ring down your finger so you can give whoever *else* wants to spy on you a nice three-fingered salute."

I looked over and noticed a few synapses misfiring. But a little confusion wasn't the end of the world. So I showed him something from his favorite social media outlet. Youtube. The very same he'd used with Tor, something even he could see the wisdom of employing. It was a classroom lecture called 'Don't Talk to Cops'. Nothing to do with cell phones, mind you, but everything to do (or not to do) when a couple of G-Men show up at your house making unruly demands.

The day after that, I beat him to death with every opsec trick I knew on how to truly be anonymous on a smartphone, be it Android, Blackberry, iPhone... anywhere, at any time.

And what I showed him that day is what I'm about to show you. Right now.

CELL OPSEC AND THE POWERS THAT BE

"No one cared who I was until I put on the mask."
- Bane, The Dark Knight Rises

Why The Government Hates Anonymity

Most governments hate anonymity. They hate encryption too, but mostly anonymity since it covers a much broader range of the mutiny they fear. Every time someone learns how to communicate *anonymously*, that iron death-grip that they hold on a person's life loosens like you wouldn't believe. The media paints it a different color, of course. They say that it's *anonymity* that drives all the internet's ills.

You've heard it all before. Sexual harassment. Bullying. Date rape. Hackers. Identity thieves. Flying purple monkeys. And that if only we give the powers that be more reach or a longer vine into our private lives, then every bully and ogre'll burst into pillars of salt (instantly!) while the world trips right into a land of rainbows, unicorns and yellow submarines with a lofty lolling Ringo Starr leading the charge.

You already know it to be fake, of course. As fake as Data's artificial thumb.

But, I'll let you in on a secret not many know. And that is this. Anonymity encourages objectivity. Seriously, it does. It forces you to judge a person by the merits of their words alone.

Think about it.

How many times have you heard an interview of some new jazz artist or guitarist whose Randy Rhoads-like riffs made your hour long commute more bearable, but somehow lacked that one ingredient that'd make them perfect in your mind's eye? You find yourself never fully satisfied with what you know of him, so you dig deeper. And deeper.

It's About Control

You want to know every dirty little detail of his life, then weigh those details against his opinion. Little details like

- His politics.
- His religion.
- His favorite foods.
- Which websites he likes and which he hates.

What movies he watches. What car he drives. What sexual preference he likes. You could go on forever nitpicking the poor guy.

And it's dirty ethics to judge a person's merit in this way. But that's the way the global elite do it, every day, every hour. They prefer you make snap judgments because it reveals a ton of things about you as well. Things that are all easily trackable.

Let's face it.

It's so much easier to blow someone's idea off if they happen to be favoring the other guy running for President rather than judge a person by what is said. So they focus on the man's upbringing. Or race. Or gender. Or which side their ancestors fought on during the Civil War. You can get to a point where you run out of ad hominem's to hurl.

It's About Power

Dangerous ideas are good for anonymity. Try saying something outrageous on a political forum during an election year, but under a pseudonym. Use a cell phone without the aid of Tor. Note the hesitation you feel when you think of writing under your real name and saying something only someone like Smaug from the Hobbit would have the red-hot balls to say. That's the power I'm talking about. Anonymity grants that to you. It allows you to share controversial thoughts without fear of your house being firebombed with Molotov cocktails filled with flaming manure. And there's a few more perks I'll add to the bonfire.

- Anonymity prevents you from getting fired for disagreeing.
- It prevents Google from getting your private data and selling it.
- It prevents you from being the target of stalkers, hitmen, and even an angry former lover intent on showing the world the raging alcoholic she lived with some 17 years ago - never mind that you've given up booze for ten years straight, all because she doesn't like the guy you're campaigning for (yes, yours truly).

The reason why people are opposed to anonymity is that they want to bully, harass and oppress people they disagree with. It's because it's always easier to discredit the man than his ideas. When you get right down to it, total 100% honesty can only be accomplished anonymously.

"Well," you start to say. "You don't need security if you aren't doing something illegal."

But that's how they want you to think.

It's like saying you may as well not lock your door unless you're a thief. Same thing. We all have to take action to protect our families and assets from those who steal, harm or burn. It's risk versus payoff, and where your freedom and peace of mind is concerned, the payoff is *always* worth it.

Imagine that you live in the Ninth Ward in New Orleans, hurricane season. A city with thousands of law abiding citizens (and maybe 10,000 criminals). You install a good lock on your front door because it's wise to do so. Likewise, you should install one on whatever portal you use to connect to the Internet. In most people's case, this means their cell phone.

That brings up the dirty word called encryption. That is, encrypting your connection. All connections, but cell phones especially. Most people shy away from this because they think they need to be some kind of super-hacker or that real hackers only target celebrities like Jennifer Lawrence.

For example, if Facebook forgets to encrypt your data, any governmental agency can use this data to corral dissidents like you and I and those who'd make bitter enemies in the event of a revolution - all into a nice little easy-to-read Matrix-green display for a round-up when the proverbial crap hits the fan. This isn't all. Questions like "Who was your best friend in high school?" can lead to other accounts being compromised.

It's the same whenever I have to shred sensitive documents. Taxes, transcripts, copies of old love letters, copies of passports. I can say 'screw it' and shred only a few things since I hate sorting them all. But all it takes for my security model to collapse is one broken link in the chain. Much less headaches to shred EVERY sensitive document and gain peace of mind over having to sort each and every one of them.

Therefore it's best to learn how to encrypt everything from the beginning instead of trying to cherry pick which is the 'best' document to be encrypted. You avoid not only government agencies like the IRS and DEA but also stalkers, vindictive ex-spouses and former business partners. It's much easier to lose a fully encrypted device than one with only a few encrypted folders. Encryption is not just about preventing eavesdroppers from reading data. It also prevents them from changing it.

ANONYMITY AND PRIVACY

Anonymity:

Noun an·o·nym·i·ty \ a-nə- ni-mə-tē\: the quality or state of being unknown to most people : the quality or state of being anonymous.

Good ol' Webster, who never fails to give us a watered down definition on how to not do something of paramount importance. The word itself comes from Greek and means 'without a name', but that doesn't really tell us how to be invisible. Two points to make on this.

First, if we're talking about *true anonymity*, the kind where you're really off the grid and can stay off the radar even if a Delta Force team is sent in to capture you, then you're not only nameless but *traceless*. This book will be of little use to you because you're a Houdini already and Houdinis rarely like to have helpers. They prefer going it alone. It's the same if you're a famous old timer with old money, celebrity status or fame who can buy your way out of the country without a passport.

But traceless anonymity - which many believe an impossibility on cell phones - gets harder to maintain just as a boat's navigation wheel becomes harder to control in a thunderstorm. One jab in the right place will sink a boat just as surely as if Zeus himself lit one up in her backside and it won't matter how much you spent on polishing her tushy. The same happened to me when Hurricane Katrina slammed home in 2005.

Katrina

A Category-5 hurricane, also known as the 'finger of God', came pretty close to sending me and my frizzy cat up to the pearly gates on a lightning bolt.

The wind barely took off a few shingles at first. No big deal I thought. It happens in most heavy storms after all. Then the kitchen window shattered. Then another. And another. Then the darkness came, only before I could panic I heard a propane tank blow up in the garage.

BOOM.

I know what you're thinking. Propane tanks don't just explode or implode or rupture or come apart on their own. In fact, an exploding propane tank is a rarity and doesn't happen nearly as often as the zombie movies portray. Only this one did because in a Cat-5 hurricane, anything's possible.

Truth be told, I didn't care about the tank. I was more worried about the darkness. That darkness was so thick you could feel it crawl onto your skin like some tar-covered gelatinous monster straight out of The Thing. I looked out onto the street and I remember thinking a lot of fat good anonymity did in this situation. I couldn't see or hear squat but I could worry. Oh yes, on that I was an ace, the top of the class. No question.

I tried to calm myself but it only got worse as I couldn't remember where I'd put the candles the last time this happened. I did know broken windows were replaceable though. They were, right? Yes, of course. Besides, how many times had the electricity gone out when it rained? Every afternoon if you lived in New Orleans and it seemed to happen all the time no matter Mardi Gras or Jazzfest or how many crocs swam down the street when the sewers clogged up. You could set your watch by it.

Soon I had two feet of water in my living room and Fritz the cat was looking pretty pathetic, like a wet hamster who'd stuck it's paw into an electrical socket. Panicked, the meows began to sound like those wailing police sirens on CSI. I couldn't understand a thing and to be honest he sounded a lot like Charlie Brown's teacher after a smoke and a stroke. He wanted out as did I.

I looked out to see the marina sailboats bobbing like bathtub ducks when the howling wind began to whistle and whirl through every room in the house, with a couple of my favorite anonymity books floating out the front door. Bad luck or poetic justice?

"Screw these shenanigans!" I said. Who'd ever gamble that this storm was the whisk-you-off-to-Oz variety? Not me. And not the cat as far as I could tell. Only a moment later, it got worse. A lot worse.

The storm began to blow in a lot of small objects from the street up and over the gutter. Pine cones. Coke cans. A Mardi Gras necklace that'd been stuck on the telephone wire for ages. Stripper panties. A nuke-green Hand Grenade drink container from Tropical Isle, New Orleans most powerful drink which admittedly was pretty tasty though it looked like an alien sex toy. At any rate I was in for some serious wind-based PTSD.

And with so many holes in my home, something struck me. I realized that any passerby could see inside and get a glimpse of my goods. All of em. I was unarmed and, God help me, without a Rottweiler to fend off any looters. Dead man walking. The looters I'd scared off during the previous flood might return for seconds if the storm got bad enough, and this time I was sure it would. Fritz and I were sitting ducks so I grabbed him in all his wet tuxedo fur and jumped into my fire-engine-red truck and headed off to the Northshore an hour away. The cat was now down to 3 lives.

First Point:

The first point is that one weak point can kill any security perimeter you thought you'd set up just as surely as my own broken windows killed mine. Maybe it was bad electrical lines. Loose ones. One lightning strike ended it. Boom and done.

With only one window gone a vagrant (or varmint or mutant) might've peeked inside for shelter and quickly deduced from the street garbage that it was an abandoned house. With <u>every</u> window gone, that same bum doesn't have to peek inside. He can see from the street what I've got. No guns? No dogs? Nothing? Oh but he sees the display case with a lot of shiny objects inside that he can pawn.

Why, even a brass lantern that'd fetch a few coins. Later I'd return to see a floating corpse, one straight out of The Walking Dead, floating near my house. I never quite recovered from that grisly sight.

In any case, I knew I couldn't sleep there since it'd be like using multiple layers of condoms given by an ex-stalker. Each one with small holes. What did help me was having walkie-talkies at my disposal. Not Tor.

And not Skype or Google Chat or any other corporate solution, where the entirety of my conversations gets sold on a silver platter to the highest bidder. Those guys have only their own interests in mind, none of which involve my safety. They care up to the point when they can make truckloads of cash. That and the act of filing away those conversations into stealthy databases and mined for future patterns and trends. Trends on me, my lover and dog and cat.

So you don't owe Microsoft or Google or Apple anything. But it's in your best interest to learn how to live without them, for when they day of reckoning (perhaps by a lightning strike) finally comes, it'll come like a thief in the night.

<u>Second Point:</u>

You're a one man show. You and you alone are responsible for whatever outcome you find yourself in. Luck favors the prepared and you'll survive a storm far and away better if you prepare beforehand. Don't be the guy who thinks that good opsec involves bubble-gumming his 3.5 floppies to the duct work behind the vents in his room.

<u>Third</u>: Absolutes where good security is concerned don't exist.

It's impossible to achieve 100% anonymity just as it's impossible to get 100% hack-proof data centers or 100% non-casualty rates on the battlefield no matter how good your opsec.

There's always a way in. There's always a leak, somewhere, waiting for a couple of fishermen to discover. A good security planner will weigh risk and apply his resources accordingly but good anonymity by way of phones, *especially cell phones*, comes down to who is trying to be anonymous from what and for how long. Disappearing from Google is not the same as disappearing from the NSA.

Take Tor, for instance. Tor is far easier to maintain anonymity on a laptop or PC using Linux than it ever will on Android. It's a nice enough tool but there are many apps that bleed your IP. Apps like those dealing with torrents.

If you're planning on using Tor on your phone to download torrents, stop reading. Return this book for a full refund. Other than clogging up the Tor network and making the Tor experience a rotten apple for other users, it is hell on anonymity services since it routes your REAL IP ADDRESS to destinations unknown. It does so anonymously of course, in the same way an envelope may be delivered by anonymous couriers. But with your real name and phone number on the inside of that envelope, well what's the point?

The first basic tactic is to change IP addresses, and do so frequently. Depending on the tool you use, most IP capable devices have the ability to set their own IP address. This tactic does come with a penalty though, because the frequent changing of IP addresses is highly anomalous. Depending on the internet service you're using at the time, it may be noted faster than you think. And if you're using Skype, well if they wanted to they could easily stream your voice to two locations at once, and there's nothing you can do to prevent that.

As well, any site that allows anonymous (or at least, accountless) posting can pretty much only block visitors by IPs. Then some of those people who got blocked are going to find a way to mask their IP (proxies, Tor, etc.) and get those IPs blocked too. Eventually you'll learn as I did that the problem isn't the websites, it's the jackasses that got them blocked. Your milage may vary. ·

The second basic tactic is to spoof and twin an IP address. With the first method you are using IP addresses that are valid for your local node, but are currently unused. For a 'spoof and twin' you want to use an IP address that another node is currently using. This method only works when your network adapter can be put into promiscuous mode and read traffic destined for other IP addresses. It requires that your device time transmission so as not to interfere with the target device, and that it continue reading open traffic until the target device receives a reply from whatever server you sent to.

Even if I provide you with the best available anonymity methods, if you are doing something that would attract the attention of law enforcement, those methods will only delay your eventual de-anonimization. Anyone with the capability of enlisting the help of large national or international telecommunication companies will find you in hours. That said, I will show you ways you could (in theory, say) prevent this event from happening. Read on.

8 DEADLY MYTHS OF CELL PHONES

We need to dispel a few myths before you learn how to go off the grid Michael Weston style. The first one is that smartphones are better at hiding you because of all the stealth apps available. It just isn't true.

Myth 1.) <u>Smartphones are better than older 'dummy' phones.</u>

Smarter, yes but better at hiding you? A very loud no with arms waving wildly from the rooftop. Consider for a moment why Russia decided to revert to typewriters after the NSA scandal broke over the German chancellor, Angela Merkel, found out that the NSA had been listening in on her calls for years. If you think it'd be much harder for any bureaucrat to spy on you if you reverted to 'the old methods', you'd be right.

Flip 'dummy' phones are superior to smartphones for good operational security, period. For any kind. They don't like to 'phone home' for one thing, and the less apps they support, the tighter your security. The reason for this is that most hacks and exploits target the most commonly used operating systems, like Windows and Android. And the 'superhackers' at the NSA love it when you use two dozen apps that you know little about. Take a hint from the Russians.

Myth 2.) <u>Home is safe as long as you're using Tor.</u>

Wrong again, a thousand times wrong. Home is a radioactive minefield as far as anonymity is concerned. Imagine yourself trying to handle a barrel of green radioactive goo without a protective suit. It's dangerously gooey stuff. Though I'll grant you'd survive it maybe long enough to call up HQ and tell them you botched the mission. Keep your phone somewhere distant even if all you want is to keep the wife out of your business. No need to leave a loaded gun around.

Myth 3.) <u>It doesn't matter where you activate your phone.</u>

Whenever I activate a phone, the opening scene from my favorite film, 'The Abyss', rolls in my head like an old film projector full of nostalgia and greasy engineers. One scene still haunts me to this day years after seeing it. It's that horrific opening scene where an underwater alien ship speeds too close to The Montana, a U.S. Navy nuclear-tipped submarine operating deep in the Cayman Trough in the Caribbean Sea.

The sleek, alien thing glides along at a whopping 130 knots. I still remember the Captain's words.

'Nothin' goes 130 knots!' he yells just as the power goes out.

The velocity of the alien ship knocks out almost every navigational instrument on the sub, sonar included. A few nail-biting seconds go by and when the power returns, the sub smashes nose first into a cliff and before anyone can breathe, the whole ship dives to the bottom of the ocean floor. But not before an officer launches the sub's emergency beacon.

That beacon breaches the surface in a flurry of little beeps and pulsing red light in the thick of midnight as ten foot waves crash all around. Picture a tiny red blip on a ten foot whitecap going Beep. Beep. BEEP. It's scary to think that the Navy found them. But find them they did.

It's not all that different when you activate your phone in any random place, where the **activation** itself will send such a signal to multiple parties interested in making your life, well, not very private at all. Maybe not *initially* mind you. It's the slow boiling frog scenario for most. First they'll want to know things like

- Where you live.
- Which sites you visit.
- What keywords you're punching into Google
- Where you're using your Mastercard.
- And who's related to you on all the social media sites.

All of this is tracked very quickly unless you've taken action beforehand to limit who gets this 'emergency beacon'. So how do we get around it? There's a few no so obvious ways.

One poor man's solution is to pay some starving English major at the local college ten bucks to activate it for you at a crowded college library you'll likely never visit. Be polite of course, but know that this fellow mustn't have any hard data on you except for any fake data you provide. If he starts asking questions, find some other urchin who isn't so nosy. Also know that this isn't the ideal solution. It just sets the stage for a very long process of *fogging up the trail*.

Myth 4.) <u>Untraceable Burners Can't Be Bought Online (at least not anonymously)</u>

This one is false as well. The problem with buying things on the Deep Web isn't that doing so requires you to be incognito. It's doing so without getting a lemon. You can in fact buy burners on the Deep Web (more on this later). For now know that one option is to use the Tor Browser Bundle to purchase anonymous burners, though like everything else on the deep web such as drugs, iPhones, Cuban cigars, you may be better off using *offline* proxies to purchase anything electronic. Chinese counterfeiting is popular on Darknet sites as you'll soon see. They fool enough buyers to leave glowing reviews at first, so it's buyer beware most of the time. That said, you can just as easily find a diamond in the rough offline.

Myth 5.) <u>Using Cash to Purchase Burners at Retail Stores is Always Anonymous.</u>

Little mom and pop stores are one thing, but big retail stores are truly privacy-hating places, especially where the Big Box Corporation has run off all the little shops in town. Those little shops made great places to forge alliances. That said, if you bought a burner from a big box store you should wait a month before you activate it. When I worked in security we'd rotate the footage daily, but did no firm deletions until 30 to 45 days out. You also must not be seen talking on-campus with that college English major we discussed. Again this depends on the level of opsec you require, but this is at a most basic, elementary level. We'll get more advanced as we go along.

Myth 6.) <u>No One Cares About Your Contact List</u>

Two things to say. The first is that contacts are *dangerous*. They create a pattern that, when lit up on a giant NSA screen, is like lighting a stick of dynamite with you being on the end of that stick. Boom again.

Much like a 'hidden' partition on a hard drive that stores two operating systems (one real and one fake a' la Veracrypt), you want to set up false leads to make it look like you have contacts where none exist. This fogs up your trail. One burner must not have the same contacts as the next. Any contacts provide less risk on paper than in a phone list since most SIM data will often give you away.

The second thing involves triangulation and pattern matching. Intelligence agencies favor "mirroring" devices over all others because of unique identifiers involved. Over time you can give yourself away by repeatedly using the same pattern, such as this:

House ---> Subway ---> Verizon (or your usual workplace) ---> Girlfriend's House ---> Home Again

Taking this route over and over establishes a mobility pattern. If anyone of importance comes looking for you, they'll find you whether you use a burner phone or not. The way to prevent this is to know your surroundings. Conversations are almost always the same length of time. That is, when talking with the same people in the same place.

Think about it. Your mother calls you on days when she doesn't work or when the hubby is at work, usually for the same 45 minute stretch. Your best friend John, probably 15-20 minutes since there's less emotional rambling. Men tend to not beat around the bush when talking other men, but over a month's time this creates a pattern of recognition if paired with other calls you make. All it takes is three or so matching patterns and it's game over.

Myth 7.) No One Cares About Broken Phones in Alleyways

Unless you want to go interrogating every bum from your home to the city limits, never throw out your phone 'as is', and especially not anywhere near your home. They should be securely wiped and then broken down piece by piece as though it were some ancient arti-fact belonging to some undead wizard.

Myth 8.) You're Anonymous on any Wireless Network (as long as you don't do anything stupid)

This is the most deadly myth. It has to do with using WiFi networks *securely*, and you wouldn't believe how many high school geeks think they're masters at Tor and hacking only to find the police show up because they threatened the wrong person online from the wrong dorm. On more than a few security sites, I see apps like Macspoofer and the like being recommended. Using any of these wonder-apps may prove detrimental to your freedom.

If your MAC address is in a constant state of identity crisis (or, always changing), you're narrowing the search parameters available to any adversary who wants to find you. For a group it draws massive unwanted attention. How? Because the access point is connected to multiple MAC numbers over a short period of time. It looks suspi-cious. Any administrator worth his salt will look into it. Better to look like everyone else rather than paint yourself black when surrounded by white sheep.

Mobile anonymity is difficult, frustrating, bothersome and generally a pain in the neck. Harder still is severing the link to your everyday life because depending on technology to do it all for you is a fool's game. A dead end. You need a good security mindset, diligence and the stamina to develop a *mental trigger* to predict accidents before they happen. We've all heard of what happens when a loaded gun is left on a table within arm's reach of a youngster. You need to anticipate this before it happens. To that, ask yourself the following:

Who do you need to hide from and why?

How much hard work and maintenance does it involve versus doing little?

Does it pass the effort to payoff test?

How much work is it to do it right versus getting caught and suffering the embarrassment of being under the spotlight and, heaven forbid, the family?

Whether you use Linux Mint or Windows 7 or a Mac, you need to kill any application if you entered any personal info into it that can aid in tracing you. Usernames that you used on forums should never be used in your anonymous phone or anonymous (like Linux Mint!) laptop.

Also, phone numbers, places of work, nicknames, hangouts, girls you've dated, online games - all of these are part of your real persona that leaves a trail right to your front door. That real persona needs to go into a coffin the moment the anonymous You comes out. Only then can we know ourselves well enough not to be bothered with worrying if we did everything correctly. By that time, we've done it so many times that it's an automatic timepiece in our subconscious. Do this and we'll see our true enemies more clearly, one of which is the NSA.

HOW THE NSA SPIES ON YOU

Let's say a few words on how the powers that be trace calls to begin with. It's a little technical but then it's always preferable to know the enemy's capabilities.

If you're like me then you've probably rolled your eyeballs enough times whenever a bad guy on Burn Notice or CSI had twenty seconds or so to taunt the FBI before his location was traced. It's all baloney, and it happens in *every single cop show* on TV I've ever seen. They think we're lemmings. Well, a few of us are.

The Rockford Files, CSI, and Burn Notice. I love every one of these shows but it just doesn't matter how much I love em because you can't love it when they get it wrong. And get it wrong they do aplenty. They get it wrong because the writers are not detectives themselves and many just want to get the script done asap, so they never shadow any in their day to day operations at all. But best-selling authors like James Patterson do their homework. Go figure.

Phone signals came inline some forty years ago and back then how you got connected was very different than today. A call was setup from one switch to the next, and the next, and then the next until finally a connecting-circuit relayed your voice.

These days most switches are simultaneous since most calls are over SS7 (that is, the Signaling System which manages calls). Each calling station is traceable at the beginning too, so the trace countdown you see on most cop shows really does stretch the truth. But it makes for a suspenseful police drama and, let's face it, most people don't mind suspending disbelief for an hour if they can get good entertainment.

I've trouble doing this though. Perhaps I'm just an impatient guy when it comes to police procedural shows but one episode on CSI came across as gut-wrenchingly sloppy. It showed a low-level programmer realigning a satellite from his laptop *without any assistance from any other agency*. I nearly fell out of my chair. It takes an insane amount of teamwork and coordination between other agencies to do something of that technical caliber.

Mobile phone tracing does require more resources than a landline since a cell phone number is not connected to a single switch. But it isn't impossible for a mobile phone provider to locate which towers the phone used or what region the call was made. One way of doing it is by comparing signal strength and then correlating that with the antenna that held your signal. If you've got an unencrypted non-burner phone, the GPS chip inside will give up your location to any who are in possession of it.

I bet you're wondering how come you can't trace a mobile phone like your cell phone company can.

The reason is the same reason that you can't identify individuals by IP address alone. Only the telephone company knows because they have the logs. They own the equipment. They have easy access. Even police need a subpoena to get subscriber access from a VPN, (or virtual private network). They can't hack the system for one individual without risking their job (or political career). Well, the NSA can I suppose, only that's a whole other enchilada. But for the internet itself no node within it is any more special than any of the others since it uses the same band.

Unlike phones.

Wait a second, you say. If that's true, then how am I supposed to prevent my phone from being tracked?

The short answer is: You can't without the right opsec *and* the right mindset. If you're using towers then you can be traced, generally speaking. But this isn't a perfect world and those towers aren't perfect either. They produce false positives just like our anti-virus programs do, albeit differently. But you can toy with the triangulation angle a bit to obfuscate the trail.

One method involves using a PBX system to delay identity discovery. Notice I said *delay*, not eradicate. The way to do it is to connect with a company's PBX system via dial-up. This will have them looking in the wrong spot. It's still possible for them to trace you given enough time but not without going though the company logs. That takes time too and to be honest they'd rather not bother unless ordered to do so by a higher power.

You can also do it by creating false leads using radio waves (yes, a radio) that links your voice to your phone. Do it right and the guy who is chasing you will end up chasing the wind. You can set the signal to whatever you want. A hundred feet becomes a half a mile and now Mr. Smith's area to catch you has suddenly become much larger. Much larger means more time, more money and more resources. However, neither of the above methods mean anything if you are either one of three things:

- Lax with your metadata (i.e. those you regularly contact).
- Lax with your situational awareness.
- Lax with opsec.

THE NSA FINGERPRINTS CELLS

Bob from accounting claims one burner is as good as the next. Tom agrees somewhat, but insists you need a voodoo doll and a crazy formula he read on an Ars Technica thread to really make it anonymous. The new girl in programming, one sexy Carrie-Anne, insists it's really what you do outside of a phone that matters. Whom do we trust? Bob the Yes Man, Tom the Tax Expert or the goth-chick-turned-hacker Carrie-Anne? What is 'good enough' anyway?

It depends on where you are. One burner can be as good as the next in Southeast Asia if that's where you're headed. Or it may be 'good enough' if you're trekking to the South Pole or diving in some bombed out Japanese sub off the Philippines and aren't really hiding from anyone except Great White sharks.

But Bangkok and the Philippines aren't North America or the UK. It's tough defeating towering bullies over small badgers though both pose a serious threat. I know because I've tried – and failed. When you get right down to it, it mostly depends on who you're trying to hide from.

But regardless of who that 'someone' is, there are two main types of cell technology we can work with. The first is GSM, which stands for Global System for Mobiles, and CDMA which stands for Code Division Multiple Access.

You and I can't cross them, which is why I can't use my AT&T cell on Verizon's service. Most of the major carriers make it simple for LEOs to trace calls because they separate burner phone traffic from prepaid traffic. A Sprint executive may say it's because they need to prioritize traffic. Only what he doesn't tell you is that it's used by the NSA and law enforcement to track down 'anonymous' callers.

The NSA does this by 'fingerprinting' every call. Fingerprint analysis is based on the contacts unique to each caller. That is, *your* unique contacts, as well as how long you talk to those contacts and how long they talk to *their* contacts. It all adds up to a nice fat profile on you that is shady at best and outright evil at worst.

Let's say our friend Jerry talks to Kramer, George and Elaine every day as he sits down with his Wheaties. He has several phones, different carriers, only the info he adds per 'Friend' per contact makes for one helluva traceable target. Every bit of data on these contacts (that is, Kramer, George & Elaine) are placed on the SIM card and match the exact contact data on any other burner he uses. For federal law enforcement to track him down would be laughably easy.

For the NSA, a few clicks in the Prism system and from there it'd be no effort at all to find his geographical location.

LOCATION, LOCATION

So then, how to solve this problem? Well first we need to define what 'location' really means to the Big Data players.

Carriers like Verizon store data based on your phone's signal-strength. That is, the 'weight' of your call between you and the nearest cell tower. It stores a mind-boggling amount of numerical data on your behavior and, at the simplest level, this is known as 'tri-angulation' locating. The GPS functions in your phone use it more often than you realize. Apps like Google Earth and Maps.Me use it as much as they can and provide your whereabouts to distant servers - and as a side hustle bonus are better able to target you with ads based on that data. It's a real juicy side of income if you've got Google's or the NSA's data centers to sort it all out.

The second thing to note is the Christmas Day error. Come one wintry Christmas morning when the cardinals and sparrows flutter about in the snowy front yard, you open your presents to find a fancy smartphone, one loaded with gizmo after gizmo. It cost a fortune and you can't wait to hit the ignition. What's the first thing you do? What's the first thing *anyone* does?

They'll call up that number to activate it. Lickety split.

They're way too sloshed to realize it, but doing that is like a tipsy mouse nibbling a morsel of cheese in a trap with the cat watching from the cover of darkness.

Before they can kick back another shot of Jack Daniels and eggnog, they blurt out their full name, home address and their mistress's password in front of the wife. From that point on it's near impossible to spoof anything because of the correlation of that phone with their real location - and all the locations and profiles of every phone user in the house. Why do they need your contact list now that you've connected to everyone in your household?

And it ain't just the NSA either.

HOW THE IRS SPIES ON YOU

It's not just the NSA that uses Stingray surveillance technology to spy on the citizenry. The IRS now uses it as well to capture metadata from cell phones. They're a part of the Big Data empire too, and they demand only the best tools of the trade: the most expensive *and* the most invasive. They use something known as *IMSI interceptors* (or cell site simulators).

Worse, IRS agents now have the same authority previously held only by judges. This power gives them authority to install Pen register devices so they can spy on people they suspect aren't giving their fair share. Or anyone that challenges them for that matter.

Historically, these were used by the FBI to capture recordings by Mafia members or Mexican Cartel leaders in Juarez. You know, real criminals. Nowadays everyone with a U.S. passport is fair game and if they run out of real criminals to prosecute, well by golly they'll just invent a few more to keep the the gravy train running full-steam. There's even rumors flying that student loan defaulters will have their passports revoked. Not too far fetched since they do the same with child support obligations, and that's only $2500, not $50,000.

Anyway. From the eagle's viewpoint you can see the IRS'

Stingrays are high-tech doppelgangers. They are clones of a cell tower that can force any phone within reach to silently connect so that any metadata can be siphoned off.

Kinda like one of those parasites you see in PBS nature documentaries, where the plant benefits and the parasite benefits in a kind of symbiosis that's a pain to study in a college textbook but fun to watch. Only where the IRS is concerned, the benefits flow in one direction only.

The kicker? That parasite will die far sooner than the plant. Think on this for a moment. What do you think's going to happen if your country suddenly finds itself unable to borrow from anyone? If you've studied history you already know the answer. They steal their own citizens' wealth in a very, well, parasitic-like way. We've seen this in Argentina, Poland and France.

Don't believe for a minute the IRS will only be using this spy tech on the millionaire fat cats living abroad. Those guys are small potatoes. If they were to seize every fatcat's funds in every country on Earth, it'd be enough to pay for Medicare for a scant 3 years. Then they'd be right back where they started. If you don't believe it then allow me to quote a rather well-known statesman on this topic:

"If you will not fight for right when you can easily win without blood shed; if you will not fight when your victory is sure and not too costly; you may come to the moment when you will have to fight with all the odds against you and only a precarious chance of survival. There may even be a worse case. You may have to fight when there is no hope of victory, because it is better to perish than to live as slaves."

- Winston S. Churchill

HOW GOOGLE SPIES ON YOU

Google loves you to death. They love everyone actually, or more to the point, everyone's private data. There's gold in them ones and zeros and most people offer em up quite willingly for their daily digital fix.

Google loves to store data about you when you're not looking. That's what happens when you invite a vampire into your home. Tough as nails to kick out and they leave a trail of confusion and mayhem when they finally do hightail it. Like little cousin Eddie whose long since outlived his welcome.

As a fairly strong privacy advocate, I like to manage that online privacy by controlling the data I make available online. The problem is that Google's been getting smarter at meta-managing me by my own keywords on other search engines. The only option is to enact whatever privacy controls are required yourself. Or don't use any of Google's services. And that my friend is a very long list that includes:

Google Search
Gmail
Google Plus
Google Alerts

Google Books
Google Finance
Google Groups
Google Hotel Finder
Google Flight Search
Google Translate
Google Trends
Life Search (or Google China)
... and a host of others.

The master list of course is a lot longer. The data-mining operations for each of these services cost millions each day. Google's algorithm tries to predict what you'll want tomorrow or next Christmas. That's fine with some people because it's legal after all and they've been doing that since forever.

The problem is that they share this with any government who pays them or allows them entry into the country. This becomes a problem overseas if you need to use online storage. Enter Google Drive.

Google Drive

Google Drive makes for one helluva solution for business travelers who need to protect sensitive files from cross-border guards. Guard who love to confiscate laptops and pen drives because, well, they want to look competent.

Just upload the data to Big G before you hit the US border and you're good to go. This also works if you have to travel to out of the way places like Philippines.

Well, most of the time. So what's the problem then?

Google is the problem, just as iCloud was a problem for a few celebrities who got hacked. It happens every year. Just ask Jennifer Lawrence how she feels about tossing her pics 'in the cloud' after her nudes got hacked and leaked. There's plenty of other risks too:

- Law enforcement can access it with a judge-signed warrant.
- The NSA can give the FBI full access to your files.
- Any alphabet agency can access it. Agencies like the DEA, ATF, CIA, & the IRS *if* they have the NSA's ability to bypass Google's encryption (which Google only beefed up after the media revealed that the NSA was siphoning data from their tailpipe.)
- Employees may upload personal info in the cloud which, if hacked, cause financial issues and maybe even a lawsuit.
- Any bank you deal with may deny you any reimbursement of lost funds if you store bank details in the cloud. They'll consider it 'negligence' on your part.

It's more effective to use an encryption app like Veracrypt or PGP to *work with* Google Drive. What I do is:

- First fire up Veracrypt or Truecrypt 7.1a
- Create a storage file,
- Pick 2 algo-based encryption schemes with SHA-512 keys
- Put all my sensitive files in there.
- Then and only then do I upload the encrypted files to Google Drive.

When I need to alter my work, say update a new draft of a novel I'm working on but don't want Google scanning it for 'offending' terms, I just copy the encrypted doc out of Google Drive, update it and then re-encrypt and re-upload to Google Drive. If I ever want to delete it, I just delete the encrypted storage file. It's easy peasy and it'll be eons before Google has Skynet's quantum computers to crack the encryption key.

Encryption and Google

As I mentioned, any governmental agency can and will access your cloud storage via a subpoena sent to Google. But what are the consequences if law enforcement confiscates your phone? Your laptop? It happens. And as it so happens you may be arrested on a totally separate case but they've insufficient evidence.

Except your laptop and phone are now in their hands. Here are the risks, number one of which is:

- Doppelgangers. Enemy numero uno. Any login cookies for Google services (like Google Docs) can be copied to impersonate you, or they can login to all Google accounts in Firefox or Chrome and act as the Real You.
- They can steal your password from the browser's password storage file if you've no master password set.
- And with your password they can reset it in Google and all Google services.
- Chrome might cache parts of files or documents the last time you logged in.
- Or they can use Data Recovery Tools to retrieve your deleted files.

You can avoid each of the above scenarios by using a full-disk encryption program. As long as your phone or laptop is powered off when they take it (and you're not in a jurisdiction where they can beat the password out of you), you're safe as long as the country in question respects your right to remain silent.

As for a searching solution that replaces Google outright, I use and recommend DuckDuckGo. It's not as laser-refined as Google is, but they must operate exactly as advertised. One thing they're very clear on is their privacy policy, which states:

- They don't track you.
- They don't sell your search data to other websites
- They don't require cookies.

- They don't collect metadata on you
- They don't store your search history.

It's black and white without a lot of legalese that most people just skip through anyway. Clear and plain as day. If they ever decide to embrace the dark side (as Google has) then the FTC can file a lawsuit. The main thing is that if a company has a privacy policy, then they must *stick to it*. No matter what.

Google Chrome

Google Chrome's a lot like Stephen King's Christine, a 1957 Plymouth Fury who loves it's owner a bit too much. She runs fast and hot and horny and like that hellspawn of a car, Chrome'll resist any temptation to tinker, mod or otherwise tighten her steel gaped maw because she thinks she can do the job better than you can. Besides, why should she take orders from some lowly peon, anyway?

But I'll tell you how it all ends: It ends with the kid owner paying a high price for putting a speed demon ahead of his family. Chrome, like Christine, 'repairs' herself without permission a little too often for my liking.

She's certainly fast though, just like Christine. But she's not that fast. And there are some serious consequences to not looking under the hood. Here are a few gems that are considered 'benefits' to the end user by Google:

- Each web url you type is sent to Google for the auto complete function - without telling you.
- Each file you download gets sent to the Big G too. They verify it against a master 'white list' then link your IP address to that file for months.
- Chrome checks every hour on the hour a list of blacklisted URLs to 'protect' you. Even opening Chrome tells Google where you are.

- When you logon to Google Gmail, they know everything about your browser: Tabs, History & all Bookmarks. Then they store it in one of those giant data centers of theirs.
- Will load a site before you finish the address.

Remember: If you are getting it for free, you are not the customer. You are the product.

HOW WINDOWS 10 SPIES ON YOU

Windows 10 is the flagship of Microsoft's cloud-centric vision, and written under the hood is the hope that you'll one day depend on that cloud for more than just accessing game saves. In the meantime, Windows 10 is not a particularly happy operating system unless it's looking online for drivers updates, patches and the like for your supposed benefit. It wants to put a smile on your face.

It all sounds well and good until the real goal becomes apparent: looking for people who fit your own social circle and 'buying' habits and corralling everyone into a nice trackable pen... all without asking you first.

Yes, I know. Microsoft's spying on the masses is hardly news. It's old hat and they're not the only ones doing it by a long shot. Every company you give money to channels your money into some kind of marketing analysis with the laser sights focused somehow on you and your stuff. Supermarkets like Winn-Dixie or Wal-Mart use them to such a laser-refined edge that they know when your daughter is pregnant before you do. It seems like a decent man just can't escape this dragnet without going off-grid and living like Jeremiah Johnson (I've tried that too, and failed spectacularly when I ran into a grizzly. More on that later).

But let's not fall on our sword just yet. You *can* in fact escape any chance of law enforcement, governments or hackers getting a hold of that data, and that's our aim, as when your data is shared with governments or criminals that abuse this information, well, a lot of nasty surprises come down the pike. Below is Microsoft's privacy statement and FAQ regarding the Diagnostics Tracking Service that comes with Windows 10:

"As you use Windows, we collect performance and usage information that helps us identify and troubleshoot problems as well as improve our products and services. We recommend that you select Full for this setting."

- Full data includes all Basic and Enhanced data, and also turns on advanced diagnostic features that collect additional data from your device, such as system files or memory snapshots, which may unintentionally include parts of a document you were working on when a problem occurred. This information helps us further troubleshoot and fix problems. If an error report contains personal data, we won't use that information to identify, contact, or target advertising to you. This is the recommended option for the best Windows experience and the most effective troubleshooting.

Them's Microsoft's words, not mine, and note also that only on Enterprise Edition can one turn Diagnostics Tracking Service off completely. Diagnostics Tracking Service consists of these files:

telemetry.asm-windowsdefault.json
    diagtrack.dll
    utc.app.json

utcresources.dll

It's not likely anyone can lockdown Windows 10 enough to know what they send or don't send either by laptop, PC or cell phone. As Ars Technica has found out, it's impossible to know why Windows 10 can't seem to stop talking to Microsoft's servers. Furthermore, Windows takes system files or memory snapshots, which may inadvertently include PARTS OF A DOCUMENT YOU WERE WORKING ON when a problem occurred. Note that Android isn't much different. It has a similar data collection policy as does Mac OS.

Windows Privacy Settings

Windows 10 comes with some privacy settings turned on and some turned off. You can open up the Settings app and tic off what you like or don't, but know that they're all tied to your Unique Advertising Identifier. This Identifier is shared across other apps you use to allow Microsoft to spy on you and show you targeted ads in much the same way Wal-Mart does with your Sam's Club card. Corporations share this with each other and some sell it outright for truckloads of cash - as do Search engines like Bing and Google. With Bing Search sitting there in the start menu, you can bet you rubber-flesh copy of Evil Dead that any search queries will not stay private. They'll be outed just as if you typed them into Bing itself. Even URLs get sent to Microsoft for validation purposes so it goes without saying that some cellar doors should remain shut. Permanently.

Cortana

Cortana comes with Windows 10 automatically enabled after install. With this on you consent to Microsoft to grant a personal assistant of sorts, one that'll send data about your activities (including applications you run, GPS locations, browsing history) back and forth between your PC and Microsoft. It also includes your handwriting and voice imprint. You can disable these within Speech, Inking & Typing within Privacy settings, but know that Cortana isn't unique in this kind of privacy abuse, as Google Now and Siri do the same thing.

It should be obvious that this is a Very Bad Thing if you plan on doing anything remotely shady on the Deep Web. If you absolutely must use Windows 10 (which I strongly recommend you do not), you must -above all else- disable *data logging*. Here's how.

Disable Data Logging in Windows 10

A few of these fixes are a bit overkill, and if you're not sure what to do then stick to the "before installation" and "after installation" parts. DON'T start mucking about with the Powershell or the registry editor if you don't have at least a good idea of what you're doing though. This goes a bit farther than merely being 'computer literate', obviously, but it illustrates how dangerous Windows really is to anonymity.

Before/During Installation

Do not use Express Settings. Hit Customize, and make sure everything is turned off. It's strongly preferred that you use a local account with Windows 10.

After Installation

Head to Settings > Privacy, and disable everything, unless there are some things you really need. While within the Privacy page, go to Feedback, select Never in the first box, and Basic in the second box.

Head to Settings > Update and Security > Advanced Options > Choose how updates are delivered, and turn the first switch off.

Disable Cortana by right clicking the Search bar/icon.

(Optional) Disable web search in Search by going to Settings, and turning off Search online and include web results.

Getting More Complex

Open up the Command Prompt by launching CMD as an administrator (hit windows key or click start menu button, type "cmd" then right click on the command prompt icon at the top of the list and select "run as administrator"), then enter the following:

sc delete DiagTrack

sc delete dmwappushservice

echo "" > C:\ProgramData\Microsoft\Diagnosis ETLLogsAuto-Logger\AutoLogger-Diagtrack-Listener.etl

Open up the Group Policy Editor by launching gpedit.msc as an administrator (same method as cmd).

Go through Computer Configuration > Administrative Templates > Windows Components > Data Collection and Preview Builds. Double click Telemetry, hit Disabled, then apply.

While still in the Group Policy Editor, go through Computer Configuration > Administrative Templates > Windows Components > OneDrive, double click Prevent the usage of OneDrive for file storage, hit Enabled, then apply.

Open up the Registry Editor by launching regedit as an administrator (yet again same method as cmd).

Go through HKEY_LOCAL_MACHINE\SOFTWARE\Microsoft\Windows\CurrentVersion\Policies\DataCollection, select AllowTelemetry, change its value to o, then apply.

First, download the Take Ownership tweak here: http://www.howtogeek.com/howto/windows-vista/add-take-ownership-to-explorer-right-click-menu-in-vista/ and enable it.

Then, head to the Hosts File by going to

C:\Windows\System32\Drivers\Etc,

and take ownership of the hosts file, then add the following IPs into it (using notepad or whatever text editor you prefer).

127.0.0.1 vortex.data.microsoft.com
127.0.0.1 vortex-win.data.microsoft.com
127.0.0.1 telecommand.telemetry.microsoft.com
127.0.0.1 telecommand.telemetry.microsoft.com.nsatc.net
127.0.0.1 oca.telemetry.microsoft.com
127.0.0.1 oca.telemetry.microsoft.com.nsatc.net
127.0.0.1 sqm.telemetry.microsoft.com
127.0.0.1 sqm.telemetry.microsoft.com.nsatc.net
127.0.0.1 watson.telemetry.microsoft.com
127.0.0.1 watson.telemetry.microsoft.com.nsatc.net
127.0.0.1 redir.metaservices.microsoft.com
127.0.0.1 choice.microsoft.com
127.0.0.1 choice.microsoft.com.nsatc.net
127.0.0.1 df.telemetry.microsoft.com
127.0.0.1 reports.wes.df.telemetry.microsoft.com
127.0.0.1 services.wes.df.telemetry.microsoft.com
127.0.0.1 sqm.df.telemetry.microsoft.com
127.0.0.1 telemetry.microsoft.com
127.0.0.1 watson.ppe.telemetry.microsoft.com
127.0.0.1 telemetry.appex.bing.net
127.0.0.1 telemetry.urs.microsoft.com
127.0.0.1 telemetry.appex.bing.net:443
127.0.0.1 settings-sandbox.data.microsoft.com
127.0.0.1 vortex-sandbox.data.microsoft.com
127.0.0.1 telemetry.*

Additional Fixes:

Replace Microsoft Edge/Internet Explorer with Firefox, Chromium, or any forks/variations you want. Note however that if you install Chrome, you're just choosing to have your data stolen by Google instead of Microsoft if you're surfing naked (i.e. without Tor).

Replace Windows Media Player with VLC or MPC-HC.

Replace Groove Music with Foobar2000, Winamp, or MusicBee.

Replace Photos/Windows Photo Viewer with ImageGlass or IrfanView.

Some of you are shaking your heads at this, and I agree with your assessment that this barely scratches the surface of what Microsoft's nefarious operating system is capable of doing. This plugs just a few holes but there are just too many to fill if you need rock-solid anonymity. For this reason alone you should use Linux (Tor with Tails) if at all possible.

HOW TO TELL IF YOUR PHONE IS TAPPED

A phone tapped with a keylogger is a bomb waiting to go off since the keylogger secretly records (and emails) every username and password you type in. Keyloggers aren't foolproof though. There are a few signs that may give clues that it isn't just your eyes seeing the screen.

1.) <u>Unexplained Data Spikes</u> - Are there any unusual spikes in the size of data being stored on the device? A lot of spyware programs pack data under the hood when you're not looking so it can be sent out later in bulk. Efficient spy payload you might call it. My Data Manager is good at monitoring this but the best spyware apps will evade detection since the footprint is becoming ever smaller and the size of devices ever bigger.

2.) <u>Unusual Phone Activity</u> - Things like turning itself off or your lock screen suddenly flashing on when you're not using it.

3.) <u>Line Noise</u> - If you're in the Philippines and making calls, line stability is often terrible in provincial areas like Davao or Dumaguete. That means tons of noise. If you're in a first world nation, a constant stream of 'clicks' and 'beeps' can signal that someone, somewhere, is listening.

4.) <u>Encrypted Emails</u> - This can happen with poorly designed spyware, where you receive odd messages that make no sense and are filled with strange symbols. Spy applications are known to be buggy little critters and not even keyloggers used by the FBI to capture keystrokes of mafia members are perfect.

5.) Odd Files in Directories - It's often easy to see spyware's been installed on your device by just looking into a few subdirectories on your Android or iPhone. Often I find if I do a Google search for the name of the file, someone somewhere has likewise found this exact same file. Better still is that they've opened a forum thread asking for help. Most of the time the file turns out to be quite old. This saves me the trouble of using expensive forensic software like Paraben's Device Seizure or UFED Physical Analyzer.

HOW TO STAY ANONYMOUS
OVERSEAS... IN ANY COUNTRY

You've won the Powerball lottery and Uncle Sam awaits his cut. Problem is, so are some ugly long lost relatives who've managed to track you down and are now throwing down an epic guilt trip by sleeping in a van next to your mailbox. They're threatening to sleep down by the river too.

But that's not all.

A guy named Eddie you remember from 3rd grade claims to have been your best friend. Except that he really wasn't. All you remember is that he gave you back a chewed up No. 2 pencil that looked fresh out of the hamster bin at the pet store.

You need to get away from this heat. Settle down somewhere and let things simmer down so you can think clearly. So you take aim and throw a dart at a world map on the wall and it lands smack dab in the middle of Zamboanga, Philippines. You hop on Google Earth and think, my my, it looks an awful lot like Maui. Then you get all googly-eyed at those turquoise-watered beaches.

Only it isn't quite that.

There's a few terrorists walking around (real ones, not the old grannies the TSA likes to pull aside to interrogate). What could possibly go wrong?

To be honest, everything. You're a walking ATM in the Philippines and most of the locals know it, though by how much is debatable. But they all think you're rich. If you can afford a $1500 round-trip flight at the other end of the world well then you're as rich as Trump, by god. Now, not everyone is looking to rip you off, but the cab drivers certainly will and if you're in Zambooanga, watch out because that's the danger zone of all danger zones.

Americans, British citizens and Canadians alike are kidnapped routinely whenever they venture too far into Mindanao territory. Especially Zamboanga. You'd never know Zamboanga houses terrorists because it looks like Cebu and even Manila. How safe are those cities? Not very. For this reason you better get ready to lie your tail off before you ever set foot on a plane. Nice guys get killed over there. Quickly.

The first thing you need is a Fake Name. No way around it. You have to know your lies inside and out before you're airborne. Then you need to build a foundation to support this lie in the event you're discovered. We'll use Philippines as an example since that's where our dart landed and also because it's the most socially networked country in the world, bar none. And I don't mean online.

1.) First things first, make up an email account using first name.last name@whereever.com. The name should obviously be fake and be something common to your country but not to your city. So if you're from Chinatown you better pick someplace else. John Smith is perhaps too obvious for most tall white guys. You must never use this email for any connections to your real name because the aim here is to muddy the trail when anyone goes looking for the real you. They'll perform reverse-image searches, phone numbers, white pages, and maybe even Usenet and Ars Technica forums looking for your favorite Skype nicknames.

Never let this fake name connect to social media that's connected to the real you. Ever. As well, never use this name on the same IP address if you can help it. Use a VPN on a laptop specific to this fake name. Signup for Facebook if you must but realize that if you login from the same IP address as your Real You, Facebook will know it and will broadcast it to the world.

2.) Women will almost always ask 'Is that your real name?' when they talk to you on Skype or some other chatroom. IF you have to you can tell them you work for the CIA or that you're the next Stephen King and your publisher's threatened to string you up from the nearest tree if you reveal your real name. If anyone online asks for an address, sever all communications immediately. They're likely either a stalker or an identity thief.

3.) Listed here are the primary things that'll give up the goose: airport luggage with your real name on it, business cards, laptops, tablets, iPhones with your real life pictures of you as a baby scattered about, and receipts. Anything in your wallet is a dead giveaway unless you have a prearranged DECOY wallet. A professional liar's wallet.

4.) Never post old photos to a fake Facebook page. Any photos have to be made exclusively for that profile and nothing else lest they see old photos from your real Facebook page.

5.) A problem area is check-in at the Marriot with a nice girl at your side, the same you just lied to. Only the cute emerald-green eyed girl at the desk asks for your real name. Do you lie? That breaks your cover. How about holding up an ID card? Nope again. She could easily ask you to pronounce it because not everyone there speaks perfect English. So now your goose is cooked. What to do, what to do.

Well for starters you can reserve a room by phone beforehand and not online. She'll ask for ID no matter what so you have to be ready. That means:
    - Preparing a business card beforehand with your website and

fake email and hand it to whoever asks. Just don't act nervous giving it out or you'll find out like Jim Rockford did in the 70s that bad liars are an embarrassment to everyone involved, so be as supercool as Mr. Orange was in Reservoir Dogs.

- Put everything with your real ID in a safe in the room. Passports too (you did email yourself a copy in the event it's stolen, right? Those Pinoy trikes have a lot of sticky fingers). If she or he asks what's in the safe just say the next War and Peace manuscript. Gold to you but worthless to them.

- Only put your fake email on your luggage tags, not your real name.

- Duct-tape your passport and a few hundred dollars to the inside of your suitcase lining. Sew it back up so the baggage handlers don't get suspicious.

- Ensure the 'location' feature of any phone is turned off. You shouldn't even bring a phone like this but for the sake of argument there was once a pinay who could see that was on E 85th and 3rd. She was a few blocks off but close enough to see where I was staying.

THE 10 BEST PHONES FOR ANONYMITY

Admittedly, smartphones and burner phones can mean different things to different people depending on the laws of their respective countries. Sometimes a burner is just a prepaid phone to Joe survivalist: cheap and good to go for when a natural disaster strikes. It'll get the job done. But that isn't the case with Fred the ex-CIA guy. The word smartphone is a bit of a misnomer too, like 'cat owner', because in reality the phone will own *you* if you get sloppy with your opsec.

One advantage that you want in a burner is being able to ditch it *fast*. Prepaid doesn't always fall into this category. So you need to be clear at the outset what you intend to do if the heat gets too hot. Plan B, to say.

Ditch it in the river? But ditching a Blackphone near to where you live may get you a longer sentence than actually handing it over to the police. For this reason it can really pay to invest in good mobile security.But first let's run through a couple of sloppy scenarios so you have an idea of what not to do.

. . .

SCENARIO #1: Bad Weed

All weed is bad if the opsec is bad. But let's say it isn't and we live in a perfect world where everything goes according to plan. Let's say you buy a burner phone that Otto the bus driver recommended. He wants a bag of weed. You commit to it. You buy it on the Deep Web and do so far away from home. You then dispose of it and consider that number 'burned'. Okay then, that seems smart enough. Only what works for the Deep Web doesn't fly so straight on riskier outlets. Outlets like Craigslist.

After getting that bag of reefer, you get a sales itch.

You've smoked the bag yourself and figure to get another one only when you do you're as high as Tommy Chong and order another round using a non-burner with ties to your real number on the clearnet. You used a burner, true enough. But not an isolated burner. You accessed Tor using your real phone. Now you're not only at risk of an LE arrest, but the sheer number of certifiable psychos out there that make Quint from Jaws look like Pollyanna may just show up on your doorstep because you used a credit card over Tor. Not smart.

SCENARIO #2: Bad Dates, Good Dates

Burners make excellent date screeners too. No, not the date Indiana Jones came close to swallowing. I mean romantic dates. You save yourself tons of hassle using a burner in case the date goes sour and you believe you should part ways amicably (but the other party doesn't). A burner number thus can be untraceable, rendering any stalker a non-threat - as long as you didn't invite them to your house.

We're not interested in buying a burner for dating, obviously.

We're interested in what it'd take to get away with buying something on the Black Market in a country that doesn't like Black Markets. You know, a control thing, the peasants vs. The Man. So as you flip through these phones you need to ask yourself if you can handle the heat that'd come down if your identity happened to be compromised.

- If you're a vendor of big crates of contraband (crates filled with those little green Toy Story aliens which are filled with, uh, green stuff), even the high-tech super spy Blackphone will be of little use since if you're pulled over by the cops, they're bound to bring a sniffer dog that'll give the a-okay to strip your car to the bone. They'll find something. They don't need the burner (though granted it'd be nice to see your customer list - any one of which will rat you out).

- Ditch your Glock before your encrypted phone. Getting caught with a handgun while dealing *anything* shady is like getting caught with one in Canada. They'll throw away the key after they throw you in a cell with snow gremlins.

- Cops love 'knock and talks'. That's when they just want to have a 'little chat' to get you to incriminate yourself. Never answer the door if they knock. If they have a warrant they'll likely come in anyway and bombard you with questions while they search. And on that topic, always, always make sure all your lights work before driving. Otherwise expect a 'talk' on the interstate.

- Get a legal side hustle, hobby, or side dream to shoot for. With straight-shooting friends. If you engage the cops for a living to feed your kids, say selling guns to rival gang members or even those granny biker gangs from Fury Road, you'll do serious time sooner or later. Lady luck favors those with more to lose.

- Never, ever break two laws at the same time.

- Bragging can get you 20 years due to this little thing called 'gossip' - your uncle Spanky, your siblings, your girlfriend. More on the finer details of Dark Personas in later chapters.

- If you're the best business in town then people will talk. Your name will be passed around to undesirables. Burner phones cannot prevent this.

BLACKPHONE

Designed by an entrepreneur, a technology expert, a cryptographer and a former Navy SEAL, the Blackphone does just what it claims to do. It protects you from the prying eyes of the NSA and a few more of it's Big Data brothers. Unfortunately this protection comes at a high price: $629. Not cheap. But for rock-solid security you could do a lot worse.

It uses PrivatOS, an operating system that gives you 100% control over who or what an app talks to. Another plus is the preventative measures that kick in when you power it on: Protection from hackers and identity thieves or just some back-alley kid whose eying your phone in Wendy's like Gollum's fishing buddy.

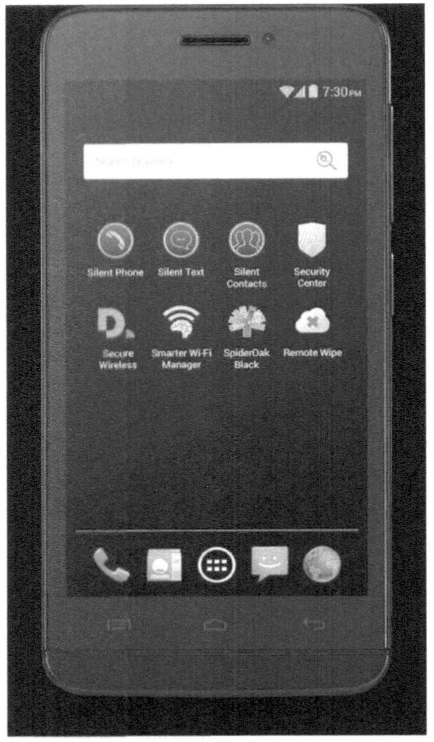

THE SPECS ARE AS FOLLOWS:

SCREEN SIZE: 4.7" (1280 * 720)

Display Technology: 4.7" IPS HD

Technology: Capacitive >4 point multi-touch

Camera

Sensor size main camera 8 MP AF

Type of camera flash: Flash LED

Front camera 5MP FF

CONNECTIVITY

Single micro-SIM slot
Bluetooth Class 4.0 LE
Wi-Fi 802.11b/g/n
Micro USB
3.5mm audio jack

Hardware
Processor: Quad-core 2GHz System on Chip (SoC)
Platform: NVIDIA Tegra 4i

NEED a good camera to give to a scout in enemy territory? Try the Blackphone's 8 megapixel rear cam. It's not top of the line but then the front cam is 5 megapixels and 16GB internal storage, so it's sufficient for surveillance work. The other plus is the CPU: an Nvidia Tegra 4i chip.

As a rule most cameras aren't terribly friendly to privacy to begin with, considering the metadata available within the images.

Then there's the GPS stamps. But the device has to be compromised before it can be abused. If it's compromised, anything else you do on the device is no longer private anyway.

So how anonymous is it? The short answer is *very anonymous*. But like I said, it's pricey, but at what cost security? To that I'd say that as far as anonymity goes all the apps bundled with the device (if you bought them individually) would cost you more than the phone itself. Things like:

- an included 1 year membership to Silent Suite

- A 1-year "Friends and Family" Silent Circle Subscription

- 1 year of encrypted web browsing from Disconnect, 1GB/month

- 1 year of secure cloud backup from SpiderOak, 5GB/month

· · ·

IT ALSO HAS the ability to remote wipe. The PrivatOS got this one right.

Granted, you have to create an account for this to work. But it's like holding a handheld nuclear launch code device. If your phone's been stolen, if you've loaned it to Harry whose been suspiciously absent from meetings for the last few days, or your sister 'borrowed' it and loaned it to her best friend's golf partner's brother-in-law, then fire and forget. Remote Wipe is a dream option.

There's also the Kismet Smarter WiFi Manager. This app memorizes your trusted networks by triangulating cell towers within the area. It comes preconfigured to make any kind of spoofing of your network very very difficult. If you travel out of any established circle of 'trusted networks', the app turns off WiFi and your MAC address.

Since the app can turn off WiFi that means you won't be broadcasting your home network name to every Joe Schmo within earshot. Lots of random attacks by bored hackers and script kiddies tend to undo people who don't care. If they know your network's name they can spoof it and begin running all kinds of scripts that sniff every byte of your traffic. That leads a trail to your front door.

If you bite the bullet and purchase this, check out the Disconnect Secure Wireless service, a VPN that encrypts everything you do online. What this app does is send all traffic via proxy to kill any tracking data inserted into, say, Supercookies. One click and done.

Two other must-have apps come preinstalled. They are:
- Silent Phone
- and Silent Text

I WAS skeptical of both of these until I learned that the designer was none other than Phil Zimmermann of the original PGP encryption suite. So I trust the crypto behind it. Any video or chat session can give you encrypted messages. Better still is the 'Burn Notice' function, a Silent Text feature that allows users to decide how long a message is available before deleting it from both the sending and the receiving device. According to designers at Silent Circle, the burn timer works differently for the sender and the receiver of the message:

- For the sender, the timer will start as soon as the message is sent.

- For the person receiving the message, the timer will start once the message as been displayed on Silent Text's conversation screen.

These are the highlights.

Unfortunately, opsec isn't a product one can buy. It's a 24/7 mindset where 90% of the reasons you'll get caught have more to do with your offline self than anything you do online. Most newcomers to the philosophy of opsec aren't able to do this because we humans are wired to trust rather than doubt.

All of this is not to suggest the Blackphone is perfect. It's not. In fact when it debuted in 2014, a fair share of bugs had come out and more than one site pointed it out. Remember though that whenever these issues are found, they are fixed promptly.

BLACKPHONE 2

Blackphone 2
____

Far from being a 'burner' phone that you'd toss away, the Blackphone's successor just may be the most unhackable smartphone to ever come along. But unhackable to whom?

That's the million dollar question you need to answer before you plop down over $700 bucks for one. Are you a secret agent? Double agent? Hacker? NSA escapee? Or are you just a businessman on his way to China who needs something hack-proof?

Right out of the gate you'll notice it's based around a Google operating system. You're shaking your head, I know. So was I. Avoid Google. Full stop. Go with something like Gentoo Linux with SELinux if you want a secure smartphone. And you're right. If you need serious security to avoid any state surveillance, that's the golden route. In fact if you've got an alphabet agency after you, don't use a smartphone at all. But for everyone else out there whose last name isn't Snowden, read on.

The phone itself is a miniature version of the black slab in 2001: A Space Odyssey, the one that killed the entire team. Monolithic and eerie looking, the specs are a decent upgrade from it's younger brother, but as we'll see the real meat and potatoes is the ease of use it gives you.

Display Screen: 5.5inches, 1080p LCD

CPU: octacore Qualcomm Snapdragon 615

RAM: 3GB

Storage: 32GB; microSD slot

Operating system: Silent OS 2 built on Android 5.1.1

Camera: 13MP rear camera, 5MP front-facing camera

Connectivity: LTE, Wi-Fi, Bluetooth and GPS

Dimensions: 152 x 76 x 7.9mm

Weight: 165g

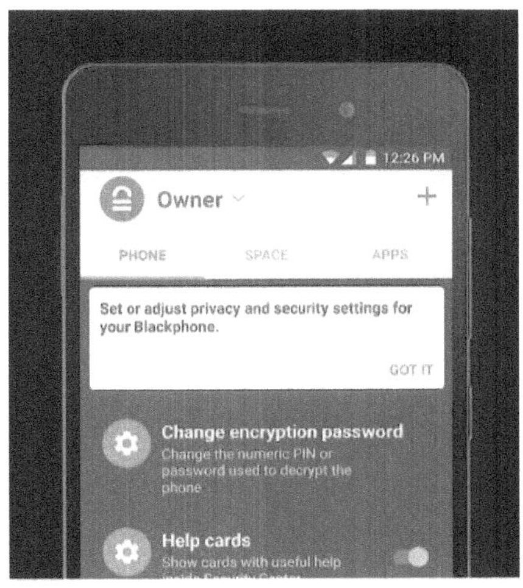

THE GOOD:

Multitasking: A dream! The Snapdragon 615 handled everything I threw at it except for games, and there's little sense in those since that's not what you're buying the device for.

CHARGE: Lasted me almost a full day, but the way I bounce around apps drained a lot of juice from the device, so I had to use it sparingly to not have to charge it every day.

USEABILITY: There was little visual difference from stock Android, with no penalties in the Google Play Store. What's available on my Samsung Galaxy Tab 4 is available here.

SECURITY: The Stock Android appearance is misleading. There's tons of security settings under the hood for you though. You don't even need the Security Center app to hold your hand either (though you can if you want). You can set any app to only have access to location data, the web, or nothing. Up to you.

It reminded me a lot of the <u>Cyanogen OS</u>, which I highly recommend if you're unfamiliar with it. A few of the goodies are as follows:

- Define 'spaces' where Google cannot tread. Within this space, it is 'jailed' in a sense, and one space cannot share data with another. I had one for my contacts, work data, writing docs, taxes and email, with each being in their own 'space' and not able to reach over the fence, so to speak.
- Manage which apps live in each space.
- Quarantine any app if you only want to test drive it. That way if a catastrophe ensues, the damage is contained. Think of what the bomb disposal guys do with the bomb. Similar effect of running a suspicious app in a VM (virtual machine).
- Security updates are quick and easy to install.
- Though pricey, you pay for the software's development and ecosystem which fuel the many features it has. Sure, an iPhone is a snuggier fit for the average Joe than this phone, and as the hardware is faster and sleeker, it's easy to learn, and access to the iOS system is unmatched. But then the Blackphone never claims to take the place of the iPhone for end users anyway, and it's not a patch on the Blackphone if what you really need is security or anonymity.
- According to Silent Circle they had a high level of cooperation from Qualcomm, and are working on having a fully audited baseband. But for now they treat baseband as a hostile router and encrypt Silent Phone voice, video and text before it goes out over radio.

THE BAD:

- WiFi: 4G speeds were better than I expected, but the WiFi was laggy. On some days it was more laggy than others. It wasn't as bad what you'd get in Manila but considering the price I expected better. Not a deal breaker though.
- Encrypted messages & calls are only for Silent Phone users, though you can call others who don't own a Blackphone. Just not encrypted calls.
- Rear camera (13-megapixel) shoots dull indoor pictures. Outdoors is much better.
- Price is $799 (US). If you're not the privacy-minded type, you'll likely buy something else.
- If 'Google' is on the front screen, it's usually a red flag.

THE Ugly

Having lived in Niagara Falls I could write a book on my encounters with Toronto police and how invasive and downright horrifying it can be to get a snarky one on a rainy day, double that for a border officer. That snarkiness gets worse if you get sent to secondary inspection. The kicker is that this is just the phone to get you there all the quicker if you take the bait they'll drop - which they always do.

Visually, it's a remarkable little security device. You can bet the ranch they'll make a remark or two about this little black beauty as merely possessing it may ruffle a few of their federal feathers the wrong way.

Investigation going on? You'll experience heightened scrutiny. What're you hiding? Border guards on terrorist alert? Shakedown time. I see cars turned inside out as I drive into Buffalo, NY from Canada all the time, though I see many more if it's a national holiday.

If I were driving into Canada, Mexico or Europe, I'd stick the Blackphone in the most innocent, ridiculous looking Hello Kitty phone covering that I could lay my hands on, or even put it's electronic innards into a rival phone's chassis so as to look as boring as possible to any border guard. These guys put up with a lot of juvenile acts every day and the last thing you want is to whip out a pricey, hardened, hackle-raising security phone if you need to be low-profile.

They *want* to see a phone like this. It makes the hot summer day all the more bearable and giving you a hard time is the icing on the cake.

BOEING'S 'BLACK' PHONE OF SELF-DESTRUCTION

III. Boeing's 'Black' Phone of Self-Destruction

BEFORE YOU WHIP out your wallet, know that this phone cannot be purchased by end users like you and I. But if you're an employee with security clearance, that means you've already consented to have any online actions monitored anyway so it's likely game over before you even fire up this baby.

The insides are nothing special:

- a 1.2 Ghz Cortex CPU, a 4.3 screen and average 1590 battery. What's unusual is the 'trusted module' satellite-uplink ability along with hardware-designed storage for encrypted data. It's pretty neat if you can get it but becomes outdated rather quickly.

Then there's the 'Pure Secure' security design by Boeing which resists all forms of spoofing or modding - which means no root access. So much for making it non-trackable to the NSA.

THE SPECS MAY SEEM LACKING but for a government employee there's probably acceptable specs for whatever the government wants him to do. For all we know they won't come in contact with the internet at all. Maybe email and productive apps like databases and NSA slideshows. Who knows.

Side note:

At the other end is the transparency for a big name corporation. Take a company like Lockheed. Now think of an outfit like Northrup Grumman, a leading global security company that provides products in unmanned systems, cybersecurity, C4ISR, and other slick services.

Would it be a terrible thing for an intelligence agency to intercept some lackey at Northrup who conspired with a Lockheed employee to send a text to the Peruvian embassy? Maybe he offered to exchange some interesting maps for the secret of ceviche? Well maybe he did. Maybe he didn't.

Nonetheless, whenever you get a phone this specialized, it's almost always used for other big hardware that no one else has. If it's stolen, most of the time they can't use it.

But I thought you should know of it in case you're wandering around the Boeing plant one day and happen to see some fuzzy-mustached manager named Bucky Goldstein yakking into one of these. Know that he's got a good piece of tech in his hands that he's not likely to loan out - but no way is he evading his Big Brother the NSA.

BLACKBERRY

IV.) BlackBerry

BLACKBERRY MADE headlines last year when it acquired Secusmar, the German-based voice-data encryption company with a penchant for waging war against well-funded eavesdroppers like the NSA. Prior to the acquisition, they'd worked together to pad Black-Berry devices with high security for a few high-profile politicians, one of which was Angela Merkel.

Yep, that Angela Merkel, Chancellor of Germany.

The same Merkel that the NSA spied on and who later rightly told Obama off by phone, BlackBerry to BlackBerry.

Notifications: Android has a far better notification system than other devices. Anonymity programs like Orbot and pretty much any security app rely on notifications for mission-critical network issues.

KEYBOARD: Hands down, Blackberry offers the best typing experience on the market. They are at the top of a very short list of makers who design physical-keyboard phones these days. In fact I've noticed my words-per-minute increased quite drastically the more I used it. This may be insignificant in a dangerous country like Iran or Zamboanga, Philippines, but while most average Joes want some level of security on their phone, it usually comes second to features and usability.

FUTURE CUSTOMERS & Support: After spending a month researching the BlackBerry market I can tell you that I was taken aback when I discovered how much they've cut back on marketing and administration. They dropped from almost $400 million to $200 million. People who don't follow markets might think that's par for the course, but it isn't. That's big bucks. Huge bucks. In fact it's almost as if BlackBerry doesn't want to grow. And they *need* to grow but with these kind of budget slashes it's unlikely many new customers will be forthcoming in future years.

So what does this mean for security?

It means patches to exploits and security holes will be filled sparingly, if at all. A bad thing. The silver lining is that, much like a few non-Windows systems, BlackBerry may simply cease to be interesting to most hackers out there. There simply won't be enough people using them to justify exploits or hacktivism or extortion-by-virus dry runs. But that isn't nearly enough to make up for the bad.

There's also the fact that much of the top sales come from South Africa. For the record I don't think that it's CIA operatives either. More than likely it's teenagers being able to talk incognito without fear of the parents butting into their business. Teenagers who'd rather use a *physical keyboard* than a touch screen. Teenagers that use BB7 phones rather than the BB10s. The handwriting on the wall seems to be that within 5 years we'll see BlackBerry folding up the big tent and heading elsewhere.

As to Blackberry's security abilities in the here and now, read on to the next section.

BLACKBERRY SECURITY

If you're an Android user you may wonder just how secure BlackBerry really is. What makes the network itself more secure than Android?

Well the truth of it is that security is tough to implement and *tougher* to stay on top of. The king of the fortress must protect every entry point in the entire estate, while any foreign invader only needs one vulnerability to exploit. That's because they only have to get lucky once. Security even on BlackBerry is only as strong as its weakest link. That's *you*, my friend.

It's not entirely different than electricity or a home invader, for both follow the path of least resistance. But if you lock down your fortress with airtight security and fill your moat to the brim with piranha yet forget about the secret entrance leading up from the sewers, well there goes your security plan. Right out the window. The best guard in the world can't defend against an arrow to the back of the neck.

To it's credit, BlackBerry has something called COPE, which stands for Company Owned Personally Enabled Devices. You can read why this is good security elsewhere but suffice it to say its what your security needs are that counts.

A friend of mine in Korea says he as well as his family all receive malware-phishing texts on a daily basis. Usually they're the kind with fake links, but look like the genuine article. If you click on the link using an Android phone, your screen gets sent to the thief. Now he can see it all. He says this is a widespread problem in South Korea, but only on Android phones. Not so in a BlackBerry.

JAILBROKEN PHONES

One of the biggest differences between Android, iPhone and BlackBerry is that BlackBerry is designed with good security from the first layer on up *at the hardware level*. For many others such hardened security begins at the app level - the surface of an operating system. If you jailbreak your phone then that trust-module is broken and any hacker worth his salt can, on his worst day, grab data housed between the operating system level and the application level *but only if you don't take steps to secure it yourself.*

That's the tradeoff with a jailbroken phone. You get more flexibility and convenience but at the cost of security. It works the other way around, too. With more security comes less flexibility. Take your BBM messages, for instance. It's very difficult, unlike on Android, for contacts such as those in an address book to be sent elsewhere without your approval. You're the one in charge of who you converse with. Deny them or accept them. Can you deny the government?

Yes, you can, by using whatever standard of encryption you desire on a BES server. That said, you can be compelled by a judge to fork over your password as is the case with many who were arrested for tax evasion. The way around this is to never allow your IP address or *any other identifying information* about you to find its way into the hands of an adversary. And these days, learning how to hide your IP address is the kindergarten equivalent of learning the alphabet.

ENCRYPTING FILES ON BLACKBERRY

There exists several different encryption apps you can use on BlackBerry for anonymous messaging. My personal favorite is PGP, but then its an app that's had over a decade of development. Thought it works beautifully on BlackBerry, there may come a day when you simply want to encrypt files natively without the help of any third party apps. Here's how:

- From your home screen, swipe down
- Choose settings, security and privacy - encryption
- From here you can choose any of these:

Set Device-Encryption to On

Set Media Card Encryption to On

Set your device's password (required)

You will find that it's not possible to select files/folders by themselves to encrypt but rather the entire device/media card.

DECRYPTING FILES

Choose Settings, then Encryption

Move slider to Media or Device from On to Off

Enter the password you set previously

<u>Important</u>: Know that implementing the above gives you an encryption key native to your phone so that if you erase this device then the key *gets erased as well*. If that happens, any data that was on this device is unaccessible without that key. To put this in perspective, if you lose your BlackBerry but still retain your microSD card that has your encrypted files (encrypted by the system that is now in the hands of someone else), you **cannot** get your files on the microSD back either, even if you use a new BlackBerry. This is linked to the system password on the device itself.

The following apps come highly recommended should you need a third-party app that encrypts individual files:

Keepsafe Photo Vault – Hide Pictures And Videos

Titan Files

Max Hide & Encrypt

Secret Keeper

One thing to note is that when you encrypt your entire device, any caller's name won't appear once the device goes into a locked state. You'll see their number but not their identity. The reason for this is because the device memory becomes partially-encrypted with each instance of unlocking the device. Some users choose to encrypt only the microSD card for this very reason.

Once again, let me restate that wiping your device will render the microSD card UNRECOVERABLE unless it is decrypted first. The password is only used to encrypt the key, and the key is randomly generated. This is why the entire device doesn't have to be re-encrypted when you change your password.

HOW TO DISABLE AUTOMATIC OS UPDATES ON BLACKBERRY 10

If there is one thing I've always hated about operating systems out of the box, it's automatic updates. I *loathe* them. Android is notorious for this and it was the first thing I changed when buying a Samsung Galaxy tablet a few years back.

BlackBerry isn't much different and many encryption users simply don't like auto-updates since they tend to break personalized settings and heaven only knows what else. Where security is concerned, you want full control over your device since one update can destroy your anonymity.

Often whenever a new update is released, if the device is WiFi-connected the update is downloaded in the background and installed automatically. Then the user is suddenly asked to restart. Not good.

He could be in an important business meeting in the middle of a presentation when this happens. Or on a stakeout and get the update just when the crap is about to hit the fan. Not fun for a device that brags about being the best around at security when it never *asks* you for permission to start with.

So here's how we turn it off:

- Choose Settings, then Software Updates. Look towards the bottom of the Updates page and choose Options.

- In the Options page, the slider is present to Enable/Disable Updates. Choose according to your needs.

OLDER & GENERIC BURNER PHONES
(AKA CHEAP PHONES)

Need an emergency phone? Then you don't need an expensive Blackphone. Give the TracFone a spin. They own Net10 & Straight-Talk, both prepaid carriers, and make a few 'bare bones' phones that'll do the job just fine. The trade off is limited support. We'll discuss those at length along with a few phones I've used that aren't really phones at all. That means no GPS, 3G or even LTE. But you get a much longer-lasting battery. There's pros and cons to every one of them.

If on the other hand you need something for *special* emergencies, then GPS is the last thing you want. Here's why.

Let's say a cell tower pings your burner phone's location every 15 minutes or so, then saves the geolocation data and time stamp. A determined adversary might be able to query events where phone A (your super secret prepaid phone) was within 30 feet of a not-so-secret phone B for 6 hours or so, with work/driving time factored into it too. How do we prevent this from happening?

The simple way is to never leave Phone A powered on anywhere near your real-identity phone (phone B). In fact secret phone A should always, without question, remain stored at a distant location even if it's in a storage unit with your real name front and center.

As long as the battery's taken out.

This battery only gets removed if you need to 'go dark'. That's when the real phone is far away from you and believe me there's far less risk this way. If you neglect to do this, an adversary with sufficient resources (pretty much anyone with a shiny badge these days) can pinpoint both signals and correlate them to your real identity.

At any rate, as we go through these cheap phones, remember what your security needs are and that no amount of cash is too much for good security. You get what you pay for in this life, and good lawyers are more expensive that good phones and good opsec.

NOKIA LUMIA 520

This phone makes a great burner phone as it's so cheap. Being a Windows phone, you'll have to tweak it to whatever anonymity services you require. Add to that there's a mile-long list at the end in the next section where I cover anonymity apps. The bonus is that it's a steal at under $50 bucks on Amazon. When searching for a phone, I typically read the 1-star reviews first to gauge whether it's a deal killer or not. Now for the stats.

Cons - Not all that glitters is gold. In other words, don't expect the gold standard for such a small price. This phone is lousy for hikers on the Appalachian trail in need of good GPS, but for cloak and dagger purposes it fits the bill nicely.

<u>Odd Camera</u> - Flash is non-existent and there's no front camera either. Photo quality is also quite poor for those photographer-tourists who always seem to wander into North Korea.

<u>Limited Customization</u> - The 520 doesn't sport too much in the way of separate profiles with different settings. I like to keep my work profile separate from my home profile, with each having a distinct ring tone (my ghost phone has no volume setting). The volume settings on the Lumia refused to allow me to make the two distinct. Mind you it *does* offer volume, just not for many profiles.

<u>App Inferiority</u> - You get what you pay for. The many apps for the Lumia 520 are quite humble next to what's offered for Android. And that's the silver lining. Modern, whiz-bang apps found on Android often have trackers that are difficult to disable and like to 'phone home' far too often for my liking.

<u>**Moto G**</u> - Prepaid Version

Another great burner phone. It uses Android and comes at under $100 at <u>Amazon.</u>

Specs:
4.5 inch 720p HD TFT display
Quad-core 1.2GHz processor with 450MHz
UMTS HSPA+, CDMA EVDO Rev A
5MP rear camera, plus front facing camera, 8GB Internal Memory

This is the one you want if your on a budget. When I first test drove this I wanted to see if I could use it as a WiFi mini-tablet. I skipped activation and ended up giving them no info at all and it's worked fine ever since. Just swipe off-screen and go into options, then turn airplane mode on. After doing this it didn't access any mobile network and never prompted me at all, so I just set wifi to on or off manually.

It's a nice little mini tablet. Good for privacy. Security? You can do better, and a Samsung Galaxy Tab she ain't. But it has decent resolution and can be used with Flixter, Amazon App store, Google Play and even games. You'll get two free texts with Verizon so you'll know if it's working or not.

MOTOROLA EX-431G

The next excellent burner is the Motorola EX-431G, a TracFone that comes with a keyboard and triple-plus minutes for life. The price varies between twenty and forty dollars and like before, you get what you pay for. This is a feature phone and not an Android phone. That means no unlimited talk, text and internet, so if you want a plan like that then you'll need to use their sister company, StraightTalk. The stats are as follows:

Full QWERTY Keyboard
Double/Triple Minutes (depends on model)
2MP Camera
MP3 Player
MicroSD Card (up to 32GB)
Mobile Web
Bluetooth
Hands-Free Speaker
FM Radio
500 Entry Phone Book
Voicemail, Caller ID, Call Waiting,
Alarm Clock

MOTOROLA MOTO G (3RD GENERATION)

A bit expensive for a burner phone, but at $179, I peg this little phone mainly for those needing sanity over anonymity, like parents with kids since it's waterproof, but can also be great for grandmas, bathrooms with soapy floors and cars in need of better communications. It's not for special ops or survival scenarios.

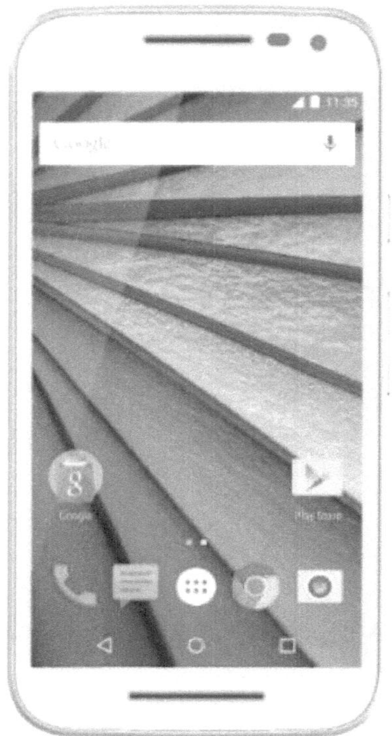

Specs:

- Advanced water resistance
- 13 MP camera which includes a color-balancing dual LED Flash
- 5" HD display; Brilliant display quality and the strength of Corning
- Gorilla Glass
- Quad core processing power in a great value product
- 5MP rear camera with a VGA front facing camera
- 24hr battery performance with a 2470mAh battery
- Expandable memory; Slot for an microSD card with 32 GB capacity.

- 4G LTE Speed; Browse, stream music, watch video, and play games at blazing speed.

The display isn't the best and 1GB is pretty minimal but it handles like a much more expensive device and as expected Android didn't cough up any problems. The camera too plays nice with the owner and since it ships with IPX7 - which allows for half an hour submersion in water w/no damage - you could do a lot worse. One major con though is that the battery is NOT removable. Remember what we said about the NSA being able to track phones with the battery still inside.

MOTOROLA I355 RADIO/CELL PHONE

This is the survivalist's dream phone. It's cheap at around $15 at most places like ebay, and fast. It also supports Direct Talk. Direct Talk in case you're wondering is when a phone has the ability (like many Nextel phones) to grant 2-way radio chat, effectively *bypassing the cell towers*. It needs a sim card to be able to do this, but the sim card doesn't actually connect to a network/tower.

The older DirectConnect involved two phones connecting to a cell tower and from there all messages were relayed to wherever. But Direct Talk bypasses cell towers completely. This came about because many Nextel customers found their jobs bringing them to areas that required walkie-talkies. This solved that problem nicely.

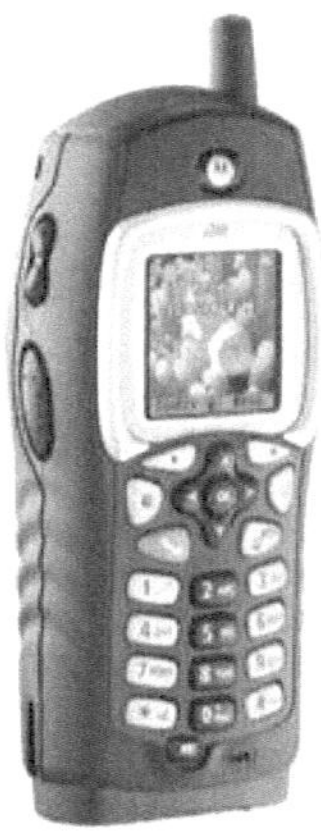

Points to Note

The range varies but 3 miles out is not uncommon. Believe it or not, having a good antenna (that is, extending it) helps this range considerably.

- Incognito one-on-one calls are supported, even group calls. You can even have twenty users participate in a group call if their close enough. This is ideal for everyone but hunters since the 'blip' sound is fairly loud.
- The i355 was once one of Nextel's babies on the iDen network (now defunct and why they're so darned cheap now). To use a sim from a different network you must have an unlock code which is about twenty bucks or so from an online 'unlock shop'.

This isn't to say the i355 is the only DirectTalk phone. There are others that support it, mostly Nextel phones.

Nextel ic402
Nextel ic502
Nextel ic602
Nextel ic902
Nextel i275

Nextel i315
Nextel i325
Nextel i335
Nextel i355
Nextel i365
Nextel i425
Nextel i455
Nextel i560
Nextel i570
Nextel i580
Nextel i615
Nextel i670
Nextel i760
Nextel i776
Nextel i850
Nextel i870
Nextel i880

SAMSUNG S150G (TRACFONE)

Next up is the Samsung S150G, also a TracFone. In the also-bought section at Amazon, you probably saw like I did that some phones advertised as 'Prepaid' aren't so cheap. The price sometimes doesn't justify what you get as you don't need to spend $50 dollars for a burner phone. This Tracphone though can be had for as little as $10 bucks. Not quite the i355, but then few are.

On the Samsung SGH-S150G you'll find a large keypad with large buttons that make dialing numbers and typing text messages easy. And that's a lifesaver in a hard storm with 50MPH winds. The specs are as follows:

TracFone Double Minutes features an LCD color display
Auto redial
Keypad lock
Alarm clock
Phonebook with up to 1,000 entries
Polyphonic ringtones
Talk Time: up to 15 hours
Standby Time: 10.4 days
Includes battery, charger, activation card and services guide

DISASTER PREPAREDNESS

I bought one of the aforementioned pre-paid phones in 2015 in Ontario, Canada with cash just to see if I could be truly anonymous in doing so. Wal-Mart was the buying place and I knew there'd be security cam footage that could identify me as the buyer, both in the store, in the parking lot and on the streetlight cams.

If I'd wanted to I could've rigged a fairly good disguise that'd throw off a decent investigator I suppose but I wasn't engaged in anything shady (sigh) so I just waltzed in like a wino off the street. When I activated it at a nearby college, something struck me as it began to rain.

These types of phones are ideal for being disaster-prepared as the charge outlasts fully-fledged smartphones and tablets by a country mile. If you want some extra insurance, you could even buy a couple of additional $10 phones to get the extra batteries (what they'd cost on most sites anyway).

In a looting and flood situation where you've got gangs roaming the streets and breaking into BestBuy to steal LCD TVs (a la Katrina), these simple cheap burners could be life-savers for your entire family. Better yet, several families joined at the hip and coordinating

security and ration procedures might save everyone involved from
ending up like those poor Joes stranded at the New Orleans Super-
dome during Hurricane Katrina.

Another reason to have several is the FCC. They require that all
cell phones must have 911-call ability even if you're not with any
carrier. For this reason I rarely throw out my old devices. Many can
still dial 911, with the Emergency Dialer usually located at the
bottom of the locked phone.

Points to Note

- You may find yourself stranded in a hurricane. Or a civil
  war. Voice may be down, so you need to learn how to
  text or get a UHF & GMRS radio to contact family and
  loved ones. Cell phone companies usually install just
  enough equipment to handle normal peak usage. So if a
  large number of people all try to talk at once it can cause
  a lot of issues even when everything is working
  optimally.
- When the Cincinnati bridge collapsed in 2007, cell users
  could only initially call for help. After a few minutes cell
  phone voice calls were either too congested or blocked for
  use by emergency personnel. However, text messaging
  still worked, even though there were some delays.
- Data travels on a different network than voice calls and
  because of its nature, can be retransmitted by the
  network until it finally reaches your phone. So, even in
  the event of a brief data interruption, the network will
  continually try to send your text messages until they
  reach your cell phone.

This makes it ideal for emergency notification, especially in the
initial stages of an emergency.

If you are trying to get a message to a group of people, set up a group email list on your email service so you can broadcast instructions.

Yes, I realize that your internet service might be down but you could even set this up on your email service right on your cell. Also realize that nearly ALL cell phones now have a way to receive a text message unless they are over 10 years old. Yep, a lot of people think they don't have that service, but they do. There are limitations on some of the cell phones in getting messages of course. Some are limited to about 100 characters so if you're sending a broadcast, you'll want it to be short and precise.

Anyway, you can build all sorts of scenarios as well as your own color alert system to help get the message out in a short number of characters.

<u>Personal Note</u>

In 2015 I decided to buy a handful of these cheap prepaid phones, only I swore to myself I'd keep them activated in case something Really Bad happened (which later did) and I needed something other than my usual cell phone. I found that if you add twenty bucks or so to them every few months, they'll stay active and give you a nice stack of 'emergency' minutes as long as you don't go hog wild with talk time. I keep one in every vehicle as well as a charger in case I'm on a trip without my cell. For strict anonymity though this comes up a bit inadequate. But it will give you a line of communication with the wife, kids or other family members who you may need to call in dire situations.

Each of these phones is connected to a different carrier's network, like Sprint and Verizon, in case one of them goes down in an Armageddon-like scenario. As stated before, these prepaid phones have amazingly more battery-charge (and can withstand drops/spills) than your average smartphone.

<u>Craigslist</u>

The value of Craigslist is heavily dependent on your region, but some very nice phones can be acquired using it.

One thing though. Always *always* carry a burner when you deal with anyone on Craigslist and especially when buying expensive items like gaming laptops, cars or rare firearms.

Come armed if you can. Let a friend know where you're going. Not that you're doing anything shady, but you've no idea if you're meeting the next Evil Dead fan who wants to pick up where the cabin demons left off. The level of evil out there is escalating. You want to leave as few digital breadcrumbs as possible. Never let strangers know you've got a nice gun filled basement with a safe full of cash and i355 phones.

National Guard Sergeant Jim Vester from Indianapolis was killed while trying to complete a Craigslist transaction for an iPad. It was a setup from the start over what amounted to $400. Such a tragedy may have been averted if he'd arranged to meet in a public place for the transaction. Sadly, he did not. RIP.

If you must use this service however, when posting the ad, do not allow email contact. Just put your contact info in the ad body itself. i.e. the phone number and specify *calls only*. This eliminates scams and weeds out the not so serious buyers as well as stupid "Is the BBQ pit in the background for sale?" and "what lowest price take for?" emails.

Scams

And beware of the Paypal/eBay/Craigslist scam. It goes like this. They send you a fake email that looks like a PayPal email would. You then click the link in said email, which then directs you to a website that looks *exactly* like PayPal, only it isn't actually PayPal. You enter your username/password in said website and viola, they now have your login info.

This scam has been around for years. A safer bet is to stick with thrift stores and yard sales. Burners are one thing but for selling weapons and related stuff, you're probably better off using Armslist.com.

There's another scam, too. Avoid any craigslist buyer/seller of costly items that cannot meet you face to face. I've met dozens of scammers buying and selling fast cars and other expensive items. Only deal with locals who have cash in their hands, ready to buy. In God we trust, all others pay cash.

QUESTIONS AND ANSWERS

Where to get the best burner phones?

If you need traceless burners, anywhere you don't usually shop that doesn't have cameras is probably a good idea. That means not in your hometown. Forget Amazon and eBay.

Burners are cheap with a few being only ten dollars or so, but if you're the truly paranoid type you can buy one from a different mom and pop store every time you need one, use it once for whatever security operation you need, then wipe the device and disperse the pieces in multiple locations.

Flea Markets are a good secondary source for burners. I've bought a few and they're 'just as good' as the Big Box store kind with the only caution being you need to ensure it isn't tracking you from the outset. You'll need new a SIM card as well. Failing that, there's also a few sources on the Deep Web, aka the Darknet, using Tor and Bitcoins to purchase one.

If I can't store it at my house or my office then where am I supposed to keep it? A safety deposit box?

No. In fact, never store it at a bank at all or any place secured with your ID. Store it at a friend's house instead. Oh but he doesn't want it there either because if he's your friend he probably knows all about your top secret operation and doesn't want the liability. Do you have a secure HQ set up? Somewhere private and away from cell towers where members meet? One possibility is storing it at an abandoned site, possibly in a rural setting.

What about batteries?

Batteries are a problem but not if you don't activate the phone prematurely. One solution is to keep them somewhere safe until the day you need it. Store in a PVC tube and hide in a tree with tree bark super-glued to it. If you live near a lake you'll see many places where one could be stored under a pier in a waterproof bag. Of course, you don't want to store *everyone's* batteries or phones there.

Good opsec is *hard work*.

FARADAY CAGES

A faraday bag or 'cage' is a storage place where radio waves are forbidden and by extension data, since data uses radio waves to relay messages. A nice place to hide a phone, though I can't think of even one home appliance that lends itself to simple modification for an effective Faraday cage. Microwave ovens make for one unreliable cage, believe me. Just put a burner inside and try calling it to see for yourself.

The holes are the problem. They're tiny enough to prevent the wavelengths that the microwave uses from passing through. Shorter wavelengths though (ones with more energy) *will* pass through. My twelve-year-old nephew once came over and asked what I was doing. I told him flat out then looked at him. This blank expression came along his face.

I hadn't seen him in a good long while so I showed him the same phone I saved from 1983, the same year Return of the Jedi came out. His eyes lit up.

"Wow,' he says. "I bet it's got all kinds of illegal parts," only then he grabs it and starts mashing the holes like they were smartphone buttons. He'd never seen one that required 'dialing'.

Moving on.

You'll have to buy a radio frequency shielding bag that blocks every signal to and from the cell phone, or go to PrivacyCase.com and get one from the pros. They're asking more than everyone else, but their product works quite well. They had it lab tested and the thing doesn't leak, period. No cellular, no wi-fi, no GPS, nothing.

Another option is if you own a gun cabinet made of metal. Line the inside with a 1/4' wire mesh and tin foil. Secure the tinfoil with foil duct tape. Now you can store your emergency electronics/burners with your weapons, though admittedly this is time-consuming. There's something else you outta know, too.

That cell you're carrying is constantly being tracked by this cell tower or that tower even when you turn the GPS function off. Whenever your phone breaks contact with these towers, it'll increase power to the transmitter to reestablish a connection. Power consumption goes UP and drains the battery.

Then there's the digital footprint of your cell going off the grid and then popping up somewhere else. Maybe even data related to *why* it went down. Certainly *where* it went down.

Then Barney the bored TSA guy wants to know what the deal is. He's in the airport and thinks he's Michael Weston before he got 'burned' by the CIA. He'll say, "Well lookie here, some taffer tryin' to get all stealthy. We'll teach 'em to mess with us!" Then you've got problems.

What about hiding phones in a fridge?

Edward Snowden suggested using a fridge as a kind of faraday cage. True, a few may block sound, but that has no bearing on a radio's frequency. In some models the seal-gap can even act as a rudimentary antenna! Microwave ovens aren't the solution either since the door seal blocks RF only at 2.4 ghz - which is not a cell band.

It's hard work and hard to maintain. If you slip up with any of the above, you best consider your opsec broken. Once broken it *cannot be unbroken*. It cannot be repaired since you don't know how many now know your identity. All numbers, accents, purchases, addresses and trails are now linked to you and you cannot unlink them.

It's why CIA agents work so hard at keeping a low profile. They offer verifiable (false) data that deceives outsiders into thinking something exists when it really doesn't. Unfortunately many of them lose friends and family over it, so they end up in a 'bubble' that's very hard to break out of. It's like that Eagles song: "You can check in but you can never leave."

Earlier I mentioned that your greatest weakness is yourself. There's another side to that coin and it's this: the NSA's greatest weakness is itself. They tend to rely on signal intelligence for everything at the expense of everything else. They rely too much on technology with not enough eyes on the ground. This is in your favor because they can only see what you give them, like using your burner to call your girlfriend after all mission burners have been activated.

It's an elaborate chess match of move, countermove, attack, but if you prevent them from getting near your queen, they cannot say *checkmate*.

Let me repeat it. Good opsec is hard work!

20 GHOST APPS FOR SMARTPHONES

Call me paranoid, but I've never trusted Android to completely remove *everything* an app may leave inside my phone. The uninstall process seems a little 'off' to me, as though something rotten has been left to fester underneath and the OS just doesn't care if I know about it or not. Windows is a *little* better, but with Android there's always some cryptic legalese about painless network access and maybe what it intends to modify, only it's in a kind of gnarled and twisted doubles-peak that even I can't untangle. Or maybe I just suck at deciphering legalese. I suck at deciphering Egyptian hieroglyphics too, but then Tutankhamen isn't spying on my internet habits.

Nevertheless, a research paper came out last year that shed a lot of light on the subject of just what goes on under Android's hood. They called it Taming the Android AppStore: Lightweight Charac-terization of Android Apps.

Here's what they did.

They tested over 2000 of the Play Store's free apps in every cate-gory using a Samsung-Galaxy S3 phone with Android 4.1. They accomplished this using a VPN which dumped IP addresses and other data using TCPdump - which monitored every app on the phone. The result wasn't pretty.

They found that many Android apps connected (without permission) to at least one of five hundred unique websites without leaving a trail. That's right. No popups. No emails. No opt-out. It connected to all sorts of things that kill anonymity outright to say nothing about general privacy.

Ad trackers. Behavior analytics. Click trackers. Tracking servers. The whole anti-privacy enchilada with Google sitting fat and happy at the top of the heap with that crooked Joker's grin. So why did they not engage in a little *transparency*?

My theory is that it isn't that they don't have this ability from a technical standpoint. They do indeed. It's that they need to grant the application developer access to your private data on a consistent day-to-day basis.

Speaking of private data, I've found most privacy advocates to care less about staying 'hidden' from the NSA and more about hiding from corporate entities. Bragging about that hot new IP over an open mic network like Skype is, to put it mildly, crazy business.

When you get to the point in your career when you're discussing business startups, the first line of defense should always, without exception, be privacy focused. That's because Microsoft, Apple, Google and the like care zero about protecting you. You are considered by them to be their product. Their bottom line. That includes every bit of hearsay, gossip, or stock details that zip around on Skype which, if you sign on the dotted line in their Terms of Service agreement, is fair game.

In the end, it isn't patents, copyrights, and lawsuits that shield your ideas and ventures and marketable products. It's trade secrets - and that requires you to kick their corporate noses out of your tent. And your business.

So what follows is the absolute end-all-be-all of must have addon apps that'll turn your gremlin-built Android phone into a veritable fortress of doom, from which *nothing* gets in or out without your express permission. Sort of like DungeonKeeper for mobile phones, except you call the shots.

SIGNAL

First up is Signal, the popular messenger and private calling app on the Google Play Store designed by Whisper Systems. It's the combining of two very secure encryption apps called TextSecure and RedPhone, both built by the same. Both apps began on iPhone and now have been brought over to Android. Several bonuses right off the bat jumped out at me.

- The code is open source, reviewable by experts. That's a big one.
- No ads to speak of.
- Anyone can use this to communicate instantly and privately.

Friedrich Nietzsche
+1 415-557-5757
11:18

Jul 2, 06:24 PM

We should consider every day lost on which we have not danced at least once. And we should call every truth false which was not accompanied by at least one laugh.
Jul 2, 10:14 PM
Send Signal message

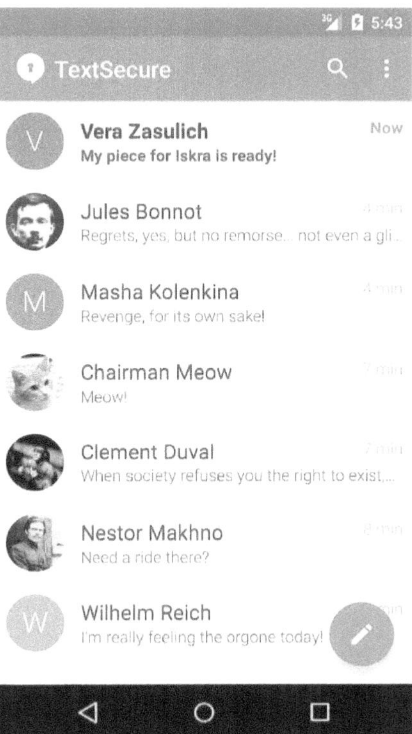
TextSecure
5:43

Vera Zasulich
My piece for Iskra is ready!
Now

Jules Bonnot
Regrets, yes, but no remorse... not even a gli...

Masha Kolenkina
Revenge, for its own sake!

Chairman Meow
Meow!

Clement Duval
When society refuses you the right to exist,...

Nestor Makhno
Need a ride there?

Wilhelm Reich
I'm really feeling the orgone today!

ORWEB

Orweb is a web browser created with your privacy in mind. It's newbie-friendly and, when coupled with Orbot, can shield you from network analysis, supercookies and all without running Flash, the same Flash that can introduce exploits into your Android system.

It does this by routing your traffic through international computers remotely rather than going directly into a VPN or other proxy service. It's slower this way, but ensures a level of security above that of the average user.

The problem is that it's now outdated. Obsolete. As of now it has been upgraded to Orfox status. As for the old version (i.e. Orweb), the developers had this to say:

"Orweb is built upon the bundled WebView (Webkit) browser component inside of the Android operating system. This has proven to be problematic because we cannot control the version of that component, and cannot upgrade it directly when bugs are found. In addition, Google has made it very difficult to effectively control the network proxy settings of all aspects of this component, making it difficult to guarantee that traffic will not leak on all devices and OS versions."

ORFOX

Orfox: Tor Browser for Android

Designed with source code from Tor Browser, a few enhancements have been added to make it a rock-solid browser for Android. With NoScript, HTTPS Everywhere and Tor Browser Button added in, it's a rock-solid tool for anonymous browsing.

Differences to note:

1.) Other than the fact Orweb is outdated, Orfox is vastly superior to Orweb as Orweb focuses on minimal browser-fingerprinting and cookies with fewer writes to disk.

2.) Orweb takes up less than 2MB. Orfox comes in at 27MB. This is mainly due to Orfox becoming a more robust browser with a longer feature set.

From the Developer:

"Orfox is built from the same source code as Tor Browser (which is built upon Firefox), but with a few minor modifications to the privacy enhancing features to make them compatible with Firefox for Android and the Android operating system."

- Orfox **REQUIRES** Orbot app for Android to connect
to the Tor network.

In as many ways as possible, we adhere to the design goals of Tor Browser, by supporting as much of their actual code as possible, and extending their work into the additional Android components of Firefox for Android.

The Tor software protects you by bouncing your communications around a distributed network of relays run by volunteers all around the world: it prevents somebody watching your Internet connection from learning what sites you visit, it prevents the sites you visit from learning your physical location, and it lets you access sites which are blocked."

TELEGRAM

Telegram

Telegram is a message app that focuses on security. It's fast, simple and ad-free. A few of the benefits they offer are:

- Cloud Storage: Telegram syncs across all your devices so you can always access your data. Your message history is also stored in the Telegram cloud.

- Group Chat & Sharing: you can form large group chats of up to 1000 members if you need to.

- Secret Chats: These are messages that, according to Telegram, can be programmed to self-destruct automatically from both participating devices. This way you can send all types of disappearing content: messages, photos, videos and files. Secret Chats also use end-to-end encryption to ensure that a message can only be read by its intended recipient.

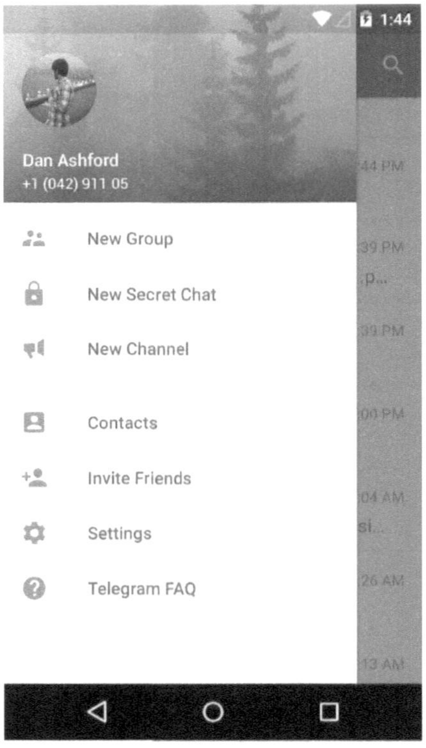

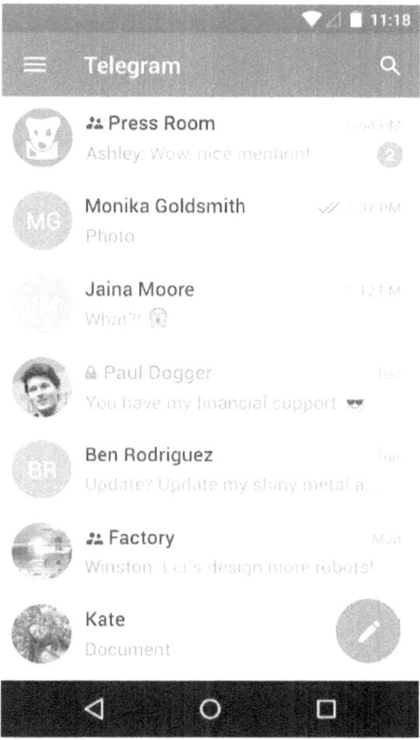

So how secure is it? That largely depends on your security needs. If you require rock-solid security like the kind political dissidents in China use, then no. There's lots of questions floating around on the lack of peer review as well. But if you only want to keep Google (or the spouse) out of your affairs, then yes.

Using an app that has end-to-end encryption is better than non end-to-end and that uses closed source (i.e. Whatsapp), with no way to peer review it. Telegram also does not store your secret chats, and the data stays encrypted until it arrives at the receiver's phone.

However, it uses non-standard crypto. Though there are those in the security community who become nervous whenever a developer does this, the bottom line is that you and you alone must determine if this app fills your anonymity needs, or whether you need some other app like CryptoCat.

CHAT SECURE

ChatSecure is an open-source chat client that supports encryption over XMPP. Previously known as 'Gibberbot', it's progressed to be a fairly reliable chat app for privacy. The downside is that it cannot stay connected or in an 'always-on' state since Apple forbids it. The upside is that it's free and works on every platform: Android, iPhone, Mac with Adium, Linux with Jitsi, and Windows with Pidgin.

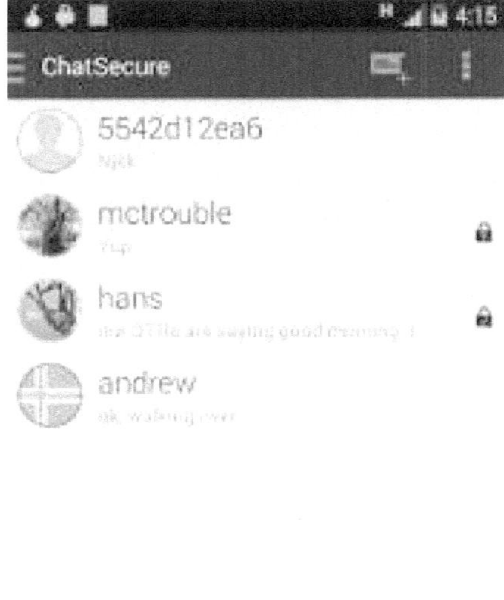

Features:

- Every message you send with ChatSecure is private so long as your recipient uses an OTR-compatible IM client

- Delivers audio, photos, files and text.

- Messages sent aren't stored in your phone's memory.

- If used with Orbot, it can bypass many firewalls and blacklists.

- Supports multiple accounts

ENCRYPTED E-MAIL

<u>K-9 and OpenKeychain: Encrypted E-mail</u>

<u>K-9 Mail</u> is built upon Android's native email application, but is open-source. It's main advantage for you is simplifying email management. If you've got multiple accounts and need encryption, K-9 is your baby since it uses OpenPGP via OpenKeychain for encrypting messages.

<u>OpenKeychain EASYPGP</u> integrates with K-9 and strengthens anonymous communications. The encryption it uses ensures that any communication can only be read by those with the proper key. When your recipient opens your message, they can see it is digitally signed by you (or not). In fact that's the whole point of PGP, also known as Pretty Good Privacy. For your eyes only. That's to ensure you're speaking with the right person.

You can also search for other people's keys online. Just remember that PGP is useful for two things:

1. Privacy and Security, and

2. Authenticity.

By privacy, I mean that you can prevent people from seeing things you don't want them to see. For example, you can encrypt an email to someone or encrypt a file with a list of passwords.

By authenticity, I mean that you can ensure a message was sent/written by the person you think it was and that it wasn't modified by a third party. Of course, these two can be combined.

I like to remember the opening scene from Wargames, where two missile silo operators have to turn their key simultaneously before inputting the nuclear launch codes.

Points to Note:

Don't worry about reverting to your old email should K-9 not be to your liking. This is easily done by uninstalling or going to

Settings --> Applications --> Manage Apps -->

and choosing your app before clicking on "clear defaults". This resets the default app for that function. It's sort of like installing a new browser. Chrome over Firefox, for instance. If you uninstall Chrome, Firefox will still be there for you.

The other thing is that if you want to export the K-9 settings somewhere, you will need to reboot your phone, after which the *com.fsck.k9* directory should be accessible at the topmost level of the Android system.

KEYSYNC: SYNCING TRUSTED IDENTITIES

KeySync allows you to sync identities between OpenPGP and ChatSecure as well as GnuPG. The app needs to do this for purposes of establishing trust between different apps on your Android device. Trust certificates, say, for Pidgin and Adium, need to be converted to ChatSecure so that there's no conflicting identities. It's sort of like having the same name and identity that matches all your credit cards.

You can use Discover and MasterCard at the same place because of the identity match. Same concept here.

Syncing to ChatSecure

Now then. Let's say you wanted to sync between ChatSecure on your phone and maybe an app on your PC or laptop. Here's what you'd have to do:

- Ensure your phone is connected via USB.

- Powerup KeySync and let it detect your system.

- If it fails to find it, it will store the *otr_keystore.ofcaes* to your phone's SD card. From there, ChatSecure can locate it.

Within ChatSecure you can go to your Account screen & choose "Activate KeySync." Then you use the QRCode that you can see in KeySync to complete this process. And that code acts as the key/passphrase to your keystore, so don't lose it or email it to anyone. It all sounds very convoluted, but you'll see it isn't once you go through it.

LASTPASS PASSWORD MANAGER

LastPass Password Manager

I absolutely love what I can do with LastPass. What does it do? Well you can use LastPass to store logins, create complex passwords and keep track of any team members passwords you have to keep under lock and key. You only need to remember one password however: *your* LastPassword.

It fills in logins for you and syncs passwords & passphrases anywhere you need it. That's not all. Some other neat things you can do (though admittedly a few break your anonymity!), are:

• Save and autofill usernames/passwords for all online accounts

• Streamline online shopping with Form Fill profiles (danger Will Robinson!)

• Store memberships, credit cards, & sensitive data in Secure Notes (Risky!)

• Search for logins and notes from your vault (useful)

• Organize sites by folders (very useful)

• Enable multifactor authentication to lock down your LastPass account.

• Share logins with friends/family (This is an absolute no-no unless you want to kill your anonymity outright.)

• Audit the strength of your passwords with the LastPass Security Challenge

In light of the above you may think what's the point since several features use services that are known to be hostile to privacy. Well, you don't need to use LastPass then. Many don't for the simple reason it is web-based. Try a Keypass database instead for offline activity, or sync with Dropbox.

Actually come to think of it, that's risky too since if you're unencrypted laptop or PC gets stolen, then you must consider *all* passwords compromised.

But let's compare an offline password manager like Password Safe with an online manager like LastPass for a moment. Weight the risks, so to speak.

Believe it or not, offline password managers carry risk just like online managers. Some believe that the password 'safe' file acts as the mother of all risks since it's the bottom ace card in a house of cards. But that's true for your PC too since all it takes is one keylogger to compromise your system.

Without any manager at all a keylogger can record every pass you use. With a manager app, you can conceivably lose ALL of your passwords in one fell stroke. For this reason I suggest you pick one or the other. They both harbor strengths and weaknesses with one strength being that you can use your passwords on anyone's computer. That's pretty convenient under almost any scenario.

Alas, there's always a hacker lurking around, and make no mistake that an online database can be breached by him and him alone. In that case, everyone goes down. Tens of thousands of users just like you. In this there is the safety in numbers element unless the hacker in question decides to sell every bit of data to the highest bidder. The silver lining is that you'll know about such a breach almost immediately from your online provider (assuming the company doesn't want a class-action lawsuit.)

LINPHONE: ENCRYPTED VIDEO AND VOICE OVER IP (VOIP)

Linphone (short for Linux phone) is a free voice over IP, or VoIP service, and SIP client, currently developed by Belledonne Communications in France. It's now available for AppleiOS and Android as well as PCs, with the biggest advantage being it isn't limited to voice and video. You can send texts, chat, make multiple calls and even call up your friends for an audio conference.

Three major new capabilities have been added: a text messaging feature (chat) with delivery status notification, multiple calls and audio conferencing. In addition, Linphone supports audio with speex , G711 ,ILBC, GSM, SILK, G722, OPUS, and video with the VP8 codec.

If you want to talk to your partners using Tor then you'll need to use Onioncat at both ends since Linphone uses UDP. Instructions on using Linphone for anonymous VoIP over Tor can be found here, at the Whonix site. Just remember that Tor adds considerable latency so it will not be like those crystal clear calls Jason Bourne gets in a fire-fight in some back alley in Pakistan.

OBSCURACAM: THE PRIVACY CAMERA

Like Pinta and Gimp, ObscuraCam allows you to blur faces in any photo or video that could lead to your identification. Use pixelation or blackout or even a funny nose/glasses combo to edit out your identity. The app itself is designed by the GuardianProject and Witness.org, a human rights training organization.

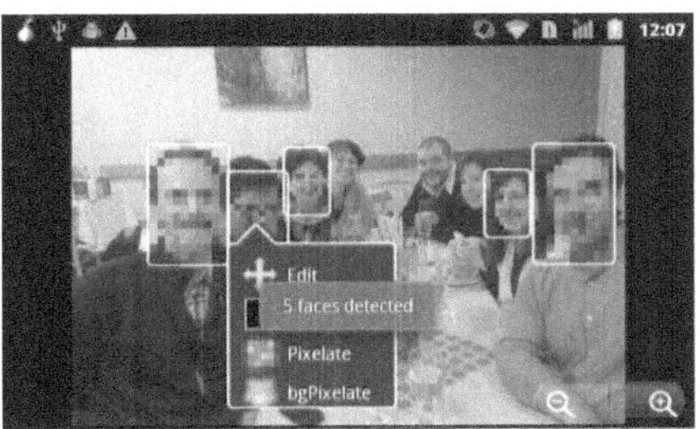

Unfortunately the ObscuraCam app itself does not encrypt files in transit. For that you'll have to resort to some other encryption app like PGP or Veracrypt and then go through the usual encryption routine like so:

- Install the app

- Create an encrypted container after choosing a container size for encrypting

- Send the file (along with the password your recipient needs via PGP). Simple.

What I find lacking in many online guides however, is the lack of metadata discussion. So allow me a short tangent on this important topic.

METADATA

Put simply, metadata is used by search engines, intelligence agencies and even grocery store chains to track you. Obscuracam removes this. Things like GPS coordinates, time/date of image, phone owner's name/nic, and phone model aren't recorded. In my view this is light years better than being able to blur faces on Facebook -which you should not be on anyway if you want privacy. The Exif Data Firefox plugin also makes a great companion tool as it can delete metadata from jpegs. Now onto some questions.

What else does metadata cover?

In theory the amount of metadata available on a person is near infinite. But they don't have quantum computers yet which means the amount of data on any one person is limited. We aim to limit it even more since even a single file can reveal a lot about you as a person.

What kind of files contain metadata?

Any kind. Word docs, jpegs, bitmaps, mp3s. Everything and anything that carries a digital signature or hash can tell them where you live, what you listen to, who dumped you and whether you squirt your ketchup on your fries or on the side at the In n' Out burger.

I'm a novelist. I don't care about any of that.

Sorry to tell you this but novelists have a lot to worry about too, especially if they're self-publishers. Actually traditional pubbers too, since French writer Grégory Delacourt was sued by Scarlett Johansson for 'stealing' her image. But that's another tale.

Novelists, writers and copywriters have to worry about privacy just like Stephen King. The master of horror storytelling once revealed his biggest blunder. He was asked if there was anything in his career that he regretted doing or saying, other than writing Maximum Overdrive. He said, "That damn American Express commercial from the eighties. Once I'd done that, people all over the world knew my face."

ORBOT: PROXY WITH TOR

Orbot encrypts your internet traffic with Tor so that it cannot be traced. It does this by relaying traffic through relays around the world. No other tool does this like Tor, and makes it a useful privacy tool. Even the New York Times praised it.

"When a communication arrives from Tor, you can never know where or whom it's from."

Okay, fair enough. But you must decide which is the bigger risk: Your cell provider or Google. I'd say both carry equal risk but, when you hand them your identity on a silver platter, well, they don't even need a judge to take you down. Only a thinly-veiled reproach. Of course some countries carry more risk than others when you take your threat model into account. Next question.

Is there a way to hide the fact I'm using Tor (Orbot) from my ISP?

Hiding Tor usage from your ISP provider isn't that hard. They'll know you're using Tor soon enough, just not what you're doing with it. They can also monitor you till the cows come home but have no idea what hidden services you're accessing nor do they have a clue which content you send or receive from while using Tor. It can be detected, however, from the Tor relay node via the IP addresses you connect to.

To hide Tor usage itself from them you'll need to use a Tor bridge, or pluggable transport bridges) to prevent them from seeing you are on the Tor network.

OSMAND: OFFLINE MAPS AND NAVIGATION

Osmand (OSM Automated Navigation Directions) is a navigation app used in conjunction with OpenStreetMap (OSM). It makes a stellar replacement for Google Maps, but it isn't anonymous unless you're offline the whole time. It uses maps from OpenStreetMap and can be downloaded using Tor.

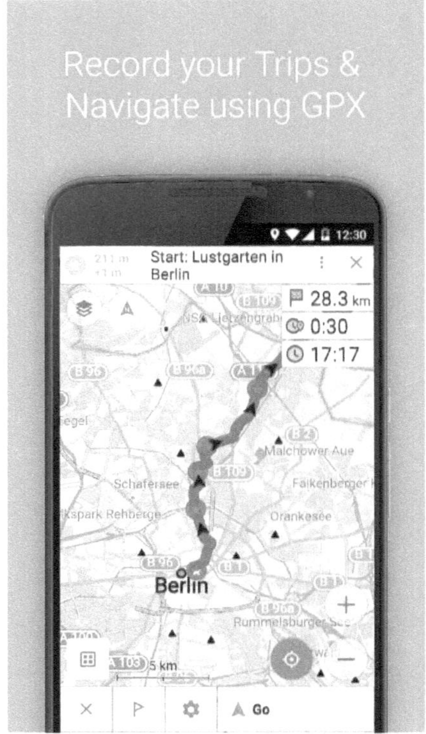

Features:

• Works online (fast) or offline (no roaming charges when you are abroad)

• Turn-by-turn voice guidance (recorded and synthesized voices)

• Optional lane guidance, street name display, and estimated time of arrival

• Supports intermediate points on your itinerary

• Automatic re-routing whenever you deviate from the route

• Search for places by address, by type (e.g.: restaurant, hotel, gas station, museum), or by geographical coordinates.

One downside is that while the screenshots on the Play Store make it look simple, it's not. In fact it's fairly complex and the controls are somewhat unintuitive.

OSTEL: ENCRYPTED PHONE CALLS

Ostel is a product designed for keeping your calls private. So private in fact, that it offers end-to-end encryption at both ends. And if you believe the United States to be the only one data mining everything on the internet, I've got a friendly rattlesnake to sell you.

I've got some mixed feelings about Ostel and I'm sure you will to. To begin with you must register for an account at Ostel.co. That was the first red flag. From the dial pad I had to key in 9196 then click the green icon in the corner before I could speak. Then came the echo test which I found similar to Skype's test. All in all, its a hit and miss scenario, but I concede your luck may be better than mine. The pros are as follows:

- Supports: Android, iPhone, Mac, Win, Linux & Blackberry/Nokia
  - Integrates well with CSipSimple app for Android
  - Supports end-to-end encrypted using ZRTP & SRTP.
  - Makes for a great privacy tool

Cons:

Encrypted phones sound intriguing to just about every

anonymity enthusiast out there, especially beginners. The problem? Configuring some of these apps can be like toying with a rattlesnake itself. Technical hurdle is putting it mildly indeed. Besides that, encrypted voice apps are really a hit and miss and here are a few reasons why.

Apps such as this one, based on my use of it, reveal a lot of counter-intuitive design decisions that don't mesh well with the Android interface, nor with what Android users are accustomed to. This isn't a problem for a technically minded person but beginners will have a hard time navigating around since a lot of these don't follow Android design specs.

Case in point: No activity light. Remember when almost every PC came with one so that you could see the hard drive being accessed? That's absent far too often these days. There's a few other red flags, one being the guessing game as to when the encryption actually began and when it ended.

Confusion. Ostel was as different to Linphone as the sun is to the moon in the directions. I'm quite good guessing games but even I tended to wander around like I was in a fog, patting my hands like a blind person. I can imagine how confusing it would be for someone new to encrypted voice calls. In one instance I ended up making a call through my normal phone line with the dial pad. There was no indication this was taking place until I ran some tests to confirm it. Strike one.

Setting up an account at Ostel.co was uninspiring, with the SIP provider not being clear on just what their definition of anonymity is, which bothered me. Throughout the process I kept thinking that newcomers will abandon ship when they realize they cannot call Skype anonymously (you need to call someone with a SIP client to ensure the call is private). That should be loud and clear on the front page.

Cannot call landlines from Ostel and have it encrypted. This was a deal killer for me, but I'll waive the strike since you may not need to call them at all.

Metadata. The app is bad at hiding it from others. Contacts, call history and such, seemed to be not terribly high on the app's priorities, unlike the Tor Browser Bundle. I admit that to compare Tor with encrypted phone use is perhaps premature as it *is* in it's infancy, but metadata is the hook, line and sinker of the NSA and thus must be executed as a priority one mission objective.

They log data. They claim to log enough data to run the service, but it sounds like the same ploy I hear from VPN providers looking to cover their backsides. We know VPN companies are great at offering privacy but for anonymity, many come up lacking. Strike two.

No Tor support. Also a deal killer, but this may be due to the prematurity of the service and not related to the company itself. Voice over IP doesn't work well with Tor anyway due to the way Tor works (torrents as well), which means Orbot won't work well with it. Strike three.

TEXTSECURE

TextSecure (now Signal) is an open-source communication app that allows you to avoid SMS fees and share media with colleagues, friends and the like, privately. We list it here if you're a little uneasy about using Signal.

So how secure is it?

Very secure, though obviously not as secure as the newly

revamped Signal app. An interesting (though insanely technical) research paper is available online and is called 'How Secure is Text-Secure'. It's put out by the Horst Institute for IT Security and their conclusion was that three apps outside of Tor outshine all others for anonymity: Threema, Surespot and TextSecure. You can draw your own conclusions, but I've tested every app and found TextSecure to be a great tool to use for any operation that requires staying off the grid.

PIXELKNOT: HIDDEN MESSAGES

Pixelknot allows you to send a short message within a photo that only the recipient can read. The practice involves what is known as 'steganography', or the act of embedding a hidden message in any format. In that vein it's somewhat similar to PGP, but uses the F5 algorithm to obscure your message. The developers (i.e. The Guardian Project) issued this standard to strive toward:

- Have the original image appear, to the trained human eye, unedited.
    - Have the bytes of the image appear, to a trained analyst, undistorted so much so as to arouse suspicion.
    - Have the complete message be recoverable no matter how it is transmitted.

I've used it for other types of communication but let's look at one in particular: Usenet. My favorite stomping ground since 1983.

Let's assume for a moment you want to send an anonymous message to someone on Usenet, perhaps in one of the many Mp3 newsgroups, and let's also assume you don't want Google indexing that message for all eternity. (Well actually, they will anyway).

You'd first pull up the app, choose a picture to hide the message in, and send it using a Usenet posting app knowing that even though the picture itself is quite visible to others, what is encoded *therein* is not. In fact, they could not even tell that it is a picture manipulated by Pixelknot. It's true that Google will index this for eons, but until quantum computing becomes widespread, won't be able to decrypt it.

If on the other hand you post an encrypted message using PGP, well, it's obvious you don't want others to see it if you post it in designated *encryption* newsgroups. The same is true for the popular encryption containers like those of Truecrypt or Veracrypt. Any extension (unless you change it) often gives away the app used and by extension the intent of the sender.

YOUR SECURITY NEEDS ARE NOT MY OWN

Admittedly, some of these apps don't quite cut the mustard anymore. Perhaps you tried a few and for whatever reason they just didn't float your boat. The apps mentioned herein aren't the only ones of course. They're just the ones that provided for *my* security needs. Yours may be different. Of course, I was a little worried about the authorities mandating a 'back door' in a few but then I realized that using plain old run-of-the-mill SMS is almost always intercepted by local sheriffs and municipal police to begin with. Everywhere.

Between using SMS and an open-source app by one of the most respected security researchers in the world, you probably know which one to use. My skills aren't really up to tracking the changelog on GitHub and recompiling it myself for Verizon's SMS, so I'll just trust WhisperSystems instead.

As a side note, as soon as Microsoft paid 8.5 billion for Skype, it found itself in a much deeper U.S. jurisdiction than Windows settled for. Skype makes voice calls to the PSTN (i.e. the public switched telephone network) and when that happened, it fell under the CALEA Act. That's the Communications Assistance for Law

Enforcement Act, an act initiated by the US Congress to facilitate wiretapping of U.S. domestic telephone and Internet traffic.

Skype encryption is not end to end.

And now that Microsoft lives smack dab in the middle of every conversation uttered over Skype in the USA (and even abroad), they have a nice intercept point to eavesdrop from their servers. By contrast, TextSecure (now Signal) does not own a voice service. So there's no intercept requirements. If TextSecure were ever to resort back to SMS, then law enforcement can sniff the ciphertext. But without the key, its pretty useless.

GHOST APPS FOR THE BLACK MARKET

First up is GRAMS, the Darknet Search Engine

Grams's engine was designed to be used primarily for exploring the Deep Web. Announced on Reddit over a year ago, it has made some great strides in indexing things you cannot find on the regular web. But like Google in 1996, they're in a very early stage of indexing things, so it's not perfect and offers nowhere near the complexity that Google does.

It does share some of the traits of Google's algorithm though, like having a scoring system based on how long the listing has been up, how many transactions, and how many good reviews any one site has. That way you'll see the best listing first - similar to what you'd see using Google.

The Grams Infodesk can be reached at the Onion site here:

http://grams7enufi7jmdl.onion/infodesk

You will need Tor to access this onion site.

Duck Duck Go

DUCKDUCKGO

DuckDuckGo strives to become the next great internet search engine that protects user's privacy and avoids the filter bubble of personalized search results that Google is so famous for.

The results are a compilation of about 50 sources including Yahoo! Search, BOSS, Wikipedia, Bing and its own Web crawler, the DuckDuckBot, among others. The best part is that while the regular search site is at DuckDuckGo.com, you can use the Duck onion site to perform a clearnet search, which adds yet another layer of security to your regular web usage. The link is at:

http://3g2upl4pq6kufc4m.onion/

Note: Obviously you will need to be connected to the Tor network for the above onion link to work.

Pros to Using DuckDuckGo

- In March, 2015, DuckDuckGo retrieved more than 9 million searches for the first time since she set sail. That month also saw the search engine retrieve more than 250 million searches. Where there are great numbers, there is camouflage. Plus, their competition could set new common rules for privacy among web service providers, which would include Google.

- You can always precede a search query with g! to see what Google's results would be. For instance:

"Mustangs !g" -> search for Mustangs on Google.
"Mustangs !gi" -> search for Mustangs on Google image
"Mustangs !yt" -> Youtube
"Mustangs !b" -> Bing
More here: https://duckduckgo.com/bang

- When DuckDuckGo lists results that it got from Yahoo or Bing, your phone or laptop isn't getting cookies from Yahoo or Bing.

Cons to Using DuckDuckGo

- DuckDuckGo labels itself as a privacy search engine, so it won't be terribly helpful to use it for things requiring location. A search for "air conditioners for sale in New Orleans, LA" will give you a craigslist-like site, followed by a contractor's webpage, and a link to YellowPages. The same search on google gives the names of some local and major-chain businesses who sell and install air conditioners.

And in case you're wondering if 'incognito' mode stops Google's tracking that results from your Google searches, the answer is no. A loud no with arms waving no. Only a non-tracking search engine like DuckDuckGo (that can guarantee your privacy) does that. Bing and Yahoo and Google will still record everything you do regardless of any incognito mode, as it affects the browser options and not the search engine of choice.

Another thing about our beloved Google, whose name keeps popping up like some handle-bar mustached villain in a bad play. Google knows your preferred home temperature *and* your work schedule when you're away at Six Flags *and* when you go to sleep and wake up, all thanks to the Nest Learning Thermostat. That, coupled with Google Pictures (which logs images on your phone or PC) makes for one very bright laser red dot on your back. People love convenience over security, even before Ben Franklin wrote his famous quote on liberty and security.

Google Wallet? Again, convenience. They keep all data related to every purchase you make, every sale, and coordinate it all with every email message you write. Remember what Google founder Eric Schmidt said some years ago?

"Google will soon know more about you than you know yourself!".

They now have far more data on you than the NSA does and that data is only a warrant away. Rest assured they will not offer 1/10th the privacy that DuckDuckGo does.

NOTECIPHER

<u>NoteCipher</u> is a simple notepad app. All notes created and stored by this app are saved fully secured using 256-bit AES encryption. They are never stored in an unencrypted state on the disk, only in memory. It was ported to Android in 2011 by the Guardian Project.

NoteCipher Locked
NoteCipher
Open

NoteCipher
Secret note..
this is my secret
note

APG

OpenPGP is another good privacy app for Android. It's open source and its goal is to provide a similar OpenPGP implementation as GnuPG.

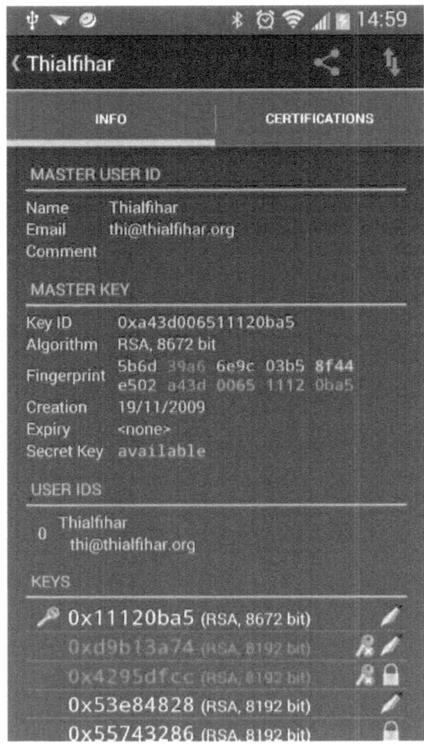

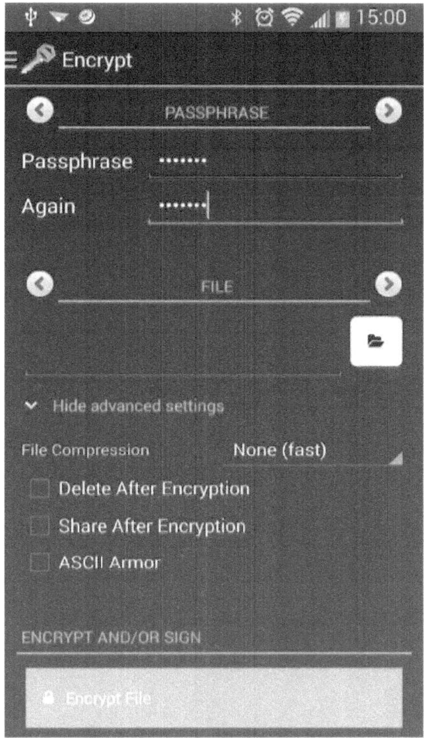

If you're browsing Darknet Markets you may run across the occasional vendor whose key wont work with APG. But this is rare. In any case you can use GnuPrivacyGuard to help.

As a side note, if you're worried about the app broadcasting that you're using Apg v.1.1. whatever (yet don't want anyone knowing you use APG), you could always edit the version before sending out any message. Example: Put Version: GnuPG v2 and anyone else would assume that's the encryption program you are using.

BITCOIN WALLET

Want to have your Bitcoins always with you? Check out Bitcoin Wallet.

You pay by quickly scanning a QR-code and if you're a merchant, you'll receive payments reliably and instantly. Bitcoin Wallet is the first mobile Bitcoin app and arguably one of the most secure.

• No registration, web service or cloud needed. This wallet is decentralized.

• Display of Bitcoin amount in BTC, mBTC and μBTC.

• Conversion to and from national currencies.

• Sending and receiving of Bitcoin via NFC, QR-codes or Bitcoin URLs.

• Address book for regularly used Bitcoin addresses.

• When you're offline, you can still pay via Bluetooth.

• System notification for received coins.

• Sweeping of paper wallets (e.g. those used for cold storage).

• App widget for Bitcoin balance.

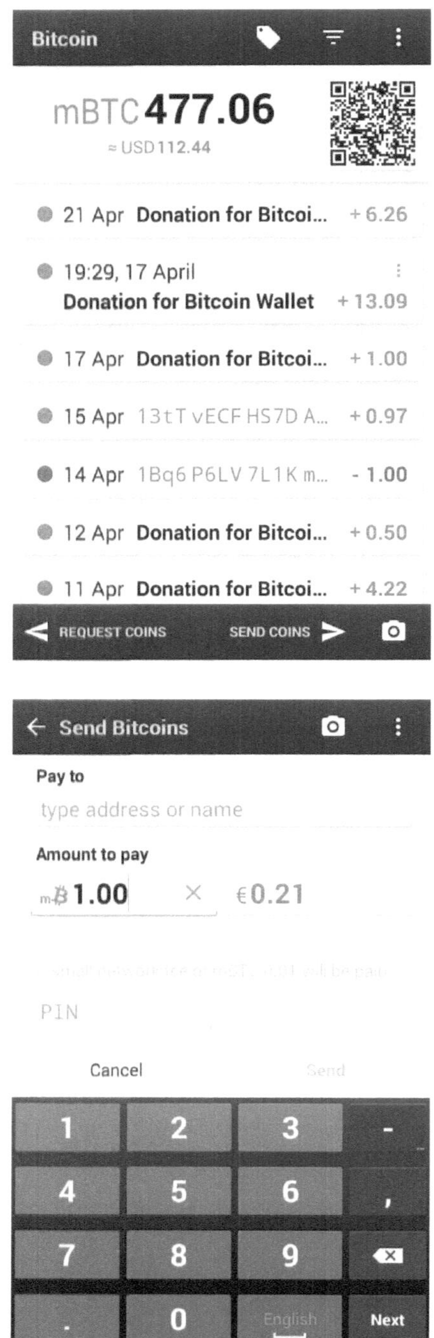

CHATSECURE

ChatSecure is a free and open source messaging app that features OTR encryption over XMPP. You can connect to your existing accounts on Facebook or Google, create new accounts on public XMPP servers (including via Tor), or even connect to your own server for extra security.

Unlike other apps that keep you stuck in their walled garden, ChatSecure is fully interoperable with other clients that support OTR and XMPP, such as Adium, Jitsi, and more.

Strong Cryptography

ChatSecure only uses well-known open source cryptographic libraries to keep your conversations private. Other apps may make claims about "military grade" security but, without publicly auditable source code and verifiable end-to-end encryption, you cannot be 100% safe.

Some of what it offers:
- XMPP with TLS certificate pinning.
- OTR for verifiable end-to-end encryption and forward secrecy.

- Tor to help bypass restrictive firewalls.
- SQLCipher to locally encrypt conversation logs.

Anonymouth

Recall earlier what we said about looking *like everyone else* when using Tor. Enter Anonymouth.

Stylometrics is the study of a person's writing 'style'. It analyzes your writing and creates a trackable profile out of it. In other words, your 'voice' in your writing or the way you phrase simple statements, word length, word choice, misspelled words and so on. Where cell phone opsec is concerned it can be impossible to predict who has this ability and where and when and what you can do to blend in without *looking like you're trying to blend in*. It can be a double-edged sword but, there are a few pearls I can dispense with here.

Long messages are just bad OPSEC any way you slice it. To counter this, Edward Snowden used short and punchy messages to throw off anyone trying to trace his NSA leaks back to him. This was good since if one used Tor and nothing else without care of what was previously published, it'd be pretty easy for the NSA to link him to previous documents he'd written on the open net.

As for us, we have the option of using Anonymouth. It's a tool for anonymizing every word we spit out on the open web. It's not simple to use but like PGP it can be a life saver if you need protection for any sensitive data. How does it work?

It uses Java to analyze previous works with present-day works, compares them and then tips you off to overused words, then suggests fixes to help you 'blend in'. You can even tell it to scan a folder or group of docs you'd like to 'anonymize'.

For instance. Let's say you are an Iranian political dissident using Tor. You also happen to be a journalist. Although your anonymous by way of IP address, the government in Tehran could (in theory) still analyze your anonymous posts and compare them to your known writings, say on your public blog. Same with leaking emails from a corrupt business. Maybe they'll compare what you mailed to a newspaper to all emails on a corporate server.

There's plenty of scenarios where this could be useful. It can be downloaded from the Github website at:

github.com/psal/anonymouth

GHOSTERY

Ghostery is very popular at the moment. What does it do? It reports all tracking packages detected (and whether Ghostery has blocked them or not) in a "findings window" accessible from clicking on the Ghostery Icon in the browser. When configured, Ghostery also displays the list of trackers present on the page in a temporary purple overlay box.

With the "Ghost rank" reporting feature enabled, Ghostery transmits the full HTML code of the page visited to Ghostery, Inc., and takes note key data such as the advertising distribution systems that users encounter and the speed at which these load on the page.

I recommend this app if you need to hide from Google. As for the NSA or Iranian government? Not a chance. According to a few online sources, they sell your data. To whom or what is anyone's guess. And there are claims of this app being spyware.

But, you can prevent Ghostery from doing this by opting out of the Ghost Rank feature. The feature is opt-in so if you didn't already opt in there is nothing you need to do. If this feature bothers you, there's a few others I can recommend. One of which is PrivacyBadger. More on that one in a bit.

FLASHCONTROL

FlashControl gives you control over which sites are allowed to display the Flash player or the HTML5 player. With FlashControl installed, web content that requires Flash plugins will be disabled by default. You then enable content by clicking on a blocked area on any given webpage, or via Flashcontrol's address bar icon. You can also reblock content that you've unblocked.

This can help reduce CPU load and provide some security control so that content isn't automatically loaded without your permission. You can get it at the Mozilla Addons site.

Sidenote: I tend to walk among the block-all-flash and then click-to-play guys, but I just wish some of the video-streaming providers that use Flash would dump it and use HTML5. Then I could lead a very Flash-free life.

PRIVOXY

Privoxy is a *non-caching* web proxy with filtering capabilities for enhancing privacy, manipulating cookies and modifying web page data and HTTP headers before the page is rendered by the browser.

It's a privacy *enhancing* proxy. That is, it filters Web pages and removes advertisements. Privoxy can be customized by users for both stand-alone systems and multi-user networks and can be chained to other proxies.

It's frequently used in combination with Squid and can be used to bypass Internet censorship. Get it at the Privoxy homepage at privoxy.org.

TACO

Taco stands for *Targeted Advertising Cookie Opt-Out.*

This app auto-blocks hundreds of web beacons, bugs, and other tracking technologies that advertisers and others use to track you. Sounds like Ghostery to me. What it amounts to setting permanent opt-out cookies for Google and 25 others, even if those cookies are deleted by Firefox.

Now a word from our sponsor.

You need to understand something about so-called "opt-out" cookies and their respective apps, which I think can be a little misleading. A couple of thoughts.

First, if you read the fine print of virtually every company's privacy policy regarding cookie use, you'll find that they promise not to display targeted ads to you based on your personal web history. That is, you'll see ads that a person would see if they were not being tracked. However, many still track you. When you start digging around in their lawyer-speak agreements you'll often find that they rarely promise that they won't track you 100%, just that they won't show you personalized ads based on their data. They still use these opt-out cookies to do any of the following:

- Track your movements, as in what sites you visit.
- What you click on.
- What you buy with credit cards or even Paypal.

Secondly, they then use this data for their own marketing purposes and may decide to sell it to other companies. So in terms of privacy, this addon by itself is inadequate without the aid of a lot of the other addons we mention - primarily because it gives people the false idea that somehow their privacy is being protected by opt-out cookies when it's not.

ADBLOCK PLUS

<u>Adblock Plus</u> for Firefox is the most downloaded browser extension worldwide and winner of the About.com Reader's Choice Award, as well as the Linux New Media award for the Best Open Source Firefox Extension. Whenever I've had to re-install an OS, this is the first addon I install after Firefox.

Depending on the filter lists you have activated, you can even block YouTube video ads and Facebook tracking. Filter lists are created by members of the open source community and free to use. If you don't want to rely on filter lists you can create your own blocking rules to customize your web experience. It all sounds like a lucid dream for the budding privacy advocate.

However.

AdBlock introduced the Acceptable Ads Program a few years back. That means various companies can pay AdBlock so that their ads are added to a long 'whitelist', so that you see them in your browser. They've actually been doing this for a good while now though not many users know about it.

NOSCRIPT

NoScript allows JavaScript, Java and other executable content to run only from trusted domains of your choice. Things like your home-banking web site, guarding your "trust boundaries" against cross-site scripting attacks (XSS), cross-zone DNS rebinding / CSRF attacks (router hacking), and Clickjacking attempts, thanks to its ClearClick technology.

That's not a simple description, obviously, and for good reason since NoScript isn't a simple addon. It's very complex, but like chess is easy to learn, hard to master.

My biggest reason for using it is that NoScript users are less vulnerable to exploits than non-users. And it does a lot more than just whitelist what sites can run scripts. It also offers protection against clickjacking and cross-site scripting even if you whitelist sites. A few users even run it while globally-allowing scripts by default simply to get a few other benefits. So it's more than just a privacy tool. It's an *anonymity* tool. It comes bundled with the Tor Browser for good reason.

Another aspect I like is that the permissions function is very domain-specific. You can allow google.com to run scripts, for instance, but deny google-analytics.com or gstatic.com. Or you can allow maps.google.com but deny all other .google.com sites. And you can even (temporarily) allow sites you'd normally deny if you need them for a specific task.

So what's the worst that could happen if you retain No Script while allowing scripts globally?

You're more vulnerable to exploits that aren't being guarded against, for one. Even if you visit a website you don't trust, scripts will still run. There'll just be some protection against dodgy techniques that you wouldn't otherwise have. And some scripts have an easier time "phoning home" and fingerprinting you. Then there's the badly-coded sites that eat up your RAM and CPU cycles.

Though there's a slight learning curve to NoScript, it isn't hard to figure out. You can block most web bugs from Facebook, Google and Twitter and the like. The 'like' button on Facebook is one such web bug. Every time you visit a site that has that button (you need not press it), a lot of data goes back to Facebook about your online habits. Same with Twitter's 'Tweet' buttons and Google's G+ buttons.

In the beginning, my biggest nitpicks were:

- Dealing with sites that want to run a gazillion scripts from a huge number of different domains, and
- How hard it was to judge the trustworthiness of third-party domains.

Obviously you must judge each site yourself according to your own opsec needs, but I solved the above two issues this way for general open net browsing:

Whenever you hit a new website, enable enough of them to get basic site functionality. Usually this means you'll allow the ones with the site name in them and work outward from there to some of the legitimate-sounding ones. Enabling past this point defeats NoScript's purpose, but you'll eventually get a feel for what you need to enable to get the site working.

UMATRIX

uMatrix is a point-and-click matrix-based firewall. Just point & click to forbid or allow any class of requests made by your browser. Not only does it block javascript, but also cookies, css, plugins, images and more on either a per domain or global basis. The interface is pretty easy, too. It exists as a plugin for both Firefox and Chrome.

Personally I like to keep NoScript for the XSS protection. uMatrix will still block javascript very well but once you allow some javascript, it will step aside. NoScript will still scan allowed javascript for obvious XSS attempts and prevent it.

uBlock Origin

uBlock Origin is a content filter by the developer of uMatrix. It shares a bit of the same functionality of uMatrix but is better suited to blocking ads. It can use the same filter lists as Adblock Plus. There's two versions: the original by Raymond Hill which has been renamed from uBlock to uBlock Origin, and a fork by Chris Aljoudi which retains the original name, uBlock.

You can use all of the above since NoScript and uMatrix often strive for the same goal. They're just fundamentally different. NoScript only blocks scripts but uMatrix blocks whole connections.

From a *privacy* perspective, uMatrix is the way to go because the connection never gets established.

From a *security* perspective, NoScript is superior. You must decide if you want to run each script. With uMatrix you can only decide on a per connection basis and NoScript won't stop third parties from connecting. Either one presents their own unique hassles. But even so, I recommend installing Privacy Badger and uBlock.

For more tools on anonymity (and a lot of other useful information) see the following link at the addon switchboard:

https://github.com/gorhill/httpswitchboard/wiki

CELL KEYLOGGERS

Keyloggers are a mixed breed of dog, and like any mixed breed I have some mixed feelings about them. They can save your hide by defending you to the death, or they can get someone's reputation or way of life destroyed. So what's a keylogger?

It's an app that secretly records keystrokes and sends them by way of sleuthy internet magic to some evildoer on the other side of the world. Or your dad could use it to catch your mom spying on him.

They really have a million uses and, right or wrong, it is parents that are the only ones truly equipped to play Big Brother, and do so *ethically*. Certainly they've got the know-how to reign in a reckless teen who's too street-smart for his own good. Dad know the limits because Dad knows the kid inside and out. Not government. Not the FBI. And most certainly not the police.

We've seen what happens to sexting teenagers who pass around nude photos like baseball cards. It ain't pretty.

Courts and cops trawl em, raid em and jail em and then claim to 'help' the kids by throwing them on the sex offender's list because, well, that's what they like to do to *other people's kids*. I don't know about you but I think the parents can do a much better job than any bureaucrat. So below are a few I recommend if you've got a 14 year old experimenting with car jackings or gang related activity. You know, serious crimes.

For other things like weed, curfew breaking and voyeurism, I'd not recommend any of these, especially for older teens. Reason being is because they may find out their being spied on. Call it a sixth sense. Then they'll Google all kinds of ridiculous things just to toy with you. Search terms like:

- Sex change operations.
- How to make a PB&J with the crusts cut off.
- How long would a rubber duck float in the Gulf of Oman.
- My cat wants me to get an abortion.
- Is narcissism genetic?
- How do cows scratch their knees if they itch?

Stuff like that. And if you've got a kid whose intelligence rivals that of Neo in The Matrix, then you've met your match. He could get a USB stick, put a live install of Linux on it and boot from the USB drive. Keep the USB drive hidden when he isn't using it.

It's a reverse whammy unless you somehow take his stick, guess his password, figure out Ubuntu *and* find a way to install a Linux keylogger. Even if that happened, he can just format it and put a fresh copy of Ubuntu on it again.

Anyway for the uninitiated, here's the first one. It's called <u>Spy Bubble</u>. It monitors cell phone use on any mobile device you can think of.

After you install it, monitoring begins instantly. It'll monitor and record information on the target phone in complete stealth, giving you complete access to any sensitive information you could be looking for. At $50 bucks, it ain't free. But it's a helluva lot cheaper than hiring a lawyer.

The downside is that SpyBubble can't track stored videos or

calendar events. It can't block phone numbers, websites or mobile apps. It can't set keyword alerts to send notice if the phone is used to access inappropriate material. You also can't use it to see BlackBerry Messenger chats either.

Second up is Spyera.

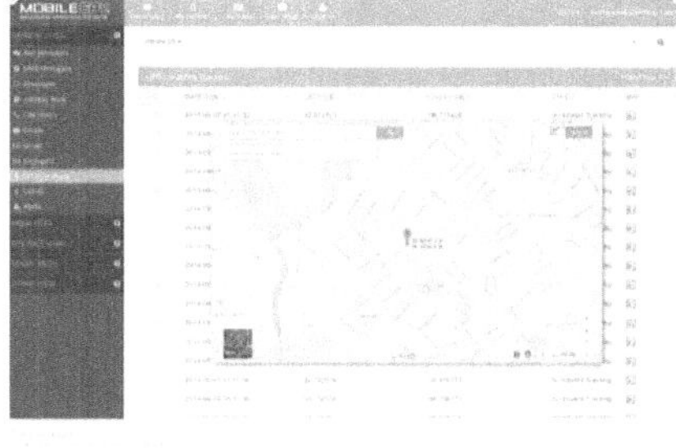

Third is MobileSpy.

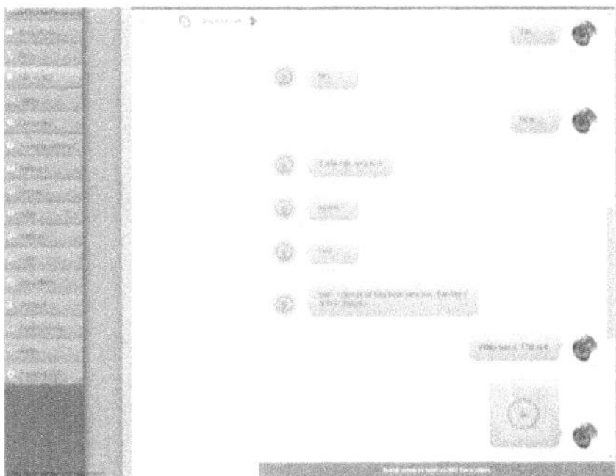

Fourth is Flexispy

Fifth and last is MobiStealth.

All of these keyloggers basically do the same thing: spy on your kids, or the competing used car lot owner across the street.

Detecting Keyloggers

Detecting keyloggers isn't exactly brain surgery. You just need to know where to look. Sometimes it's difficult, but there's usually others online who've gone through the trouble of posting a thread on a forum somewhere. So help abounds. Here's a few ways you can check for keylogger modules that may have wormed their way (with a little help from the Mrs.) into your system.

Most keyloggers use a kind of DLL-injection to get under the hood and stay there without you seeing it. That means that a DLL will show up mapped to a process's address space, as seen below:

The pyd (python extension) file sits at the top in the second section under 'Name'. This one's been loaded right into Windows Explorer's address space, which means it'll run every time Explorer is run. For anything you need Explorer to do. That makes it hard to get rid of without dedicated anti-virus software that knows what to look for.

DLLs like this want to see *everything* you type, so they typically load themselves into every target address space available. For a smart cookie who knows his PC like the back of his hand, he'll likely see odd DLLs here and there that look suspicious - files he can't link to any products he's bought or uses. He can bring these up in a list for every process. Geeks do this enough every day to where they begin to see anomalies, or 'ghost files' that shouldn't be there. They don't like to rely on anti-virus programs alone.

That's one thing that kids are lousy at: noticing things like a tiny switch (or GPS device) hooked under the car ignition. Spyware companies depend on kids being uninformed.

Solutions?

1.) You can study the 'drivers' folder for any strange files.

2.) Create a debug boot file with BcdEdit and hook up a firewire cable and hit a break point when the module loads and study ALL modules, every one, filtering details as you go along. Any DLL/driver can't do squat about you looking at it before it's loaded into Windows. This is, of course, the complicated way of doing things.

3.) Almost all keyloggers phone home somewhere else. So connect to a transparent proxy and note connections not familiar to you. You may see something along the lines of 'myspy.ukraine.com' rather than just your usual VPN address.

4.) Purchase an 'anti-keylogger' program. There as numerous as anti-virus vendors, but not all equal.

Obviously if you're using this spyware to monitor your kids, they won't have half the brainpower to do any of the above unless they've got a few whiz kids in their circle of friends. Better safe than sorry, I'm with the parents on this one.

TOR AND CELL PHONES

Tor users generally fall into one of two categories: The average Joe who can't be bothered to expand his knowledge of security past an intermediate level is one of them. He's super confident, and generally he likes things easy-peasy. Press a button and go. Many Mac users used to fall into this category but now many Windows users get over-confident in their own security abilities.

The other group are Tor superhackers who can smell a Tor honeypot from Hong Kong to Longview, Texas. They know when the cops are around. Hounds, they are. They can smell the red-blue, red-blue of a police cruiser's lights long before they come on.

While their numbers are few, they're also the restless types since they can't sleep unless they've plugged every security hole imaginable and chained enough proxies to circle the moon. Even then they're generally the most paranoid obsessed micro-managers this side of a psych ward. We aim to be somewhere in the middle.

But you should know that even with the anonymous Tor browser, anonymity on a cell phone is harder than on a PC because of how phones are now entwined with social media applications and your real identity. This, along with how Google loves to track every move you make (even if you whistle a copyrighted tune out your backside), makes smartphone opsec very problematic indeed for the survivalist and anonymity enthusiast.

But first, a refresher on the basics.

Tor & IP Addresses

I'll repeat this a million times if necessary: Your IP address is worth GOLD to social media giants like Facebook and YouTube.

Think about the long-term effects of monitoring you for years on end for a moment.

Your browser alone, never mind all the leaks of data your OS gives, provides all kinds of data on your lifestyle by way of web analytics. Things like where you like to shop, what you say and to whom you say it and how often. Which political or religious forums you frequent. Your pets names. Your hairdresser. Your fixer.

And that's not all. It links your family history on social media sites. It links your favorite book genres, your favorite sexual fantasies, your eye color. The list goes on and on. Therefore it is most crucial that we hide it as much as possible as we build out our cellular fortress of doom from which nothing can penetrate. If you don't know what Tor is, I highly recommend visiting the Tor website to learn the dirty little details.

The gist of this is that any packet sent by Tor is stripped of the sender's originating info. Tor is able to remove who sent the packet and who the intended recipient is. Think of it this way:

Imagine you sent an envelope to person A, and in that envelope was an envelope to send to person B.

- Person A then sends the letter to person B.

- B gets the envelope from A, and in that envelope is *another* envelope to send to person C.

- Person C gets that envelope from B, then looks up the information that is requested. Then that person sends the response in an envelope addressed to person B.

- Person B puts that in an envelope for A and sends to A, which then puts it in another envelope to send back to you.

Tor routing works like this, except you also know the public keys for A, B, and C ahead of time, so that when you send a message to person A, the only thing that A can decrypt is the fact you are sending a message to B - only the message itself is **still encrypted** and **only decryptable by Person C**. Meanwhile, Person B receives, decrypts, and relays the message to C but never knows you sent it, and C has no idea who you or "A" really is.

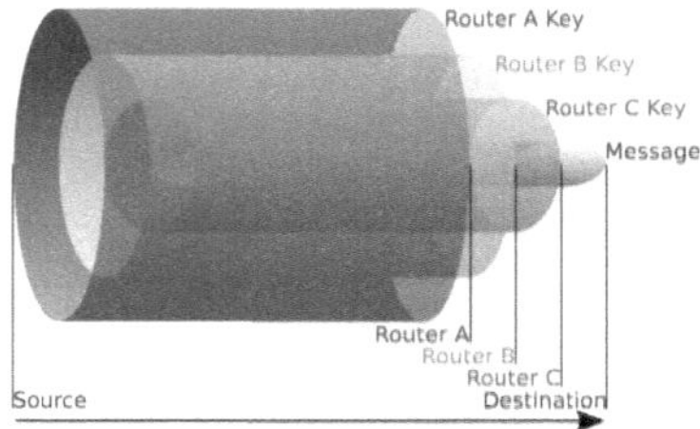

If you're in the United States, there's some bad news to hear, and it's this: Tor is generally safer for citizens that don't live in nations with lots of alphabet agencies (i.e. intelligence) running Tor exit nodes that sniff traffic. If you're in the USA and run Tor - as long as no one is deploying high statistical traffic-analysis on you, your IP address is generally safe for the session. Given enough resources and time/funding, Tor can be not-very-safe if your doing anything illegal.

That said, this leaves a lot to be desired when we need good opsec. So many ways exist that could out your identity. If you open Hotmail for instance while surfing with Tor, any alphabet agency can, with sufficient resources, correlate that address with Tor activity. Keyloggers can too. They can record keystrokes outside of Tor and send them online to destinations unknown. From Russia with Love. You could even run into a site that has an XSS security hole and have your identity stolen right out from under you. A million things could go wrong.

For this reason, we need to set a few ground rules for using Tor. It doesn't matter what you're using it for. Americans have been arrested for sarcastic comments left on Facebook. So anything done on Tor must never be connected with any social media outlet. Ever.

10 TOR RULES FOR SMARTPHONE USERS

The way we go about securing our phone with Tor is to assume everything you run is compromised. Plug all the holes so to speak. And the basic guidelines are the same.

- **No Browser Customizations** - That is, no customization based on emotional whims. The Tor Browser can't fix your personal imprint that drip-feeds intel onto the net, which leads to your front door in the same way a wolf leaves dribbles of urine back to it's lair. Plugins like Flash, QuickTime and Firefox Personas can reveal your IP address. Load up Firefox with a dozen social media plugins and you can kiss your anonymity goodbye. This also means no YouTube. No Facebook. No Twitter. No LinkedIn.

- **Avoid Chrome and Internet Explorer -** There's no reason to use these at all since Tor comes pre-bundled with a very fine-tuned Firefox setup. Chrome isn't built for Tor. It's built for tracking you. That's what Google does. Google didn't build a billion dollar search empire by playing nice. Just as Samsung when they tried to sneak an Adblock-like app into the Play Store. They did reinstate it later, but not without some heavy oversight.

- **Never Open Executables** - If I absolutely must run an executable file, pdf or document, I transfer it to memory stick and carry it by hand to a computer that is not online. I then copy/paste it to a virtual machine like VMWare with Windows installed (aka sandboxed) so that if a virus does exist, it's ability to do damage is limited. Think of a nuclear weapon going off underground out in the Nevada desert.
- **Use Tor Bridges** - If Tor brings to much heat, use a Bridge Relay. While vanilla Tor does a good job, it's not perfect. It can't prevent an NSA data center with huge resources from doing traffic analysis to determine if your using Tor. If you want to hide the fact you're using Tor, then opt for a Tor Bridge Relay instead of a direct connection to the same Tor entry point everyone else uses.
- **Act Like Everybody Else** - Tor relayed this to me that when I maximized Tor Browser:

Maximizing Tor Browser can allow websites to determine your monitor size, which can be used to track you.

The solution is simple. Always use the default options whenever possible unless it enhances anonymity, such as disabling Javascript. One comment on the Tor Blog illuminates why this is the case:

"Using an unusual screen resolution was sufficient to identify me uniquely to Panopticlick.com. With my portrait mode screen resolution of 1200 wide by 1920 high, the default window size of 1000x1765 was **unique**, no resizing or maximizing needed."

A website can find out information about your screen that includes width, height, DPI, color depth, and even font smoothing. A 1080p resolution isn't so bad, but the worst thing you can do is to resize the Tor browser to a random size instead of maximizing it. Any adversary won't have a clue about the hardware you're running, but you'll probably be the only person with that browser size on each site you visit.

This is bad since it means your activity can be tracked - the adversary will know that sites A, B and C were visited by the same person despite the fact that Tor used three different IPs to access those sites.

Therefore, act like everybody else.

- **Never enter your real information online**. Perhaps this is obvious, but don't enter in anything that may reveal your identity online. If asked for your personal details when signing up for a web site, lie.
- **Take extra caution if you register a domain name**. If you want to set up a site of your own, you may be tempted to register your own domain. Be careful. Domain name registrars collect a lot of information and reveal a lot in WHOIS records. If you register a domain name, do so anonymously.

ANONYMOUS ANDROID

Strong anonymity takes a lot of hard work as you'll soon find out. It's like something out of Pandora's Box.

Securing a leaky, soul-stealing privacy-eating gremlin-toothed operating system like Android can unleash hell quite easily. And all it takes is one mistake, a simple curiosity, a little peek that leads to another, and another and before you know it you're one cocky, self-absorbed son of a gun who can do no wrong when the inevitable happens. You take unnecessary risks.

What happens to those on a motorcycle who take risks? Gun owners? Athletes?

The day you lose respect is the day you'll wind up beneath an overturned gasoline tanker. Like chess and motorcycles, it's just not an easy platform to master. In fact, Android is a pain in the ass to lock down, a beast that doesn't like chains and being told what to do. Just when you think you've got her figured out, she shapeshifts.

Changing Android's Hardware (firmware)

Your phone or tablet has two operating systems. One on top, such as iOS or Android, and one beneath that deals with all things radio. That's the beast in the basement we must deal with if we are to sail the flagship named Anonymity.

It's housed in firmware and gets its meat from a baseband processor, so it's a little difficult to access without modifications. Make that, *dangerous* modifications.

Most of them run on the ARM processor but that's of little consequence since you can replace the Android operating system itself if you so desire. You can do this by installing CyanogenMod along with Team Win Recovery Project.

Required apps:
- CyanogenMod
- Team Win Recovery Project image
- F-Droid package
- Orbot from F-Droid
- Droidwall from F-Droid
- Droidwall Firewall Scripts

HOW TO ACCESS HIDDEN ONION SITES ON THE DEEP WEB HOW TO ACCESS HIDDEN ONION SITES ON THE DEEP WEB

Onion sites are those sites with an .onion extension that can only be reached by using the Tor Browser. You cannot reach them on the open web. Accessing them is just like accessing any other site over the Tor network as long as you know the address.

To that end, Reddit holds a repository of interesting darknet articles and a massive number of darknet links in the sidebar. You can find it at:

https://www.reddit.com/r/darknetmarkets

DeepDotWeb is another site where you can harvest many .onion addresses. They even have comparison charts of all the hidden sites that can be accessed over Tor, with pros and cons and even reviews of each vendor or outlet, updated monthly. After installing Tor I recommend you set your homepage to

https://wtfismyip.com/

or the Tor IP check (check.torproject.org). That ensures your IP is masked.

LINUX DARKNET EDITION

Linux Darknet is just a fancy term for Tails, The Amnesic Incognito Live System. It uses the Linux operating system and comes highly recommended. Bruce Schneier and Ed Snowden along with a host of other well-known security experts cannot praise it's strengths enough. It's cheap, fast, and untraceable even for those new to the Deep Web. As a matter of fact, it's the perfect incognito tool for doing *anything* on the Deep Web.

What You Need:

- A PC or laptop capable of running a live operating system via USB/DVD.
- A Blank DVD or USB Stick
- A 4GB Stick for Persistence (In case you want to create a persistent volume in the free space left on the device by Tails Installer. The files in the persistent volume are saved encrypted and remain available across separate working sessions).

One of the great things about Tails is that it forgets *everything* at shutdown. All files, settings, and RAM are cleared. When you need permanent storage, a USB or SD card can be used. More than likely you *will* have sensitive info on this storage, so it should also be encrypted.

How to Setup Tails

Warning: Never run Tails in a Virtual Machine. Doing so jeopardizes your security as you put yourself at the mercy of the host operating system. Whonix is a much better option for this, which I go into detail in my Tor & the Dark Art of Anonymity book. One reason is spelled out on the Tails website:

"Both the host operating system and the virtualization software are able to monitor what you are doing in Tails."

Which means "If the host operating system is compromised with a software keylogger or other malware, then it can break the security features of Tails".

Another reason is that traces of your Tails session are likely to be left on the local hard disk. For example, host operating systems usually use swapping (or paging) which copies part of the RAM to the hard disk.

- Download the Tails ISO image from the Tails website.
- Verify the image

Now choose which to boot from. You've 2 choices: USB or DVD.
If DVD:
Burn the iso to DVD.

You now need to edit the Boot Order. Depending on your computer you should see an entry for removable drive or USB media. Move this to the top of the list to force the computer to attempt to start from your device before starting from the hard disk. Disable Fast boot and Secure boot, then click save and continue.

You should see the Tails operating system after rebooting. Now feel free to hack the Pentagon to see if Area 51 really was the site of a crashed UFO.

On system shutdown, make sure everything you need is saved either to an external encrypted drive or your Persistence. Upper right corner has the power off button. Click and select shutdown to turn off.

- Alternatively: Remove USB to initiate shutdown.
- Wait for the RAM to be wiped.
- Done. You have completed a secure session with Tails. Everything not saved has been lost and is irretrievable.

Tails is the most respected privacy app out there for good reason. It leaks the least data of every system in existence and is scrutinized *mercilessly*. Whonix is also a good choice, but it is less used and thus less scrutinized. Therefore you should use Tails as a starting point on your journey that is the Darknet Marketplace - which we'll descend into next.

BYPASSING WEBSITES THAT BLOCK TOR

I'll keep this short and sweet. By now you know that Tor isn't foolproof, especially on cell phones.

It's just a lock on your shed after all, a lock designed to make you a harder target than the next guy. Websites know this, even adversarial ones who do not like Tor users.

Plenty of websites will block any IP address associated with Tor, even if it is not an exit node. The sites you want to use may already be listed in there.

But exit nodes are not hidden. In order to hide your Tor usage you need to proxy-chain a VPN so that any traffic coming out isn't coming from a known Tor node. You can see a list of exit nodes here:

https://check.torproject.org/cgi-bin/TorBulkExitList.py?
ip="YOURIP"

In most cases they may only be able to block the largest and most used exit nodes, but if you cannot access a particular website, use their own tools against them by configuring Tor (via the torrc file) to use an exit node that recently joined the network (up to a few hours or days, whichever you need).

You'll sneak into the castle and past the anti-Tor drawbridge because it takes time for a website to update the Tor block list.

If on the other hand you'd like to setup Tor to only use exit nodes from a specific country (like the USA for example), then you need to look for the torrc file inside the Tor Browser directory (Data/Tor/) and add this line to the torrc file using a text editor:

ExitNodes {us}

GOVERNMENT TRACKING OF TOR USERS

<u>Can the government track which sites I visit over Tor?</u>

<u>Tor's design document</u> Section 3.1 states:

A global passive adversary is the most commonly assumed threat when analyzing theoretical anonymity designs. But like all practical low-latency systems, Tor does not protect against such a strong adversary.

If you've got three-letter agencies after you and they have a special interest in obtaining your data, it'd be easier to just deliver a payload remotely by way of a keylogger and, failing that, done covertly with assistance from local LE where they may send out an unmarked car to initiate surveillance of your property.

These days, especially in the United States, any judge will gladly take the two seconds it requires to sign a subpoena if law enforcement waves a few colorful alarm words at them (terrorism, child porn, survivalist gremlins), with many judges not bothering to ask whether or not you're simply using Tor to help the network out.

For most users, Tor provides the best available protection against a well-resourced

observer. It's an open question how much protection Tor (or any other existing anonymous communications tool) provides against the NSA's large-scale Internet surveillance. On its own, Tor can't protect against attacks against vulnerabilities on your computer or its software.

If the adversary is the NSA, a seriously strong SIGINT entity, the best offense is a good defense – being a pain in the neck to target. That's the goal. You must look and act like everyone else because it disrupts the intelligence-gathering cycle. A well-funded SIGINT entity like the NSA won't waste time going over your cleartext communications since your metadata & ID patterns are good enough. That's why any agency worth its salt will be much better at *targeting* than crypto-analysis.

For this reason you should always use Tor on something other than a cell phone if you can help it. Reason being is that they monitor everything they can get their paws on before feeding this data into the beast system for whatever endgame their planning. There's no doubt anymore on this.

And until the night of the long knives and we see enemies of the state strung up by their feet (like those old black and white photos), there will be no end to data harvesting.

Onionscan may be of some use to check for security holes.

TOR & SMS VERIFICATION

Like the annoying buzz of a fly, Tor users have to deal with SMS verifications to register for a website on occasion. Hidden services as well, it seems, must deal with it, even merchants.

Be very careful with this. Optimally your threat model should not require any such 'verification' outside the usual opsec tools. Exposing yourself (by way of a cell) in this way not only grants the media sites you visit a nice gourmet of your metadata, but any network operator, law enforcement or hacker may join in for a bite if you use the same cell to login to social media sites. Until we have traceless SMS, I'd avoid that site for anything requiring anonymity.

But for Darknet Marketplaces, take a gander below. It's a hypothetical scenario involving a Tor user who wants to buy from a Black Market vendor. Who cares what he wants to buy. That's his business. But the vendor in question has a decent reputation on Agora Marketplace, so the customer sends over his PGP info (encrypted of course).

Vendor: That PGP data didn't make it through. Use SMS4Tor ok? (he sends the link).

Customer: I'll just resend PGP using the profile key you gave.

Vendor: Still ain't workin, pal. Dunno why not cuz you ordered last week.

Customer: Last week? Wasn't me as I've never ordered from you. Will you resend that public key again so I can import it (again) and re-send?

Vendor: Methinks you're using a different PGP app. Same as last week. (he then issues more demands)

Notice anything off about the above conversation? I do. The vendor is an incompetent clown. Two PGP apps not compatible? That's something either a cop or hacker might say to get more information (i.e. fishing). It's the same tactic Homeland Security uses when they infiltrate chat rooms and try to fish for some new meat who's a first-time buyer.

Whether incompetence comes by way of a hacker or an incompetent stooge vendor, never jeopardize your safety by assuming they are just having an 'off day' and blow it off. Follow your gut, always. If something doesn't smell right, RUN.

TOR PRANKS & CELL PHONES

There are a lot of bored college students out there who believe Tor makes for one seriously strong suit of armor against any and all would-be opponents, and an invisible one at that. An invisible knight is, well, pretty formidable foe. Maybe these jesters just feel they were born in the wrong century. Regardless, we can learn a lot from their folly. You, o' anonymous traveler, must use the gift of discernment to rightly divide fantasy from reality because what works in the world of Faerun doesn't squire well with the real world.

A Harvard kid decided he wasn't quite prepared for final exams, so he emailed a bomb threat to get out of taking them. He used Tor and a throwaway email account to cover his online footprint, only little did he know that all the school officials had to do was search through the campus lab's logs to discern who accessed Tor at that time. It led them straight to his dorm room.

It probably didn't help that he used Harvard's WiFi to access Tor. He was the only one who did at that particular time.

If you are at a Mardi Gras party and everyone else has removed their masks except you, you're going to stand out. If you want to be anonymous, then use tools that enable you to look like everyone else *when everyone else is using it.* Our Harvard friend did not. Imagine yourself paying cash for something small. Cash is considered king for anonymity but can backfire if you're the only one using it to pay for a brand new Camaro in a 200 mile radius.

Recall what Kevin Mitnick (hacker wanted by the FBI) said upon his arrest; that Tsutomu Shimomura, a computer security expert, had broken the 'rules' by helping the Feds nab him instead of relying on his technical expertise – and nothing else. He thought it a game and any attack vector would come through Tor and Tor alone. For this reason you mustn't think of anonymity as some fantasy game with a ruleset. Cops do not play by the rules. They play dirty. They break the rules. They break the law. Then they break you because you think they are confined by their own laws. Only they are not.

Any action, especially a cell phone prank like that of our Harvard genius, leaves breadcrumbs for others to follow. When you use WiFi at Starbucks for example, then you are there in the flesh doing the deed and in well range of CCTV surveillance. There are fingerprints on your coffee cup; the same you pitched into the trashcan alongside your slightly used comb.

So blend in to the detriment of comfort. Avoid layers of anonymity that produce complex requirements yet produce more visibility. Ninjas in ancient Japan did not look like the sort of ninja Chuck Norris went toe to toe against in The Octagon.

They didn't wear black pajamas. They looked like your neighborly rice farmer, one among dozens of other rice farmers. Sort of like SAS wearing burkas to sneak into ISIS HQ.

BLACK MARKETS ON THE DEEP WEB

Here are a few things you can buy on the Deep Web you may not have heard about.

- Rare Opsec Manuals for Survivalists
- Rare Special Ops Guides
- 3D Printed Guns and Bullets
- Drugs for Cancer
- Japanese Manga
- Books on How to Overthrow Governments

Top Darknet Markets

THERE ARE two types of Blackmarket Drug emporiums on the Deep Web. Those you trust and those you don't. Below is a list of some of the more popular black market outlets. One or two may be gone already by the time this book goes to press. In five years all of them may be gone. The point here isn't to steer you into any one of these in particular or even that I want you to buy illegal drugs (I don't), but to remind you that none of these sites will last forever just as Google and Microsoft won't last forever.

Something will come along to replace the behemoths just as surely the same as AltaVista, Infoseek, Napster and Divx were replaced. It can happen quick. My grandfather's motto: Never gamble or invest more than you can afford to lose.

Agora Marketplace

Established: Dec 3, 2013
Invite (Required)

Abraxas Market

Established: Dec 13, 2014
Invite (Required)

a AlphaBay Market

Established: Dec 22, 2014
Taken down by the FBI in 2017

Dream Market

Established: Nov 15, 2013
Invite (Required)

Nucleus Market

Established: Nov 24, 2014

East India Company

Established: Apr 28, 2015

Established: Dec 29, 2013

Established: Dec 22, 2014

Middle Earth Marketplace

Established: Jun 22, 2014

Oxygen O_2

Established: Apr 26, 2015

Established: Unknown

The Russian Anonymous Marketplace (aka RAMP)

Established: Unknown

MARKETPLACE INVITES

You may have noticed that a handful of these markets, such as Agora, require invites. What this means is if you're a new buyer or vendor or even just a nosy parker lurking around, you cannot register without an invite link from an already registered user. That's just how it is with some of the more established outlets.

Also, don't assume that because a website's been around longer than the others that it is more secure, and never assume that a closed door means it is closed forever, or for even a long time. At Agora for instance, you'll sometimes see this error:

"Cannot register at this time, user limit reached. Please wait until full time release."

It's confusing because it's meant to be. They try to be as cryptic as possible to throw off anyone looking to take them down. The first option is to either sit tight for a few hours and give the server time to catch it's breath, or...

- Visit the forum of the marketplace you're trying to reach and ask for an invite. Failing this, you can

- Visit the Reddit subforum of the market in question.

Two points to say on this.

First, if you're using a long term account and login using Tor, then your activity can build a profile of sorts, all based on what you do on the Reddit site. Tor can't really prevent this from happening so if you want to *preserve your anonymity*, you must keep your 'real' identity and 'hidden' identity completely separate. One way is to never log into any account with both identities.

The second point about Reddit is merely a suggestion:

Beware of *phishing* links there, both on related as well as non-Darknet related subreddits. I'd not recommend using any link in any subreddit, for example, unless you recognize it. Many are plagued with phishing links that comprise more than half of the help desk's 'can't login with password' topics. All referral links are safe as long as the link begins with the official Agora URL. Anything else is likely a phishing link. And the person whose referral link you use doesn't get any "notifications" or anything letting them know you used it, nor can they see how many people used their link. You are completely anonymous to them.

If you can remember two phone numbers, then you can remember 16-characters for an official link. If you still can't be bothered, there's a third option.

3.) Visit clearnet sites that spell out where the site is and even have rating systems in place. One such place is DarknetMarkets.org, but there are others you can Google for yourself that will also have the forum .onion address you need to access them.

Just be warned that they, like many hidden servers across the Deep Web, come and go like the tide. Some will even change their .onion address for security reasons and some will go down as felled trees because of DDOS attacks, hacking attempts or that gut feeling you get when the spider you threw behind the dresser in the wee morning hours is now looking at you from across the room like he wants to skate down your spine with a flamethrower.

In other words, always assume someone is watching.

THE BLACKMARKET SUPERLIST

If you're curious about what other sites exist further down the rabbit hole, you can find the Superlist at:

https://i.reddit.com/r/DarkNetMarkets/wiki/superlist

It's a list of "all currently known, operating markets and tumblers" with the disclaimer that "all markets listed should not be taken as endorsements or confirmation by the moderators that a market is trusted. Always confirm links before you use them."

Requirements for this superlist are as follows:

- The Market must have been up for at least a week after announcing themselves on Reddit's Darknet Market page.
- The Market has to have at least 20 listings from active vendors.
- Their service must have at least 50% uptime over the span of a week, under moderator discretion.

- Users must be able to withdraw their bitcoins (or other relative currency).

DARKNET DICTIONARY AND OTHER DARKNET TOOLS

If some of the technical words in these chapters confuse you (and I readily admit to throwing them around like Mardi Gras beads), don't despair. Check out DeepDotWeb's Darknet Dictionary on various terms and phrases. It's really a godsend because even the most ardent and astute darknet administrator doesn't know everything there is to know about the Deep Web. You can find this dictionary at

https://www.deepdotweb.com/2014/03/02/deepdotwebs-darknet-dictionary/

SHIPPING & RECEIVING: THOU SHALT NOTS

What follows are a few pearls of wisdom from which you may benefit, chief among them being the use of your real-life details; things like your name, address, phone number, Facebook profile, what have you, that many newbies pass around like skittles. Too much transparency can be catastrophic to any Darknet Marketplace or even a single purchase, especially when dealing with a place like Agora.

- If the doorbell rings and you give the delivery guy a fake name, a warning bell is going to go off in his head that you're the next Silk Road admin looking to fill his coffers. He knows your real name already, so don't lie unless you want him to file a report. If your wife has sticky fingers from opening your mail, buy a private box at the UPS store or post office.
- It's okay to use a fake name if you've got the credentials to back it up. Fake passports can be bought online as gag gifts that wouldn't fool a TSA officer but *would* fool the mailman and maybe even the UPS store employee. I

rented one in Canada and the female employee looked to be no older than 23 years old. She wasn't very observant with details. They won't call the cops on you either way.

- Agora cannot send Amazon drones to deliver your package. Therefore you need to realize that sensitive materials requiring anonymous services take longer. If you order in December, expect a delay but don't pester the help desk people unless it's been two weeks since you ordered. For every commonsense person out there who can follow instructions, there's a million pigeons who have the solution right under their beaks. The solution is a little dove called Patience.

- Use PGP for any and all messages. This is because your address is connected with a Darknet Marketplace and by extension, a vendor who sells items of dubious legality. A hundred things can go wrong. One being the site can be imaged by police with your fancy cul-de-sac address being front and center along with every sentence you've uttered (use short sentences!). A few vendors won't even talk to you if you refuse to encrypt. So use GPG4USB to save yourself the rejection slips. It only takes 20 minutes to learn.

- Bitcoin Tumblers. Assuming you bought Bitcoins connected to your real-life identity, you should wash or 'tumble' them BEFORE you buy. That means putting those coins through a tumbler like Coinbase first before any depositing goes on at the Agora address. If you withdraw from Agora, it's the reverse procedure:

Agora account to tumbler to Coinbase and *then* into your Bitcoin Wallet.

- Which Bitcoin Tumblers, you ask? Well, the most stable ones you can find. For 2016 onward, Grams Helix Light is the top choice, al though you're hit with a 2.5% fee for the total cost. BitBlender is also a good choice but they require account setups. SharedCoin is yet another but I found it makes it harder to figure out who sent bitcoins to what address. It uses a different method of relaying than the others. This is primarily for small buyers, not for someone looking to pack a warehouse with marijuana bricks in Chicago, Illinois.

- It may come to pass that you've ordered something and haven't received it yet. It's been ages. Have you been scammed? Locked out of your account? Or maybe your bitcoins never showed up in your Agora account? Don't fall on your sword just yet. What you need to do is message the market admins, not any forum at Ars Technica or Reddit or anyplace else, and send a (private) message to 'Agora' detailing your problem. The backlog of tickets is considerable but they will get back to you in 48 hours, usually. They tend to bump you further down the priority list if you go overboard and start issuing threats, however, so don't burn any bridges by giving them any catitude.

TO FINALIZE EARLY OR NOT?

I explored this topic in my Tor and the Dark Art of Anonymity book and I'll mention it here, albeit briefly.

Opsec lessons can be costly. Finalize Early, which means you pay a vendor *before* you receive the magical goods, can wreck your life like none other. In general you should avoid ever doing this since the risks alone will give you an ulcer.

Many before you can attest to getting ripped off to the tune of five figures or more. Vendors can build up trust a long time before they bolt with the bitcoins, a scheme called Exit Scamming. That's when the vendor, a sneering twirly-mustached little man works his black magic and makes off with the loot. *Your* loot.

Newcomers like to trust them implicitly not to rip them off, until they do. Then they spam Usenet, Reddit, Ars Technica and every other tech site with doom and gloom as though said evil man set off a tactical nuke in New Jersey.

Amazon, eBay and Newegg all have trackable systems in place that, when linked with those utilized by credit card companies and banks, can save your hide and get you your stolen funds back. Sometimes. Darknet Marketplaces don't however. If you get robbed then it's highly likely you won't be getting your money back *and* you'll likely not be alone in that regard.

400 positive feedbacks sounds like a lot of happy customers. Only it isn't. A vendor with thousands of deals under his belt would be a lot of happy customers IF he has a good rating to boot and IF you've done your research, but even then it doesn't justify losing every coin you own.

INTERNATIONAL VS. DOMESTIC ORDERS

I always like to remember that verse when I travel overseas. It's to remind myself not to get too cocky in foreign markets.

Do you travel overseas? Have a passport? Bank cards? Email? Imagine that every day you wake up every little thing that happens to you has to be looked at with suspicion. Emails from family. Your new girlfriend. Whenever the phone rings. That's what it is to be a slave, a slave to your own ego.

You may think there's something magical about buying illegal items from international ports of call. Don't believe the hype. It's the same tune but with twice the headache. Whether international falls into the "Thou Shalt" or "Shalt Not" category is up to you of course, but how many migraines do you want? One lump or twenty? Can you lose it all without losing your sanity? Do you want it quick or safe and secret?

Turkey and the Netherlands brings with it more potency but

increased security. Increased security means higher risk. Higher risk means more intense pain.

Content from these exotic locales draw unwanted attention and stand out from other packages unless some extensive pre-made cover has been setup. Australia comes to mind. It's riskier than other places. The biggest risk is where the Deep Web intersects with the international Real World - and getting the stuff delivered to you - and keeping you and your family safe.

A few pointers:

- NEVER check the status of a package through Tor. Packages tracked via Tor are automatically flagged.
- Never send contraband from a state where it is legal (i.e. Colorado).
- If you're a vendor, never plaster your site with the word "Cheap!!" and then try and slide in heavy shipping costs at the last second. Customers hate that.
- Don't use first.last@gmail.com as your email address, as other dumb people have (though granted Ross didn't know he was creating a Black Market Amazon, nor did he have any knowledge of the Snowden/Prism/Lolsec revelations).
- No teams. EVERYONE cooperates or you can't operate = not likely. Also, any website that must rely on distribution via US mail is going to have a very bad day. Couriers are better.

An international buy is much the same as domestic except it comes with substantially higher risk and has the added value that you can be extradited to the other country after the U.S asset forfeiture laws clean your carcass of any link to humanity - assuming there's anything left since the U.S.A is the prison capitol of the world.

(Now I'm off to finally get those rocket launchers in my car reloaded.)

BLACK MARKET ARRESTS

We've seen what happens with money and ego. One always prevails over the other. Watch the film Heat starring Al Pacino. One guy on the team of thieves, the new guy, gets everyone else killed or close to it. His bad opsec destroys everyone else's good opsec; the rotten apple or yeast parable applies here: A little bad ruins the whole dough.

There's one site I found quite informative in this department. It lists every black market arrest imaginable. Interestingly the list omits a glaring data set: one that involves each darknet market operator's OPSEC - admittedly hard to quantify. Take Silk Road for instance. From the link we can deduce that opsec just isn't that high a priority for some users.

"No single theme emerges reading through the many arrests. Some people are busted through sheer bad luck in being randomly pulled over or their packages inspected; some are undone by other peoples' mistakes, and some have no one but themselves to blame for talking to a policeman and blurting out all their secrets; some are undone by their trust in others, and some are undone by lying to federal agents; some are undone by signing for packages, while others are undone by a

stray fingerprint; some followed the OPSEC rules and some engaged in mind-boggling follies like using their real return address or accepting payment to their own bank account or running their own clearnet site; some clammed up, denied everything, and saved themselves, while others kept records of everything (perhaps in the misguided belief it would earn them clemency in the worst) and only condemned themselves; some were busted at home, others in the totalitarian zones of international borders; some were busted through high-tech browser-based deanonymization, but most through low-tech methods like a customer or friend snitching; some sellers' packages are spotted during Customs inspections, and some are noticed only when delivery fails & the bogus return addresses explode."

OPSEC FOR BUYERS

Mark Twain once said, "I don't like to commit myself about heaven and hell. You see, I have friends in both places."

OPSEC is more important than anything else when it comes to buying Darknet product. You can never have enough, so it's a little like ammo. If you were in Ukraine when the Soviets invaded would you be better off playing the part of sniper or just cutting bait and running? Sometimes you just have to do both. Allow me to run through a few truths that make this a little more applicable.

Your Machine is Your Fortress

Tor is a fine tool for playing cloak and dagger with small purchases, but it isn't suitable for large orders or running from the FBI. Given what's happened in the U.S. and UK over the last 5 years even small orders may be detrimental to your freedom. And free speech. Government bureaucrats have all but guaranteed they respect neither the Constitution nor our laws.

So then. What can we learn from Silk Road? Well first off, there's evidence that Silk Road's servers were misconfigured and revealing IP addresses and that they were doing it repeatedly. The index page gave away the IP address for several minutes via a print_r debug message printed to every requesting browser. That's the online goofs, but you can screw up offline, too.

Silk Road Lessons

1.) Your encryption keys to your drives are as sacred as your PGP keys. Do not give them out. Not to your roommate, your girlfriend or your mother, and especially not to your friends. Not even your business partner Eddie.

2.) Leave your PC unattended at your own peril. With your OS booted and up and running, anyone from thieves to cops to jealous girlfriends can access anything on your hard drive that isn't nailed as tight as a coffin (i.e. encrypted containers).

3.) Talk at your own PERIL. That is, never mention darknet marketplaces to anyone. Feign ignorance. While you needn't do a disappearing act like Bilbo Baggins did, telling one person will almost always have the same effect as telling a dozen people, all strangers. And it almost always is valuable to someone, somewhere.

4.) Keep your Darknet Marketplace username/pass under lock and key. Write it down in a text file but encrypt it with Veracrypt or PGP. No stickies.

5.) Use different username/passwords for different markets.

PSYCH TRICKS

The following are merely suggestions, nothing more, and are more apt to apply to creative types over say, mathematicians.

Music: Certain kinds of music reproduce specific kinds of behavior. Stephen King listens to AC/DC when he writes. He cranks it up. Personally I feel an aneurism coming on if I try to write to that. So I listen to Steve Roach, ambient composer with titles like Dreamtime Return and Early Man. Dreamy wispy music. It works. If I switch it up then I lose focus and get distracted too easily.

Light/Darkness: In almost every scene in The Matrix, Neo can be seen always working in the dark. Even his display glows a matrix-green with cryptic lettering, the only brightness in the room being that of his monochrome skin. Works for me too. Almost like a sensory-deprivation chamber and it's amazing how much better I sleep because of it.

Locale: Stephen King once said that you don't need a glamorous 'study' to write good stories. You just need something familiar. And he's right. Having traveled to a few countries I can tell you that writing in a new city every week is not remotely possible for me as there's just too many distractions. You need a spot like Neo did - a place your identity always goes but never goes *outside of* either by doorway or otherworldly portal.

Drugs: Caffeine, nicotine, sugar highs, but no prescription drugs. They put me in a state of mind that gets reinforced daily, though I do toss and turn at night. Alcohol, Stephen King once stated, helps immensely with epic fiction writing but kills you in the process. I can vouch for that.

Scents: My girlfriend used to light caramel candles to scent up the room whenever she'd come over from the ER, usually when I was just finishing up a mindblowing chapter. After the breakup I had trouble finishing chapters.

The point of all of this is this: the more opsec you employ on a daily basis, the more your brain will, IF put into action, develop an opsec-focused mindset that doesn't have to be turned on every day. It just kicks in. Automatic. Razor sharp as piranha teeth. It does this because it's burned in like ram on a motherboard. Like pushing a button to boot Linux, you open your eyes and it's there, waiting for orders. It'll be there especially when any dangerous developments present themselves. Develop and hone this and you won't mistake that woodpecker at 6 AM for a group of angry white-hot stormtroopers.

Engaging in shady deals is a little like gambling. The house always wins if you keep playing. If you can't work the opsec well then the only winning move, as Matthew Broderick found out in Wargames, is not to play. If you continue to play recklessly, it'll be tough to find a lawyer who takes payment in bitcoins.

VENDOR OPSEC

You get what you pay for, and playing cheap gets expensive if you're caught. For any Tor hidden server operator, that means never letting the reins fall into someone else's hands. Not your associates, your girlfriend or cousin Eddie because it's you and you alone they're coming after, lock stock and barrel.

One torpedo can wipe out an entire battleship and they only have to get lucky once. You can't afford a lucky strike, so you as captain need to sense when something's 'off' so you can pull the plug without having to explain why. Partners will demand to know why of course, but it's better to run silent and deep.

Ross Ulbricht failed in this department. But we can learn a lot from his mistakes.

Looking through the court details of his arrest one gets the impression that he was not only lax in basic IT security, but that he knew nothing about how search engines track users at all. So Lady Luck never really had to come into the FBI's playbook at all. The guy was just sloppy and might as well have slapped on the cuffs himself.

Ross was caught long before Silk Road grew mega-popular. Court documents reveal security mistakes that a rookie drug dealer on

Miami Vice might have made, not someone in charge of a multi-million dollar Deep Web drug operation. Here are a few of Ross's opsec blunders.

- Advertising openly on the Bitcoin Talk forum that he needed an IT guy for a hidden Tor service - and then using his real name for a Gmail address *and* his Silk Road Wordpress site, a site he connected to from outside of Tor.
- Ross's Google Plus account connected to his Gmail with a list of his favorite Austrian economic theory videos, the same theories he'd bragged about using for Silk Road on more than one clearnet forum.
- Using code for SilkRoad from a public programming site (i.e. StackOverflow), from an account never accessed with Tor with his IP address being out in the open for months. Any law enforcement official could track these breadcrumbs at their leisure.
- Using his real identity on LinkedIn, with links to Silk Road musings on his Wordpress blogs.

These are just some of the mistakes he made, to say nothing about his lax hidden server settings. Besides these, there's a lot to be said for smart vendors who know good security.

Vendor Guidelines Part I

These are just like the buyer opsec rules, except in reverse. Short and sweet.

- Use a sanitized laptop, cash bought, with only a Linux distro configured to run Tor and *only* Tor, with no other outgoing connections allowed.

- Dissolving your real-life persona and using different usernames on every forum visited with no non-Tor IP addresses exposed.
- Not residing in the USA. This is a big one.
- No ordering of fake IDs in the USA (vendors only) or any other contraband that'd raise suspicion with authorities.

Vendor Guidelines, Part II

You've read this far and want to be a vendor, or at least know what it takes to be one and not get caught (cue Miami Vice theme).

This is **very shady territory**. Mostly illegal. The risks here carry an awful lot of pain if you screw it up, and it's far more pain than what the Shady Acres Homeowner Association would give you for not curbing your dog.

There's no accidents here.

No 'accidentally' slipping on rings found in dark, damp caves. No 'but I was only looking for UFOs' excuses. Success in the black arts tends to fuel a life of it's own much like Sauron's ring of Power. It's knowledge that *wants* to be abused. Before we discuss the criminal element, let's discuss the business side of things.

- You have to be a businessman. If you're smart you should consider investing $500 and take an introduction course at the university. Do it online. You'll need to know the ins and outs of mail-order, accounts and ledgers (and when to dispose of them), and how to replenish your products. Doing it all anonymously raises the difficulty by a factor of ten. It's hard work even when it's legal products.
- Sell fakes at first. Cubic zirconium rings. Flour. Fake credit cards. Not to real customers but to *yourself*, and long before any real product matures.

- Money talks. Invest in a site that charges a fee for vendors. People take you seriously when they know you've got startup capital.
- Create a Dark Persona. This is the hardest part of all, as this person must be the opposite of the real You in every detail: Politics. Sexual taste. Movies. Style. Age. Locale. Accent. If you're confused on what this means, watch The Matrix. Neo lives two lives and the Agents know it. It's why it was so hard to track him down. One is a hacker who specialized in obtaining contraband and the other works in a respected software company and (in my best Agent Smith impression)... helps his landlady take out her garbage.

Like Neo your offline security should get Top Billing, meaning the little pigtailed girl across the street should not think of you as 'that quiet, creepy dude who's cat Lucifer wails like a police siren at dinnertime' and keeps her up at night. They need to think positive thoughts.

They should trust you but not know *too* much. They only need to never suspect anything shady is going on - that you're good at fixing broken computers, bikes and love big dogs but you'd never do anything to hurt anyone. Never anything to do with any of the following: Tor. PGP. Freenet. I2P. Darkcoins. Especially Darkcoins or whatever flavor of the month they come in since they too change like the wind.

Pay cash for everything.

Avoid social media outlets like the Black Plague.

You know the ones.

Facebook. Twitter. YouTube. Instagram. Pinterest. These are locales polluted with diseased gossip that'll turn any normal person into a zombie walker given enough time with an unrooted cell phone.

Neighbors gossip mainly about those they don't know. They fill in empty gaps with guesses and nonsense and sometimes outright lies.

To prevent this, go to social engagements or pop in at backyard BBQs and be the one that has the best fireworks on the 4th of July, the same who bought expensive beer for everyone.

Be a volunteer at a shelter. A no-kill cat shelter. The Salvation Army. It doesn't really matter what as long as your neighbors think you're 'Nice Guy Eddie'.

Help the neighborhood kids find their lost dog by going door to door with his pug mugshot you ripped off the telephone pole. Find him and they'll forgive you for accidentally launching a nuclear weapon in a Pentagon hack attempt (not possible by the way).

You get busted, you'll want these people to speak up for you. Do all of the above and they'll form a standing army at your beck and call. Just never mention Tor, PGP and the rest, not even to dear old Dad who you can be quite certain will brag at every BBQ you go to that you're Snowden's long lost brother.

Change PGP keys frequently if and when your business grows. Avoid using any of your own handwriting on anything. Neither your name, address, favorite colors, nicknames you use on various forums.

Research the following:

Cashing Bitcoins

Mail Anonymity/Stealth

Stealth Materials

Competitive Pricing

Customer Service (i.e. How to keep your customers coming back for more).

Sales copywriting. Read Cashvertising, a book on writing copy for anything.

Research the best lawyer to have for whatever it is you're selling.

POSTAL DROPS & CONTROLLED DELIVERIES

Now for the real black market opsec. The first topic we'll discuss is controlled deliveries, a term used by those on both sides of the law.

What's a controlled delivery?

It's a way for law enforcement to dupe you into accepting a package containing illegal goods. It could be anything. Drugs. Guns. Japanese manga that involves underage 'cat' girls. All in the hopes you'll accept the package and make some off-the-cuff remark about the contents. They hope.

Then they can search your house. They need only establish you knew the package was coming, what it contained or what you intended on doing with it. Smoking it, of course, but one out of three is usually sufficient to get a search warrant. Let's dispense with a few myths first prior to counter-surveillance techniques.

Myth #1: If a person receives any type of contraband in the mail, he can be arrested on the spot. Guilt by association.

FALSE.

If receiving anything illegal in the mail is enough to send a guy to the Big House with Bubba, every school bully in existence could get sent up the creek by just ordering a few Scooby sheets of LSD to his house. It doesn't work that way. The police need proof that you know what's inside, otherwise it's a no-win case and they know it. If you're a cool level-headed, logical thinking kind of guy like Mr. Orange in Reservoir Dogs then they've got a problem. If they see your stone-cold blue eyes are filled with an Iron Man resolve, then they know their only recourse is to get you to flap your gums before the adrenaline 'fight or flight' rush wears off. To this end, there's a couple of effective ways they'd like to deal with you. Both involve deception.

The first is by taking the **'Nice Guy'** approach. You'd be shocked at how well they can get a stranger to spill his guts by playing up the nice guy angle. Be his friend so to speak. His father confessor.

When the heat is on and you've got a few stormtroopers stomping around your house with muddy boots, well, you want them to leave. I would too. And that's what they tell you. We'll leave, they'll say. Then the dirty tricks start. They make any newbie *want* to talk if only to relieve stress. Only he ends up spending *years* in prison instead of a measly three stinking days because he never kept his mouth shut.

Police officers and DEA agents in particular have had years to perfect the art of persuasion by deception. That means lying their ass off.

If you've ever seen Black Hawk Down then you know how ferocious a night raid can be, where they may have to 'clear' a house by going room to room and scaring the living hell out of anyone living there. It's scary stuff. The cat's smart enough to hide under the bed but Rover gets shot in the leg.

But it doesn't always go down that way.

You're usually seated in cuffs when the nice guy routine kicks into high gear. That's what they want to try first. Nice guy *then* mean guy and not the other way around since it's far easier to upgrade then to downgrade on the poor sap's emotions. Police usually say something like this.

"We only want the dealer, not you kid. Look, you're small time. We know it and you know it and your supplier knows it. You're useless to us. But your partner, your boss, he's the one we're after. The Big Fish.

The Don. We see your family here and understand your situation, we've got our own. You're poor. You wanted to escape for an hour, maybe two. That's all. We understand. No trouble for you if you coop-erate and tell us your source. Where'd you get these drugs from?"

You give Barney Fife a long silence as you fidget and glance around the room at where your hidden stash is. They'll say, "Talk so we can go home and you can get back to playing The Witcher on your laptop over there." (This is the part where they'll lie and say they're fans of the game themselves).

Should you talk?

Can they be trusted?

Then out of nowhere, when they see the synapses firing in your brain that tell you to keep your big trap shut, they bring out the **'Bad Guy'** routine. Nice Guy's evil twin brother whose tone sounds an awful lot like the mouth of Sauron in the Lord of the Rings.

"Look kid, you're life's over. You're done. Cooked. You'll lose your kids in the next room over and your job and your car and your house and maybe even your cat sitting under the bed. She'll be put to sleep long before you get out of jail. Unless you just give us the name so we can cut you some slack, kid."

What's the first thing that's going to pop into your head if you're new to this?

- You want these clowns out of the house. Yesterday.
- You want a clean rep so the family doesn't think you're Jabba the Hutt.
- You want to believe them. They're dressed nice after all. Clean shaven. Shiny boots. Nice haircut. But then so was the Terminator when he went looking for Sarah Connor and her rebellious pain-in-the-ass son.

Bottom line: Don't fall for any of their lies. You see, when you're raided at some ungodly hour say at 6 AM, all the blood in your system goes to your legs and arms and you get what's called *brain drain.* You become a moron. A Ferengi or drunk Klingon say instead of a logical Vulcan who thinks clearly and invokes that God-given gift to all men called *discernment.* It's fight or flight time and the cops know most people won't use their brains at 6AM because they're used to seeing scrambled eggs. They'd rather fight, run away or just sign on the dotted line to shut em up so they'll leave, leave, LEAVE!

Don't let this happen. It's like walking right into Hell with both eyes wide open.

Don't talk to cops. Don't sign anything. Don't agree to anything.

Oh but you say you'd end up in jail? You'll end up there anyway regardless of what they tell you, only what they don't tell you is that 90% of the time, *if you keep your trap shut,* the prosecutor'll drop the case for insufficient evidence. Most evidence comes from a confession, not from what the cops see or pick up on site.

Therefore never admit to a thing nor sign any 'apology' letter or anything else. Note that they'll try to get a confession before taking you down to the station. That's the whole point.

Myth # 2: You Should Always Use a Fake Name or ID for a postal box.

FALSE.

We briefly mentioned this one a few chapters ago, but it bears repeating. Whether you're using a UPS Store rental box or the post office, never ever use a fake ID or a false name. If one package of yours becomes compromised then you could be looking at a worse situation on account that they will know you lied. It'll look suspicious. Probable cause is much more likely a given if they know you're a liar. Be honest with non-law enforcement types. Honesty and silence work hand in hand but if you lied at some point along the way it'll be hard for you to deny any bad intentions with the rented box.

After 9/11 fake IDs get you into heaps of trouble these days, but doubly so for ordering darknet stuff. Now they're linked to everything from terrorism to identity theft to Silk Road-level drug empires. So in light of this, use your real name.

MYTH #3: Retrieve the package quick! Before anyone notices!

ALSO FALSE. You need to let it sit for a couple of days if at all possible. This is because the package is still 'hot'. Granted, police don't have unlimited funding that allows them to survey the store 24/7/365 days a year, even for a small fish who needs a break. But if any bust is going down it'll likely happen fast.

From there you can take it to a neutral spot and open it somewhere safe. Or you could wait a few days later to add that extra layer of plausible deniability about the contents of the package. Again this goes back to our opsec mindset and living out that opsec mindset day to day, hour to hour, by taking action beforehand. That is, having a clear plan ahead of time as well as a Plan B, a Plan C, etc.

ESCAPING THE WEST!

The gauntlet's been thrown down. The challenge issued. You've got about six months to cash in a few assets to get your money and your sorry-you-ever-married-a-Toronto-girl hide out of Dodge for good or else a court judgment will fly down like a bolt of lightning from Zeus to your arse that'll leave you wailing like those alley cats on Bourbon Street.

You've been over it a thousand times. If you don't hightail it you just know a police cruiser will be along at any moment to arrest you for whistling a copyrighted tune out your backside - and then you'll be seeing red-blue flashbacks with every trip to the john.

Six months. Six *months.*

What's a decent guy to do? How do you start a brand new life abroad with only a U.S. passport and less than a hundred grand to your name? Where do you go and how do you prevent a tail? Is the

IRS's long reach an urban myth? Student loans? Child support for that illegal you shagged in Phoenix?

Extradition laws vary but you've little desire to learn Thai or Vietnamese and zero will to fight off the Zeta cartel's pack of little league brigade in Monterray. You need an escape plan.

Let's assume you've no qualms about breaking any further laws at this point. Being thrown beyond the pearly gates, there's little reason to keep playing that rusty old harp so you'll break a few laws on the way down hoping no one Really Big will take notice.

The first thing you must do is *change your identity*. There's a few ways to go about it. The simplest way is to steal someone else's. Someone who won't care. Someone who, frankly, isn't here anymore. A baby. Yep that's right, a baby whose gone up to the pearly gates but on the way up managed to drop that shiny new social security number when his wings popped out.

Thousands of babies never make it past a year in this world of rain and failure. They pass on, greener pastures and all that, God Bless em, but the names of those tykes are still in the system. Your system. The same one you've been paying your hard-earned money into for all your life. So you need to research deceased citizens who died when they were young, preferably around your age. This is the one time in all of human existence when Google is really your friend.

You get the number and that's the number you'll use for a new driver's license, passport, bank account or even credit union. Combine that with and off-shore holding corp and you may have a winning combination.

It may be that the deceased is in fact listed in the Social Security Administration's system as 'deceased'. Not always, but sometimes. Your mission is to keep trying until you get one that isn't in this beast of a system. Getting a 'new' number isn't easy. The brigands that run that maniacal ship often require an in-person interview before they give it. Again, not always, and it'd be quite embarrassing to explain how you got by the last 30 years without one or a driver's license.

But if the illegals can do it, so can you IF you've got nothing to lose. Nothing is set in stone where the government is concerned and for the record they catch more rule-followers than rule-breakers.

That said, read again the disclaimer at the top of this chapter. Sneaking into Canada (even if you're Canadian citizen) without stopping into the checkpoint is also a felony, one that's punishable by a $5000 dollar fine.

SNIFFER DOGS & CASH

When going through customs checkpoints, keep in mind that there are dogs that are trained to sniff out money. Some dogs are gifted that way. Some of them can even sniff out cancer. People not living near the border think these dogs are out all the damn time. It isn't true. I live in Canada and can tell you I've seen a dog twice, both times on sunny bright flower days and happy as a clam. But on a rainy day? Here's a little police secret: cops hate working in the rain just as much as sniffer dogs.

State troopers in particular would rather sit in their police cruiser and wait till the rain stops on the interstate from say, New Orleans to Phoenix, to resume ticket writing or searches. That's why if you're a smuggler or just a guy who likes to bring a little reefer along on a long beach trip, you leave on a rainy day. Same with customs. On some days, the rain and snow fly in *sideways*. Can you picture a cop (any kind) enjoying writing out a stack of tickets that way? I can't.

Back to sniffer dogs.

Snoopy can separate scents so hiding cash or drugs in mustard isn't going to work. His big wet nose can smell weed even under your nails to say nothing about clothes. Most of these dogs though are trained to sniff out the serious drugs, drugs like heroin, MDMA, cocaine and every other drug imaginable. And cash. Oh yes. Cash has quite a strong scent. Take out a couple grand from your bank account and when you get it home, take a long whiff of it. It's potent stuff and I read one account that said there's traces of cocaine on every $100 dollar bill in the US.

A sealed ziploc bag will get you through 50% of the time though, provided the bag is washed thoroughly and any residue on the outside has been rinsed away. The problem here is that weed, like cash, gives off a very potent odor and given enough time the scent will permeate through the plastic. So you must do this within hours of travel. The longer it's in there the more risky it gets that the smell has permeated through the seal to reach the dog's wet nose.

One thing to remember though:

It's that the primary function of a sniffer dog is to act as a **legal prop,** regardless of what you're carrying. Yes, a legal prop.

Let's say you get profiled.

You're a twenty-something, college aged, black-skinned, black-haired tattooed-up probable drug user. You get pulled over on some pretense to secondary inspection coming into Canada. You refuse consent to any search. The cop brings a drug dog and that dog ALERTS (according to the cop) like you've got Cheech and Chong hidden in the trunk with 100 pounds of coke. Now the cop has a probable cause for a warrantless search.

"The dog barked so he must be a terrorist!" (though they don't generally alert by barking).

Regardless, it's almost always the officer who targets you in 95% of the cases and it almost never matters whether the dog can smell anything or not, just that the dog was present and the cop "testifies" that it alerted. This is true with cash, drugs or the preggo alien in the back seat from Men in Black. Doesn't matter what it is.

Also, you don't legally have to wait for them to bring the drug dog because doing so would constitute a detainment - which they cannot do unless they are arresting you on specific grounds. If they threaten you with it you should ask if you're being detained. When they inevitably say "no," that's your cue to leave. Just make sure that any other issues (like a speeding ticket) are already taken care of so that the cop doesn't go back to his/her car and just sit on your driver's license until the dog shows up.

Sailboats

Sailboats can be an effective way to disappear, with a few caveats. Do you hold a US passport? If you do then why do you need someone's permission to leave the coast? Hire a skipper you trust (and a first mate!) if you can't sail and just need to get from point A to point B. Blue water boats you can buy on the cheap (relatively speaking) for about 20 grand. You'd want to go someplace with a less than reliable immigration control system, obviously. A place without an extradition treaty with the U.S.

Laos?

It's your port of call but sailing around southwest Asia is about as low-key as a guy can get without kicking off a new career as a Tibetan monk. The downside is that you can get a little too comfortable in other places like the Mediterranean and end up exposing your new identity to first world officials and their beast systems. You don't want to end up in someplace that's quickly turning into a shadow of the USA.

Are you broke?

Don't sweat it. It's mostly a mental barrier which, if you get to a safe harbor somewhere abroad, you'll see it never was a barrier at all. If you lack cold hard cash and need to flee with little in the way of records being assigned to your hot name, lots of boats lack enough crewmen to do the job. They've got their own safety to worry about. If they not enough men, they don't sail. They'll take you in if you ask with a smile.

'Hop aboard!' they'll say after you've promised to pay for the cheap beer. You can forget about getting paid like the rest, though they'll probably throw you some scraps. That's good enough. The real hurdle is to hop on a boat that won't create a paper trail (as in no centralized system). Somewhere that doesn't assign you a number to track you to your dying breath. A place like Cambodia now that I think about it. If you've ever seen Cambodian border checkpoints then you know how lax they can be.

Either way, be sure to record your adventure on camera: Boarding a ship, working as a crew member, adventure unknown.

CONCLUSION

'Do not go gentle into that good night. Rage, rage against the dying of the light!" - Dylan Thomas

DARKNET

How to Stay Anonymous Online
A Beginner's Guide

INTRODUCTION

"If you want total security, go to prison. There you're fed, clothed, given medical care and so on. The only thing lacking ... is freedom" - Dwight Eisenhower

Friend,

My name is Lance and I am the author of this book on encryption security and anonymity. I have been an encryption enthusiast as well as writing about security in general for over a decade. I have been a member of many security and encryption forums since the 1980s, and have been involved with computer technology long before that (yeah I know that makes me an old geezer). But if there is a security or encryption program out there, I have used it and experienced its strengths and its shortcomings and (more than likely) attracted the attention of the authorities (more on that later).

I was there when PGP first arrived on the scene and when Napster was the dominant method of p2p trading. I have used most versions of PGP, Drivecrypt, Bestcrypt, Truecrypt, Tor, Freenet, I2P and every spinoff and copycat you can think of.

Let's face it. Today we are constantly bombarded with news by the media of those trawled, raided, arrested, imprisoned, tortured and humiliated because they weren't necessarily breaking any law but because they did not know the difference between privacy and anonymity. I waited and waited for some smart hacker to put something up on Amazon to prevent this from happening.

Didn't happen.

So I decided it would be me. I stepped up to the plate pronto, though truth be told I had been meaning to put together some of the rudimentary elements of encryption security in such a way that a person without any knowledge of security encryption or anonymity could become familiar.

It is not a particularly advanced book, but rather a portal from which a beginner can step through with the assurance of anonymity when he is online. To that end I present a few tools (mostly free) at your disposal to accomplish this lofty goal. If you're an advanced user, you just might learn some hidden vulnerabilities in your favorite anonymity program.

A PhD in computer science is not required to use encryption. Neither are you required to be a programmer of any sort. You only have to know your way around your operating system and be able to follow directions to the letter. If you know how to install an operating system, or for that matter, any application at all, then you can safely use encryption programs to preserve your own digital data and safety.

PRIVACY AND ANONYMITY

If you're like one of the many billions of people on the planet who use the internet to surf the net, check email, download programs or do any kind of online work, then you probably know there are risks associated with being a habitual internet user. That's just how it is. But it is not *your* fault that there are so many latent traps and pitfalls associated with online spelunking, in whatever form that may be.

It is just a fact of life that the Good lives alongside the Evil in our lives, offline or online. This book is meant as a beginner's guide to distinguish between the Good and the Evil, and to conceal your online footprint. To be a ghost on the internet, that is our aim.

This book is not necessarily for the advanced, such as those who teach computer science courses, but rather it is for those who would like to learn to surf without compromising their identity, or having their online habits tracked 24/7, and who engage in some risky speech against their government once in a blue moon. It is also for those who might not know about some of the little known vulnerabilities in their favorite "anonymous" software programs. In the end, you just might learn there is a vast difference between "anonymity" and "privacy".

Let's start with the basics. I'll just put this out there so you know the weight of the privacy situation entirely. As of 2014, you are always being tracked on the internet in just about every way you can imagine. Search engines, cookie managers, download managers and everything you do online has the potential to make someone, somewhere, a LOT of money. Most of the time, this is because laser-targeted advertising is extremely profitable. The more they know about your habits, the more money they make.

How?

Simple. If they know more about your fears, your likes and dislikes, and how and where you spend your money, they can deliver targeted advertising to you. Laser targeted advertising. That means more power for them, less for you. Now, advertising in and of itself is not such a bad thing, but neither is a loaded gun sitting on top of the fridge. By itself it can do nothing. However it is the method of execution that defines its usefulness.

If you type any medical search term into a major search engine such as Google, Yahoo, or Bing, soon enough you'll start to see targeted ads. If you search for "how to cure a hangover", you might not see anything right away, since hangovers generally don't last that long. However if you were to type "how to cure herpes", you will likely be typing variations of that sentence over the course of a few weeks or months since it is not an easy condition to treat. Eventually you would see pay-per-click ads start to manifest themselves in your search engine results in the top corners. These ads might be selling all manner of snake-oil remedies for the cure to herpes, or they might be referrals to medical specialists.

The bottom line is this: why do they think you have this disease? The answer is because you repeatedly typed it into the search engine over the course of days/months. Over the course of a year, how much do you reveal about your medical history and identity to your favorite search engine? Do you ever wish you could keep this information private?

They like to "bubble" your identity based on how you search: the time between searches, the time of day, your country, your area. With the help of a very specific item in your internet portfolio called an IP address, they can even find out where you live, who your ISP is, and chart a course right to your very doorstep. With the help of Google Maps, and a whole plethora of other mapping applications, this can potentially lead to some very annoying and/or embarrassing situations. Do you think this information would be valuable to door-to-door salesmen? Or perhaps a company that sends out mailed advertisements? Of course.

But first things first, let's briefly say a word about the difference between privacy and anonymity since many would-be geeks confuse the two. They are not the same thing. Not by a long shot.

<u>Anonymity & Privacy - The Differences</u>

WHILE WE SHOULDN'T WASTE time splitting hairs here, it is probably a good idea to distinguish between the terms "privacy" and "anonymity". The two terms are not really as interchangeable as you think. Let's say that you have Firefox running, and you are working from home with a direct connection to your ISP. You don't want anyone knowing what you're doing, so you select the "private mode" tab in Firefox. This disables cookies and inhibits the ability to store any remembered websites (unless you choose to do so).

However this privacy only goes so far. It does nothing for the IP address problem we discussed earlier. Search engines still see it, as does your internet service provider. Both entities know which sites you visit and for how long, based on your IP address. In short, they can see everything. Your wife can't, however. That is why the privacy mode in web browsers were built: to keep the sites you visit private and out of the public view.

Is this privacy enough for your needs? You certainly have some level of privacy, but anonymity is another matter. Anonymity takes privacy to an entirely different level, where the IP address, and thus anything you do online, is extinguished like a wet cloth to a candle's flame through layer after layer of digital barriers. If you want to have privacy, use Firefox's private mode, or use a VPN service provider in conjunction with this feature to ensure no one else in your household can see your online footprints. This assumes that they do not have access to your laptop or PC.

If that's the case, it's game over.

If on the other hand you want anonymity, there are several tools are your disposal, one of which is to use the Tor network. In doing so, you will guarantee yourself strict anonymity and be assured of simple privacy as well, provided you don't do something stupid like blurt out enough info (on a forum, for instance) that narrows you down to a city or state.

THE ANONYMOUS TOR NETWORK

"If money is your hope for independence you will never have it. The only real security that a man will have in this world is a reserve of knowledge, experience, and ability."
    Henry Ford

Every Internet Service Provider assigns an IP address to every user who logs into their network. From there, you can connect to the millions of websites, newsgroups, and online applications that you enjoy most. IP addresses are like phone numbers. They tell your computer where to connect and send packets of data. They need this information to not only send data, such as html code, but also flash code so you can watch Youtube videos. These are targeted with ads, too. And if you bring up task manager in Windows, you can see Flash player running. Do you think Adobe is not sending data back to them about your habits? Let's continue.

So, if the security of online privacy involves concealing the IP address between two computers, how do those two computers talk to each other without a direct connection? If you hide the phone number, how do you make the call? The answer is simple: you have someone else in another country dial the number for you. This is the first step to being anonymous online. Do not use the IP address (yours) as a direct connection. Hire a middle man to do the talking for you. How is this possible? There are several ways. You can use the free online program called Tor, which acts a relay point between you and your online destination. There are also paid services called VPNs (virtual private networks) as well as other anonymous networks like Freenet and I2P, but we'll get into the specifics of those later.

First and foremost, let's talk about Tor.

It is the quintessential solution to online privacy since it masks your IP address. The websites you connect to have no way of knowing where you live, which ISP you are using, or what your browsing habits are. When you connect to the Tor network, you are establishing a conduit whereby if you connect to a website (Google for instance), it connects through several layers of IP addresses, or "onion layers" to reach its destination. You send out a message, email, or some type of communication. The message then goes to Bob, Jane and Herb, then finally reaches the end of the line...your favorite webpage. It routes data (backwards/forwards) through an onion later of IP addresses, so that no one adversary can see who sent what without very significant resources.

As you have probably guessed, there is a small speed hit in doing this. In order to hide your IP address, several "hops" or intermediaries, have to be jumped through. Like portals. Without going into too much technical detail, let's just say that these hops serve a very valuable purpose: to keep your private communications out of the hands of those that intend to snoop on you. Since your IP address changes every time you login to the Tor network, they can't "bubble" you effectively and target you with ads because you look like a different person from a foreign country to them each time you login. The Tor relay will end up giving you a different country to "pop-out" from with each session of your Tor browser, thus making it impossible to know your origin or where you will go next.

Let's examine an analogy between Tor and regular internet usage. You're sitting in your living room browsing anonymously via the Tor network. Your wife on the other hand is sitting in the kitchen on her Macbook, browsing without Tor. You might wonder if her browsing habits break your own anonymity. They don't...up to a point. While your isp doesn't know what *you* are doing online, they certainly do in regards to your wife.

Imagine yourself driving down Main Street in a Mercedes with tinted windows. No one can peer inside to see what you are doing at the stoplight. Not even the cops. Your wife on the other hand has non-tinted windows. People can glance over without any effort and tell if she is smoking a cigarette, listening to her iPod or talking on her phone. You are anonymous. She is not. The ISP along with any websites she visits can see everything she does online. They can't see what you are doing, however.

Firefox (and many other browsers) talk to different hosts, with the router acting as the traffic cop. An example:

Your machine: Port X, Machine A (Tor: all encrypted traffic)

Your wife: Port Y, Machine B (without Tor: all visible traffic)

It's like shooting fish in a barrel, and for the NSA, even easier than that. This same concept also applies with other things you may do on your machine while using Tor. If you use BitTorrent, your ISP can still see what you do on the P2P network even if you are running Tor simultaneously. But it cannot see the contents of the Tor network.

Thus, don't do anything on your P2P network that you wouldn't want your ISP to know about. Tor however is a different story since they cannot see what is going on between Tor relays. For all intents and purposes, Tor is like a cloak of invisibility that shields you from the sight of all onlookers, unless you have accidentally ripped a hole in the cloak (i.e. turned on javascript). If you are thinking, "Wow, it might be cool to run BitTorrent through Tor so I won't get sued". A nice goal, except BitTorrent devs aren't falling over themselves to implement this feature with Tor, and the Tor network can't really handle the bandwidth anyway. You'll just make everyone else miserable by downloading those 720p Blu-Ray rips you can easily get from Usenet (and with SSL, you're not likely to get sued.)

It might be prudent to spell out some of the best practices of using the Tor network should you decide to use it. First, although the Tor package comes with a preconfigured Firefox browser, there are still some rules you should follow that might not be apparent.

- Never give any compromising information on the Tor network that could be used to identify you. This means using your credit card for purchases, accessing your bank account, or logging into a social media site like Facebook. Card transaction are traceable. Tor, in fact, may even result in flagging transactions done via a tor exit node.
- Never mix browsers. Don't use the same browser you browse every day to Facebook and your ISP email as you do to access the Tor network. Super cookies can give away which sites you visit outside of Tor and can lead to a correlation attack on your identity/IP address.
- Always disable Javascript. The reason for this is that exploits can be utilized to reveal your IP address through using flash. Flash videos such as those on Youtube only work if this is enabled. After installation of Tor, ensure that the settings in the NoScript plugin are ON and not off by default in the plugins options screen.
- Install a bare minimum of browser plugins. You want to be as vanilla as everyone else. Too many addins, plugins, games, etc., can act as an identity beacon--fonts you use, time of day you use certain features, can all be used to build a profile on you. BE VANILLA.
- Disable any automatic updates in the browser's options tab. This also includes updates for any addons. You should update manually, not automatically.

TOR AND TORRENTS

A word about torrents and the Tor network. It might seem on the surface that running your torrent client through the Tor network would be an obviously beneficial idea. After all, if Tor can cloak your regular Firefox downloads, surely it can do the same with torrents too, right? Well, yes and no. Yes, you could route your traffic through Tor using your favorite torrent client, however this is not a good idea for several reasons.

The first is that Tor was never developed to withstand the kind of punishing traffic bandwidth that usually comes from torrenting.

Secondly, most torrent clients like uTorrent, BitSpirit, and libTorrent are not coded properly to make you anonymous on the Tor network. They often will ignore their socks proxy settings since UDP protocol is heavily involved with torrenting, and will send your real IP address to the tracker, thereby defeating the purpose of using Tor completely. Tor in fact still does what it is coded to do: send whatever packets anonymously through the Tor network to your destination. However, it sends your IP address within the torrent tracker right along with it...anonymously.

It would be like sending a secret message in an envelope directly to the person you are attempting to hide that message from. This is not a problem with the Tor application, but rather the way torrent trackers are coded. The only fix would be if the torrent application coders themselves rewrote their applications to work harmoniously with the Tor network, something they probably will not get around to doing anytime soon (and much to the glee of Tor developers).

Tor Onion Sites

ONE OF THE most secretive elements of the Tor network is the existence of Tor Onion websites, which are pseudo top level domains acting as anonymous hidden services. In other words, they are hidden in that they can only be accessed by the Tor users themselves residing within the Tor network, rather from the open web. The motive for the creation of such hidden sites is so that the admin of the site as well as those accessing such sites cannot be traced. Since onion sites that are based on the hidden service protocol cannot be accessed from the regular internet, the address of the onion site you are looking for must be known. You can connect to an onion website on Tor just as you can a regular website, by typing the address into the address bar. For example, you might want to go to Tor2Web, in which case the address is:

http://tor2web.org/

A warning about tor2web: it is intended to offer one-sided security, that is, to protect the identity of those publishing content on Tor, not those browsing it. If you want to be secure while browsing you'll need to install the Tor application. Convenience and speed should always take a back seat where security is concerned.

Needless to say, a hidden network would not stay completely benign of nefarious webmasters if it wasn't indeed anonymous. To that end, the Hidden Wiki was developed, a singular .onion page with a wikipedia-like structure outlining in explicit detail everything from political activists to every conceivable criminal group imaginable. There are links to hundreds of various .onion sites dealing with everything from how to obtain illegal drugs, warez operations, virus creation, anonymous use of Bitcoins, illegal pornography, hacked Paypal accounts and even how to hire contract killers. Needless to say, some of these sites need to be taken with a grain of salt.

Be aware of your own country's laws regarding what can legally be obtained. What goes around in Amsterdam or Japan may not fly straight with the authorities in the USA. Remember that information that exists in Deep Web is just that: information. By itself, the information can do nothing. Words are just rearranged letters to get your point across. Pictures and videos are simply ones and zeros moving across your display. It is what they are eventually used for that define their ethics.

At the core of it, the Hidden Wiki is not terribly dissimilar from any run-of-the-mill black market operation offline. It just so happens to be online, and accessible by anyone with a little search engine sleuthing capability. Not all of the information in the Deep Web is used for nefarious purposes. Like Freenet, there are a lot of different sites that concentrate on exposing human rights abuse, political corruption, and government scandals involving high-level politicians. In the end, it is what you do with the data that determines the criminal element.

Testing your IP address visibility on Tor

WHEN YOU HAVE INSTALLED TOR, you may want to test your IP address to see if it really is broadcasting your Tor IP and not your real IP address. If you installed the default package of Tor, then Tor will show you the IP you are broadcasting as your start page. If you want to check it yourself, then go to

http://whatismyipaddress.com/.

This will show you not only your IP address, but your internet service provider as well, and where it is located on google maps. It will also show city and country. When you are using Tor, you will see a different city/country than the one you currently reside in. Mark down what your IP address is outside of Tor, and check this site when your launch Tor if you're especially paranoid (I am).

VPNS

The last few years have seen an emergence of many different VPN (virtual private network) providers with server farms in just about every country. What a VPN does is somewhat similar to what the Tor network does. It sends a different IP address to your destination, whether that is a webpage, usenet provider, or webhost. There are some pros and cons to this. First, it is not free. A VPN will cost the same amount you would get for Usenet service: about ten dollars per month. This amount fluctuates from provider to provider. Sometimes it is a little more, sometimes a bit less, but all providers have you login to their service the same way you would an ISP. Most of the configuration is automatic and doesn't require any technical wizardry to setup. Five minutes, give or take.

Another major difference is that while Tor provides anonymity, and is free, a VPN will provide you with *privacy*, but not necessarily *anonymity*. This is because the middle man, the VPN in this case, knows your real IP address. They have to know this information in order to forward your requests. The VPN service is built upon a different technology than Tor. It is built for *speed* and *stability*. Torrenting, you say? Knock yourself out.

Further, let's say that you're a Chinese dissident. You don't like the way your country is headed in regards to free speech and human rights. You can't exactly criticize the Chinese government in the Saturday paper can you? Of course not. So what is a good, law-abiding dissident to do? You build a news website using a VPN in another country and relay your dissent through that internet portal. You don't necessarily have to build a website. You could simply setup your newsreader to access Usenet via the VPN connection. In that way, the Chinese government could not determine the origin of any anti-governmental messages through the use of the IP address (unless of course you hint of incriminating personal information that narrows down your location).

You can also access forbidden places by the Chinese government, such as Facebook, Skype, private chat rooms and even Usenet. The reason these kinds of places are blocked by the Great Firewall of China is precisely because they are fertile ground for free speech enthusiasts. While this may sound like an easy way to circumvent the Chinese police, remember that most VPN providers offer connections through almost every civilized country you can think of. If you are a Chinese dissident, I wouldn't connect to a VPN located in China, but rather Canada or perhaps a country hostile to China. Most VPN providers offer a selection of many servers to choose from in which to route your messages and traffic.

On that note, let's talk a bit about law enforcement and VPNs. Many in the past have erroneously thought that a VPN carried with it a strong dose of anonymity, similar to what Tor offered. It doesn't quite stack up that way. A VPN service offers privacy, not anonymity, as we stated. They do not route your data through intermediaries the way Tor does. Depending on which VPN you choose, you could end up with one in Switzerland who will not cave to anyone's request for subscriber information outside of Sweden. On the other hand, you might have a US based provider who will bow down to the whims of any judge's warrant for subscriber information in a New York minute.

While most are perfectly safe for purposes of torrents and the like, one should think twice about using a VPN in a western country for felonious offenses, as they will most likely give your name and address up to law enforcement in order to stave off any fines and/or trouble by the government. There are of course ways around this, such as not using your credit card and paying anonymously, however sometimes it is better not to use a VPN at all for those kinds of purposes (think hackers, smuggling, illicit banned goods, drugs etc). Vpns have never been built with anonymity in mind. Tread carefully.

TOR RELAYS

"Who can you trust? Nobody, cause nobody wants you here."

Those words, uttered by Sean Connery in The Untouchables, are as appropriate for darknet discussions as they are for the mob. But let's be realistic for a moment. There are, as you read this, ten thousand more organized crime syndicates spread out over the net than you will ever come across in the "Deep Web". They run the same secure, enterprise-grade software that Wall Street banks use and cloak themselves better than Ringwraiths. No outside eyes peer in unless the alphabet agency has a guy on the inside. Cartels like these rake in millions in drugs, arms, counterfeit pharmaceuticals, mercs and excel at human trafficking.

The Deep Web is similar, but not that similar. But those who are for outlawing it completely are really advocating for more control rather than for less crime, as was the case with Prohibition. They claim the negatives outweigh the positives. Let's say a guy in North Korea gets curious as to why his government is censoring information from him. He wants to know why. So he uses Tor to access websites blocked by the North Korean regime (Facebook for instance, to hook up with an uncle who may have escaped to S. Korea). And he does so anonymously. So that is one positive trait.

But this, they say, does not outweigh the child porn, contract killers and heroin runners. They say, people aren't going to Tor to discuss ways of avoiding the mine fields on the border and neither are they discussing the latest enlightenment from Tibet. Yes, anonymity has its meritorious moments, but someone who wants to hide almost always does so at the circumvention of the law. There are only so many North Koreans, after all.

They assume, quite wrongly, that those criminals engaged in the above activities would cease to exist. They are wrong. These were around before Tor and the Deep Web were even a spark in the developer's minds, and will thrive regardless of what government regulations are cooked up by congress critters. The same as it was during Prohibition.

Hazards of running a Tor Exit Node

In 2012, an Austrian named William Weber, an IT admin, was arrested for running Tor servers that route anonymous traffic over the Tor network. The charge? Distributing illegal images. Police detected the data coming off one of the nodes he ran. A police raid ensued. Searched his home. Confiscated his Xbox, iPods, all drives and miscellaneous electronics and even his legally owned firearms. The court order revealed one of the Tor exit nodes (he ran seven) was transporting the data.

Notice, we did not state that *he* transported the data. The data in question is going to come down on some node, be it his or someone else's. That is how Tor works: via encrypted traffic that gets piped through servers on its own IP address, through various layers (hence the term Onion layer) and decrypted back into its initial form. An ISP cannot discern the contents in transit. However, law enforcement can see the contents coming out of a node that was sent from the other side of the globe. Holding a Tor node operator responsible would be like holding a forum administrator responsible because some anonymous poster said he was going to kill the president.

Misuse of Tor end nodes are fairly common. Back in 2008, a man was arrested by German police after bomb threats passed through his Tor node, and similarly, they confiscated all electronics--hardware, software, and threatened imprisonment because someone abused his generosity. These kinds of cases bring up a few parallels. Should the Austrian government sue Google for having illegal data flowing through its servers? We're not only talking about images or bomb threats. Warez, kidnapping, extortion, bribery, espionage, a long laundry list of crimes occur on a daily basis via their search engine, and though Google cooperates with law enforcement (as Weber did), when was the last time you heard Google's servers confiscated by a court order?

And then there is encryption. Should Drivecrypt and Truecrypt developers be held liable for helping illegal enterprises? Truecrypt is a software used quite heavily by Mexican cartels as well as organized crime in the United States. Law enforcement, particularly the FBI, tends to shoot first and ask questions later. Maybe. If they're in a good mood (or ordered to by a judge). Meanwhile, your electronics are confiscated and your reputation damaged.

The entire ordeal has been setting dangerous precedent for years, as any average Joe who just happens to pass some part of an illegal data packet through his connection (or unsecured WiFi) can be prosecuted. Furthermore, police are not known for their technical aptitude, in Austria or anywhere else. They took his Xbox360 and anything else plugged in that looked about as complex as a toaster. We mustn't allow Tor node operators to be scapegoats. If Tor dies, innocent people die. They won't get the word out about corrupt government actions without risking their own lives. And they shouldn't *have* to risk anything to get the word out.

As of 2014, no one has been sued or prosecuted in a U.S. court of law for running a Tor relay (unlike those using BitTorrent). Furthermore, using Tor as well as running a Tor relay is perfectly legal under U.S. law.

Benefits of Running a Tor Exit Node

We've talked a little about the risks of being a Tor exit mode. You might be saying, well, the risks far outweigh the benefits. And in some places, you're right. But it depends on where you live, the laws, the bandwidth, your setup, etc.

So what are the benefits?

- Help people all over the world browse the net anonymously (esp. censorship-prone countries)

- Provide support for the network

- Exit nodes are always scarce. Your generosity supports development.

- Defeat tyranny (what's that? Well, North Korea for one)

- Prevent websites/search engines from tracking you

- Help others get beyond the Great Firewall of China

- Join the Rebel Alliance (yeah right)

At this point it might be prudent to relay my own experience. The first time I used Tor, I was already fairly good as not only admin of several websites and hosted machines, but quite good at encryption. My frame of thought was, if I was no slouch at encryption, Tor would be a piece of cake. And it was...for a while. I had plenty of bandwidth available, so I jumped right in.

Being in North America at the time, it would be a few weeks to get up to speed on all the pros and cons of Tor relays, and not from the technical standpoint, but the legal. I envisioned Blackhawk helicopters and car chases involving white vans with license plates that read "NOTOJ" should I be so unlucky to screw up my configuration. Putting my paranoia aside, I finally got it running full speed, and studied the network logs like a hawk to see what it was doing. And I was well-pleased. Full of pride, you might say.

Tor traffic trickled in like a sprinkle before a storm, and after three days my node had spread just as the bandwidth limits I had preset kicked in. The feeling was euphoric. Addicting. I envisioned some tech-starved villager in North Korea accessing something verboten by the Korean government. I kept thinking about Matthew Broderick in WarGames and the famous line, "The only way to win the game, was not to play." Well, I tweaked it to add, "...by the Man's rules." It was all good.

Until a week later when my ISP ordered me to cut the Tor umbilical. It was polite, but stern. It seemed a few complaints sailed their way. As my luck would have it, that North Korean villager turned out to be a swarm of torrentors using Tor to evade the trackers setup by the record industry. It hampered Tor's bandwidth like a hurricane had set upon it.

"Torrents?" I said. "Really?"

Yes indeed. And even though I lived in Canada at the time and wasn't worried about a torrent of lawsuits, I still did not want other Tor users to be hindered by greedy users. The problem I ran into was that filtering torrent traffic is a bit counterproductive since BitTorrent is able to run on any standard port. I tried blocking ports 80 and 443 (web traffic). It wasn't a silver bullet, however, since torrent users could still use other ports. BitTorrent clients like uTorrent and BitLord can run on any port, almost all randomly chosen. Thus every port you add to your exit node can connect to another client listening on that same port. Some users even enable a range of ports, thereby increasing the chance of getting a DMCA takedown for you.

Hence, we come to the Reduced Exit Policy of Tor, an alternative to the default exit policy. You are still able to connect and at the same time block TCP ports (usually) used by BitTorrent users. Below are a couple of port lists to check against BitTorrent clients:

https://secure.wikimedia.org/wikipedia/en/wiki/
List_of_TCP_and_UDP_port_numbers

http://www.speedguide.net/ports.php

What should become clear as crystal at this point is that you should not run an exit relay from your house, with emphasis on *should not*. Why not? Because of the aforementioned scenarios with law enforcement. As we've seen in prior cases, it is quite easy for them to get a judge's signature (a judge who knows squat about Tor) on a no-knock warrant in the USA should they start sniffing your traffic. Not only will they take your computer, but everything with connectivity, which these days includes TVs and monitors. Much better to run the exit relay from a commercial provider (and there are many). A few in the U.S. who are not only knowledgeable about Tor, but have the support needed to deal with abuse cases are as follows:

Amazon Web Services (AWS)
    AmeriNOC
    Arvixe
    Axigy
    ChunkHost
    Team Cinipac
    Cyberonic
    Ethr.net
    Evolucix
    Future Hosting

A full comprehensive list is available at the Tor Wiki that covers many countries, each with their own subset of laws dealing with anonymity services (and extensive comments on each).

https://trac.torproject.org/projects/tor/wiki/doc/GoodBadISPs

In the event you do decide to run a Tor relay from home however, make sure you inform your ISP and ascertain whether you have their full support (i.e. no surprises a month down the line). The abuse complaints will come sooner or later, just as they did for me. The Tor forums have a list of ISPs that are friendly towards Tor and are knowledgeable about the network, in addition to ones that are not.

FREENET

Freenet is unlike any other anonymizing beast on the entire internet. It takes quite a wizardly mind to crack its protection and to that, it is a bit like chess: easy to grasp the basics, long and difficult to become a master. Built in 2000, Freenet is a vast, encrypted datastore spanning thousands of connected computers across the globe, all distributing encrypted contents from one computer to another. To this end, it is somewhat similar to a P2P program like Emule. Except with eEule, every file, whether it mp3, rar or iso is out there in the open for weeks, months and years, along with the IP addresses, trumpeting who downloaded and uploaded every file. You know what you upload, and what you download, and so does everyone else.

Freenet is different in this regard.

While your IP address is visible, what you are uploading out of your datastore is not. You initially setup the size of the datastore for others to download from you. This datastore is encrypted. You have no idea what will eventually be inside, as the contents are encrypted. It is a bit like a postal worker delivering the mail. He has no idea what is in the package he is delivering. That is not his job. His job is to deliver the contents to its destination. Therein is the strength of Freenet.

While you can see your downloads merrily trickle their way down to your laptop, there is no way to decrypt your datastore's content and see what it is you're passing along to the nearest node. And to that, the bigger the datastore, the more efficiently Freenet runs. After one inserts a file into Freenet, the user is free to shutdown their pc. This is unlike torrents in that the stability of the torrent file is dependent on the length of online seeds. Thus, high reliability is a factor with Freenet files, as the file is spread between encrypted blocks residing in the Freenet system.

Freenet is slow. So slow in fact, that you may not see any measurable progress in download speed for a couple hours or so after install, and it may be a day before you can see extensive progress with old (unpopular) files. Don't get discouraged because of this. It will speed up gradually over time.

Now, with your IP address out there in the open, you might be tempted to think it is not very anonymous. Nothing could be further from the truth. Whatever you download is encrypted from one end of Freenet to the other, and decrypted on your PC. No one looking in from the outside can see who requested which file or message. No one on the inside knows either, except you. For this reason alone, it is extremely censorship-resistant. This level of anonymity requires each node that requests data to operate in "hops", from many intermediaries, similar to what you would see in Tor.

However, no node knows who requested which file, thus giving a high level of anonymity. This requirement carries a price in that downloads as well as uploads are initially extremely slow, especially for new data inserts.

Let's say you want to share an iso dvd image on this network. You fire up Frost (a front-end addon for Freenet), then hit insert, then select the file. Then depending on how big your file is, you could be waiting for a long time, say several hours, for the file to finish. If this file had been inserted three months prior, and was very popular, with dozens of users trying to fetch said file, then that file would download very fast. However this is not usually the case with new files since every kernel of data on Freenet operates faster if and only if it is a popular file.

There are two types of security protocols that Freenet offers: Darknet and Openet. For Openet, you connect to other users, called "strangers". There is nothing sinister about this, as this is what the Freenet developers envisioned that most beginners would use. The IP address of said strangers is visible, but the anonymity of Freenet isn't nested in the security of the IP address like Tor, but rather it is nested in the encryption methods of the distributed datastore.

The other security option, which you are given at installation, is Darknet, where you will connect to "friends" rather than "strangers". These will be Freenet users that you will have (presumably) previously exchanged node references, which are public security keys. With Darknet mode, it is assumed that you will have a higher level of trust, as your node reference is related to your online Freenet identity. Needless to say, this mode is not to be taken lightly. You really do have to TRUST those you add to this protocol. That is, the darknet protocol.

Within Freenet, there are no censors. Every kind of free speech is allowable and often encouraged. The very way in which Freenet is programmed makes it impossible to remove any message from the system by a censor. Individual users may opt to erase certain comments from the frost system, for instance, but this is only at the local level, on their machine, and not the Freenet network itself. Thus, no religious group for instance can force others in the network to conform to their belief and discussion system. No one on Freenet may deem information so offensive that it must be removed. Not even Freenet developers.

Needless to say, this has some negative consequences in that anyone may say anything to anyone at any time. Some Freesites on the Freenet network are plagued by spammers, identity thieves, terrorists, molesters, government anarchists and software pirates. The

Freenet developers have stated this is a necessary evil of sorts in allowing 100% free speech to reign free. It could be argued that one should not allow illicit digital goods to be exchanged between users just so people could speak freely, however one of the stated purposes of Freenet is to preserve such a system in the even of societal collapse or oppression.

While there are no rules to govern Freenet by in the sense of censoring unsightly posts, a few guidelines have been posted in scattered parts of Freenet that should probably be heeded:

1.) Never give anyone on Freenet your node-reference, as this contains information that could be exploited to correlate your Freenet identity with your IP address.

2.) Same rule as Usenet: Don't give in to trolling activity. Trolling by its very nature flourishes with the more responses it receives. Ignore them.

3.) Never give out any personal info: your location, where you grew up, which restaurants you like most, what kinds of clothing stores you shop at, as these could zero-in on your location

4.) Take notice of different regionally spelled words (labor vs. labour, color vs. colour: these could reveal your home country).

5.) Never use any nickname that is the very same unique nickname you use for opennet forums. Use popular nicknames like Shadow, John, Peter and the like.

THE HIGHEST SECURITY setting can be a bit foreboding, but perhaps necessary in countries where criticizing the government could land you a lifetime in a work camp. It has an encrypted password option to encrypt Freenet usage. This setting is in the security configuration, along with a host of other options of varying system requirements. The higher the security setting, the slower Freenet will run as it will use more resources to cover your footsteps.

When first installing Freenet, it will likely take no more than a few minutes, while asking you which security level you would like to operate at (normal up to maximum). After that and a bit of time allowed for Freenet to find nodes to connect to, you'll be presented with a previously hidden world where a Freenet index lists every possible combination of Freesites available. Everything from anarchy sites to Iranian news, to pirated copies of books, films and game roms and even a few political how to documents describing how to protest a corrupt government without getting caught will be indexed.

These are the types of things typically either censored by Google in China, or deindexed altogether. The only thing missing is a disclaimer at the bottom of the screen welcoming you to the deepest, darkest depths of the internet, known as Darknet.

Optionally, you may run Freenet from an encrypted Truecrypt container file. You will need to create a Truecrypt volume that is sufficiently large enough to hold whatever files you intend on down-loading from Freenet. Remember to keep in mind that when Freenet asks you how large you want the datastore to be, the size you choose could be a benefit to other Freenet users. The larger the datastore, the more efficient the Freenet network operates.

That is not to say that downloads will *always* come down faster, but rather encrypted data will last longer on the network. This is similar to the retention times that Usenet providers talk about when they try to sell their servers to you. The higher the data retention, the longer the files on the network will last. There is also another bonus to having a large datastore, say fifty gigabytes or so. Files that you may request may already be in your datastore after having run Freenet for some time, thereby shortening the time to retrieve them.

With your Truecrypt container you can run Freenet with the volume mounted and not worry about your Freenet activities being used against you in case of your computer being confiscated. You can also do the same for your Tor browser as well. Install Tor browser bundle to a mounted Truecrypt container and only run the program when mounted.

Frost

FROST IS a separate application than Freenet, which acts as a front-end. It makes browsing on the Freenet network more akin to browsing Usenet newsgroups. Download at:

HTTP://JTCFROST.SOURCEFORGE.NET

AFTER RUNNING FREENET, you can optionally run Frost simultaneously to download inserts from the Freenet network. It is not mandatory but it is incredibly helpful. Run Freenet, then Frost, and then wait an hour or so for Frost to find some groups, and then hit the globe button at the top panel to subscribe to groups. These groups all have discussions going about every topic under the sun. Some of them are fairly dead, with almost no discussion at all, and others swarm with activity.

Frosty Tips

1.) If you started downloading something in Frost, finish it in Frost

2.) Like Usenet, don't troll the boards. It will get you put on user's "ignore" list and they will henceforth not see any messages from your nick.

3.) Never reveal your node reference to anyone on the Frost boards, as it could be used to locate you.

4.) Set days to download backwards to 60 (or however long you wish). Just be aware that it may take several days to retrieve all messages if you select a very large amount of days.

5.) In the options/preferences tab, you may adjust the setting to ignore comments from users with less than four messages attached to their nickname. This is very effective at eliminating most spam messages on the board.

TRUECRYPT, VERACRYPT, ETC.

There are two types of encryption: one that will prevent your sister from reading your diary and one that will prevent your government. - Bruce Schneier

IT WOULD BE FOLLY if we went to all this work of laying out the security options to keep our online footprint out of nefarious hands and not say something about our offline footprint. Put simply, you should tread carefully with your offline habits just as you should your online persona.

Let's say you're in your favorite cafe. You're sipping your ice cappuccino with your laptop in the corner of the coffee scented shop and have to make a break for the restroom. It'll only take a minute or so, right? While you're in there, the guy sitting at the next table decided to insert a USB key into your laptop and upload a keylogger virus into your machine. This keylogger is ridiculously small in size, and can hide undetected by most users. It can even disguise itself as a windows service and look just like any other svchost process, all the while taking snapshots of your screen, recording everything you typed for the remainder of that day, and emailing them to whomever installed the virus.

You would be a bit worried if you knew about it.

However, most don't realize they leave themselves vulnerable to such attacks in public places. Some experts have referred to this as the "evil maid attack", after a scenario whereby you are in a hotel and briefly step outside for a moment and at which point the maid comes in and has physical access to your running machine. They now have access to every cookie stored by your browser in addition to any credit card numbers you have used, possible phone numbers/emails of friends, and the like. How to prevent this?

For starters, to prevent identity theft you need to seriously consider full-disk encryption. This is not nearly as complex as you might think. It is ridiculously easy encrypt your boot drive and costs you nothing, and potentially saves you from months of headache.

There are several encryption apps at your disposal: the paid programs, such as PGP, Drivecrypt, and Phonecrypt, and the popular free versions, PGP and Truecrypt. There are a few differences between them but the one thing to take away from both free and paid versions is that they prohibit anyone from booting your computer, laptop, or phone without the password.

Truecrypt is free, and does this by creating a 256 AES encryption key. You install the application, select your drive you want to encrypt, and select your passphrase and create an encrypted key. Simple.

How does this benefit you? Well, the next time that thief who stole your laptop tries to boot up the hard drive, without the password he'll be out of luck. He is presented with this password field before windows even boots, and if it is not keyed in correctly, the drive halts. The password, if sufficiently long, is enough to withstand almost any brute-force attack, even by the NSA. Just make sure to use a passphrase that will be easy to remember, but long enough to thwart any attacker: 15-character passphrase with upper/lowercase letters with a number or two.

Just how strong is Truecrypt? It is considered impossible to crack, on the order of millions of years. It would take quantum computers eons to crack even a moderately length passphrase using brute-force methods. In all likelihood the absolute weakest link is *you*.

Keyloggers can obtain your password if you are unlucky enough to get one. However, these are a fairly rare occurrence if you keep your operating system, anti-virus and anti-malware programs up to date. The other weakest link is your passphrase. You would be surprised at just how many people use their own personal information in their passphrases. Doing this might make the password easier to remember, but also easier to crack.

A good passphrase is made up of lower and upper case characters in addition to spaces, which lend more entropy bits to the protection. At each instance a bit is added to a passphrase, the computational crunching requirement to crack such passphrase is doubled. If I were living in North Korea or China, for example, I would seriously consider a passphrase that was at least twenty characters long, with some keyboard symbols thrown in for good measure. Most people do not like to remember a twenty character passphrase however, so they use a less random one.

Drivecrypt is another encryption program, but it is not open-source and is not free. I have used this program for eight years and have to say if money is a concern, then go with Truecrypt as it has many of the same functions that Truecrypt does, and for zero cost. Drivecrypt has an option called "bootauth" which is short for boot authorization. The install process is similar to Truecrypt, though the bootup passphrase screen is a little different. You boot your hard drive, and then type in the passphrase to boot the OS. Truecrypt has this function as well.

As stated, it is not open-source. What that means is that it cannot be studied by the public sector (read: security users) to determine if any backdoors have been coded in. Like Truecrypt, it offers the option to create an encrypted operating system that holds a hidden operating system as well whose existence can be denied to those trying to harm or prosecute you. This is especially beneficial if you live in the UK, where failure to hand over a passphrase to an encrypted hard drive can get you two years in prison on a contempt of court charge. However you could give them the password to your decoy system. There is no way they could know if you were concealing a hidden operating system without a keylogger in place.

Truecrypt and Drivecrypt give no hints or leak any data regarding the existence of hidden files. The only way to mount said file is to know the password, and there are two you create with such an option: one for the decoy, and one for the hidden container/operating system.

Truecrypt and Drivecrypt also support the use of encrypted container files, which when clicked will mount the file the same way a mounting application like DaemonTools or Nero mounts an iso image. Prior to mounting, the application will ask you for the password. Mistype the password and the container does not mount at all. This can be very handy as there are a plethora of private items that you could conceal from government or any kind of prosecuting institution, such as medical records, tax records, school transcripts, business correspondence and the like.

Veracrypt may also be an option if you don't mind the Truecrypt interface. In fact, they look and act very similar.

VeraCrypt main features:

• Creates a **virtual encrypted disk** within a file and mounts it as a real disk.

• Encrypts an **entire partition or storage device** such as USB flash drive or hard drive.

• Encrypts a **partition or drive where Windows is installed** (pre-boot authentication).

• Encryption is **automatic**, **real-time**(on-the-fly) and **transparent**.

• Parallelization and pipelining allow data to be read and written as fast as if the drive was not encrypted.

• Encryption can be hardware-accelerated on modern processors.

• Provides **plausible deniability**, in case an adversary forces you to reveal the password: **Hidden volume** (steganography) and **hidden operating system**.

SOME TIPS FOR TRUECRYPT/VERACRYPT users:

1.) If you have one, disable the firewire port, as this can be used to reveal the encryption keys.

2.) Never leave any containers mounted on a laptop when crossing a border station, unless you want your private information in said container to be shared with the guards.

3.) Never leave your PC powered on and unattended for any lengthy amount of time (public wifi spots, cafes, libraries, college classrooms, etc). All security goes out the window when an attacker (or anyone else) has physical access to your machine. Neither Truecrypt nor Drivecrypt can protect your data in such a case, as the attacker can install a keylogger that can record your keystrokes.

Thumbnails

IF YOU POSSESS any incriminating snapshots (flings, Wikileak photos, informant docs) then at a later time delete the images in the folder, be aware that a shadow copy still exists. In windows XP (yes, legions of users are still clinging to this OS), thumbnails of jpegs are stored within each folder of the image's location. So if you have a folder called "government office snapshots", you will have thumbnails enabled in the folder settings tab for any pictures (jpegs, bitmaps, etc), and a hidden thumbs.db file will be present that shows a mini version of the picture in question. So even if you delete the jpegs, this hidden file will still reveal to anyone what the contents of the original folder were.

The only way to see or disable this hidden file is to go to Tools – Options – View and set the option to "show hidden files and folders".

Until this is done, every single folder with pictures in it will store a mini-snapshot of the pictures unless this is disabled. Windows 7 is a completely different file system to Windows XP. Instead of keeping the thumbnail cache within the folder where the pictures reside, it stores it in a central location

(%userprofile%\AppData\Local\Microsoft\Windows\Explorer)

I HAVE FOUND it much better to just leave the thumbnail option off in Windows 7, as the images load fairly quickly without the need for a cache to speed things up. There are other files, like text, audio and the like, that are also at risk of being discovered if you do not take precautions to securely delete the file. That does not mean deleted from the *recycle bin*, however. When you delete any items from the recycle bin, all that does is tell the operating system that the space previously occupied by that file can be written to again. It does not delete the file permanently until that space is overwritten to again by some other program.

Government agencies have programs that can *undelete* a file. The way around this is to use various programs to securely delete a file, such as Ccleaner. This app has an interesting wipe utility as well, in that it can wipe the free space of any previously deleted contents on the hard drive. You can even do this while the operating system is in use.

Needless to say, if you have a 2 terabyte hard drive and you're only using 20% of the drive, with 80% being "free space", then it will be a few hours for it to finish the wipe process, dependent on the speed of the hard drive and what other programs you have running. It does not touch any installed programs that exist already on the system unless you tell it to, and then only that free space that is allocated for use.

Swap File

LET'S talk briefly about the "swap" file that most operating systems use. What this means is that sometimes during heavy PC usage, you will run low on system memory, and then the operating system will use your hard drive as a temporary ram storage device. This is what is called the "swap file", which increases the speed of computer operations. This swap file can be a veritable gold mine of data to someone with nefarious intentions.

Text files, video thumbnails, and word document fragments can exist herein, enough to print out a pretty good snapshot of your past. There have even been court cases where people were convicted in court using nothing but thumbnail fragments.

You can disable the swap file windows uses by going to control panel, System & Security, System, Advanced, Performance, Settings, Advanced, Virtual Memory and click Change. Choose "No Paging File". Reboot.

Note: Some resource intensive games use the swap file to speed up their games when there is not enough ram. If you run into any slowdowns with normal PC usage you can always switch this option back on, then reboot.

I2P

I2P, otherwise known as the "Invisible Internet Project" is another option that people can use to hide their online IP address. It shares a lot of the same characteristics of other networks in that it routes traffic through neighboring peers. The developers have stated that their main goal is not necessarily one of 100% anonymity (a goal some say is impossible), but rather to make the system too troubling and expensive to attack from the outside. It is an *anonymizing* network with several layers of encryption wrapped around all the data that travels through the system.

I2P VS Tor

YOU MIGHT THINK this sounds a lot like Freenet, but the similarity is actually more like Tor's network. I2P offers interactivity with websites, blogs, forums, chat, search engines and all without the need to install any of them locally. Such are the hallmarks of I2P. Websites that exist in the I2P network are called Eepsites, and are hosted anonymously with I2P being a strict requirement to access these websites. In that vein, it is similar to the .onion sites accessible only via Tor. Every PC that is connected to the I2P network shares in the forwarding of encrypted packets of data through proxies prior to the final destination. Each *subsequent* proxy prunes a layer of encryption at various intervals until encryption is removed. The bottom line is this: No one knows the origin of said packets, a trait also shared by Tor. While it is true that both Tor and I2P have different goals in mind, there exists many similarities:

- Both exist as anonymizing networks
- Both use layered encryption to funnel data
- Both have hidden services
- Tor has Exit Nodes and I2P has Outproxies

Benefits of Tor over I2P

- LARGER USER BASE THAN I2P; support from academic sources, constant improvements in stability and resistance to attacks
- Funding is sourced from many countries around the globe
- Large number of Exit Nodes
- Translated into many languages
- Optimized for Exit Traffic
- Memory more optimized than I2P
- Written in C

Benefits of I2P over Tor

- HIDDEN SERVICES much faster than the Tor network.
- Not as many DOS (denial of service) attacks as Tor.
- Compatible with peer-to-peer file sharing (Tor is not).
- Tor tunnels last a long time compared to I2P. This ensures less attacks as the number of samples a hacker may use are limited.
- Every peer routes data for others.

- Offers TCP/UDP.
- Written in Java.

AS YOU CAN SEE, both networks are safe enough for anonymity, as long as you aren't a world-hunted target. To this, a user's anonymity is typically broken due to their own sloppy behavior--their overconfidence being the weakest link in most cases (using the same login names on many websites, mixing these with Tor and non-Tor websites, and enabling JavaScript/Flash).

Since I2P is not built to act as a proxy to the WWW, you should use Tor if you want to surf anonymously. The outproxies on I2P, as you've probably guessed, are similar to the exit nodes on Tor, but they do not have the greatest support and tend to be unstable. Thus you should use Tor for anonymous web browsing and I2P for I2p eepsites. One option is to use Foxy Proxy to test it yourself. Be aware however that since there are fewer outproxies than Tor exit nodes, it may be easier for an adversary to identify your activities. It all depends on how much risk you want to assume and what the ramifications are if you are caught (and in which country).

You can also use I2P for BitTorrent and iMule as well as other P2P applications. Like Freenet, you will find that I2P will grow in speed the longer you use it without interruption. Torrents will be faster. Data will come down like lightning. Tor users will thank you for it. There are already too many torrent users on Tor that clog the network and make it difficult for people in dire straits who need anonymity for their political actions far more than the next Incubus CD.

While I2P is a technical powerhouse for anonymity, it can be a bit like a house of cards. Once the Ace is pulled from the bottom layer (by you), it can be rendered moot. I2P is just a tool, as is Tor and Freenet. It is not an invisibility cloak. Do something stupid, like move too much when a pack of Orcs are looking your way, you're bound to get an arrow in a place where you least expect it. Thus, act smart by being proactive in anonymity:

1.) **Turn Off Javascript**

Yes, it bears repeating, with arms waving in the air and shouting at the top of our lungs. Javascript is the bane of not only Tor, but other networks that rely on cloaking your IP address. Leaving this beastly plugin ON allows code to be run on your machine, code that will decloak you. Look at your browser settings and disable it. Also disable cookies. Super cookies are deployed in the wild to track down Tor users. Don't let it happen to you on I2P. Javascript can reveal a ton of metrics that fingerprint a user. Display resolution, page width, font and so on can be sent to an adversary by stealth. If you're in doubt, take a look at the web API at Mozilla:

HTTPS://DEVELOPER.MOZILLA.ORG/EN-US/DOCS/ WEB/API

2.) **Silence is Golden!**

DON'T SAY A PEEP. Sure, you can talk. But refrain from discussing: the weather, your geography, your hobbies, your city politician that was just arrested for soliciting hookers. If someone says, "Hows the weather in your town?" You say: "Sunny." Every time. Alternatively, you may misinform. The CIA does it, why can't you? Their entire organization is built on secrecy and deception. Don't get too choked up about a few white lies. Spreading misinformation about trivial things like the weather and the local politics can really put a nail in an adversary's coffin. Ditto on employment. If you are asked about your work and you're a programmer, say you're a mail sorter down at the Post Office. They're not going to ask you about the latest Elvis stamp.

3.) **Rotate Usernames/Nics**

The desire for convenience often gets people in trouble. They use the same usernames on multiple sites/forums. That's fine for the daytime, open web. Not so much for the darknet. It breaks anonymity. Take forums for example. When your username becomes infamous for a wealth of knowledge, change it. Create a new one. Don't tell anyone. Entropy rises when many users swap information like this on a frequent basis. Maintain separate personas: one for the darknet, one for regular internet. Memorization is better than writing it down.

4.) **Never turn off your router**

I never turn mine off. Ever. If it is constantly going on and off while Freenet, Tor, I2P or IRC is running, after a while clues will surface as to who I really am, provided a sufficiently determined adversary has the resources to do it (NSA). The cost in power is negligible, so don't go cheap with anonymity. As the saying goes: out of speed, anonymity and reliability, you can only pick two, but make up for the lost component by acting *smart*.

5.) **Power in Numbers: Bandwidth**

Don't be stingy with your connection. The more you participate in the storm of users (Freenet, I2P), the more cloaked you will be. It is better to run 24/7 if you can. This makes it more difficult for an adversary to discern if you sent a file to someone else, or if you are merely the middle man to some file sent by a total unknown on the other side of the globe. Besides this, leaving the program running just makes it a lot faster network in general for other users. Think *Safety in Numbers*.

6.) **Optional (but smart)**

In the browser settings, set browser.safebrowsing.enabled and browser.safebrowsing.malware.enabled to false. Search goliaths like Google and Microsoft do not need to know the website URLs you visit.

Get into the habit of flushing the cache--cookies, etc. You can set this to do it automatically upon exit of the browser.

Refrain from using Foxy Proxy to selective proxy .i2p links. You don't want to be sent to the clearnet. If an I2P website is a honeypot, your Firefox browser can send a unique identifier in the referrer, in which case... anonymity broken.

At this point you're probably thinking this is way more headaches than it is worth. And you'd be right...in the beginning. But anything worth doing is usually hard at the outset. I as well as my colleagues do all of these things only because we have done them for years.

We do them every day.

Are we thinking about them?

No, not in the least on account of smart habits done daily. Do you think intently about starting your car? Pulling out of the driveway? No. But it's a good bet you were petrified to do it when you were sixteen. And pulling out of your driveway is a very complex action, as are the aforementioned suggestions. Just one of your brain cells is more complex than a 747. Don't waste any of them.

Torrents and Eepsites

FIRST THINGS FIRST. Install not only the NoScript plugin, but also the Cookie Whitelist (Buttons). Ideally you want to block everything when surfing Eepsites. There are a multitude of add-ons on the

Firefox site but you do not need all of them. You only need the ones that preserve your anonymity.

INSTALL QUICKPROXY, also at the Firefox site. Restart. Then open the proxy settings using the edit tab and then browse to "Preferences" and "Advanced". Then "Settings". Change your proxy settings to:

127.0.0.1 for HTTP Proxy, Port 4444 and 127.0.0.1 and port 4445 for SSL Proxy. Ensure Socks v4 is checked.

CLICK "OKAY" and exit out. If you've configured it correctly you should be able to click the QuickProxy icon (lower corner of browser) when you browse Eepsites. You can also paste in .i2p websites and hit "Go" the old fashioned way.

Torrents

AN OPTION for torrents is to use I2PSnark. If you're a beginner, ensure the service is running by opening a terminal and inputing:

$ i2prouter status

IF IT IS NOT RUNNING, start it with:

$ i2prouter status

THEN BROWSE via Firefox to

. . .

HTTP://LOCALHOST:7657/I2PSNARK/

AT THE MAIN I2PSNARK PAGE, you can see it running. Now you can create a torrent. Move a torrent and the data into

~/.I2P/I2PSNARK

THE OTHER OPTION is to paste the data you want to seed to the same directory, and in my case, this is usually PDFs and technical manuals. At the Tracker option, you can choose whatever method you wish or create an entirely new torrent. I2PSnark will create the new torrent and set it in a queue. All that remains to be done is to click Start in the top corner and away you go.

Get your torrents from Postman's tracker:

HTTP://TRACKER2.POSTMAN.I2P/

TORRENTS MIGHT BE slow at first, but do not get discouraged. You will have far faster downloads on I2P than you ever will Tor. One can never have enough good karma in this world.

FACEBOOK AND OTHER MISFITS

Facebook is a bit of a mixed bag where ethics is concerned. On the one hand, it is immensely popular and profit-inducing for a reason: people love to chat with relatives, old neighborhood friends, girlfriends, mistresses and political liaisons, all in real-time. People love connections. The feeling of unity and solidarity. The benefits are fairly immediate if you're the type of individual who likes instant gratification. There is nothing quite like the feeling of seeing old friends on your friend's list who you have not seen in twenty-five years, now instantly accessible for a chat session at just about any time of day.

It used to be that Facebook didn't rely as much on the IP address as a P2P network did. Times have changed. Nowadays, all of your personal information is theirs for the taking, and in some cases offered up on a digital platter by endusers. Your real name, phone number, who your past and present friends are, and even your pets are all valuable data as it can be targeted with advertising tailored to every atom of your personality. What could go wrong, you ask?

One problem facing Facebook users is that it is all too easy for Facebook to give this treasure trove of data up to the highest bidder.

Worse, Facebook acts not as a protector of the 4th amendment, but as an destroyer of it. Many government agencies and local law enforcement have relied on Facebook profiles to establish alibis, reveal private emails, and prove or disprove acts that may be criminal or not. Read the Facebook privacy policy for yourself:

"WE MAY ALSO SHARE information when we have a good faith belief it is necessary to prevent fraud or other illegal activity, to prevent imminent bodily harm, or to protect ourselves and you from people violating our Statement of Rights and Responsibilities. This may include sharing information with other companies, lawyers, courts or other government entities."

THEY'RE MANDATED by the government to abide by subpoenas for user information data except any private messages that are unopened and are less than 181 days of age (these require a warrant). The problem is that the Supreme Court never recognized a 4th amendment right to privacy. That is, data being shared with third parties, so the government pretty much has a blank check to engage in "shooting-fish-in-a-barrel" type expeditions for subscriber information that may or may not have anything to do with any criminal acts.

State and corporation are thus conjoined at the hip in a quasi-fascism that is difficult to defeat and predict, nevermind the fact that the government often, when it has nothing else to do, creates laws that are meant to be broken--over and over (speed limits, anyone?).

Thus, outside of discussions on anonymity, there is a not much to do when the enemy's archers are standing upon the castle towers with flaming arrows aimed at the exposed king. But we'll try nevertheless.

Be mindful of what you type on Facebook. Actually, be paranoid, unless you are one of the king's fools. This should go without saying, but the neverending stream of fools on Facebook often don't even recognize your need for privacy or anonymity to say nothing of their own. They get so accustomed to the personalized interface that you start to think they've got in it for you with their shouting your real name across the internet.

You are not anonymous here, or on any other social media site-- Twitter, Pinterest, Google Plus, etc.

In fact, a new Facebook account has even less privacy than one on a P2P network like Emule. Where emule is concerned, you only had to worry about the ip address. With Facebook, your private life belongs to them unless you take drastic action to prevent it. Yes, you may have heard more than a few complaints from a few peasants about the lack of privacy on Social Media. It hasn't failed to reached the ears of the ivory tower executives at Facebook, Inc. But what do they really think of anonymity?

THE ANOMALY: **Anonymous Facebook Login**

IN APRIL OF 2014, CEO Mark Zuckerberg announced that Facebook planned to implement "Anonymous Login" for all users. It was a misnomer in the same way that "cat owner" is a misnomer. It offers more privacy, certainly, but not anonymity. It doesn't come close to anonymity since you cannot login to Facebook *anonymously*. What it means is that, using your Facebook login, you can sign in to other websites, say at Ars Technica or Wired, and make comments without having to grant access to the treasure of data Facebook holds on you: your list of contacts, relatives, friends, favorite cereals and the fact you hate cats with a brimstone passion.

Presently they are testing this so called "anonymity" service with a smattering of social sites and forums so as to better "benefit the end-user", as Zuckerberg claims--grant more control to its userbase on some of the data that gets transferred. Notice the word "some"... of the data. Not all.

And herein is the fallacy: most people, especially those on social media, do not know the difference between anonymity and privacy. Thus the masses will gobble it up. Certainly signing up for a new service can be cumbersome--email, check link, clink on link, fill out forms, click another link in email, fill out more forms. It's a breath of fresh air to know simpler times are in the pipeline, but let's call it what is: efficiency, not anonymity.

Most people will think Facebook will stand true to their anonymity statement, but the truth of it is that they lied to their user-base right out of the gate, trading the mundane term *privacy* for the much loftier goal of *anonymity*. Facebook knows all about these third party sites you visit, and is willing to offer the data up to the highest bidder.

Your behavior, your identity, your favorites, all are a win-win for Facebook, and a lose-lose for the third party sites and *you*. If a nosy judge wants to uncloak you on a third party site over some "slanderous" comment you made, they need not go to the third party site. They will go to Facebook. They know the name you signed in with, the time you made the comment, the IP address you used to bounce to the discussion. Checkmate.

In an interview with Wired's Steve Levy, Zuckerberg had this to say about their new vision:

"WHEN WE WERE A SMALLER COMPANY, Facebook login was widely adopted, and the growth rate for it has been quite quick. But in order to get to the next level and become more ubiquitous, it needs to be trusted even more. We're a bigger company now and people have more questions. We need to give people more control over their information so that everyone feels comfortable using these products."

SOUNDS SUSPICIOUS, does it not? Well, that's not to say it's good for the goose either. In this case, the third party. Website developers who decide to use Facebook's API to expand their readership will have that decision come back to haunt them since Facebook "controls" the client that uses the API login. They can shut off the API for the developers just as Nevada can shut off water piping out to California. To counter this, they will be ever more vigilant in mining user data and be hesitant, if not fully opposed, to using this new "anonymous" setting as it grants Facebook absolute rule over its userbase. That is, if they were *smart*. Many are not.

HOW TO BE **Anonymous on Facebook**

FACEBOOK IS ALLERGIC TO ANONYMITY. You've probably heard that they frown on anonymous accounts. It is not entirely diffi-cult to understand why. They can't target you with advertisements if they don't know who you are, and that's their bread and butter. From your behavior come the metrics, the things you buy, the places you enjoy visiting, your family links. From their own lips:

"WE REQUIRE *everyone to provide their real names, so you always know who you're connecting with.*"

THIS IS a roadblock that fortunately can be overcome, since genuine names are not yet tied to any form of government ID schemes like driver's licenses or social security numbers (though they will be some-day). And even then, the rules of supply and demand would dictate even this would not dissuade the need for full anonymity.

When you are neck-deep in the account creation process at Face-book, you need to enter as much false data as you can. The email address in particular needs to be created in complete anonymity. The big mistake most people make is assuming that clocking the IP address is a sufficient means to the end. However there are many tracking mechanisms--complex algorithms designed to match behavior patterns and preferential choices--that all the big social media giants employ. Just one slip up, a broken link in the chain such as connecting to a website that knows your real identity (BBC, for instance) can destroy your every effort. Before you know it, all the others have been alerted by bots, warning pings and moderators that you've talked to in that session. Endgame.

Ask yourself this: Would your closest friends refer to you by name if you attended a popular masquerade in New Orleans during Mardi Gras? You bet they would, masked or not, even if you had pleaded with them to protect your identity. Some of them might whisper your name, not really even thinking about their prior oath of secrecy.

Then before you know it, another who happens to have the ears of a fox overhears your name being called. In much the same way, Facebook identifies you by your acquaintances just as others might do at the masquerade. Who is he talking to? A woman? Young or old? Tall or short? Do they talk with their hands? Ah, that's Maria from Rome. It's really not too difficult, and neither is it for Facebook. Friends and family lists are hardline identifiers in Facebook and Google's algorithms. The facial recognition Facebook employs can only get more advanced as it scours the web for matches elsewhere: Flickr. Google. Amazon. Twitter. Mugshot sites. Surveillance videos. Then there are photos of you to worry about: photos your friends have that are out of your control.

Facebook installs super cookies on your machine (or one of their many 3rd party enforcers) that tracks you in a number of ways: by Sid number, MAC address, etc. It continues to track you even after you've logged out of all your social media sites. There can be no such event as 100% anonymity just as there can be no such thing as a perfect human. We are the weak links.

But fear not, young Jedi. All is not yet lost.

While true anonymity is difficult, it is not impossible. We can approach 98% anonymity with some smart decisions. First things first. Invest in a VPN account. The more walls we have between us and the target, the stronger the cloak. Visibility is cloudy in a VPN as they shield many of your moves. Location awareness is difficult to detect using a VPN, but avoid free public proxies as Facebook and every other site has been spammed to death with them and have shielded themselves from those range of IP addresses. Thus, a proper (well-respected) VPN is the way to go. You will want speed to blend in with other non-anonymous users. Every metric counts.

You will need to disable most cookies from third-parties but allow Facebook for each session. Using Firefox portable, you can set the browser to auto-clear them upon exiting each session.

Set up your false data. Everything must be different from anything you've set at any other forum. Ars Technica, Wired, WSJ-- they're all in bed with Facebook to one degree or another. Ensure complete uniqueness, and under no circumstances give them your mobile phone number, as this will nuke your anonymity before it gets off the ground. That number, along with the IP, is used primarily for targeted advertising as well as by law enforcement. You may have noticed that Yahoo now requires it for new accounts. The reason is that it makes things easier to identify you.

Avoid a large group of friends and NO RELATIVES. This can't be stressed enough. Relatives, especially the elderly, love to gossip and spill details about the retched veal you cooked last night, or the cat you sprayed with the garden hose last week. What you don't hear in other's chat boxes at Facebook can harm you. Politely tell (never ask) others not to tag you or refer to any events that may compromise you: pictures, videos, music that your "real self" enjoys. Three bread-crumbs is enough to raise the eyebrow of the algorithm. Insist on them calling you by a nickname. If they refuse, remove them.

Never use the same browser for your VPN that you use for non-VPN sessions. Install Firefox portable in its own directory with its own shortcut and configured to the VPN BEFORE creating the

Facebook account. Never mix them up. You don't want cross-cookie contamination.

Be cautious on other social sites as well: Google, Twitter, Pinterest, MySpace. Facebook will not invest in the resources to find you unless you hand them crumbs of data yourself, which can easily be done on other sites you are careless with. So avoid being too specific about things related to your hardwired beliefs on those other sites, too: Religion. Politics. Ethics. Switch them up. Be a Buddhist for a session or two. Or a non-practicing non-denominationalist. Just be mindful of stirring up a hornet's nest. A friend in Thailand (an American) who was well known in Freenet insulted the Thai king on Facebook, prompting them to take a magnifying glass to his account. The end result? Facebook changed his name without his authorization--to reflect his *real identity*. Embarrassing. He'd posted a link to his page on Freenet as well and as you can imagine, his entire identity was uncovered by this loud behavior.

It is not possible to convert your existing Facebook profile into an anonymous one no matter how many tweaks you make. Changing the name will do nothing. The algorithm (think of the sentinels from The Matrix) will still have records of your online behavior as well as your IP address. Privacy, however, *is* obtainable, in case you wish to shield your identity from nosy coworkers or other misfits. In this case you need to change your username, that part of the profile others see then tweak the privacy settings accordingly with how invisible you wish to be. It is a bit of a double-edged sword since this will make it harder for others to see you--those you may *wish* to see you. You'll have to seek them out yourself and add them. And this, too, can reveal your true identity. Nothing typed into Facebook is ever truly invisible from the bots at their disposal.

TAILS

Edward Snowden. The name rings a bell for most people around the globe. In tech circles he is a visionary. As for the non-techies, a few labels come to mind: Whistleblower. Hero. Traitor. Regardless of what you pin him with, one thing is certain: He hates censorship and loves anonymity, the kind of anonymity that calls for untrackable execution. Before discussing anything, he insisted liaisons use not only <u>PGP</u> (pretty good privacy) but the end-all-be-all of anonymity tools:

<u>Tails</u>

It is a simple tool that frustrates even those in the upper echelon of the NSA. And for good reason, since even they do not know the wizard who designed it.

Where Tor is the worm of the anonymous fisherman, Tails is the fishing box. The fish at the other end have no idea who is inside the boat, watching, listening. It's a hacker's tool but also a patriot weapon. Using it is a breeze: install it on a USB stick, CD, whatever, boot from said stick and find yourself cloaked and shielded from the NSA, provided that you don't out yourself. And if you're using Tails, you're smarter than that anyway.

Built upon the shell of Linux, it acts as an operating system and comes with an assortment of nukes to launch under Big Brother's nose: Tor browser, chat client, email, office suite and image/sound editor, among others.

Snowden preferred Tails on account of its no-write rule: no direct data writing. A breach from a remote adversary? Not going to happen. Forensics investigation? Nope. No trace is going to be left on the DVD/USB. Obviously this is a no brainer to use if you're an NSA employee looking to spill the beans on unconstitutional spying, as well as a must-have for political dissidents and journalists. It is armored with plausible deniability, the same as Truecrypt.

Tor runs like warm butter when you boot with Tails. There's not much of a learning curve, and no excessive tweaking required. You can use it in the same PC you use at work. Boot from USB or DVD. Do your thing then reboot back into your normal PC with no record or footprint of your Tailing. For all intents, you're a ghost on the internet. And speaking of ghosts, the creators of Tails are anonymous themselves. No one knows their identities. But what we do know is that they will not bow to governments trying to muscle a backdoor into the code.

Linus Torvalds, creator of Linux, said in 2013, "The NSA has been pressuring free software projects and developers in various ways," implying that they had made the effort, and all with taxpayer funds. A bit like the cat saying to the mouse, "Transparency is good for you. Sleep out in the open and not the damp and dark, flea-infested mousehole." They don't like secrets.

You might be asking, how do we *know* that Tails does not already *have* a backdoor? How do we know that the NSA has not already greased their hands? The evidence is twofold: the code is open-source (anyone can audit it), and the mere fact that the NSA made an effort to sideline end-users says they fear such a powerful package. They cannot peer inside to see what the mice are doing. Snowden claimed that the NSA, while he was with them, was a major thorn in the side of that organization.

At the time of Tails conception five years ago, the interest had already started to build up in the Tor community for a more cohesive toolbox. "At that time some of us were already Tor enthusiasts and had been involved in free software communities for years," they said. "But we felt that something was missing to the panorama: a toolbox that would bring all the essential privacy enhancing technologies together and made them ready to use and accessible to a larger public."

PGP is also included in package. You owe it to yourself and peace of mind to learn it. Spend a Sunday with it and you'll be a competent user. Spend a week and you'll be an enthusiast.

As well, KeePassX can be useful if you want to store different info (usernames, pass phrases, sites, comments) into one database. These two are like a good set of gauntlets no aspiring black knight would do without. And don't think the blacksmiths have just smelted down some cheap metal, either. The designers have gone to a lot of trouble to modify the privacy and security settings. The more they do, the less you have to.

This is not to say you should use Tails every day. Only use it in those times you feel anonymity is warranted. As mentioned before, if you start mixing up services, operating systems and mac addresses, you may blow your cover. Though Tails is packaged with programs that one wouldn't normally associate with anonymity (GIMP, Open-Office, Audacity, etc) you don't want to leak info where an adversary might build a profile on you. You'd be shocked at how many applications these days "dial home" without your knowledge (hint: almost all of them).

But the true Achilles heel is the *metadata*. Tails is really lousy at hiding it. It doesn't try to. It doesn't clear any of it nor does it encrypt the headers of your encrypted emails. Are you an ebook author? Be careful about PDFs and .mobi files, as depending on which software you use, it can store the author's name and creation date of your work. But this is not really the fault of Tails. Rather, it is the wishes of the development team to stay compatible with the SMTP protocol.

The other problem with metadata is pictures: JPEGs, TIFF, BITMAPS and so on, which again, depending on the software, can store EXIF data--data that stores the date the picture was taken as well as the GPS coordinates of the image. Newer cameras and mobile phones like Samsung Galaxy are notorious for this, and even keep a thumbnail of the EXIF data intact for nose parkers with nothing to do all day but to sniff through other people's property. A fake GPS spoofer may be useful but even that won't eliminate the exif data. You'll need a separate app for this. You might even go so far as to only use formats that don't store any metadata at all. Plain-text is one option, though even that can be watermarked.

You might think, "Can I hide Tails activity?" The short answer is: maybe. It depends on the resources of the adversary. And just who is the adversary? The government? The private detective? The employer? The fingerprint Tails leaves is far less visible than what Tor leaves. And yes, it is possible for an administrator to see you are using Tor, as well as your ISP. They cannot tell what you're doing on Tor, mind you, but there are Tor Browser Bundle users, and Tails users. It all comes down to the sites you visit.

We've seen how they can build a profile on you from your resolution, window metrics, addons and extensions and time zones and fonts, but to alleviate this the Tails developers have tried to make everyone look the same, as if they were all wearing white Stormtrooper armor. Some fall through the cracks, making themselves easier for a correlation attack by installing too many addons and thus marking themselves in the herd: A purple-colored stormtrooper, if you will. Such and such user has a nice font enhancer while no other user does. This alone does not break anonymity, but with a hundred other factors and sufficient resources, it might be the one detail that breaks the house of cards. Death by a thousand stings.

You might find Tor bridges (alternative entry points on Tor) to be a good investment in reading, as they can better hide you from your ISP. In fact, using a bridge makes it considerably harder for your ISP to even know you are using Tor. If you decide this route (and you should if merely using Tor can get you arrested-- a case in which you should NOT use the default Tor configuration), the bridge address must be known.

Be mindful of the fact that a few bridges can be obtained on the Tor website. If you know about it, others do too--even adversaries like the NSA, but it is still stronger for anonymity purposes than the default Tor config. Like Freenet, it would be optimal if you personally know someone in a country outside the USA who runs a private obfuscated bridge that has the option *PublishServerDescriptor o*. As always, luck favors the prepared.

HOW TO DEFEAT THE NSA

It needs to be said: The time is nigh for the NSA to dissolve. If not dissolved, then at least broken up as Nazi Germany was after WWII. Yeah I hear your eyes rolling. Comparing the Nazis again? Please.

But mission creep, the expansion of a project beyond its original goals (often after initial successes) has reared its ugly head once again as the NSA, once known as "No Such Agency", has far surpassed its original purpose: to secure American communications while gathering intel on our enemies. Unfortunately, it seems *we* have become the enemy. We, the path of least resistance, so to speak.

Intelligence gathering is now such a high priority to the NSA that it has gone global at the expense of sovereign security. The Tailored Access Operations (TAO) directive makes this obvious. Install spyware/backdoors on the enemy's computers... well and good until Snowden revealed that they do the same to their own countrymen. It's called *bulk surveillance*. The more data they have, the louder they are on claiming victory over the usual boogeymen: Terrorists. Drug lords. (how long was it to catch Bin Laden?). Emails, calls, even video is collected without your consent. You could say it is a system ripe for abuse, if it were not already rotting from the inside out due to the

Patriot Act (section 215). The very notion that the NSA can shield itself from Congress and the taxpayers who foot the bill should appall most Americans.

So, what to do when the mother eagle turns on her chicks? Answer: Build your own nest. First things first, however. Understand that if you are a high value target like Bin Laden or a Mafia don, the NSA will hack your internet-connected computer or phone regardless. There's no getting around it. If you're thinking, "Well, I paid a hundred clams for Drivecrypt and Phonecrypt and so it is safe from those hucksters," there is some bad news for you to swallow, cowboy. It is far from safe.

Drivecrypt is commercial software and closed-source, and considering the free offerings out there (Truecrypt--open-source and *audited*), the best case would be that you're only paying for the name. Worst case? The NSA has a backdoor within the code, or at least knows of an exploit no one else knows about. You can thank the NSA's BULLRUN program, which attempts to "insert vulnerabilities into commercial encryption systems, IT systems, networks and endpoint communication devices."

In an ideal, pro-Constitution country, the security of the citizenry against foreign threats would be priority one. Instead, we are faced with a well-funded behemoth that considers the monitoring and data farming of *citizens* priority one. Again, think "least resistance". Hacked accounts from Blizzard to Kickstarter to Yahoo occur every month and the NSA seems helpless to stop it. Only the truth is a little different than they led us to believe.

They do have the means to stop it, as it turns out. But it would require a significant rerouting of resources so that citizens are protected and not monitored and assumed guilty of some obscure crime. Worse, the positions of authority and influence are unbalanced and skewed. Cyber Command should not be integrated with NSA priorities at all. Their priorities should be focused abroad, *like all other military operations*, and not focused on citizens like some Eye of Sauron that creates crime out of thin air.

Luckily, a few have leaked enough data from the NSA's coffers to mount a counteroffensive. One man cannot undo the damage they've done, but a nation can: the millions can overpower their overreach and send them back to their proper place.

How?

Knowledge is power. This hardly changes over time and for the NSA, the knowledge resides in the network itself. That's where the NSA loves to probe and plant their bugs. To this, they farm all the data. Everything. Then hire analysts to sort it all. They monitor phone calls, satellite messages and even listen to the oceanic cables running to and fro to our allies. They tap the waterfall at the source, high above, or beneath our feet if need be. Good intel, ripe for the sifting.

But what is good intel to them? Well, it's whatever sets off the most flags: the people involved, their countries, the language they use, their religion. It all gets prioritized based on profiles their algo agents categorize. The more red flags, the higher up the totem pole it goes... into a wellspring of *metadata*. It is easier to cherry pick targets by examining metadata than to study complete emails and conversations. It saves time. It saves money. Metadata to the NSA is like cocaine to a drug dealer. It's valuable stuff.

The Systems Intelligence Directorate does the data sifting and sorting in this case, and is given billions by Congress to optimize its operations every year. They are always updating and honing their capabilities. Testing what works and what doesn't. A security group exists for each directive handed down by the brass. They do nothing but look for ways to streamline each infiltration tactic. Make it all blood simple with the push of a button, a button that has global outreach.

NSA agents can infiltrate at will, but they especially love non-updated hardware like routers. When was the last time you updated your router encryption key? Right. The NSA knows this as well. They have a backdoor for many of them and entire teams devoted 24/7 to finding exploits for every brand of router and password encryption scheme. This is all accomplished by the TAO (Tailored Access Operations). Once inside your PC, they can easily install a custom-made keylogger that records your keystrokes and will send them quietly under the radar. Your anti-virus will not detect it. Once this is done, it doesn't matter how complex your password is. Thus, it is easy to see how valuable prevention is.

But how does one prevent such an intrusion from a well-funded entity? The answer is **encryption**. Encrypt your email. Your data. Your boot pass phrase. Most people will not bother with email. Some might bother with data. And fewer still will bother with encrypting the entire OS as it can take hours for a 2TB hard drive.

A few strict security suggestions:

I) The NSA does not like Tor. It's expensive to track users. When a lot of money is asked of Congress, they start asking questions and demanding results. They don't want *anyone* asking questions. So use Tor. However, do not say anything in an email that you would not recover from if it was broadcasted on network TV. And do not access your normal email account or bank account using Tor. Can you see why?

II.) Invest in an offline netbook or laptop for mission critical data. Make encrypted backups: Blu-Ray, USB, SD. Never allow the data onto your internet PC unless in encrypted form: Truecrypt containers/PGP encrypted, etc. Only decrypt messages offline and away from the internet. Learn about SSL/IPsec. Many Usenet providers offer SSL for free but leave it off by default. Turn it on.

III.) Whenever possible, avoid commercial encryption packages. The proprietary software is almost never audited, unlike Truecrypt. What does that tell you when they are afraid of people looking at their code? They're hiding something from you. When an encryption program is open-source, it is more secure, not less, because others can verify its security and detect any back doors. Word spreads like wildfire when a backdoor is discovered, but not if the door is nailed shut from the other side.

IV.) Your screen lock does not have to be perfect. It won't keep out any government agents but it may keep out nosy wives and friends. If however the OS is not encrypted and your laptop is stolen, all your data is theirs for the taking. Use an open-source app like Password Safe to secure them all from prying eyes.

You're probably thinking, why do you need all of these tools for privacy? Shouldn't Truecrypt or SSL for your Usenet be enough? The short answer is: it depends. It depends on your own level of risk. What you can live with if all is lost. And your loss is the NSA's gain, through threats of lawsuits and coercions and unconstitutional spying. They've almost succeeded in turning the web into a vast Orwellian looking glass-- with themselves as the only keymasters. They can only succeed if good men do nothing.

Trust encryption like you trust ammunition. And like ammunition, it can be learned in a weekend. Mastery however takes some time and effort, but know that by itself, it will do nothing but allow tyranny to flourish unless used for its original purpose.

Endgame

Hopefully if you have read this far, then you are now aware of some of the dangers that await us in the future. Clearly, having an exposed IP address is only a drop in the ocean next to the coming power grab. Unfortunately, there are always going to be up and coming social networks and applications that try to go above and beyond the use of the IP address to monitor you. We have seen it happen with many personal applications over the years: Internet Explorer, Napster, Limewire, Myspace, Facebook and the like.

These make their profits by subverting your personal choices and then targeting you based on those choices, and when you get right down to it, the longer you put off protecting your individuality, the less choice you will have in the long run. However, you now have at least an effective arsenal of tools in which to minimize this subversion. If enough people take notice, it may stem or even reverse the tide of fascism coming over the hills.

More and more we are seeing a gradual erosion of privacy. Some employers reject applicants to entry level positions based on credit score. Some employers demand Facebook usernames and passwords before hire. Some fire employees for words on a Facebook post. In the end it is all about control and eroding individual choice. For there is no one in the universe more unique than you. You are worth more than all the stars combined, and they know it. And want to control it. And there is no such thing as controlling just a little bit of a star.

Stay safe, always.

TOR & THE DARK ART OF ANONYMITY

TABLE OF CONTENT

PREFACE

You want what you want.

Invisibility. Anonymity. Ghost protocol.

You've taken the red pill and have seen the truth, and you don't like it. I don't blame you. I didn't like it either. But what I thought I knew about Tor and other incognito tools was only a drop in the ocean next to what's really out there. Stuff you don't find on many tech forums. They're whispered in private, of course, and it's all been rather invisible to you unless you hang out in hacker forums or Usenet. That is, until now.

Which brings us to you and I, or rather what I can do for you. It's amazing what a guy can learn in a decade when he rolls his sleeves up and gets his hands dirty. Private hacker forums. Usenet. Freenet. I scoured them all for years and what I've learned isn't anywhere else on Amazon.

Equally amazing is what you can learn for a few dollars in a weekend's worth of reading. That's me, and soon to be *you*. Where you will be by Monday is where I am now, only without the years of mistakes. Mistakes I made using Freenet, Tails, PGP. You name it, I did it. And boy did I make BIG ONES. Mistakes you'll avoid because after you read this guide, you'll know more than 85% of the Tor users out there, and know more about anonymity than most Federal agents. Yes, even the so-called superhackers at the NSA.

If you don't come away satisfied, return it for a full refund.

But I know you won't. Because once you've taken the red pill, there ain't no going back. You can't unlearn what you've learned, unsee what you've seen, and you'll want more. Much, much more.

First off, we're not sticking with the basics here. If all you want is Tor for Dummies, look elsewhere. Where we're going is dangerous territory. It's shark territory when you get right down to it. But not to worry. We've got shark repellant and everything you need to surf safe. You'll reap benefits you've only dreamed of and by the time we're done, you'll have gained NSA-level anonymity skills with a counter-surveillance mindset that rivals anything Anonymous or those goons at the NSA can counter with.

Speaking of which, they won't have a clue as to how to find you.

Secondly, for a few dollars you will know every exploit those superhackers like to wield against Tor users and more: How to avoid NSA tracking. Bitcoin anonymity (*real* anonymity), opsec advice and Darknet markets and Darkcoins and, well, it's a long list frankly but by the time you're done you'll be a Darknet *artist* when it comes to marketplaces and buying things incognito.

Third, we'll go over many techniques used by the CIA and FBI to entrap users. False confessions. Clickbait. Tor honeypots. It's all the same. You'll learn the same techniques used to catch terrorists, hackers and the group Anonymous and couriers for Reloaded. Baits and Lures and how to spot an LEA agent from a mile away. I break it all down into simple steps that you can understand. A few dollars for this info will save you a LIFETIME of grief. No, you won't find it on Reddit or Ars Technica or Wired. If you're mulling this over, don't. You need this now, not when you're framed for something you didn't do.

Fourth... reading the dangerous material herein requires you take ACTION. The Feds take action. Identity thieves take action. Hackers take action. Will you? Make no mistake - This is not a mere guide. It is a *mindset*. It's professional level stuff meant to keep you and your family safe for a decade out, going far beyond apps and proxies. And it's all yours if you do two simple things: You read, then act. Simple. Because you know what they say: Knowledge is power.

No, strike that. Knowledge is *potential* power. *Your* power. But only if you act.

Fifth... I update this book every month. New browser exploit in the wild? I update it here. New technique for uncloaking Tor users? You'll read it here first. We all know how Truecrypt is Not Safe Anymore, but that's only the beginning.

Besides, freedom isn't free.

Lastly... The scene from Jurassic Park with Dennis Nedry, I believe, is a nice frightful analogy to what happens if you don't take your security seriously. We see poor Dennis try to get his jeep out of the muck in the middle of a tropical storm. Lightning unzips the sky and the rain pours. The thunder rolls. A dilophosaur bounds upon him, beautiful, yet painted across his ugly mug is a deadly curiosity as it sniffs the air and cocks it's head at Nedry - moments before spraying his chubby eyes with poison. Blinded, he staggers back to the safety of the jeep, wailing and gnashing teeth, only to discover a visual horror to his right: he's left the passenger-side door ajar - wide enough to let Mr. Curious in for a juicy evening meal - which it savors with a row of sharp teeth.

The point is this: Don't be Dennis Nedry. There are far bigger creatures who'd like nothing better than to split your life (and family) wide open if for no other reason than THEY CAN, such is the nature of the elite.

Unless, of course, you tame them...

Not bloody likely.

ONE

IS TOR SAFE?

That seems to be the question alright. And to that, well, it really depends on whom you ask because there are always wolves in sheep's clothing out there who stand to gain from a man's ignorance. Many say no. A few will say yes, that it's 'safe enough'. The media, for all their expertise in things political and social, come up woefully lacking when something as complex as Tor is discussed and get a lot of things wrong.

Case in point: <u>Gizmodo</u> reported that in December, 2014, a group of hackers managed to compromise enough Tor relays to de-cloak Tor users. If you're just hearing this for the first time, part of what makes Tor anonymous is that it relays your data from one node to another. It was believed that if they compromised enough of them, then they could track individual users on the Tor network and reveal their real life identities. Kind of like how the agents in The Matrix find those who've been unplugged.

Anyway as luck would have it, it turned out to be kiddie script-hackers with too much time on their hands who simply wanted a new target to hack. Who knows why. Could be that they'd toyed with the Playstation Network and Xbox users long enough and simply wanted a curious peak here and there. These were not superhacker-level NSA members, either.

But as is usually the case with the media, this attack attracted the attention of a few bloggers and tech journalists unsympathetic to Tor and frankly, ignorant of what really constitutes a threat. The Tor devs commented on it, too:

"This looks like a regular attempt at a Sybil attack: the attackers have signed up many new relays in hopes of becoming a large fraction of the network. But even though they are running thousands of new relays, their relays currently make up less than 1% of the Tor network by capacity. We are working now to remove these relays from the network before they become a threat, and we don't expect any anonymity or performance effects based on what we've seen so far."

What those conspiracy bloggers failed to report was that any decentralized network like Tor is a prime target for attacks such as the above. But to truly stand a chance at punching a hole through this matrix, hackers would need Tor to implicitly trust every new node that comes online. That doesn't happen.

It also takes time for fresh relays to gather traffic - some as long as sixty days or more and the *likelihood* of being reported is rather high since the IP addresses are out in the open - which only speeds up malicious reporting. The *real* danger, and has been since inception, is scaring Tor users to less secure methods of communication. That's what the NSA wants. The CIA already does this in foreign countries. Now the NSA is following their lead.

RISKS OF USING TOR

The REAL Risk of Using Tor

I list them here before we dive deep into enemy territory so you'll know what to avoid before installation, and maybe get an "a-ha!" moment in subsequent chapters. As you read, remember that having Javascript on is really only a drop in the ocean next to what is possible for an enemy to kill your anonymity.

Javascript

It's widely known that leaving Javascript on is bad for a Tor user. Ninety-five percent of us know this, but the mistakes of the 5% get blown out of proportion and thrown into the face of the rest of us. Worse, many websites now run so many scripts that it seems as though they hate Tor users.

One site required over a dozen. Without it, the page was/is/will be pretty much gimped. Sometimes not even *readable*. You can imagine what might happen if you were using Tor and decided to visit that site if it was set up to lure users into a honeypot.

I remember one <u>researcher</u> claimed that "81% of Tor users can be de-anonymised."

Bull.

That 81% figure came about because the targeted users knew little about the NoScript browser add-on, and likely mixed Tor usage with their daily open net usage, providing ample data for a correlation attack. But that was just the icing on the cake. They left personal details *everywhere* - using the same usernames and passes they do elsewhere on the open net. Bragging about their favorite Netflix movies. Talking about local events (Jazzfest in New Orleans!). The weather (Hurricane in the French Quarter!). You get the idea.

Volunteering as an Exit Node

ANOTHER DOOZY, though not quite the granddaddy of all risks, but still risky. On the plus side, you as a valiant believer in anonymity graciously provide bandwidth and an "exit pipe" to the rest of the Tor users (hopefully none of whom you know) so that they may pass their encrypted traffic through your node. Generous? Certainly. Wise? If you live in the States... hale no as my Uncle Frick in Texas used to say.

It isn't that it is illegal *per se* to do so. On the contrary, but what passes through your node can land you in hot water if you live in a police state. All exiting traffic from your node (i.e. *other people's traffic*) is tied to your IP address and as others have found, you put yourself at risk by what <u>others</u> on the other side of the planet do with your node.

Lots of new Tor users fire up BitTorrent configured for Tor and suck down all the bandwidth. It makes for a very miserable Tor experience for other users. You may get served with a copyright violation notice (or sued), or perhaps raided if child porn flows out of your pipes. Think carefully and do your research before taking on such a risky charge, lest your computer be seized and your reputation ruined.

Running an Exit Relay From Home

RUNNING it from home is even worse then using cloud storage, and is infinitely dangerous in the USA and UK. If the law for whatever reason has an interest in your Tor traffic, your PC might be seized, yes, but that's only the start. In the UK, there is no 5th amendment protection against self-incrimination. A crusty old judge can give you two years just for not forking over the encryption keys (which if they had, they would not have bothered raiding at 6AM).

Use a host instead that supports Tor. There is Sealandhosting.org, for one. They accept Bitcoins and do not require any personal info, only an email. They offer Socks, Dedicated Servers, Tor Hosting and VPS as well as Domains.

We'll get into the nitty details later, but these are the Rules I've set for myself:

- Refrain from routing normal traffic through it
- Never do anything illegal (more later as it's a grey area)
- Never put sensitive files on it (financial info, love notes, court docs)
- Be as transparent as possible that I'm running an exit
- If I get complaints from The Olde ISP (or university), I use this template.

Intelligence Agencies

THEY'VE DECLARED war on Tor and its stealth capabilities, no doubt about it. And though they will fight tooth and nail to convince you it is for your own good, really what it all comes down to isn't so much national security as it is national **control**: Control over you in that they know not what you're doing on Tor, nor why.

They don't like that.

It's quite galactically pompous of them to spend so much money and waste so much time chasing you simply because they don't like you or your actions not being **easily identifiable**.

As you probably know, it's more costly to go after a high-value target. But they do not know if you are a high-value target or merely low-hanging fruit. As we've seen in the case of bored Harvard students, anyone can get into serious trouble if they go into Tor blind as a bat.

Even Eric Holder has publicly pointed out that Tor users are labeled as "non-US persons" until identified as citizens. It's beyond pompous. It's criminal and unconstitutional. It sounds as if they view ALL Tor users as high-value targets.

And by the time you are identified as such, they have acquired enough power to strip you as well as millions of other citizens of their rights to privacy and protection under the Fourth Amendment of the Constitution.

They do this using two methods:

The Quantum and FoxAcid System

HERE IS the gist of it:

- Both systems depend on secret arrangements made with telcos
- Both involve lulling the user into a false sense of security
- Neither system can make changes to a LiveCD (Tails)
- Both can be defeated by adhering to consistent security habits.

Defeating this requires a mindset of diligence. DO NOT procrastinate. Decide ahead of time to avoid risky behavior. We'll get to them all. A good, security mindset takes time and effort and commitment to develop but should be nurtured from the very beginning, which is why the RISKS are placed up front, ahead of even the installation chapter. Things tend to drag in the middle of a book like this, and are often forgotten.

Speaking of risk, if you wonder what truly keeps me up at night, it's this: What do other nations tell high-level CEOs and Intelligence agencies (Hong Kong, for instance)?

If the only thing I can trust is my dusty old 486 in my attic with Ultima 7 still installed atop my 28.8k dialup modem, then it's safe to assume *every* commercial entity is jeopardized by the NSA. And if that's true, if the NSA has to jump hoops to spy on us, how easy is it to infiltrate American-owned systems *overseas with our data on those systems?*

To that, if no corporation can keep their private info under wraps, then eventually the endgame may evolve into a Skynet grid similar to the Soviet-era East/West block in which CEOs have to choose east or west. But that's like trying to decide whether you want to be eaten by a grizzly bear or a lion.

So then, you now know the real risks. The main ones, anyway.

Every one of these risks can be minimized or outright defeated using knowledge that is in this book. The sad part is that most readers will forget roughly 80% of what they read. Those who take action will retain that 80% because they are making what they've read a **reality**: Making brilliant chess-like countermoves when the NSA threatens your Queen. If you do not take action ,but merely sit there like a frog in a slowly boiling pot of water, not only will *you* perish but your future generations will as well. Alright then. Enough of the risks. Let's get to it.

THREE

A FOOLPROOF GUIDE

Or As Foolproof As We Can Get It

NOW LET'S answer *what Tor is* and *what it does* and *what it cannot do*. You've no doubt heard it is some kind of hacker's tool, and you'd be right, but only from the perspective that a powerful tool like Tor can be used for just about anything. In fact anything can be bought (except maybe voluptuous blondes in red dresses) anonymously... as long as you're *cautious* about it.

Before you knock Tor, remember that it is not about buying drugs or porn or exotic white tiger cubs. It's about anonymous communication and privacy - with the main function being to grant you anonymity by routing your browsing session from one Tor relay to another--masking your IP address such that websites cannot know your real location.

This allows you to:
- Access blocked websites (Facebook if you are in China)
- Access .onion sites that are unreachable via the open internet

- Threaten the president with a pie-to-the-face...and no Secret Service visit!

It does all of this by a process called ***onion routing***.

Wait a sec. What is onion routing?

Think of it as a multi-point-to-point proxy matrix. Unlike peer to peer applications like BitTorrent or eMule which expose your IP to everyone, Tor uses a series of intermediary nodes (and thus, IPs) that encrypt your data all along the network chain. At the endpoint, your data is decrypted by an exit node so that no one can pinpoint your location or tell which file came from which computer. Due to this anonymizing process, you are anonymous on account of the packed "onion layers" that hide your true IP address.

It is even possible to build a site such that only Tor users can access it. Also called "Onion Sites," though technically challenging, you don't need a Ph.D in computer science to build one. Or even a Bachelor's degree. These Onion sites are unaccessible by anyone using the regular web and regular, non-Tor Firefox.

We'll delve deeper into that later, as well as construct a fortress of doom that nothing can penetrate.

Installation

INSTALLING TOR IS DIRT SIMPLE. You can download it from the Tor website at:

https://www.torproject.org/download/download-easy.html.en

If your ISP blocks you from the Tor site, do this:

- Shoot an email to Tor. Tell them the situation. You can get an automated message sent back to you with the Tor installation package.

- Go to Google. Do a search for any cached websites, including Tor, that might have the install package to download. Many tech sites may just have it in the event of all-out nuclear war.

- Visit rt.torproject.org and ask them to mirror it.

- Get a friend to email you the Tor installation. Ask for Tails, too.

- VERIFY the signature if you obtain it elsewhere other than from the main Tor site, **verify** it even if your friend hand-delivers it. I've gotten viruses in the past from friend's sharing what they thought were "clean" apps.

Now then. Choose Windows, Linux or the Mac version and know that your default Firefox install will not be overwritten unless you want it to. Both use Firefox but Tor is a completely separate deal. You'll notice it has the same functions as Firefox: Tabs. Bookmarks. Search box. Menus. It's all here - except your favorite add-ons.

On that point, you might be tempted to install your favorites. Don't give in to that temptation. Multiple add-ons that do nothing for your anonymity might assist someone in locating you over Tor by what is known as "Browser fingerprinting."

NOW YOU'VE GOT some choices.

One is to volunteer your bandwidth, which makes it easier for other Tor users but comes with risk. It is explained in-depth by Tor developers here. I'd recommend reading it if you are new to anonymity tools.

After Tor is installed, every page you visit with the Tor Browser will be routed anonymously through the Tor network. There is however an important detail you need to know concerning security, and that is that your Tor settings are merely reasonable **starting points**. They are not optimal. We're still at the infancy stage and quite frankly, optimal as Tor knows optimal is largely dependent on hardware (network, CPU, RAM, VM, VPN), and so each person's setup will be different.

WHAT TOR CANNOT DO

Now for what Tor *cannot* do, or at least cannot do very well. In the future this may change so don't fall on your sword just yet.

1.) Tor cannot protect you from attachments.

THIS IS NOT LIMITED to executables but anything that can be run by way of code. This means Flash videos as well as RealPlayer and Quicktime, if you still use it. Those babies can be configured to send your real IP address to an adversary. Not good. So never run any executable or app unless you trust the source. If at all possible, go *open-source*. This also goes for any encryption scheme which you MUST use if you're going to use Tor. It is NOT an option. Some say it is but that's like saying learning Thai is optional if you're going to live in Bangkok. You won't get far that way.

2.) Tor cannot run torrents well.

. . .

OLD NEWS, right? Thousands still do this. Better safe than sorry, they claim. Only problem is... they are safe and ***everyone else*** is sorry. Tor cannot do P2P apps like Emule and Limewire without making everyone else's Tor experience miserable. It simply sucks down too much bandwidth. In addition to some exit nodes blocking such traffic by default, it's been <u>proven</u> that an IP address can be found by using torrents over Tor. eMule, too, uses UDP and since Tor supports TCP protocol, you can draw your own conclusions about what that does to your anonymity.

True, you may be spared a copyright lawsuit since the RIAA likely won't go through all that trouble in trying to get your IP, but please spare other Tor users the madness of 1998 modem speeds. A VPN is a much better choice.

<u>3.) Tor cannot cloak your identity</u> if you are tossing your real email around like Mardi Gras beads. If you give your true email on websites while using Tor, consider your anonymity compromised. Your virtual identity must never match up with your real-life identity. Ever. Those who ignore this rule get hacked, robbed, arrested, or mauled by capped gremlins. Much more on this later.

FIVE

TOR APPS & ANTI-FINGERPRINT TOOLS

The Best of the Best

A few applications make Tor less of a headache, but they are not particularly well suited for desktop users unless you're doing some kind of emulation. But with everyone using mobile these days, some of these have benefited me in ways I never thought possible. Be sure and read the comments in the Play Store since updates tend to break things.

Orbot: Proxy with Tor

IT IS a proxy app that runs similar to the desktop app and encrypts your net traffic and protects you from surveillance and fortifies you against traffic analysis. You can use Orbot with Twitter, Duck-DuckGo or any app with a proxy feature. I've used this for a long time now and have gotten used to it. Perhaps it is time to try something else.

Invisibox - Privacy Made Easy

JUST PLUG the InvizBox into your existing router / modem. A new "InvizBox" wifi hotspot will appear. Connect to the new hotspot and follow the one time configuration set up and you're ready to go. All devices that you connect to the InvizBox wifi will route their traffic over the Tor Network.

Text Secure

TEXTSECURE ENCRYPTS every message on your mobile phone and is simple to learn. Better still, in the event you leave your phone at Marble Slab (Marble Flab to the Mrs.), rest assured your privacy is safe due to encryption. It's also open-source. Far too many apps aren't, and thus cannot be peer-reviewed by, well, anyone, unlike some proprietary apps like those offered by SecurStar (i.e. Drive-crypt, Phonecrypt).

Red Phone

THIS APP SECURES every call with end-to-end encryption, allowing you privacy and peace of mind. It uses WiFi and offers neat upgrades if both callers have RedPhone installed.

It's not for everyone. Though it's not as expensive as say, Trust-Call, there are convenience issues like lengthy connection times and dropped calls (ever Skype someone from Manila?) so it's not going to be as quick and dirty as Jason Bourne does it.

But the pluses outweigh the minuses. I especially love the two-word passphrase as a security feature: If you fear Agent Boris is dead and has been killed by Agent Doris (who now has his phone), you can request she speak the second passphrase. Simple yet effective.

Google and Tor

WHAT DOES Google think of Tor? Quite honestly I suspect they try not to.

They probably don't *hate* it like the NSA does, but they know that if every Google user used Tor on a daily basis, much of their ad targeting system would, shall we say, begin firing *blanks*. Imagine if a thirteen year old boy received ads for Cialis, or an eighty-year old woman named Bertha began to see ads for Trojan coupons, or... well you get the idea.

They don't mind donating funds, either, since this allows a future stake in the technology (sort of). To that, they've not only donated to Tor, but to Freenet as well and even Mars rover technology. All kinds of crazy things. They never know which technology is going to rocket into orbit a week or year from now so they throw money around like Scrooge on Christmas morning.

Captchas

AT TIMES you'll be using Tor and find that Google spits this requirement out in order to prove you're human. This, on account of their massive analyses on search queries, is what drives some Tor users to think Google has it out for them.

However, Google has to put up with **lots** of spammers and general thievery; bots hammering the servers with tons of queries in short amounts of time that put undue strain on the servers can be one thing, but it can also happen if your employer uses proxies - many employees working for the same company that uses one of these can set off a red flag.

When your Tor circuit switches to a new one, usually it solves itself. There are other search engines like DuckDuckGo you can use, however.

You may find websites do the same thing. Again, this is on account of so many exit nodes (all of which are publicly visible to any website admin), slamming the website with traffic such that the hammering behavior resemble those of a bot, the kind Russian and Chinese outfits like to use.

SpiderOak

NORMALLY I WARN against using Cloud Service for anything you want private. SpiderOak one exception, with some reservation. It's a decent enough alternative to DropBox as it is coded with "Zero Knowledge" (so say the developer) and when you install it, a set of encryption keys is created client-side. When you upload data to SpiderOak servers, they're encrypted on *your* computer and *then* uploaded. Again, according to the developers.

They claim that even if a subpoena requires subscriber data, they could not deliver since only you have the keys. Not bad, but I still would not upload anything unencrypted. A container file, for instance.

The other downside is that it is centralized. Centralization means a single-point-of-failure. As well your data can be deleted by them at any time (true with any online service really). Remember that between you and a judge, they will always side with the judge.

SIX

TAILS

Ever heard of a "live system"? Neither had I until Tails burst on the scene. Tails allows you to use Tor and avoid tracking and censorship and in just about any location you could want. It houses its own operating system and is designed for those on the go.

You can run it via USB stick, SD or even a DVD. Pretty handy as this makes it resistant to viruses. It's also beneficial if you don't want your hard drive to leave remnants of your browsing session. The best part is that it's free and based on Linux *annnd* comes with chat client, email, office, and browser.

The downside to using a DVD is that you must burn it again each time you update Tails. Not very convenient. So let's install it to USB stick instead.

1.) Download tails installer here. You must first install it somewhere, like a DVD, and **THEN** clone it the USB stick or SD card.

2.) Click Applications --> Tails --> Tails install to begin the installation.

3.) Choose Clone & Install to install to SD card or USB Memory Stick

4.) Plug in your device, then scan for the device in the Target-

Device drop down menu. You'll get a warning about it overwriting anything on the device, blah-blah. Choose yes and confirm install.

Tails Limitations

NEITHER TAILS nor Tor encrypt your docs automatically. You must use GnuPG or LUKS for that (included), bearing in mind that some docs like Word or Atlantis may have your registration info **within** the document itself (In 2013, Amazon self-publishers discovered pen names could sometimes be revealed by looking at the code of the above apps and finding out the real identity of authors. Ouch.)

Personally I use fake info when "registering" any app I will use in conjunction with Tor or Tails.

OTHER NOTEWORTHY STUFF:

- Document metadata is not wiped with Tails

- Tails does not hide the fact you're using it from your ISP (unless you use Tor bridges). They cannot see what you're doing on Tor, true enough, but they know you're using it.

- Tails is blind to human error. Try not to use the same Tails session to begin two different projects. Use separate sessions. Isolating both identities in this way contributes to strong anonymity for your sessions.

Chrome

FIREFOX IS HARDLY the only way to slay a dragon. There's also Chrome. Yes, it's Google, and yes Google has strayed far from it's "Do No Evil" motto, but like everything else in life, luck favors the prepared. You just have to have the right sword. The right armor. The right lockpicks. The preparations (reagents) are as follows:

. . .

I. INSTALL THE SCRIPTNO EXTENSION. It is to chrome what a mouse is for a PC, at least as far as precision aiming goes. It offers excellent control, too, even allowing you to fine-tune the browser in ways that NoScript for Firefox cannot. If you find it too difficult, ScriptSafe is another option. I've used both and came away very satisfied, though like everything else on the internet, YMMV.

II. FlashControl is a nice alternative to Firefox. In the event you don't see it in the Google Play Store, just search for "Flash Block" and it should come up (Google has a habit of removing apps that aren't updated every Thursday under a Full Moon).

III. Adblock. This one is just insanely good at repelling all kinds of malware.

IV. User-agent Switcher for Chrome. Install it. Never leave home (0.0.0.0) without it. It spoofs and mimics user-agent strings. You can set yours to look like Internet Explorer. This will fool a lot of malware payloads into thinking you really are browsing with IE and not Firefox or Chrome, thus firing blanks at you.

IT MIGHT HAVE SAVED Blake Benthall, 26 year old operator of Silk Road 2.0, from getting raided by the FBI (among a dozen other drug outfits). This was accomplished over the span of many months since they had to get control of many relays, and if you have *control of relays*, you can use sophisticated traffic analysis to study patterns in IP addresses and match behavior and browser settings with those addresses. Recall that any federal prosecutor will always try to tie an IP address to an actual person where felonies are concerned.

It bears repeating.

An IP address is considered an *identity* for the purposes of prosecution.

We're all a number to them, regardless. Those of you with student loans know this perhaps more than anyone else. This will change as time goes on of course as Tor competitors like Freenet and other apps evolve to offer what Tor cannot. Ivan Pustogarov goes into much more detail here on this but suffice to say the FBI did their homework and when all was said and done, had more resources on identifying lazy users than a typical VPN would. /endgame

V. CanvasBlocker - *And* another great plugin for Firefox. This prevents sites from using Javascript <canvas> API to fingerprint users. You can block it on every site or be discriminant and block only a few sites. Up to you. The biggest thing for me is that it doesn't *break* websites. More info here but in case you can't be bothered, here's the gist:

The different block modes are:

</canvas></canvas></canvas>

- block readout API: All websites not on the white list or black list can use the <canvas> API to display something on the page, but the readout API is not allowed to return values to the website.

- fake readout API: Canvas Blocker's default setting, and my favorite! All websites not on the white list or black list can use the <canvas> API to display something on the page, but the readout API is forced to return a new random value each time it is called.

- ask for readout API permission: All websites not on the white list or black list can use the <canvas> API to display something on the page, but the user will be asked if the website should be allowed to use the readout API each time it is called.

- block everything: Ignore all lists and block the <canvas> API on all websites.

- allow only white list: Only websites in the white list are allowed to use the <canvas> API.

- ask for permission: If a website is not listed on the white list or black list, the user will be asked if the website should be allowed to use the <canvas> API each time it is called.

- block only black list: Block the <canvas> API only for websites on the black list.

- allow everything: Ignore all lists and allow the <canvas> API on all websites.

As you can see, it's powerful stuff.

Firefox Armor

BUT FIRST A LITTLE mention of something a lot of people get wrong. You might be tempted to enable "Check for counterfeit websites" in Firefox. Don't do this as it will relay sites you regularly visit to Google's servers. Google's "predictive text-search" is also bad as it relays keystrokes to Google as well. To change it you have to do it manually by going into about:config in the address bar. That said, let's look at some other privacy settings you might want to know about.

Javascript - Avoid like the plague. You may notice it is turned on by default under the Firefox options tab, though. The reason is spelled out here by the Tor Developer Team:

We configure NoScript to allow JavaScript by default in Tor Browser because many websites will not work with JavaScript disabled. Most users would give up on Tor entirely if a website they want to use requires JavaScript, because they would not know how to allow a website to use JavaScript (or that enabling JavaScript might make a website work).

There's a tradeoff here. On the one hand, we should leave Java-Script enabled by default so websites work the way users expect. On the other hand, we should disable JavaScript by default to better protect against browser vulnerabilities (not just a theoretical concern!). But there's a third issue: websites can easily determine whether you have allowed JavaScript for them, and if you disable Java-Script by default but then allow a few websites to run scripts (the way most people use NoScript), then your choice of whitelisted websites acts as a sort of cookie that makes you recognizable (and distinguishable), thus harming your anonymity.

Ghostery and Ghostrank

NOT DEADLY, just useless on Tor since Tor disables tracking anyway. If you do use it, either could possibly alter your browser 'fingerprint', though not to the extent of breaking anonymity. Ghostery still blocks any tracking scripts regardless if you're on Tor or not. But use DuckDuckGo if you want to beef up your anonymity.

Adblock

THIS COULD ALSO CHANGE your fingerprint. Adblock plus has "acceptable ads" enabled by default, and there is also the scandals that Adblock has been in over the years, one implying that Google paid the Adblock CEO for Google Ads to be shown.

Besides, the basic idea of the Tor Browser Bundle is to use as few addons as possible. They figure that TorButton, NoScript, and HTTPS Everywhere is sufficient to preserve anonymity without the added risk of additional addons. Or um... drama.

The Panopticlick website may also be useful to you.

Whonix & Tor

IF YOU'RE paranoid that using Tor could get you into trouble (if you are hosting a Hidden Service), you might want to look into Whonix before running anything. Many power users who use Tor daily like the tighter security it offers. This is not to say that it is *better* than Tails by default. Both tools offer strengths and weaknesses meant for different purposes, and you may find one is better than the other for *your personal situation.*

Like Tails, Whonix is built with anonymity *and* security in mind. It's also based off of Debian/Linux, so it's a good synergy where anonymity is concerned. This synergy grants anonymity by routing everything through Tor. The advantages are that DNS leaks are next to impossible and malware cannot reveal your IP address. In fact, the only connections possible are routed through Tor via the Whonix-Gateway.

The question you may be wondering is: how much security is too much security? What's overkill and what isn't?

Well, you should ask how far will you fall if caught, and how much time are you willing to invest in reading to prevent it. Tails is easier to grasp, and if you do not expect attacks from sites you visit then by all means use Tails.

If you live in North Korea or China then there is a possibility of hard labor hammering worthless rocks if they see any Tor activity coming from your location that correlates to "things they don't like" activity... or anything else in the case of NK that offers hope. Guilty until proven innocent.

So if the above applies to you, use Whonix as it offers more security.

A few notable features of Whonix that make it more secure:

Anonymous Publishing/Anti-Censorship

Anonymous E-Mail w/Thunderbird or TorBirdy

Add proxy behind Tor (user -> Tor -> proxy)

Chat anonymously.

IP/DNS protocol leak protection.

Hide that you are using Tor

Hide the fact you are using Whonix
Mixmaster over Tor
Secure And Distributed Time Synchronization Mechanism
Security by Isolation
Send E-mail anonymously without registration
Torify any app
Torify Windows
Virtual Machine Images (VM)
VPN Support
Use Adobe Flash anonymously
Use Java/Javascript anonymously

THE FOLLOWING IS an example of a moderately secure system:

- Host Whonix on a memory stick with a flavor of Linux of your choice

- Use a VPN you trust (for privacy, not anonymity)

- Use Macchanger to spoof any mac address every session (Whonix does not hide your mac address from sites you visit!). If Macchanger isn't to your liking, give Technitium MAC Address Changer a try.

- Avoid regular calls of non-Tor WiFi tablets if using Cafe WiFi

- Know where every CCTV is located in the area you plan to use Tor

MAC Addresses

WE MENTIONED MAC ADDRESSES.

As technology would have it, your new WiFi/Ethernet card has something that can aid intelligence agencies in tracking you. It's a 48-bit identifier burned-in by the manufacturer. Sort of like an IMEI for your phone. If by chance you were not thinking clearly and bought your computer with Tor in mind using a credit card, you may later get targeted by an FBI "NIT" that swipes your MAC number. If that happens, you're toast.

The way to defeat this is to have a disposable MAC (the number, not the Apple product). One that you bought with cash with no security cams. That way you can get rid of it in a flash or swap it out.

They are also soft-configurable.

Believe it or not, Tails itself alters this randomly with every session. With a virtual machine, the FBI Nit may target a MAC number from the VirtualBox pool. Not really an issue unless they happen to raid your house and snag your system simultaneously. So swapping this out on a daily basis, as you've probably guessed, can be quite a pain. It's mainly for guys who run illegal markets. Guys who are *always* in the crosshairs of alphabet agencies.

But then, so can you. I've found it pays to think of oneself higher than what one is actually worth when traversing dark nets. Basically, thinking of yourself as a **high value target**. You'll subconsciously program yourself to research more, learn more, from everything from bad security mistakes to bad friendships to bad business practices. To that, you don't have to be in the top 5% of guys who've mastered network security. Being in the top 25% pool is more than enough to make The Man get frustrated enough to look for his flashy headlines elsewhere... for a low hanging fruit named Neb who lives in mama's basement, for instance.

Whonix Bridges

IF YOU LIVE in a communist hellscape where even mentioning Tor can get you into trouble, using a Bridge with Whonix can be quite literally a life saver.

What Bridges Are

BRIDGES ARE obfuscation tools to cloak your Tor usage from a nosy ISP or government who might see you are using Tor, but not know what you are doing with it. To that end, Tor bridges are alternative ways to enter the Tor network. Some are private. Many are public. Some are listed on the Tor homepage. In a hostile environment you can see the value in using it to your advantage as it makes it *much more* difficult for an ISP to know you're using Tor.

What Bridges Are Not

WHILE NOT ESPECIALLY *UNRELIABLE*, they are certainly *less* reliable than regular Tor usage where performance goes. But the tradeoff may be in your best interest. Only you can decide if the performance hit is warranted. Here's how to do it in Whonix.

Bridges must be added manually since there is no auto-install method for Whonix, but it is not difficult. You simply must enter them into the proper directory:

/etc/tor/torrc.

IF YOU'RE USING a graphical Whonix-Gateway, then browse to:

Start   Menu   ->   Applications   ->   Settings   -> /etc/tor/torrc.examples

To edit your torrc file (necessary for bridge adding), browse to:

Start Menu -> Applications -> Settings -> /etc/tor/torrc

Then add whatever bridge you copied from the Tor bridges page (or a private one if you have it). Then restart Tor for it to take effect.

SEVEN

TOR AND VPNS

There is a lot of confusion among beginners when it comes to VPN companies. They read one thing and see something else in the media that contradicts that one thing. The cold, hard truth about VPN companies is that a few want your patronage so badly that they're likely to bury the fine print on their web page where it is difficult to read. Believe me, that's fine print that can get you sent to the Big House if you're not careful. It really is a minefield where these companies are concerned.

For this reason, you need to decide whether you want privacy or anonymity. They are different beasts that require different setups. And not every VPN user uses Tor and not every Tor user uses a VPN service, but it is advantageous to combine two powerful tools; one that affords privacy (the VPN) and one anonymity (Tor). Like I said, two different beasts.

But for what it's worth, if you like this combo then find a VPN that offers 128 bit encryption and that does not store **activity logs**. That's the first rule of business.

And here's the part where the fine print comes in. Many VPN companies *claim* they do not log a thing... but will gladly offer your subscriber data on a silver platter if a subpoena demands it. Between Big Money and Your Freedom, money always wins. They will not go to jail for you, ever. So do your due diligence and research.

Obviously a VPN service is not anonymous by default. Providers love to tout that it is, but let's face it there is nothing anonymous about using someone else's line if you left a money trail leading straight to your front door.

Enter Tor, slayer of gremlins and we-know-what-is-better-for-you nanny staters. Tor makes for an extra and formidable layer of security in that the thieves will have to go an extra step to steal something from you. Thieves come in all flavors, from simple jewel thieves to border guards who want to make you as miserable as they are. So it is a good idea to ensure all the holes in your Tor installation are updated.

Updated applications are resistant to malware attacks since it takes time to find exploitable holes in the code. But... if you do not update then it does not matter which VPN you use with Tor since your session may be **compromised**. Here is what you can do:

Option 1

Pay for a VPN anonymously

THIS MEANS NO CREDIT CARDS. No verified phone calls. No links to you or anyone you know. In fact, leave no money trail to your real name or city or livelihood at all and never connect to the VPN without Tor.

For optimal anonymity, connect to your VPN through Tor using Tails. Even if the VPN logs every session, if you *always* use Tor with Tails, it would take an extremely well-funded adversary to crack that security chain. Without logging, it's even more secure.

But always assume they log.

. . .

OPTION **2**

Pay for a VPN using a credit card

CONNECTING with Tor when using a card with your name on it does nothing for anonymity. It's fine for privacy, but not for anonymity. This is good if you want to use Pandora in Canada for instance but not if you want to hire a contract killer to loosen Uncle Frick's lips a bit. Uncle Frick, who is 115 years of age and being tight-lipped on where the sunken treasure is.

Ahem, anyway, VPN services sometimes get a bad rap by anonymity enthusiasts, but signing up *anonymously* for a VPN has advantages. It strengthens the anonymity when using Tor, for one.

Even if the VPN keeps logs of every user, they will not know even with a court order the real identity of the user in question. Yet if you used Paypal, Bitcoin, credit cards or any other identifiable payment methods to subscribe to a VPN for the express purpose of using Tor, then anonymity is weakened since these leave a paper trail (Bitcoin by itself is not anonymous).

But the real down and dirty gutter downside is .onion sites. These are sites that can only be accessed by using Tor. The problem is that the last link of connectivity for these sites needs to be Tor, not the VPN. You'll understand what is involved once you connect with one which brings up our next question.

How Tor Friendly is the VPN?

THAT DEPENDS. Spammers use Tor. Hackers use Tor. Identity thieves use Tor. A few VPNs have reservations about letting users attain 100% anonymity by signing up anonymously. But if you signed up anonymously then you have little to fear since at that point it is *their* nose on the line.

There is one problem: the hardliners at the FBI do not like this attitude. In fact, they'd just as soon go after you if you use a VPN over Tor. Might a person come under twice the suspicion by using both? Maybe.

FROM FEE.ORG

"The investigative arm of the Department of Justice is attempting to short-circuit the legal checks of the Fourth Amendment by requesting a change in the Federal Rules of Criminal Procedure. These procedural rules dictate how law enforcement agencies must conduct criminal prosecutions, from investigation to trial. Any deviations from the rules can have serious consequences, including dismissal of a case. The specific rule the FBI is targeting outlines the terms for obtaining a search warrant.

IT'S CALLED *Federal Rule 41(b), and the requested change would allow law enforcement to obtain a warrant to search electronic data without providing any specific details as long as the target computer location has been hidden through a technical tool like Tor or a virtual private network. It would also allow nonspecific search warrants where computers have been intentionally damaged (such as through botnets, but also through common malware and viruses) and are in five or more separate federal judicial districts. Furthermore, the provision would allow investigators to seize electronically stored information regardless of whether that information is stored inside or outside the court's jurisdiction.*

The change may sound like a technical tweak, but it is a big leap from current procedure."

· · ·

THE NSA DOES this without hindrance. We know this from Snowden's leaks that the FBI uses the NSA's metadata from private citizen's phone records. Thus, a VPN is not a truly formidable obstacle to them.

But this takes it to an entirely different level since if merely signing up for a VPN provides a basis for a legal search, then they can snoop on any ISP's server they want with no legal grounds at all to justify it. They've done similar things in Brazil.

But here in America, it usually goes down like this:

1.) Spy on JoBlo to see what he's up to.

2.) Make justification to seize PC/Raid/Data by reconstructing case

3.) Apply pressure to the right people with direct access to subscriber info

4.) Subpoena to decrypt subscriber's data. If they've done it once, they can do it a hundred more times. No Big Deal.

Solution

IF YOU'RE GOING to go the VPN route, then use PGP: Pretty Good Privacy. Never, ever transmit plain data over a VPN, not even one that offers SSL.

1.) Talking to police will never help you. Even in a raid situation. They wake you at gunpoint at 6AM and corral your family and threaten to take everyone to jail unless someone confesses. It's all lies, all the time by these agencies. A friend once remarked that a plain-clothes officer once knocked on his door to ask him if he was using Tor, only to *make sure he wasn't doing anything illegal*. He answered yes, but nothing illegal sir. That gave incentive to go forward like a giant lawnmower right over his reputation. He was proven innocent later on but not before the cops dragged that man's reputation through the mud. No public apology came (Do they ever?).

2.) If they don't charge you for running a hidden service, walk out. In fact, if they don't charge you with *anything*... walk out. Every word out of your mouth will aid them, not you.

3.) You have no reason to justify anything done in your own home to them, or anywhere else. The responsibility to prove guilt is theirs, not yours.

But, if you are in a situation where you have to talk or give up your encrypted laptop, always *always* give up your laptop first. Laptops are cheap and easy to replace. Five years is not.

USING **Bitcoins to Signup Anonymously to a VPN Service**

BITCOINS ARE NOT DESIGNED for absolute anonymity, but neither are VPNs. They're designed for privacy. So why use them?

Well because any extra layer that strengthens your anonymity is a layer you want. But just as with any advanced tool, you can lessen anonymity if you are careless with it. Good, tight anonymity tools can be a bane or a boon: A boon provided you do your homework. If not, folly and embarrassment ensues, possibly a situation where, depending on the country you're in, you might as well slap the cuffs on yourself. It's sad that the times have come to this predicament.

So let's consider then how one pays for a VPN and obtains this level of absolute anonymity... recognizing that a VPN **by itself** will do nothing to further this goal. It is only one tool in a toolbox full of tools and Bitcoin is only one of them as well. You wouldn't try to repair a Camaro engine with only a wrench, would you?

Now then, back to Bitcoin.

Bitcoins are open source coins, a digital currency that utilizes P2P-like code, and like *real* money you can buy online products with it. Products like memory cards at Newegg or even a Usenet or VPN premium service. These are useful to us. Using these Bitcoins, you the end-user, completely bypass the need for a credit union or bank. Pretty neat. But, they're not without their shortcomings.

For now simply know that they are created from the collective CPU computations of a matrix of users (like you, for instance) who donate to their creation. Bitcoin mining is involved, and though you may have seen images of Bitcoins on websites stamped with a golden "B", they are actually not something you can carry around in your pocket.

Not in the way you think at least.

They have something in common with PGP - public and private keys - just like the PGP application, only instead of verifying your identity like PGP does, Bitcoins verify your *balance*. This is where **Bitcoin wallets** come in. Again, not a magic bullet but rather one tool at our disposal.

On that point, Bitcoin Wallets will only get better at strengthening anonymity in the coming years. They will accomplish this by breaking the trail to our real identities. Oh, and their development is constantly improving.

However as we mentioned earlier--embarrassment will result if you neglect to do your homework, for every purchase by a particular wallet **can be traced**. That's right. If you buy a new video card at Newegg with it, the same that holds your credit card details, and then subscribe to a Usenet service or VPN, guess what... you've now established a trail to your real identity. The FBI or Chinese government will not need baying bloodhounds to sniff you out.

But not if you make only one purchase per wallet.

This means never using it for *any* online entity in which you've purchased goods while your real IP is connected. It also means forgoing Google Plus, Facebook, Skype and all social media outlets with said wallet. Twitter, Wal-Mart, BestBuy and even small mom & pop stores with multi-social media buttons splattered all over their websites--these are enemies of anonymity whether they know it or not (more likely they don't). They are not our friends anymore than a grenade is your friend after pulling the pin.

A single individual might hold several addresses and make only two purchases a year, but if he cross-contaminates by mixing up (each transaction is recorded in the Bitcoin blockchain), then anonymity is weakened and in most cases, destroyed by his own making. Not good.

The trick is this: don't create a pattern. A string of purchases create a pattern; the exact sort of pattern Google and Amazon code into their algorithms to search and better target you with interest-based ads. Bad for anonymity and that's far from the worse that can happen.

We get around this problem by using **Bitcoin mixers**. These weaken the links between several different Bitcoin addresses since the history of that purchase is wiped by the exchange of Bitcoins among other Bitcoin users. There are a few options available to you. One is BitFog but there are many others.

Bitcoin Wallets

IN ORDER TO subscribe to a VPN or buy anything online with Bitcoins, a Bitcoin wallet is required. More than one type is available to us. We'll go through each and list their pros and cons.

Desktop Wallet

THIS IS what I use and for good reason: I have absolute control over it not to mention the thought of having to access my money on someone else's web server defeats the entire idea of anonymity. I would never store my encrypted files "in the cloud" and neither should you. At least, not without an insanely secure system.

Think about it. Would you bury your safe in the neighbor's yard with a For Sale sign out front? Same deal. The server could go down.

The company could go bankrupt. Any person on the other end on the hosting side can install a keylogger without your knowledge. Nasty buggers, those things. Desktop wallets aren't perfect, mind you, but they are better than The Cloud. One downside is that you must backup your Bitcoin wallet, an especially imperative task if it contains a lot of money. I do this quite religiously every week, as should you. Apologies if this all sounds like a Sunday sermon, but some of this stuff really must be taken as gospel.

Mobility/Travel Wallet

AS THE NAME IMPLIES, you carry this on you to make purchases in the same way you would a credit card. Convenience x 1000.

There are many types of wallets such as Coinbase and Electrum but I found **Multibit** to be very easy to learn. It is available in both Linux and Windows and offers a pass phrase option. Even the balance sheet looks like a PGP interface, but yet is beginner-friendly and open-source, so no backdoors. Good for anonymity.

MULTIBIT WINDOWS INSTALL

NOW WE COME to the instructions for a clean install of this work of wonder.

DOWNLOAD THE INSTALLER.

The possible problems we may run into: On Windows 7 64-bit which is the system of choice outside of Linux these days, it may be that the Java Virtual Machine (JVM) is not correctly located, or

"Failed to create a selector" is shown in the error message. A solution is to change the compatibility setting:

Choose the compatibility dialog (right click--> icon - Properties --> Compatibility)

Choose: "Run this program in compatibility mode for Windows XP SP3."

Check the box: "Run this program as an administrator"

Multibit Linux Install

IF YOU'RE a Linux fan (and you should be if anonymity is something you strive for), then download the Linux / Unix installer.

OPEN a terminal window and create an installer executable with:

CHMOD +x multibit-0.5.18-linux.jar

RUN THE INSTALLER: java -jar multibit-0.5.18-linux.jar

INSTALL.

THEREAFTER YOU WILL HAVE a shortcut to start MultiBit in your "Applications | Other" menu. If you see no MultiBit shortcut, you can run MultiBit manually by doing the following:

Open a terminal window and 'cd' to your installation directory

type java -jar multibit-exe.jar

. . .

NOW IT IS time to purchase Bitcoins. There are a few useful guides around which list possible advantages unique to your <u>geography</u>.

As you can see from the link, there are several options but what we want to do is execute an offline option; to buy Bitcoins *off the grid* which cannot be traced. Cash n' carry.

LocalBitcoins looks promising as does TradeBitcoin. But as Trade looks down so let's go with LocalBitcoins.

- After you choose a Bitcoin outfit, you must signup for the site (anonymously) but be aware of the interest charges which vary from one to another depending on how much you want to deal in. For this transaction, use an email in which you anonymously signed up. That means:

- Tor Browser/Tails

- No Facebook or other Social Media/Search cookies present on machine

- Only accessed for Tor/Bitcoins.

CHOOSE 'PURCHASE' on the seller's page and the amount we wish to buy. Remember, we're not buying a house here, only a VPN to use with Tor. Once funds are transferred out of escrow, you will be notified.

Notice that the trader you are dealing with might be able to see your financial information, i.e. which bank you use, etc., but you can always opt to meet up in person if you want. This carries a whole other set of risks.

Check to make sure the funds are in your Bitcoin Wallet.

Paying for a VPN to Use with Tor

NOW IT IS time to pay for your VPN service... *anonymously*. Let's choose Air VPN at $9/mo and who also accepts Bitcoins for payment.

First: Sign up for the service but do not put any information that you've used on any other site such as usernames or passwords. Also, since we do not need to input any banking info, no money trail will be traced to us. The email we use is a throwaway email (you did use Tor to signup, right?)

Second: Give them the wallet address for our Bitcoin payment. Hit send.

Done!

Like any Usenet service, a VPN service will send confirmation to your email with details you need to use that service. Afterward you can see the details of this payment in your Bitcoin wallet.

As you can see, a Ph.D in Computer Science is not needed for this extra layer of anonymity. The problem with the mass of people on Tor, however, is that they cannot be bothered to do these simple extra steps. That's bad for them. Good for you. Those that wear extra armor are often the ones left standing after a long battle. But there is one topic left to discuss, and it's the most important:

EIGHT

REAL IDENTITIES OUTSIDE OF TOR

This is a big one.

One that I'm guilty of breaking because even anonymity nuts can crack under peer pressure every now and then and do something dumb like use Facebook over Tor (my early days, thankfully). A question I kept asking back then was this:

What kind of danger is there in using your real name online?

Well sir, it depends.

Law enforcement and prospective employers who mine your social media presence for data are often worse than thieves who salivate when you announce on Twitter you'll be out of town for two weeks. Thieves, while unsavory and criminally deviant to be sure, rarely profess to be just. And thieves, as stated before, come in all shapes and sizes. If they take your private data without asking you first, that's stealing.

Employers can be the worst of the lot, as hypocritical as Harvey Two-Face, demanding transparency in *your* life but not their *own*. Make an inflamed political post or drink wine on vacation in Bora Bora with half-naked Filipinas twirling fire sticks and you could lose your job... or be *denied* one. Not kidding. Mention you use Tor and you may hear your interviewer ask:

"I noticed you're a big fan of Tor. Could you elaborate on why you need to use an anonymizing service? We like transparency in our employees."

Yes, I was actually asked this in an interview for a position that handled a lot of money. It came out of nowhere, but what really bothered me was the casual way it was asked, like every applicant should have something to hide if they desire anonymous communications. Maybe I was some rabid fan of Jason Bourne and up to no good. At any rate, they did not like my answer.

"Because I value freedom."

I came out of that interview perplexed, yet jobless, viewing privacy as somewhat of a double-edged sword since one *needs* an online presence for many higher paying employers. It did not sit well with me. I felt a little cheated to be honest and as I drove home, some of the mumblings I overheard later on became as loud as roaring trains in my ears:

Don't like someone on Facebook? You probably won't like working with them.

Like the competitor's products? Here's our three-year non-compete agreement for you to sign.

You use Tor? The only people that use that are terrorists, pedos and hitmen.

Soon thereafter, any time a prospective employer noticed "Tor" under the Hobbies section of my resume, it would always illicit a negative reaction. My breathing would become erratic as my heart raced, as if they were about to summon an unbadged "authority" to warn me of being *too private*.

He would dress a lot like Dilbert, only he'd be skinnier, and with a bumblebee-yellow pen and a clipboard. He'd have multiple facial tics and a quirky habit of raising a Vulcan eyebrow as if it were purely illogical to value privacy. I have no idea why he'd have a clipboard, but he always did.

My solution was to rightly divide my public and private identity in social settings and remove any trace of it on my resume. In fact, I did not give any indication on any social media site, either, that I was into any of the following:

- PGP
- Encryption, or encrypting files or Operating Systems
- Tor Relays
- I2P
- Freenet
- Anonymity in general
- *Anything* linking to Edward Snowden

Such is the nature of the masses. One simply cannot rely on Facebook or Twitter or Google to respect one's freedom to use Tor without announcing it to the whole world.

But with Tor, Google cannot mine your browsing session for ads. No ads = no soup for them. From NBC:

"The Internet search giant is changing its terms of service starting Nov. 11. Your reviews of restaurants, shops and products, as well as songs and other content bought on the Google Play store could show up in ads that are displayed to your friends, connections and the broader public when they search on Google. The company calls that feature "shared endorsements."

So I firewall everything I do. I use Ghostery for social sites and offer only pseudonymous details about myself. In fact, I try to avoid any correlation between Tor and any social media site just as one would a can of gasoline and a lighted match.

Anonymous Bullies

THE MEDIA along with Google and Facebook seems to think that if only everyone's name were known to them, then every bully from California to Florida would go up in smoke.

Vampirism, like bullying, comes in many forms, but if you've ever read Anne Rice then you know every clan is as different as diamonds are to lumps of coal. But they do usually share similar *beginnings*. Take adolescence for example.

Were you ever bullied in school? I was. I remember every buck toothed spiked-club wielding ogre who pelted me into nothing but a wet snowball in 7th grade, and it didn't stop there. How I wished it had, but not having Aladdin's lamp made things difficult. I watched as they spread like cancer, sludging upward to other grades for easier victims. Ninth on upward to 12th and even into the workforce. Bullies who'd make great orc chieftains if there were any openings, such was their cruelty and ire.

I recall one particularly nasty breed of ogre in 8th grade. He was the worst of the lot. A walking colossus who sweat when he ate as though he were being taken over by something in The Thing. Either that or Mordor. He certainly had the arms for it. When he arced an arm over me it sounded like a double-bladed axe slicing the air in half.

Harassment grew more fierce and fiery every year. Later I would learn that his entire family, perhaps his entire *generation*, grew up being the baddest of the bad - bullies that thrived on terrorizing to make a name for themselves. Every one of them went on to become cops in the New Orleans area. One died of diabetes. Another went on to join the ATF to fight the evil scourge called *drugs* (how'd that work out?).

I knew everything about these cretins and not just their names. I knew who their parents were. What they did for a living. Who they hung out with. What beers their dad's drank and with what porn mags. Gossip spread like wildfire in high school and no detail of identifying information was ever left out.

And yes, I told the principle, a great big lady named Beverly whose former job was working in some HR high-rise. I remember multiple times meeting her in that office where glitzy awards hung like a safari hunter's office and thinking if only she had an elephant gun I could borrow. Boom! My trouble's be over (so thought the 13 year old).

Meetings between my circus acrobat mother became fruitless and rather embarrassing. Absolutely nothing positive came of it. The point, however, isn't that nothing came of it, but that nothing came of it even as I knew **everything** about the scourge I faced daily. Knowing their identities did, well, not much of anything. Knowing their names did nothing. Knowing how many other kids they tormented did nothing and, let's face it, kids just aren't smart enough to band together and attack no matter how many times we watched Road Warrior.

We can see how bullying spreads on Facebook. Like anthrax. Little wolves ostracize a rejected member when a drop of fear is shown, so they crucify without knowing much of anything about him or why he's being targeted. Real names? Check. Real addresses? Yep. Everything is traceable now just as it was way back then. And still the orcs come in a blood-toothed frenzy like sharks to a wounded dolphin.

When 13 year olds begin hanging themselves in mom's bedroom to escape the torture, one thing is immediately obvious: what they really want is to *disappear*. They want *anonymity*.

But that's not something bullies think highly of. They won't allow it. Neither do they allow running away, not that a kid has the means anyway: No money. No car. No distant relatives in Alaska to run and live with and hunt moose all winter.

Anonymity is not an option. It's a requirement. It should be the law on some level but isn't. This is because if they gave us true anonymity, they would lose the precious power they wield over us. If Google and Facebook ever teamed up with the federal government to require ID to access the internet, we'd all be better off going face-to-face with an Alaskan grizzly.

<u>Email Anonymity</u>

THERE WAS a time when we didn't have to worry about what we said in emails. Security? That was something geeks did. Geeks and supergeeks who attended hacker conventions and scoured Usenet for zero-day exploits. It was the days of Altavista and Infoseek, when Google was still wet behind the ears and Microsoft was still struggling to satisfy every Dos user's whim. We wrote whatever we wanted and hit send with nary a worry about third parties intercepting it and using our own words against us. Sadly, no longer.

Advertising and search engines now tailor advertisements to individuals based on what you like and are sure to click. Trails are left. Messages are scanned. And Gmail is no different than Yahoo or Microsoft. In fact, judges wield more power with the pen than any CEO in any company in North America.

When a trailer is <u>leaked</u> or someone says something nasty about the government, you can bet IP addresses will be subpoenaed. Sometimes I imagine a lot of ex-Soviet officers are laughing at how many snitches the Internet produces on a yearly basis. Subversion to the extreme.

But... is it possible to send a message that is *foolproof* against subpoenas?

There are, in fact, many flavors to choose from to accomplish this task. Below are a few rock-solid services. Combined with Tor, they grant you a virtual fortress. Anonymity squared if your message is encrypted.

The first is **<u>TorGuard</u>**.

TorGuard allows users to use PGP (Pretty Good Privacy) in email so you needn't worry about snooping. You get 10MB plus several layers of protection with mobility support.

. . .

SECOND IS W3, The Anonymous Remailer

Connectable with Tor, you only need an email address to send the message to (preferably encrypted with PGP--more on that in a moment).

Another is Guerrilla Mail. They allow users to create throwaway emails to be used at leisure. Emails sent are immediately wiped from the system after you hit Send. Well, within one hour at any rate.

ALL OF THESE services claims of anonymity would be pretty thin if we did not encrypt our messages-- which brings us to PGP.

PGP is the encryption standard of choice for many old users like myself, and for good reason. It has never been cracked by the NSA or FBI or any intelligence agency and likely won't until quantum computers become common. It works by way of key pairs, one which is public and one private (the one you will use to decrypt your messages with).

Worry not about the term "keys". It is not difficult to grasp and will be as easy as hitting send once you've done it a few times.

The first thing you must do is make your public key available. This is only used to verify your identity and is not the same as divulging your passphrase for say, a Drivecrypt container. Your recipient must also share with you their key so you can respond in turn.

The good news?

Only the two of you will be able to read each other's messages. The caveat is if the other person is compromised and you don't know about it. They will read everything you encrypt. Here is what you need to know:

1.) To begin, make two keys, one public--for everyone else but you--and one that you wouldn't even share with your own mother. You should back this key up in a secure medium, and remember that if it isn't backed up to three different types of media, it isn't backed up. If your truly **paranoid**, send one on an encrypted microSD to your parents in case of housefire. Yes, it does happen.

. . .

2.) If however you opt to tell mom, then she will need your public key (you did publish it on a public key server, right?) Then you can read it by way of your private key. She doesn't know this key (thank the gods!)

3.) YOU CAN "SIGN" any message you want over Tor or anywhere else (Freenet, for example, the highest security setting of which demands absolute trust of your friend's darknet connection) to verify it is really you sending it.

UNLESS NORMAN BATES does a shower scene on you and takes your keys. Your mom can then verify with your public key that it is really you.

4.) Users you've messaged with (or not) can sign your public key as a way of verifying your identity. As you can see, the more people that do this, that is, *vouch for you*, the better.

<u>Important</u>

UNLESS YOU'VE GOT the photographic memory of Dustin Hoffman in Rainman, it's a good idea to store your public/private keys and passwords and also revocation-certificate to backup media so you can retrieve it five years down the line... should you need it. And believe me, you will!

Encrypt them in containers. Always print your key-file or pass phrase and deposit in a safe place. If you lose it, all documents encrypted with it are permanently lost. There are no back-doors and no way to decrypt without it. Also, consider making an expiration date at key-pair creation.

If you like nice and easy interfaces, try Mymail-Crypt for Google's Gmail. It is a plugin that allows users to use PGP-encrypted messages in a handy interface, though ensure your browser is air-tight secure and you trust it with your private key.

One More Thing

RATHER THAN HAVING to encrypt files and upload them somewhere unsafe, look at AxCrypt encryption tool. This is useful if you're used to uploading to Dropbox or Google Drive. Just remember that in the event you upload an encrypted file to "The Cloud," you will not know it if your password to said file has been compromised without setting strict security rules.

With that said, let's configure PGP for Windows

- Install Gpg4Win

- Next, create your key in Kleopatra and choose Export-Certificate-to-Server by right click so you can publish it to a keyserver. Get a trusted friend to "sign" and establish trust.

- Use Claws-Mail client that comes packaged with it or use Enigmail if you're using Thunderbird.

- Send a few messages back and forth to your trusted friend via PGP to get the hang of things.

- Optionally you can set a Yahoo/Gmail/Hotmail filter so as to forward any messages that contain "Begin PGP message" to a more private account.

Tor Instant Messaging Bundle

IT IS no secret that the NSA has Skype, Yahoo Chat and other instant message services in their hands, but as long as the Tor development team knows about it, they can do something about it.

Enter Tor Instant Messaging Bundle.

True anonymity is the goal of this application. It is built by the very same who developed the Tor browser bundle and like that application, will route all communication through Tor relays... encrypted *backwards and forwards* and hidden from the NSA's prying eyes.

There is also Torchat.

Torchat, like Yahoo's IM, offers encrypted chat and even file-sharing. Since it is built upon Tor, you are assured absolute privacy on what you say and to whom you say it. Both Windows and Mac versions are available and no install is necessary. Just unzip anywhere and run (preferably from an encrypted hard drive or USB-Drive) the blue earth symbol titled 'Torchat'.

A few more useful apps:

ChatSecure - ChatSecure is mainly used for encrypted messaging on mobility devices but they offer PC, Linux and Mac versions as well. From their website:

The Guardian Project creates easy to use secure apps, open-source software libraries, and customized mobile devices that can be used around the world by any person looking to protect their communications and personal data from unjust intrusion, interception and monitoring.

Whether your are an average citizen looking to affirm your rights or an activist, journalist or humanitarian organization looking to safeguard your work in this age of perilous global communication, we can help address the threats you face.

Telegram - This app also focuses on messaging but with superior speed and is similar to SMS and allows for picture/video sending. There are also 'Secret Chats' that offer encrypted sessions. They claim no data is kept on their servers and you can even set the app to permanently delete all messages.

CryptoCat - Billed as an alternative to social media chat apps like those seen on Facebook, Twitter and the like, CryptoCat gives you encrypted communications using the AES encryption standard. All encrypted info is deleted after an hour of inactivity.

<u>Freenet</u> - This is the granddaddy of all anonymous systems the world over, both for file sharing or any kind of secret chats. Explaining everything it has to offer goes far beyond our Tor discussion as they are two different systems, but I include it here as an alternative if you find Tor lacking.

And it is not as simple as Tor, nor is it as fast unless you leave it running 24/7. It is not for everyone as there are all manner of criminal entities that use it and you will notice this if you load up any groups. It is hard to ignore and unlike Usenet, there is no one to file a complaint with. No one to report. It is anarchy multiplied many times over in many groups, but there are ways of mitigating the damage.

But for *absolute anonymity* and freedom of speech, there is no better tool to use if you have the patience to learn its darknet offerings.

FROM THE WEBSITE:

Freenet is free software which lets you anonymously share files, browse and publish "freesites" (web sites accessible only through Freenet) and chat on forums, without fear of censorship. Freenet is decentralised to make it less vulnerable to attack, and if used in "darknet" mode, where users only connect to their friends, is very difficult to detect.

Communications by Freenet nodes are encrypted and are routed through other nodes to make it extremely difficult to determine who is requesting the information and what its content is.

Users contribute to the network by giving bandwidth and a portion of their hard drive (called the "data store") for storing files. Files are automatically kept or deleted depending on how popular they are, with the least popular being discarded to make way for newer or more popular content. Files are encrypted, so generally the user cannot easily discover what is in his datastore, and hopefully can't be held accountable for it. Chat forums, websites, and search functionality, are all built on top of this distributed data store.

An important recent development, which very few other networks have, is the "darknet": By only connecting to people they trust, users can greatly reduce their vulnerability, and yet still connect to a global network through their friends' friends' friends and so on. This enables people to use Freenet even in places where Freenet may be illegal, makes it very difficult for governments to block it, and does not rely on tunneling to the "free world".

It is not as simple as using a Usenet provider's newsgroup reader. No sir, Freenet requires **patience**. Using Frost or Fuqid (Front End apps for the main Freenet program), it might be half an hour before you can "subscribe" to groups or download in the way you can Usenet. Some groups, like the Freenet group and other technical groups will be immediately available, but with few messages. Time will solve this. So keep it running in the closet and forget about it for a day or so if you plan on subscribing to a lot of groups.

It will be worth the wait.

Frost & Fuqid

THE TWO FREE front ends I recommend are: Frost and Fuqid.

Frost has seen a lot of improvements but I recommend you try Fuqid first as it is the first external app for Freenet that acts as as an insert/download manager for files. Fuqid stands for: Freenet Utility for Queued Inserts and Downloads and runs on Windows or Linux under wine.

The Fuqid freesite is on Freenet itself at:

USK@LESBxzEDERhGWQHl1t1av7CvZY9SZKGbCns-
D7txqXoI,nPoCHuKvlbVzcrnz79TEd22E56IbKj-KHB-
W8HHi9dM,AQACAAE/Fuqid/-1/

You will need to paste the above into Freenet's front control panel where it says "Key". It can take several minutes to load if you're new to the system.

After you've installed it, right click on the left side with your list of boards and choose "Add new board". For the name put in "**fuqid-announce**" with out the quotes. You will now find a new board called "fuqid-announce" in your list of boards.

Right click this board and choose "Configure selected board". This will bring up a new window. On that window click "Secure board" to change it from a public board. Now in the section that says "Public key" paste in the key below:

SSK@qoY-E5SKRu66pmKH64xa~R~w3hXmS5ZNtqnpE-GoCVww,HTVcdWChaaebfRAublHSxBSRaRFG91qCwsa3m-GF3-QE,AQACAAE

Now you have the announce board for Fuqid added to your Frost boards. The latest releases of Fuqid will be posted to this board along with the fuqid board on FMS. Questions? Direct them to the Frost or FMS board called Fuqid.

Passwords

GOOD, strong passwords are like having a couple of Rottweilers sleeping in your den. Most intruders will leave when the chaos starts. Weak passwords are like having a Golden Retriever. Nice and friendly and easy to trust around kids, but might just let out a little woof at 3AM when said intruder comes. Then he will hide under the coffee table (the dog, not the intruder).

I've heard for years that you should never use anything personal as your password. That includes family names. Favorite books. Movies. So what's the solution?

Remix your passwords with a symbol or two. If you think a hacker won't be able to guess the name of your girlfriend's locker combination, you'd be mistaken. It is dirt simple to guess even if you mix it up a bit. Computers devoted to this practice can guess many in less than a nanosecond.

BUT HOW DO you remember a password for a site used over Tor that has symbols?

Easy. Use a passphrase that is simple to recall for you only. First write out the first letter of each word, taking not of case and position. Insert symbols therein. For instance:

LAST SUNDAY, the wife bought me a Rolex watch and it was too ugly. Which when changed is:

LS,twbmarwaiw2u

The above pass is hard for a hacker to guess but easy for you to remember... assuming you are good at substitution.

Changing Your Passwords

PROVIDED you've followed the above to the letter, you shouldn't have to rotate out your passwords every 90 days. I'm sure you've heard from both sides of the aisle their say on the subject, but I believe research has proven that keeping a strong password (unless proof of compromise) is a safe bet.

THE RESEARCH PAPER FROM ACM/CCS 2010: *"The Security of Modern Password Expiration: An Algorithmic Framework and Empirical Analysis" by Yinqian Zhang, Fabian Monrose and Michael Reiter came to the conclusion that changing passwords every few months did not, repeat, did NOT increase security:*

at least 41% of passwords can be broken offline from previous passwords for the same accounts in a matter of seconds, and five online password guesses in expectation suffices to break 17% of accounts.

...our evidence suggests it may be appropriate to do away with password expiration altogether, perhaps as a concession while requiring users to invest the effort to select a significantly stronger password than they would otherwise (e.g., a much longer passphrase).

....

In the longer term, we believe our study supports the conclusion that simple password-based authentication should be abandoned outright.

Storing Passwords in Tor Browser

YOU MAY HAVE NOTICED that the "Remember Password" option in Tor Browser is not available, or so it seems. But if you look at the privacy setting and alter the history setting to "remember history" and "remember passwords for sites," it will no longer be greyed out.

Diceware

IF YOU MUST STORE PASSWORDS, a good option for a unique random one is Diceware, (there are others, too) where you can get an expire date for any password months from the date of creation. You can copy any password to a text file then encrypt it and mail it to yourself or place on a removable (encrypted) drive or USB stick.

Remember: Tor does nothing to improve the security of your *system* to everyday attacks. It only improves security online, and even then only when used responsibly. Tor has no idea if your version of Windows is unpatched and infected with a zero-day malware payload that infected it with a keylogger.

One way in which a hacker could guess your complex password is if they linked your Tor usage with non-Tor usage and compromised your passwords from a non-Tor site. This is why you should never use the same usernames/passwords for Tor that you do for non-Tor activity.

PREVENTING **Non-Tor Activity From Being Linked with Tor Activity**

It is risky to browse different websites simultaneously and preserve anonymity since Tor might end up sending requests for each site over the same circuit, and the exit node may see the **correlation**.

It is better to browse one site at a time and thereafter, choose "New Identity" from the Tor button. Any previous circuits are not used for the new session.

Further, if you want to isolate two different apps (allow actions executed by one app to be isolated from actions of another), you can allow them to use the same SOCKS port but change the user/pass.

Another option is to set an "isolation flag" for the SOCKS port. The Tor manual has suggestions for this but it will lead to lower performance over Tor. Personally I like to use Whonix. Two instances, two VMs. One of them runs Tor and the other with Tor Firefox.

Keyloggers

YOU MIGHT WONDER what a keylogger has to do with Tor. Or for that matter, what a keylogger even is. You're not alone. In fact you'd be surprised how many people don't know and shocked how many techs consider them a non-issue.

In 2010 I caught up with an old childhood friend of mine I had not seen in over a decade. He was now an ATF agent. I was surprised and (falsely) assumed his extensive training meant he knew as much as an NSA agent when it came to computer security. Wrongo.

He replied to a post I made on a Facebook regarding the hacking group "Anonymous."

"What's a keylogger?" he asked. I waited for someone else to reply. No one did so I told him. He seemed amazed, dumbfounded, as though it were something only recently unleashed upon the net. I then told him that they had been around a long time.

But (sigh), there's a lot of confusion on what they do exactly. Some people call them spyware. Others say they're trojans. Still others, exploits. They're a little bit of everything to be honest.

They are *surveillance* software that tracks and records every click you make, every website visited, every keystroke typed. Chats, Skype, Emails. If you can type it, it can record it and all right under your very nose. It can even email what you type to a recipient on the other side of the world. CC numbers, passwords and Paypal login details are just the short list of targets it can acquire.

So how does one get in infected?

- Opening an email attachment
- Running an .exe file from a P2P network from an untrusted user
- Accessing an infected website with an outdated browser
- The NSA, if they can grease the right palms

Some employers use them to track productivity of employees. Some wives attach one via USB (Hardware version) to see who their hubbies are conversing with at night after bed. Parents use them on the kid's computer. So it isn't like they're 100% malicious *all the time.*

But they are devilishly difficult to detect. They wield an almost vampiric presence, but like vampires there are subtle signs you can glean without whipping out a wooden stake.

Vampire Signs

- SLUGGISH BROWSING speed
    - Laggy mouse/pausing keystrokes in a text doc
    - Letters don't match on display with what you type

- Errors on multiple webpages when loading heavy text/graphics
There are two types: software and hardware.

Software Keyloggers

THIS TYPE HIDES inside your operating system. They *lurrrve* Windows. Linux, not so much. The keylogger records keystrokes and sends them to a hacker or other mischief maker at set times provided the computer is online. Cloaked, most users will never see it working its dark art. Many popular anti-virus vendors have trouble identifying it because the definitions change so frequently.

Hardware Keyloggers

BOND MIGHT HAVE USED one of these. Being hardware, it is a physical extension that can plug into any USB on a PC and can be bought online by suspecting spouses or kids wanting access to their dad's porn stash. Keystrokes are logged to ram memory. No install needed.

Thus, unless you're the type to check your PC innards every day, you might not spot it until it's too late. They also can be built right into the keyboard. The FBI loves swapping the target's out with a carbon copy custom-built surveillance device. Granted, this is mainly for high-value targets like the Mafia but they're available to anyone.

Keylogger Prevention

- CHECK your keyboard for suspicious attachments. If you are an employee at X company and a new keyboard arrives at your desk one morning, exercise caution unless you trust your boss 200%.

- Use a Virtual Keyboard. No keystrokes = no logging!

- Use Guarded ID to prevent hackers from capturing your keystrokes. It works by scrambling everything you type, rendering any info useless to hackers.

- Use a decent firewall to stop a keylogger from delivering your data. A year ago, my Comodo firewall alerted me to suspicious network activity seemingly out of nowhere when I wasn't doing anything online. Turns out I had the Win64/Alureon trojan. I had to use Malwarebytes to detect and remove it. Norton was useless!

NINE

DARKNET MARKETS

Here, there be dragons.

SOME OF YOU might be wondering how safe a Darknet really is in light of the vulnerabilities discussed. The short answer is this: *As safe as you make it.*

You are the weak link. The last link in the security chain. And although you need Tor to access Onion sites, the term can apply to any anonymous network - networks like I2P or Freenet or anything else that cloaks the source of data transmit, and by extension, your **identity**.

Which brings us to the *Darknet Marketplace.*

The complete list of such marketplaces on the deep web are numerous, and the risk of getting scammed is quite high. It's one reason why you may not have heard about them. They are often taken down quickly by either a venomous reputation or a law enforcement bust. Sometimes they piss off the wrong people and then spammers ddos the site. But there are numerous places one can go if you're curious about what is sold by whom.

When I say *sold*, what I mean is... Anything you want that cannot be gained through the usual legal channels. And remember that what is legal in one country may be illegal in another. In Canada, lolicon comics are illegal and can get you in big trouble if you cross the border. But not in America. In the USA you can pretty much write any story you want. In Canada? TEXT stories involving minors are verboten.

The other difference is that there are safety nets in buying almost anything in a first world country on the open market. Think BestBuy. Mom and Pop stores. Florist shops. If customers get injured, what happens? Customers sue via the legal safety net and make a lot of lawyers a lot of money.

But the Darknet Marketplace laughs at any such safety nets. In fact, you're likely to get scammed at least a few times before finding a reputable dealer for whatever goods you seek. And it really doesn't matter what it is, either - Teleportation devices? Pets? Exotic trees? It's all the same that goes around. Whatever is in demand will attract unsavory types and not just on the buyer's end.

Therefore, research any darknet market with Tor, being careful to visit forums and check updated information to see if any sites have been flagged as suspicious or compromised. Some other advice:

- Always use PGP to communicate.

- Never store crypto-currency at any such marketplace.

- Assume a den of thieves unless proven otherwise by *them*. The responsibility is theirs just as it is offline, to prove they are an honest business. If you open your own, keep this in mind: customers owe you nothing. You can only betray them once.

Now for some examples of Phishers and Scammers and other Con men. By their fruits, ye shall know them.

1.) **Silk Road 2.0** (e5wvymnx6bx5euvy...) Lots of scams with this one. Much like Facebook and Google emails, you can tell a fake sometimes by the address. Paste the first few letters into a shortcut next to the name. If it doesn't match, steer clear.

2.) **<u>Green Notes Counter</u>** (67yjqewxrd2ewbtp...)

They promised counterfeit money to their customers but refuse escrow. A dead giveaway.

3.) **<u>iPhones for half off</u>**: (iphoneavzhwkqmap...)

Now here is a prime example of a scam. Any website which sells electronic gadgets on the deep web is ripe for scamming customers. Whereas in the Far East you will merely get counterfeit phones with cheap, Chinese made parts that break within a month, on the Deep Web they will simply take your money and say adios. Actually, they won't even bother saying that.

So then, how does one tell a scam?

Because many new darknet vendors will arise out of **thin air**, with rare products that will make customers swoon and send them money... without doing any research on their name or previous sales. A real hit and run operation. Hit quick and fast and dirty. Seduce as many as they can before the herd catches on to the wolf in disguise. Many are suckered, thinking "it's only a little money, but a little money from a lot of Tor users goes a long way in encouraging other scammers to set up shop.

When you ask them why they do not offer escrow, they say "We think it is unreliable/suspicious/unstable" amid other BS excuses. It is better to hold on to your small change than leave a trail to your treasure chest. And make no mistake some of these scammers are like bloodhounds where identity theft is concerned.

Do your research! Check forums and especially the dates of reviews they have. Do you notice patterns? Are good reviews scattered over a long period of time or is it rather all of a sudden--the way some Amazon affiliate marketers do with paid reviews that glow? Not many reviews from said customers?

If you've seen the movie "Heat," with Al Pacino and Robert de

Niro, you know when it is time to Walk Away. In the middle of a nighttime heist, Niro goes outside for a smoke. He hears a distant cough. Somewhere. Now, this is middle of the night in an unpopulated part of the city that comes from across the street - a parking lot full of what he thought were empty trailers. Hmm, he thinks maybe this isn't such a great night for a hot score. Not so empty (it was a cop in a trailer full of other hotshot cops). He walks back into the bank and tells his partner to abort.

The other aspect is time. Some fake sites will set a short ship time and count on you not bothering to see the sale as finalized before you can whistle Dixie out of your ass. After finalization, you're screwed since the money is in their wallet before you can even mount a protest.

Fraud Prevention

ONE IS GOOGLE, believe it or not, at http://www.google.com/imghp. Dating sites like Cherry Blossoms and Cupid sometimes use reverse image search to catch fakers and Nigerian scammers masquerading as poor lonely singles to deprive men of their coinage. If they can catch them, so can you. If the image belongs to some other legit site, chances are it is fake. Foto Forensics also does the same, and reports metadata so that it becomes even harder to get away with Photoshop trickery.

When it is Okay to FE (Finalize Early)

FE MEANS 'FINALIZE EARLY'. It's use online can usually be found in black marketplaces like Silk Road and Sheep's Marketplace. It simply means that money in escrow is released before you receive your product. Every customer I've ever spoken with advises against this unless you've had great experience with that business.

But... quite a few vendors are now making it a *standard practice* to pay funds up front before you have anything in your hands.

On more than one Marketplace forum, there's been heated exchange as to when this is proper. You might hear, "Is this guy legit? What about this Chinese outfit over here? He seems shady," and others: "A friend said this guy is okay but then I got ripped off!". You get the idea.

Here is my experience on the matter.

1.) It is okay when you are content with not getting what you paid for. This may seem counterproductive, but think how many gamblers go into a Las Vegas casino and never ask themselves "How much can I afford to lose?"

The answer, sadly, is not many. Vegas was not built on the backs of losers. Some merchants do not like escrow at all. Some do. So don't spend more than you can afford to lose. Look at it the way a gambler looks at making money.

2.) It is okay when you are **guaranteed shipment**. There are FE scammers out there that will give you an angelic smile and lie right into your eyes as they swindle you. Do not depend solely on reviews. A guy on SR can be the best merchant this side of Tatooine and yet you will wake up one day and find yourself robbed. He's split with a million in BTC and you're left not even holding a bag. Most won't do this to you. But a few will.

When it is NOT Okay to FE

WHEN LOSING your funds will result in you being evicted or a relationship severed. Never borrow money from friends and especially not family unless you want said family to come after you with a double-bladed ax. If you get ripped off, you lose not only the cash but the respect and trustworthiness of your family. Word spreads. You don't pay your debts. What's that saying in Game of Thrones?

Right. A Lannister always pays his debts. So should you.

MultiSigna

SOUNDS like something from Battlestar Galactica to pass from ship to ship. A badge of honor perhaps some hotshot flyboy wears on his fighter jacket that bypassed a lot of red tape.

While not exactly mandatory, it makes for interesting reading, and is something Tor users might want to know about if they wish to make purchases anonymously. Here's what happens:

When a purchase is enacted, the seller deposits money (in this case, Bitcoins) in a multi-signature address. After this, the customer gets notification to make the transaction ($,€) to the seller's account.

Then after the seller relays to MultiSigna that the transaction was a success, MultiSigna creates a transaction from the multi-signature address that requires both buyer and seller so that it may be sent to the network. The buyer gets the Bitcoins and ends the sale. Confused yet? I was too at first. You'll get used to it.

Critical

MULTISIGNA ONLY EXISTS AS A VERIFIER/COSIGNER of the entire transaction. If there is disagreement between seller and buyer, **no exchange** occurs. Remember the scene in Wargames when two nuclear silo operators have to turn their keys simultaneously in order to launch? Yeah, that.

MultiSigna will of course favor one or the other, but not both if they cannot mutually agree. The upside is that is if the market or purchaser or vendor loses a key, two out of three is still available. A single key cannot spend the money in 2/3 MultiSig address.

Is it Safe? Is it Secret?

I don't recommend enacting a million dollar exchange for a yacht, or even a thousand dollar one as they both carry risk, but ultimately it is up to you. Just remember that trust is always an issue on darknets, and you're generally safer making several transfers with a seller/buyer who has a good history of payment. In other words, reputation as always, is everything.

Alas, there are a few trustworthy markets that have good histories of doing things properly, thank heavens.

Blackbank is one. Agora is another. Take a look at the Multi-Sig Escrow Onion page here with Tor:

http://u5z75duioy7kpwun.onion/wiki/index.php/Multi-Sig_Escrow

Security

WHAT THE EFFECT would be if a hacker gained entry to the server? What mischief might he make? What chaos could he brew if he can mimic running a withdrawal in the same manner that the server does?

If a hacker were to gain access and attempt to withdraw money, a single-signature would be applied and passed to the second sig signer for co-signature. Then the security protocol would kick in where these policies would be enforced:

1.) Rate limits: the rate of stolen funds slows

2.) Callbacks to the spender's server: Signing service verifies with the original spender that they initiated and intended to make the spend. The callback could go to a separated machine, which could only contain access to isolated approved withdrawal information.

3.) IP limiting: The signing service only signs transactions coming from a certain list of IPs, preventing the case where the hacker or insider stole the private key.

4.) Destination Whitelists: Certain very high security wallets can be set such that the signing service would only accept if the destination were previously known. The hacker would have to compromise both the original sending server as well as the signing service.

Let me repeat that MultiSigna are *never in possession* of your bitcoins. They use 2 of 3 signatures (seller, buyer & MultiSigma) to sign a transaction. Normal transactions are signed by the seller and then by the buyer.

PURCHASER STEPS for MultiSig Escrow

1.) Deposit your Bitcoins. Purchase ability is granted after 6 confirmations

2.) Make a private & public key (Brainwallet.org is a JavaScript Client-Side Bitcoin Address Generator)

3.) Buy item, input public-key & a refund BTC address

4.) Retrieve purchased item

5.) Input the private key and close

BELOW IS a list of exchanges that support Multisig:

BITSTAMP - MULTISIG SERVICE: https://www.bitgo.com

ROCK TRADING - MULTISIG SERVICE: https://greenaddress.it

TERAEXCHANGE - MULTISIG SERVICE: https://www.bitgo.com

BITQUICK - MULTISIG SERVICE: https://www.bitgo.com

TEN

THE LONG ARM OF THE LAW

The Long Arm of the Law

Can the law steal funds?

Assuming you mean U.S. law, no, since the wallet does not contain the money. The Bitcoin blockchain prevents this. Hackers cannot steal it either since two private-keys are required and they will have had to steal 2 out of 3 private key holders... not likely.

WHAT ABOUT SAFETY **in using the private key?**

Never irresponsibly use the private key from your Bitcoin wallet. Create a new one instead. Give it the same love you give your Truecrypt/DiskDecryptor master keys. Lots and lots of special love that no one else gets.

THIS SOUNDS AWFULLY RISKY. **Won't I get caught?**

Here is how most people get caught, and it really matters not what it is. You could be dealing in illegal Furbies (Believe it or not, back in 1999 the NSA felt these toys might be able to record highly-classified intel). Most dealers get busted making the usual mistakes:

- Bar Bragging

- Dropping too much personal data to strangers (See Ross Ulbricht)

- Selling contraband to undercover law enforcement

- Snitches

- Committing crimes while under surveillance

- Managing an operation that grows by leaps and bounds (with loads of newbies making mistakes).

HOW FAR WILL the police go to catch you? That's a good question. The answer thought is pretty simple: As far as resources allow.

It'll probably be no worse than what Charleton Heston suffered being hogtied and dragged around the ape city, but know that some apes are worse than others.

It boils down to if what you're doing.

Case 1: In 2010, police in L.A. organized a phony sweepstakes scheme in order to lure in those with outstanding warrants. I kid you not, they did not come up with this idea themselves, but rather took it from The Simpsons.

They sent out close to a thousand fake letters under the name of a marketing group only to have a little over half a dozen show up at the La Mirada Inn for their free prize: A BMW 238. Nice, eh? Only the joke was on them as their smiles melted upon hearing those four dirty words, "You're all under arrest!"

The poor saps even brought ID to verify their identities. Dumb. They might as well have slapped on the cuffs themselves. And if they're willing to go through all that trouble just for a few misdemeanor crimes, imagine what they, along with the NSA, will do with a group of Tor users selling Furbies.

And this is an OFFLINE example. Imagine what one department can do by lying alone to an ISP or search engine. Threats of fines. Warrants. Bad publicity. Subpoenas of users. A bad reputation they are not likely to recover from soon. Police in Vegas in particular love to play dirty like this, dredging up old laws to ensure every member in that Ferbie operation has the book thrown at him.

IN 2013, a Secret Service Agent arrested several online by selling them fake IDs. The kicker?

They were all charged under the RICO Act of 1970. Originally created to put away mobsters, it allows them to lasso entire groups and charge each individual as if he committed the same crime everyone else in the group did... no matter the role.

Translation: The courier gets the same treatment as the ring-leader, as do the buyers. Individually, not much prison time in the grand scheme of things in 1970, but being charged as a GROUP? Twenty years minimum. Al Capone never saw such a hefty sentence.

It simply doesn't matter to a prosecutor if you're OS is encrypted and they can't get the data. All they need to prove is that you were part of the *enterprise* operation. That can be done outside of your shiny new Western Digital hard drive by subpoena to your ISP and a few other services you subscribe to. They've done this (and succeeded) with the newsgroup porn bust years ago in which every member of that hideous pedo group had encryption coming out of their ears.

Here was the short list of rules in that group.

- Never reveal true identity to another member of the group

- Never communicate with a member of the group outside usenet

- Group membership remains strictly within the confines of the Internet

- No member can positively identify another

- Members do not reveal personally identifying information

- Primary communications newsgroup is migrated regularly

- If a member breaks a security rule/fails to encrypt a message=BAN
- Periodically reduce chance of law enforcement discovery on each newsgroup migration by:
    - Creating new PGP key pair, unlinking from previous messages
    - Each member creates a new nickname
    - Nickname theme selected by Yardbird (Group leader)

THE AFFIDAVITS READ like a Hell's Angels list of rules. And though I disagree with his (the website owner, not Yardbird) conclusion that "there are basically no nice people who provide case studies of OPSEC practices," I believe much can be learned by studying the habits of law-abiding citizen and criminal alike, especially considering the wide net over which the NSA is casting over *law abiding citizens.*

Remember that in Nazi Germany, if you slandered the SS, it was considered a capital offense. The film 'Sophie Scholl' is an excellent example of underground resistance movement for the right reason. It won accolades for its realistic portrayal of a college woman who stood up to the SS elite and was beheaded for it.

North Korea, Now. Same thing. They'd have little issues with doing worse. Beheading might be almost too lenient for them as they prefer prolonged, tortuous environments for their subjects. China? China has done some strange things, like outlawing stripping at funerals and banning Bitcoin transactions, and I do recall the violent protests by Muslims in 2010 and thinking "Those communist schmucks will round up all those screaming fools and shoot them at dawn and not look back!"

My Chinese girlfriend leaned over to me as we watched and mumbled, "They won't wait till dawn."

I like to think of Darkcoin as Bitcoin's smarter brother. Much smarter in fact, and darker. The best part of course being that it is constantly evolving.

Like Bitcoin they are a privacy-centric digital money based on the **Bitcoin** design. It's a design that allows for anonymity as you make day-to-day purchases on, well, just about anything so long as the digital store offers it.

With Bitcoin, anyone can see who made a purchase by only looking at the public blockchain. What Darkcoin does is anonymize your transaction *further* by using *Master nodes* - a decentralized network of servers that negate any requirement for third-parties: Parties that could scam you out of your coins.

Though few outlets use it, it is one of the quickest growing digital currencies out there, with an economy breaching over twenty million. Impressive. And that's not all. It's "Darksend" feature is quite fascinating--increasing privacy by compounding a typical transaction with *two* other users.

Needless to say, this is immensely attractive to a lot of Tor users who value high anonymity. Whistleblowers, journalists, underground political movements. That's the good list. The bad list though, well, you can never have the good without the bad: Terrorists. Contract killers. Tax evaders. Fallout players with the child-killing perk.

I hear the same arguments against its use that I heard with Freenet: Bad guys want to evade detection. Bad guys trade Darkcoins. You use Darkcoins. Therefore, you're a bad guy. Cue torches and pitchforks and black cats catapulted over the moat.

Heroin dealers love to use cash yet you never hear news outlets screaming about cash-only users linking to such a crime. Besides, the most corrupt money launderers are the central banks. It is *they* that allow states to borrow from future citizens to pay *today's* debts. One need only look at the National Debt to realize this.

But that's not to say Darkcoins are without issues. A few excellent questions have arisen:

- What if these "Masternodes" eventually form centralization?

- What if Darkcoin is abandoned by the creators once the price goes through the roof?

- Who is trustworthy enough to "audit" Darkcoin? We saw an

audit with Truecrypt in 2013 which turned out to show no back-doors... except that the developers shut it down with a cryptic message saying Truecrypt was Not Secure Anymore. We can argue all day about what that meant.

These questions may never be answered. But that should not stop us from forging a new frontier in anonymity services.

Using Darkcoin for Business

IT IS MUCH HARDER to run a Hidden Tor Service than it is to open a business using Darkcoin. It's so simple really that it boggles the mind what might be available in the future... and with minimal risk to you.

If this appeals to you, then get the Darkcoin Wallet. This is used to send/receive/store Darkcoin with the benefit of using Darksend for 100% anonymity. More info here on this. Most of your patrons will want you to have a wallet, so better to learn it early in the business rather than later.

Pick a Transaction Processor

BELOW ARE a few you can research to your liking. Not every processor will suit everyone just as every bank or credit union will not appeal to everyone. You must judge these yourself, weighing your needs with whatever risk your business entails. I've tried most of these and came away satisfied but like everything else with crypto currency, what works for me may not work for you.

ALTACCEPT

Fees

Transaction: 0.25% + 0.0005 DRK; Withdrawal: 0.01 DRK

. . .

COINPAYMENTS

Transaction: 0.50%; Withdrawal: Network transaction fee (TX)

CointoPay

Transactions: 0% (coin to coin) 0.5% (coin to fiat); Withdrawal: Network transaction fee (TX)

Transaction: 0.5%; Withdrawal: Included with transaction fee.

DARKCOIN GRAPHICS (COURTESY of the Darkcoin homepage)

After this you should signup to the Merchant Directory.

Then (optionally), do some reading on InstantX here. InstantX is a double spend proof instant transaction method via the masternode network. Not exactly light reading, but the more you know...

NO SINGLE ENTITY has control of the entire system. Though the chance of an accident borders on the *not likely*, you need to remember that Darkcoin is still in development and because of that, unforeseen things happen. So a healthy dose of due diligence is required. I suggest only purchasing with money that doesn't break the bank in case bad luck happens upon you.

Frequent backups are mandatory for your wallet, more than Bitcoin since the anonymizing process executes more transactions in the background. If you've ever used Freenet, you know how slow the network can be and how much of a system resource hog anonymity often requires. Thus, make a new backup of your wallet whenever a you hit a coin ceiling.

ELEVEN

TOR HIDDEN SERVICES

How to Setup a Hidden Service on Tor

ONE BENEFIT to using Tor is that it allows you to create hidden services that will mask your identity to other users. In fact, you can have a website that is untraceable to you personally, provided you've taken all security precautions to keep your system updated. Here is an example of an onion site only accessible by using Tor:

http://duskgytldkxiuqc6.onion/

Naturally you can't access this with your Firefox browser without Tor. hence the "hidden" name.

This chapter will give you the basics on what you need to set up your own Tor hidden service. It's not meant to be all-inclusive that covers everything and the kitchen sink, but only to give you an idea of the technical know-how you need to possess.

STEP ONE: Ensure Tor Works

Follow the directions on installing Tor, securing it against exploits and security vulnerabilities first and foremost. Windows directions are here, Linux here, and OS X here. Each OS has it's own vulnerabilities, with Windows being the worst. I recommend you go with Linux after you've mastered the basics as it gives you more control over Tor and is far more resistant to attacks than Windows.

Now might be a good time to state the obvious, something you've probably realized by now, and that is this: That no two counter-intelligence experts ever do the same thing the same way all the time. There is no red pill that makes it "All Clear." No cheat sheet of Magic Opsec Sauce that everyone can master if they only gulp it down. You can't memorize every organic compound combination in Organic Chemistry. Believe me, I tried. There were far too many.

What you do however is memorize the *general principles*, from which you can derive a solution to every problem that comes about. Anonymity is sometimes like that. Your strengths will not be your neighbor's strengths. Your weaknesses will be different as well. You adapt as you go along, and I can guarantee you your skills as a hobbyist will far exceed those working on the government dole.

STEP TWO: Installing Your Own Web Server

A local web server is the first thing you need to configure. It is a bit more involved than space here allows (without jacking the price).

You also want to keep this local server separate from any other installations that you have to avoid cross-contamination. In fact, you don't want ANY links between your hidden server and your day-to-day computer usage outside Tor.

Your server must be set to disallow any data leaks that might give away your identity. So you must attach the server to **localhost** only. If you're swapping trade secrets and don't want the boss to know, use a virtual machine to prevent DNS and other data leaks, but **only** if you can access the physical host yourself. Professional web hosting services (i.e. the Cloud) are a big no-no since it is stupid easy for the admin to snatch your encryption keys from RAM.

Go to http://localhost:8080/ via browser, since that is the port-number you entered at creation. Copy a text doc to the usual html-folder and ensure it copies successfully by logging into the webpage.

Configuration

Now comes the part where most people quit. Don't worry, it isn't hard. It's just that beginners see these numbers and think "Oh no... math!" and throw the book out the window.

But that's not what you'll do... because you're a *smart cookie*.

First, set your hidden-service to link to your own web-server. You can use Notepad to open your "torrc" file within Tor directory and do a search for the following piece of code:

########### This section is just for location-hidden services ###

As you can see, the hidden services function of Tor is edited out by the "#" sign, where each row relates to a hidden service. Hidden-ServiceDir is the section that will house all data about your own hidden service. Within this will be the hostname.file. This is where your onion-url will be.

The "HiddenServicePort" allows you to set a decoy port for redirects to throw off any efforts at detecting you. So add these to your torrc file.

HiddenServiceDir /Library/Tor/var/lib/tor/hidden_service/

HiddenServicePort 80 127.0.0.1:8080

Next, alter the HiddenServiceDir to the real directory from which Tor runs.

For Windows, use:

HiddenServiceDir C:\Users\username\Documents\tor\hidden_service

HiddenServicePort 80 127.0.0.1:8080

FOR LINUX:

/home/username/hidden_service/, substituting "username" with whatever you named that directory.

RESTART TOR after saving the Torrc-file and it should be operational. Check your spelling if it throws out any errors.

Now then. Two files are created: the private_key and the hostname; private keys for your hidden service which you should keep under lock and key. The hostname is not your private key, however. You can give this to *anyone* you wish.

A descriptor for the hidden service links to other Tor servers and their respective directories so that Tor users can download it anonymously when they link or access to your hidden server.

OTHER POINTS of note

- Visitors to your hidden service may be able to identify whether your web-server is Thttpd or Apache.

- If your offline 50% of the time, so will your hidden service. Little bits (or lengthy ones, in this case) of data like this are useful to an adversary creating a profile on you.

- It is wiser to create a hidden service on Tor clients versus Tor relays as the relay uptime is visible to the public.

- Be aware that you are not a Node by default. On that point, it is advised to not have a relay running on the same machine as your hidden service as this opens security risks.

Shallot and Scallion Option

YOU ALSO HAVE the option of using Shallot or Scallion. Shallot allows one to create a customized .onion address for a hidden service, such as yyyyynewbietestyyyy.onion

On Running a Hidden Tor Server (and other Opsec Magic Sauce)

Having used Tor for many years, it came as a pleasant surprise to learn how few incidents there were in which the NSA managed to disrupt Tor. And I don't mean spam, either, but rather something that brought large sections of the network to a grinding halt. As it turns out, they're bark is much worse than their bite, especially if one is vigilant with their own secure setup.

The thing is, most Tor users couldn't be bothered. But then most users aren't interested in running a hidden server just as most P2P users don't bother seeding. Most are hit n' run downloaders. They know that as U.S. citizens they stand a good chance of getting sued if they leave their balls out there long enough. So some users opt to not further their own security knowledge. Let the Tor devs do it, they say. Can't be bothered.

Except most of the Tor advice by Tor developers I've read come up woefully inadequate. In fact I find that they aren't paranoid *nearly enough*. It's always been my belief that you can never be sufficiently paranoid as far as protecting your freedom is concerned, since the powers that be want to capture it and bottle it the way a cancer captures control of a cell: One organelle at a time with little of it's environment aware of the slow-boiling attack. To be honest... I suspect they *depend* on apathy and ignorance. And a lot of users gladly oblige.

Mr. Frog, meet boiling pot of water.

So then, what can we do? Well for starters, we can get the right security mindset.

TWELVE

TOR & YOUR RIG

Tor and Your PC

A secure computer is your best defense as the NSA mostly relies on man-in-the-middle attacks and browser exploits that deliver payloads to hidden Tor servers. That said, you should anticipate and **expect** such an exploit can infiltrate your system at any point. Things like Nits (network bugs), you have to be aware of. Thus the need to adhere to the following:

Use Linux whenever possible. Yes, I know you're comfortable using Windows and think Linux too much of a bother. But you won't if you're ISP is subpoenaed for something you said on Facebook. Something anti-feminist, for instance. So learn to use it.

As you can see in these NSA slides - they typically target the weakest system. The Tor Browser Bundle for Windows was instrumental in taking down Freedom Hosting and Silk Road because of unpatched vulnerabilities. That, and a few rogue Tor exit nodes patched unsigned Windows packages to spread malware.

If you're new to Linux, look at Linux Mint. If you're experienced, Debian is a good choice. Windows can't be trusted primarily because it is closed-source, but also because malware is more effective on it than Linux. If Linux is out of the question, consider Tails or Whonix as these apps come preconfigured to not allow any outgoing connections to clearnet.

Update Update Update

YOUR PC MUST ALSO BE UPDATED, ALWAYS. Not updating leads to vulnerabilities and exploits such as those in Windows. Optimally, you should ensure Tails is *always* updated each time you use Tor, and avoid any sites that use Java/Javascript/Flash or any kind of scripting as these execute code in ways you cannot see. Use these only in an emergency and never in your home system.

Avoid using cookies wherever possible. Consider installing the Self-Destructing Cookies add-on.

Again, you should not use anything but a portable PC since your home PC is most likely not portable enough to be discarded in a trash can in the event of compromise.

Avoid Google like the Black Plague. Use DuckDuckGo or Startpage instead for Tor sessions.

Situation Awareness

HERE WE GO AGAIN. But reading things three times often becomes a trigger in the brain later on for taking action, so here it is.

If an agency can monitor your local connection as well as the link you are browsing, then (with sufficient resources) they can apply traffic analysis to pinpoint your real location. Therefore, I recommend you do not use Tor in your residence.

Just to clarify, do not use Tor in your *legal* residence if doing any kind of covert work or anything *illegal* without strict security measures in place; the kind the average Tor user will likely overlook. Let that other guy learn his lesson. It's a tough break, but better him than you. He's a 19 year old named Jimmy who likes hacking. You're a 32 year old construction guy with two kids and a mortgage. Who has more to lose? Right, you. So study counter-surveillance and counter-forensics like your life depends on it. Because it does!

For enemies of the state-level operations, I would suggest not engaging anything even **near** your online PC at home. Certainly nothing that makes you think you need Tor to hide it. It may be fine for private browsing but not for someone planning a coup, running an illegal operation (home bible study in Iran, for instance), or trying to disappear.

Be wary of using it in hotels as well, where often there are many cams watching with 24/hr surveillance. That location can be linked to Tor activity.

Do not use Tor more than a day in any specific location. A correlation-attack can be done in less than an hour if a black van is parked nearby--a van you will not see. They may not slap the cuffs on you as you walk out of the cafe that very week, but later they might. Consider the area a toxic dump after a day, regardless if you must travel to the next shop or town.

If you want to get really cloak and dagger about it, have an app running (an MMO, for instance) while you are out and about doing your Tor activity that makes it look like you were home during that time.

THIRTEEN

TOR HIDDEN SERVICES RULES

High Risk, High Reward

CNN, along with FoxNews and a hotbed of other media outlets, has been trumpeting the defeat of certain hidden services for a few years now. It makes for good headlines. Services like Silk Road and Freedom Hosting, which I'm sure you've heard about. They are a easy target for the FBI since hidden services are not high on the list of priorities by Tor developers yet. Same for the NSA.

Both agencies know every trick and hack there is to know about running a hidden service. And so should you. This is not to say you need the expertise to match their team of <u>super hackers</u>, but that you need even more vigilance to run such a service than you do *visiting* such a service.

Priority number one is simple: if you run one, you must own one. They must not be run under somebody else's control if you can help it, because if that service is compromised, ***everyone*** goes down. That means total anonymity, 100% of the time with world-class jewel-thief stealth ability.

The Silk Road admin did not have this ability. In fact, looking through the online docs detailing the arrest, one gets the impression he was very lax in IT security procedure. He repeatedly made mistakes such that luck on the part of LE never really came into it at all. The guy was just sloppy.

FIRST

Never, ever, ever run a hidden service within a VM that is owned by a friend or a Cloud space provider. Remember, all "The Cloud" is, is someone *else's* drive or network, not your own. Encryption keys can be dumped from RAM. And who owns the RAM?

Right. The Cloud provider. Lightning strikes and there goes your own anonymity as well as the anonymity of your visitors if they are lazy in their browser habits. The FBI delivered a "nit" (network investigative technique) this way to unpatched Tor Browser Bundles in 2013. If, however, you own the machine, then it's a different story. But let's back up a few steps and assume you don't. How might you go about running it on a host system?

Well first off, you would need two separate physical hosts from different parties, both running in virtual machines with a firewall-enabled OS that only allows Tor network activity and *nothing else*.

The second physical host is the one the hidden service runs from, also VM'ed. Secure connections are enabled by IPSec. What's IPSec, you ask?

"IPSec is a protocol suite, for securing Internet Protocol (IP) communications by authenticating and encrypting each IP packet of a communication session. IPsec can be used in protecting data flows between a pair of hosts (host-to-host), between a pair of security gateways (network-to-network), or between a security gateway and a host (network-to-host)."

If an intruder agent tampers with anything, you will know about it and can shut down the service or move it to a safer place, and all while being a ghost in the machine. You can imagine how valuable this would be in North Korea.

If you were in that cesspool of a country, you would be more than a little paranoid if the server went down even for a few seconds. But you could always move it to a more secure location or even start over, and you might just want to since you would not know if a RAID failure had occurred or if some commie jackboot was sending a copy of the VM to the higher ups.

Second

If going the host route, you must ensure that remote-console is always available to you by the host, any time you want. You must do everything remotely, in fact, and change passwords frequently via https. I'd say once per day as paranoia in such a climate as North Korea would be good for your health.

THIRD

You must never, not even once, access the service from home. Not from your Nexus 7. Not from your girlfriend's Galaxy Note. Not even via Tor from your backyard using your neighbor's WiFi. Using a VPN as well is risky unless you know what you're doing. Only access it via secure locations at least ten miles away from your residence. Overkill, some might say, but then there is no such thing as overkill in a gulag.

FOURTH

Move the service on occasion. Again, look at any Youtube video on how snipers train to take out an enemy. They move place to place after each shot to conceal the true location from the enemy. How often is up to you. Once a week? Once a month? Personally I'd say every twenty-one days. You can never be too secure when running one of these.

FOURTEEN
DARKNET PERSONAS

"We've been watching you Mr. Anderson, and it seems you've been living... two lives." -- Agent Smith, The Matrix

YOU'VE NO DOUBT READ of Tor busts where an undercover agent snagged a phone number or clearnet nic from someone they were targeting because said target trusted too much, too quickly. Take it from Yoda - You can avoid this by retraining yourself, *unlearning* what you've learned.

You must consider your Tor sessions the property of your other Self. The cloned You - that shadowy thievish looking guy above. The *second* You. One that despises Incubus and loves Tool and views Neo as just another beta-orbiting punk who got the luck of the draw when Morpheus and crew unplugged him. This clone would not use Twitter or YouTube or other social gunk. He would never hang with you nor call you up for a few beers. In fact, he hates beer, preferring J&B as he hacks with John Carpenter's The Thing OST playing as mood music in the background. That's your other *You*. The smarter you.

And he must be the new You **on Tor**. And you must forever separate him from the non-Tor You.

His Facebook, Twitter and YouTube accounts are all fake, having never once used them on his home PC. His nics are different, as is his passwords, likes/dislikes and even the fonts he uses to browse the Deep Web. Mixing this dark persona with your own would be like the boy made of matter kissing the anti-matter girl...

Boom.

Further, any phone calls this person makes is done by prepaid phones that were not purchased by any credit cards he holds. He is a cash n' carry guy and then only if he is twenty miles from home. Any *SIM* cards he uses are strictly used in conjunction with Tor activity and never used in phones the *other guy* uses. And... he deliberately leaves false info wherever he goes. Kinda like the CIA does.

But to better clarify this idea, let's assume John Doe doesn't know any better. He watches a movie on Netflix. Then he mosies on over to Freenet and drops intel without even realizing it, eager to share his great cinema experience with his darknet buds (no pun).

"Hey guys, just watched a cool flick with Russell Crowe. Kinda Michael Bay-ish and Liam Neeson's cameo was too short, but makes for a good flick if you want to learn how to disappear. But those police, sweet Jesus! Those rent-a-cop guys sure are as dumb as a sack of bricks!"

Police are dumb, he says.

Metadata is collected by Netflix just as it is with Google and Yahoo. Every single user. They know every film you viewed and even which ones you hated. He's even made forum posts indicating similar weather and, though not mentioning names, has griped about local politicians being handcuffed in very geo-specific arrests, even dropping the charges!

How many Netflix fans do you think watched this movie at the time of his Freenet post? How many in cities that had local politicians arrested for embezzling? How many with similar weather depicted in the film? Most likely less than ten. Maybe not even that.

There is also the handwriting element. Does he *mispell* the same words over and over? Throw commas like daggers? Misuse semi-colons and run-on sentences? System clock out of sync with his posts? All of this leads to a great profile that ties his IP address to his identity. Often it is enough to get a warrant if he so much as whispers that he's obtained any kind of contraband.

Unless of course, all of this info is tailor-made to fit the other *You*.

We already know that the VPN called Hide-My-Ass as well as Hushmail and Lavabit stabbed their users in the back when threats by a judge became too heated ($5000 a day in Lavabit's case, until they forked over user data). And all this just so they could track Edward Snowden.

Bottom line: Learn from Snowden's mistakes. Take every company's claim of anonymity with a grain of salt. The proof is in the amount of arrests tied to said company or app. In the case of Freenet... none.

But there is always a first time. Recall that they only have to get lucky once, which more often than not relies on your carelessness.

USENET: THE ULTIMATE GUIDE (AND THE FUTURE OF ANONYMITY)

CHAPTER 1

You've probably heard the term "Usenet" floating around various tech forums of one flavor or another. Some liken the technology as being similar to P2P, while others state that it is nothing like P2P. In truth, it has a little bit of both systems in that

1.) you can find almost any kind of file therein, such as mp3s, games, movies and the like and

2.) you have the ability to upload and download anything you like

Since its inception in 1979 by two Duke graduate students, Usenet has leapt beyond all expectations in regards to not only data retention, but enhancing freedom of speech. Whereas users were once inundated with extra charges per month for downloading a handful of data, they now have the ability to download terabytes per month, and pay ridiculously small sums to do so. This has all been done with the help of not only thousands of server farms across the world, but also by legions of longtime Usenet users who upload (and leech) every kind of data file in existence. Thus, the true ingredients for the worldwide success of Usenet hasn't been so much because of

Usenet providers themselves, but by end-user subscribers who faithfully upload the latest movie, game and music releases every month to the over 100,000 available newsgroups on Usenet.

What typically happens when the average Joe off the street wants to subscribe to Usenet? He usually ends up test driving a free trial by one of the dozens of Usenet providers for a period of two weeks, and then like any P2P user, they are hooked for life. Or at least, the life of the subscription....and that subscription will likely last a long time. Why? The answer lies in the perceived value of the goods he acquires through said Usenet subscription. As mentioned, the worth of the goods acquired far outweighs the monthly fee of the Usenet provider. There are over 100,000 newsgroups, with the large majority of them being TEXT groups rather than BINARY groups (i.e. where the real meat of Usenet is stored). The dirty little secret among long-time Usenet users is this: Usenet would not be one-tenth as popular as it is if it weren't for the bulk of groups like alt.binaries.boneless, alt.binaries.hdtv and alt.binaries.complete_cd. One could make the argument that text discussions certainly have their place that benefits society in some manner, however the bottom line is that file sharing (again, mp3s, movies and games) make up the bulk of not only Usenet, but is the reason Usenet companies have been able to grow their businesses at exponential rates.

Risk vs. Reward? Usenet vs. P2P

If you've paid attention to the news media outlets over the past ten years, you're probably aware of the inherent risks associated with using P2P systems like Emule, Limewire and the like in acquiring copyrighted material. When you fire up a P2P program like Emule, you participate in downloading with your IP address out in the open, from which peers run by law enforcement (i.e. NordicMule) or the Recording Industry can monitor the source and destination with every file you transmit through the network. P2P in effect requires its participants to upload as well as download. It is not so different than downloading torrents in this regard. Usenet on the other hand, encourages leeching without uploading. While you certainly have the freedom to upload, your download speeds are not crippled if you decide only to lurk and leech from the uploads of others. What is more, you do so at your full internet speed, unlike peer-to-peer systems, where you are often at the mercy of others in the swarm.

When someone uploads a copyrighted film (Avengers, for instance) on a p2p or torrent system, it is far easier to track said uploader to an ip address which leads straight to their front door. If however the uploader used a premium Usenet provider to upload the film, the movie industry lawyer must first get his subscriber information from the Usenet company them before any action is taken. If he accessed his Usenet account through a vpn provider, and used anonymous means to pay for his Usenet account, then that adds a further layer of privacy that the entertainment industry lawyers will have to peel back in order to reveal his identity. We'll discuss later on the fruitfulness of signing up anonymously with Usenet and Vpn providers.

To Summarize:

Pros to Usenet:

- Not dependent on seeders like torrents
- Uses full bandwidth available on your internet connection
- MPAA (Movie Industry), RIAA (Recording Industry) cannot see your downloads as they can with torrents
- Can utilize SSL to encrypt data en route to your pc (unlike torrents)
- In its 30 year history, no one has ever been sued for downloading anything off Usenet (again, unlike with torrents)

Cons to Usenet:

- requires a paid subscription to access older posts
- posting/reading comments require a newsreader/not as easily accessible as torrent sites

Signing up for Usenet

For users who value privacy

For those who are simply not concerned about privacy, you may confidently resist the upselling offers of your Usenet provider's advertisements regarding SSL. At signup for some of the lesser known Usenet providers, the advertising might incline you to believe that you absolutely have to have SSL as an option, otherwise your PC will certainly be hacked by all manner of gremlins, evil gnomes and other bogeymen. Do not believe it. SSL often comes free with a subscription to the major providers, however some providers will still charge extra for it.

For users who value anonymity

Some Usenet providers accept bitcoins as a method of payment. If you are going to be uploading a large amount of legally questionable files and are based in the US, it might be prudent to sign up anonymously for a Usenet account. Do not use any kind of payment that carries personal information about you, such as your name, bank and the like.

Isn't Uploading to Usenet Anonymous with SSL Enabled?

The answer to this question is: sort of. Yes, you can download with impunity. Yes, it encrypted the data in route to your pc, from which point it is decrypted with the decryption key. Most Usenet providers do not keep download logs of what you siphon from the binary Usenet newsgroups. However, the catch is that if you upload, certain information is left as breadcrumbs to your Usenet account. Your messages, in addition to your uploads (all of them) contain unique header identification breadcrumbs, so to speak. If for instance you were part of some conspiracy group of assassins and shouted in some obscure newsgroup that you were going to assassinate the president of the United States, then the Secret Service could look at your headers and find out from the Usenet provider where you lived if you did not sign up anonymously. The nntp posting host & X-Trace lines accomplish this as it often relays the identity of the Usenet server, which in turn leads to your specific account. The Secret Service would have no idea that YOU posted it, but they would know you used Astraweb or Easynews to post it. They in all probability would not even need a subpoena for subscriber information, as most of the big Usenet providers would gladly provide subscriber information that involved terrorist threats, illegal porn or identity fraud (spam is a bit more involved, but then again, the Secret Service doesn't investigate Usenet spam).

There also exists the possibility that the header could be encrypted by the Usenet server themselves, in which case it can only be decrypted by them. The header might have some lengthy mosaic of jumbled letters mixed in with numbers. It might say "sdauhjk7tt324-=asdsad", which of course would be unreadable to anyone except the Usenet provider, as they hold the decryption key and no other Usenet provider does. It is somewhat similar in concept to the headers from a free email service such as Yahoo or Hotmail. This is how the hacker who pried into vice-presidential candidate Sarah Palin's email was arrested: by revealing the headers in the address bar. The FBI took this information from a screenshot the hacker had posted and traced it back to the source. A vpn service would not have helped in such a scenario, since they themselves are bound by the law, and most of them reside in the US anyway. The only way he would have gotten away with it (that is, bragging via a screenshot of her email account with the header exposed) is if he had used Tor to do so from step one. Ironically enough, it seems that a hacker's worst enemy is himself.

Recommended binary newsgroups worth exploring:

Alt.binaries.hdtv: This is perhaps the quintessential newsgroup that carries almost any kind of high definition material you could ever want. Documentaries, mainstream films, tv shows and the like can be found here free for the taking. Be aware that many movies here tend to be passworded. Thus, it is prudent to download the first rar file of the set, extract it, and preview it. Winrar will complain that it is broken, but extract it anyway. You'll get a ten minute preview of the film, or it will complain about the lack of a password entered. Some passwords can only be gained from private forums. If you see a movie you desperately want from the group, but was passworded, ask which forum you can join to extract the file.

Alt.binaries.hdtv.x264: Don't want to have to wait for eons for a 50 gigabyte movie to download from the hdtv group above? Try its sister group, which is a group dedicated to re-encodes of most of the popular movie and tv titles. Re-encoders will take a fifty gigabyte movie and compress it down to an 8-12 gigabyte file, preserving much of the picture quality of the original fifty gigabyte movie. Not recommended if you watch HD on a projector or own a tv that is 42' inches and above. However for those with a 27' inch monitor/tv, you will not see much difference as long as the encoder has done a decent job.

Alt.binaries.boneless: This is an all-around depositing group where all manner of files can be uploaded. Anything and everything gets dumped here, and is one of the largest groups on Usenet. Only recommended to those with very fast internet connections, as the header count often takes over an hour on an average connection. Most of the group carries everything you can imagine, which admittedly can be quite jarring for newcomers as there doesn't seem to be any "one" topic for the group.

Alt.binaries.movie.divx: This group is much like the hdtv groups, however few movies are here in HD, saving the downloader hours worth of downloading time. If you're not sure if a film is worth owning, it might prove prudent to test-drive it first with a much smaller size. Most movies here are in the one to two gigabyte size range which is sufficient for a laptop or phone, but you'll notice a substantial difference on a 28 inch monitor as opposed to a dvd with a decent bitrate.

Alt.binaries.sounds.mp3.blues: (substitute your favorite genre instead of blues, such as celtic, jazz, new-age, rock, heavy-metal, classical, christian, etc). Be aware than many of the mp3 groups have strict posting guidelines in their faqs, and will report you to your usenet provider if you spam said groups with off-topic mp3s. However, they offer a very narrowly-defined listening experience depending on your favorite musical tastes

Alt.binaries.games: The main group for posting pc-related games, yet some console game get posted here rather than their specified groups. Be weary of viruses in this group, irregardless of how big the file is. A good anti-virus program is paramount if you are going to be downloading from this group with any regularity. Disable "auto-play" in your operating system, as many a game iso will, when mounted, launch a virus at the first execution of the windows auto-play feature. The iso format itself is not to blame, but rather the file that lie within the folders themselves on the disc image can be virulent.

Alt.binaries.dox: missing an nfo file for a game? This is the place to ask. Game manuals are also uploaded here, along with most every nfo file you can imagine from every "scene" group in existence.

A word of caution concerning binary groups: You will not see much philosophical discussion in these "binaries" groups, aside from bickering about broken rars/not enough pars and endless requests. If you want political or academic debate, subscribe to the lengthy list (there are thousands) of alt groups that do not have "binaries" in the title.

CHAPTER 2

How to use Usenet

Over the past ten years, Usenet companies have made significant progress in simplifying what was originally a very cumbersome process for Usenet customers. After subscribing to a Usenet provider, it is now ridiculously simple to access the treasures that Usenet holds.

Basics of Using Newsgroups

Downloading: When you sign up for a ten dollar/month plan, your NSP (Newsgroup Service Provider) will email you three things: your username, password, and news address for the server (i.e. news.astraweb.com as an example). There are many different Usenet tools available that are similar in function to how a browser works. You can opt for the simpler method, which requires downloading an .nzb file from free sites like Binsearch, NZBIndex, or Newzbin (paid) and then importing to a newsreader or downloader of your choice. One of the simplest is an app called Nzb-o-Matic Plus. In the options screen of the application, just insert your user/pass combo and the server address with port 119, then set a destination where your downloads should reside. You can even choose the desktop. It's that simple. There are other free newsgroup tools available as well.

Newshosting Client (requires signup) Free
The Newshosting client self-repairs files for you if you have a subscription to them. However this is a bit redundant since Quickpar and Winrar are free.

Easynews Web Interface (requires signup) Free
The Easynews Interface is similar to the Newshosting client in that you can see thumbnails of the files posted, if they are pass-worded, and will check for errors automatically.

NewsBin Pro $20

SABnzbd Free

NewsLeecher $20

Binreader Free

GrabIt Free

Unison $29.99

EZ Global Search $2.99

NZB-O-MATIC Plus: Free

Nzb-o-Matic is perhaps the easiest out of all of the above tools to hop aboard Usenet. It is for downloading only however, but once you have the NZB file, you simply import, set your username/pass and download away.

Uploading is a bit trickier, but by no means are you required to upload anything to Usenet. In fact, leeching is encouraged, unlike torrents. If you are new to Usenet, be aware that anything you upload outside of a private proxy or Tor will leave your IP address exposed. Take care if you are unsure if your uploads are copyrighted or not. As they say, luck favors the prepared.

<u>How to Upload to Usenet</u>: (if you have no intention of uploading, skip this)

The process of uploading a small file is not extraordinarily different than uploading a large file. The main difference is that uploading a large file, say gigabytes in size, takes hours on a slow DSL connection. Nevertheless, let's go through some admittedly simplified steps on how to do so. You'll need some free tools to do so, though these are fairly mandatory to the entire process. They are:

Winrar – for archiving the files. You can't upload a single 25 gigabyte Blu-Ray movie to Usenet without risking it failing or timing out. Thus, it is better to use Winrar to break up your movie file in small chunks and upload those. You would be pretty angry if you spent two days downloading a Blu-Ray file only to find out that it "skips" in the middle of the film. Thus, Winrar and Quickpar solve this problem by testing the authenticity for broken parts. Once you have Winrar installed, right click on the file and select "Add to Archive" from the Winrar context menu. Winrar adds this to the windows context menu, thus with a simple right click you can archive any file no matter the size. Just be sure and choose an appropriate size to upload. One hundred megabyte chunks is sufficient for anything over 1 gigabyte in size. Smaller files like mp3s usually are fine with the mp3s non-archived, but will come with par files to repair any redundancies/errors in them. When downloaders finish downloading all the rar pieces, they can right click on any of the posted rars and choose "extract here" to the present directory, or any directory they wish. Before they do this however, they will likely run Quickpar first to check for errors, provided YOU have uploaded pars alongside the rar files of your movie.

Download Winrar at:
    http://www.rarlabs.com/download.htm

Quickpar – for creating par files. This is not mandatory for Usenet uploads (unless the newsgroup specifically asks for it...check their faq), but can be quite a godsend for downloaders as often Usenet servers will "hiccup" during the upload process. Creating parts at 10% redundancy is sufficient for most files.

Download Quickpar at:
    http://www.quickpar.org.uk/Download.htm

Camelsystem Powerpost (Windows only) - A freeware tool used to upload the rar and par files you created. It is delightfully simple to use. You will need your username and password combo from your Usenet provider, along with the port number to insert into the settings menu before your are allowed to upload.
    Download Powerpost at http://powerpost.camelsystem.nl/e-index.php

NZB Files – You can think of NZB files as being similar to torrent files that you load into a downloader program. Only instead of using uTorrent, you would import the file into something like Nzb-o-Matic Plus. The NZB file itself is the files you have selected from a site such as Binsearch or NZBindex. It can contain any number of pointers to the files you want, which may be in separate newsgroups. Using an NZB file makes it exponentially easier to manage the files you want, versus those you don't want. In the old days of Usenet, you had to use an archaic program like Agent or Nomad News to manually check-mark each rar or item in separate newsgroups to download what you wanted. This process alone could take an hour or more depending on how many files you wanted. When NZB files came along, they simplified a needlessly cumbersome process of getting what you wanted from your favorite newsgroups.

Incomplete Files – Incomplete Usenet files may look complete in your newsreader, but upon downloading the complete set, you discover that Winrar spits out an error midway through extracting the files. This is usually because the uploader has an unstable connection, or perhaps the power went out upon uploading his files, or a server hiccupped during transmission. Usenet servers transfer files from other Usenet servers, and it differs somewhat than your regular run-of-the-mill internet server. For this reason, you should install the free Quickpar program to alleviate any potential headaches this can cause.

SFV Files – SFV files can be used to verify that your downloaded file is what it is supposed to be, and if any corruption occurred along the way. It doesn't repair the file. That is what Quickpar does. This method of repair is quite different (and yet more stable) than what you might be accustomed to using BitTorrent, where pars are rarely provided with seeded files.

CHAPTER 3

Usenet Reviews - The Wheat and the Chaff

If you scout around the major search engines and use search terms like "usenet" "best usenet prices" and "usenet reviews", you will literally come across hundreds of websites all clamoring for your referral dollars as they tell you which Usenet provider is best and which ones to avoid. The thing is, most of them offer the exact same services, and by and large are just as competent as the next company. They offer similar services, ease of use, and some like Newshosting even offer their own Usenet browser that will do all of the hard work for you. Almost all of them offer free SSL and unlimited packages as well. Usenet-Server and Astraweb seem to be the cheapest, though Astraweb has had its share of problems regarding incomplete uploads in the past.

For the purposes of anonymity, going with a US based newsgroup provider probably isn't conductive to good anonymity practice. While it certainly isn't foolproof to have an account with a European provider if one is uploading copyrighted material to Usenet (or any other illegal activity), the laws in the US are more litigious and draconian than any other country on Earth that houses the server farms of Usenet companies.

The Big Five

Astraweb: Often the cheapest priced out of all Usenet providers with unlimited specials at $11, their past problems have been server downtime as well as incomplete files (as of 2012). Posted PAR files will certainly make up the difference...most of the time. However on a dual core fitted pc, quickpar can take more than an hour if a sufficiently large amount of rars are broken. In addition, their customer service is not as refined as say, Easynews or Newshosting, but they cannot be beat for the price they offer. If you don't mind a few broken files and using Quickpar on a semi-weekly basis, and price is a concern, Astraweb is the prime choice.

Usenet Server: Similar to Astraweb but more stable infrastructure. They are also a few dollars more in price however for their unlimited plan. Incompletes were not seen in over two years of using them. Thus, you really see where this extra few dollars per month went: system retention and reliability.

Newshosting: Similar to Usenet-Server, however they provide a free newsreader that makes it ridiculously easy to see which files are authentic and which are viruses/spam (hint: look at the file size...if it is a heinously small size, it is probably spam or malware). The thumbnail view is similar to what you would see with Easynews' web interface that scans the thumbs of all the newsgroups you need to view.

Easynews: One of the first companies out of the gate, and one which still does not have the unlimited offerings of the above Usenet providers. However, they are dirt cheap, have a reliable backbone of server farms since they have been in business for eons, and have one of the top forums for troubleshooting and tech issues in the industry. Their customer service is unrivaled as well. The only caveat is that if you are a power user who wants to download over a hundred gigabytes worth of data per month, they probably should not be your first choice. They are, like Giganews, extremely strict with takedown notices from lawyers. If HBO specials and documentaries are your cup of tea, be aware that they have the ability to "nuke" uploads should they deem it too "hot" to reside on their servers (i.e. Game of Thrones, The Sopranos, etc)

Giganews: Undoubtedly the most expensive of all the Usenet premium providers. They provide one of the largest server backbones, and provide similar services as the above mentioned providers. They are considered the "Harvard" of Usenet companies, however it seems rather needless to pay for the name since you get most of the benefits from the other big four Usenet companies. Giganews is also known for giving in to "take down" requests for uploaders of copyrighted content, such as HBO series like Game of Thrones, in which files were purged from the servers in such a large quantity as to make pars useless to recover them. The problem therein, is that many smaller Usenet companies use Giganews backend servers for access to Usenet. Thus, when they do comply with a take down order or request from some Hollywood law firm, other Usenet providers are affected. If money is not an issue, Giganews is a great choice for their consistently good customer service.

Others: Thundernews, Newsdemon, Ngroups, etc.

You're taking a spin on the roulette wheel with anyone not in the top five. That is not to say they all provide bad service, but it is important to note that a rock-solid business like those in the top five take years and years of backbreaking work and perseverance. The lesser known Usenet providers usually are lacking one of three key areas: customer service (usually emails from tech support), reliability/completion of files, or retention (age of files). Some of them are so newly minted that they have no choice but to rent part of their infrastructure from the likes of Giganews or Highwinds, which have many, many server farms.

In the end you might ask, what is the number one thing that customers want from a Usenet provider? It is not retention. Most Usenet companies have similar retention rates that span many years. It is not even completion of files. Most large uploads from users around the world upload a sufficient number of pars to repair any large group of posted files such as Blu-Ray movies or the like. No, what Usenet customers most want is GOOD CUSTOMER SERVICE. Customers don't want to sit waiting on the phone up to an hour for tech support to answer. To wit, they want someone who speaks the same language and in the same dialect. They also don't want to be spammed with upselling offers by the Usenet company in question (web hosting companies like Godaddy are notorious for this), nor do they like to be called on the phone with such offers.

The First Rule of Usenet (don't talk about Usenet!)

On many social media sites and forums such as Facebook, Twitter and Reddit, some users will post advertisements from the late nineties from such big box stores as BestBuy, Wal-Mart, Sears and the like that show a dramatic difference in regards to hardware costs. For example, a 1.5 gigabyte hard drive from BestBuy in 2000 cost over $200 dollars. Now however, for the same amount of dollars you can buy a 3 terabyte drive. It is not that different for Usenet server farms. As time goes by and more customers sign on for premium Usenet accounts, the business costs incurred for Usenet companies goes down. That is why you can have an unlimited data account for less than ten dollars a month. So then, why is traditional file-sharing such as torrenting more popular?

The reason is because it is eminently easier to download a torrent for free than it is to fish out your credit card and set up a Usenet account. Ridiculous, is it not? It is also easier to see comments on a torrent site than read and filter through all the spam in a Usenet newsgroup such as alt.binaries.boneless. Some interfaces, such as Newshosting's newsgroup browser will filter out most of the spam and passworded files and make it easier to use.

It is a well-known fact by most BitTorrent users that the Record and Movie industries like to unleash their armies of lawyers upon copyright works that have seeds numbered in the millions. This makes it very convincing in a lawsuit as far as who you uploaded files with and to whom you didn't. Often, a movie release for September might be leaked in August, and the swarm of users will catch the attention of the copyright holders and sue the downloaders as well as uploaders provided their true ip address is showing. This is less the case with Usenet, where it is not possible to see who downloaded which file, even in casting a wide net. Thus, if you live in a litigious society like that in the United States, it is to your benefit to learn to utilize Usenet's strengths in this regard.

On many forums you will hear users say "Usenet is dead" or "Usenet doesn't have what torrents have". Take confidence in the fact that people who espouse such nonsense don't in fact use Usenet themselves. It is not beyond the realm of impossibility that such naysayers are actually attorneys, or employee shills for the record industry who don't want legions of potential Usenet experts asking too many questions concerning what it has to offer.

CHAPTER 4

In this chapter, we'll discuss ways you can add anonymity to your Usenet connection, so that you can participate in discussion groups without fear of persecution. These methods often are most useful in situations where you may lose your Usenet account if you say the wrong things to the wrong people. Usenet companies are big business now, and unlike twelve years ago, will now think nothing of terminating your account of they get enough complaints. Simply being unpopular and taking a stand against the status quo in certain newsgroups can get your Usenet account banned (i.e. alt.privacy). However, with true anonymity, they may ban your account, but rest assured that not only will your words remain forever on Usenet, but you will not be persecuted for speaking out against a tyrannical government, or a company that you work for (which has happened many times by disgruntled employees on Facebook).

It should be stated at the outset that using Tor for Usenet binary downloads will actually strain the Tor network, just as it does with torrents. And to boot, whenever you use torrents via Tor, the torrent software actually sends your IP address to the recipient. It does so anonymously, in the same way a post office worker will deliver you your mail. Needless to say this defeats the purpose of using torrents. This problem is not with the Tor code, but rather the way that applications like BitLord and BitTorrent are designed. The torrent applications themselves need to be coded to allow anonymity. It is better to use Freenet with the Frost addon for p2p-like trading if you wish to remain anonymous. Tor is much more efficient at textual discussions and binary downloaders using your native connection, but the easiest method to do this anonymously is by use of the remailer network. By using such a method, the identifying Usenet posts are stripped away from your messages, essentially erasing the digital trail that leads back to your IP address.

As we have seen from past media reports around the world over the last several years, there could be any number of valid reasons you want to hide your identity.

- Maybe you work for a computer manufacturer, or perhaps a robotics company and are concerned about the lack of safety measures being enforced by your superiors, but fear some kind of retaliation by them should you go public, like the loss of your job. Usenet is a great place to ask advice and not worry about the consequences. Places like Facebook and Twitter on the other hand might invite retribution by the executives or CEO of your company.

- It could be that you want to vocally protest your discontent with the direction of the prevailing winds of government. Doing so in countries like the US, Iran, China, and the like could put you on a "watch" list of sorts, and before you know it, you have problems relating to "no fly" lists at airports and border stations.

- Perhaps you want to establish a free email address that has never had any contact whatsoever with your real IP address. Services like Yahoo Mail, Gmail, and Hotmail repeatedly scan emails looking for keywords or files in which to flag. Shutting down your email is one thing. Having your IP address along with the email forwarded to government entities for prosecution is quite another. Anonymity prevents this from happening.

Remailers

As a crude example, let's say you own a reporting agency that is active in most of the less-than-savory newsgroups, and you use your email from your office quite regularly. Then you see a rape victim who needs your assistance. You might not want to divulge your email address to everyone. Using a remailer will ensure that any identifying information of you will be erased from the headers of any messages you upload to newsgroups. Your message will be forwarded to the recipient without any risks of public disclosure.

Traceable vs. Untraceable Remailers

Traceable: there are some types of remailers that keep active lists of senders/pseudonyms whereby receivers can reply to mail by fictitious names. When the remailer gets a message, it consults a list and forwards mail to the sender. Thus, there is an element of privacy to this method of communication; however as was proved in previous years by the penet.fi (Finland) incident, this does not provide anonymity. Any hacker, government agency, judge, or the like can gain access to said list and discover who the sender is. In the case of penet.fi, Scientology launched a lawsuit of copyright infringement against them, in which a lower court demanded they turn over the identity of its users.

Untraceable: If no list is maintained on the pseudonyms of users, then security is increased exponentially...provided you are willing to give up two way communications with your party. Needless to say, this has some drawbacks, and is in some ways inferior to using Tor and/or PGP to communicate. In addition, there is always the possibility of hacker attacks whereby once entry is gained upon the server, anonymity is compromised. Traffic-sniffers along with a host of other tools can also be used as a method of attack, as they compare and contrast the traffic emanating from the server. Such attacks are very difficult to coordinate, but are somewhat analogous to attacks within Tor and also Freenet, whereby if a sufficiently high number of hostile nodes are controlled within the network, then probability of stripping away layers of anonymity becomes more likely. In other words, if Law Enforcement for instance, controls all Tor relays, the long-term effect would be similar if they had control of most nodes on Freenet. Though they are admittedly vastly different technologies, they do share one common goal: hiding the true IP address of senders and recipients.

Mixmaster techniques however attempt to thwart such subversive attempts by sending messages through several servers across the globe, in various countries of legality and law enforcement jurisdictions. It becomes exponentially difficult for hackers and/or government entities to bunny hop from server-to-server across the globe in order to track down where the original sender resided. Thus, it goes well above and beyond the phrase "don't put all your eggs in one basket" and is more akin to "many eggs, many baskets". Such is the skeletal framework of the onion-routing network Tor.

You may download Mixmaster here.

Things That Break Anonymity on Usenet

1.) Giving out your real email address, even one from one of the "free" services such as Yahoo, Hotmail and the like, not only can, but *will* open you up to armies of spambots, guaranteed. You would be surprised at how many new to Usenet are under the impression that these free email services are somehow foolproof to the legions of bots that trawl Usenet. A better alternative: use a fictional name and temporary "Usenet-Only" email. If you have a website, your host probably offers you the ability to create throwaway accounts. Or, go with Anonymizer Nyms at https://www.nyms.net for twenty bucks per year. SharpMail, Mailinator & Hushmail are also excellent options, however if you want anonymity as well as privacy, remember to sign up while on the Tor network, not the open web. Also remember not to use credit cards or paypal, as it leaves a money trail. Better to use Bitcoins or a money order with no link back to you.

2.) Dropping Personal Info. This is a big one, and one that is seen quite frequently on various groups where flame wars erupt over issues like political campaigns, privacy and even some mp3 groups (i.e. alt.binaries.sounds. mp3.electronic). Political affiliations/liaisons, favorite restaurants, bars, musical groups and the like can lead to some stalker building a profile on you, then hopping on Facebook, Twitter or LinkedIn and keying in all the personal data you have given over the past six months. Remember that whatever is typed in *any* newsgroup will be there for years and years. Type in "labor" as "labour" or "color" as "colour", and it is not difficult to discern your country of origin.

3.) <u>Leaving messages with your headers clearly visible</u> to the reading public. By using various search tools, they can see every message you posted to Usenet, even if you used different nyms. This of course doesn't occur if you use a service that strips away this information.

4.) <u>Signing up for a Usenet or VPN service using credit cards</u>

Realize that when you use your credit card to purchase anything like a vpn (virtual private network) or Usenet account, you are in fact leaving a money trail straight to your identity. If you are only after a small measure of privacy, such as wanting a Usenet account that doesn't monitor/log your downloads, then a vpn is fine. However if it is anonymity you want, you will have to sign up for *both* Usenet as well as the vpn service using anonymous means, either by bitcoins, money order, or a prepaid debit card with no identifying information leading back to you.

Truecrypt, Usenet and Passwords

In all of this talk of posting rars, pars and messages out in the open newsgroups, it would be a shame not to mention that you can also upload locked containers and encrypted volumes to Usenet as well. The main difference is that you have to have the Truecrypt (free) application installed, and create an encrypted container with messages or data therein before uploading it to a Usenet newsgroup. There are lots of different newsgroups that allow this and many that don't. However you can use alt.binaries.test as a means to communicate covertly with another, or share files privately with another person. The encryption is actually fairly straightforward. When you create the Truecrypt container with the data you want to send to someone else, you could then rar that one file (or files) and upload that. Then the only ones who would be privy to its contents are those with the keyfile, which you could email to them, and/or the password to the container.

The benefit of implementing Tor (for text groups, not binaries), Usenet and Truecrypt simultaneously is that you get the best of both worlds. You get the privacy that a vpn will allow, in addition to having the anonymity (different than privacy) of Truecrypt.

Always check the newsgroup's FAQ first before passwording files as many groups do not allow it. What is the worse that can happen? Your Usenet provider will be inundated with complaints and they will revoke your posting privileges, which can be quite a cumbersome ordeal regardless of whether you have signed up anonymously or not. If in doubt, ask the group, or post the word "passworded" or "pw" in the subject line. Groups like alt.binaries.hdtv, which are flooded with passworded blu-ray files, will thank you for it. There is nothing quite infuriating as downloading a 50 gigabyte Blu-Ray disc and finding out that it won't extract the files because of a password requirement. This is in addition to not having a membership to the forum where such a password was revealed in the first place.

Running Usenet from a mounted Truecrypt image

Optionally, you could create an encrypted volume, install your Usenet newsreader into that container, and only run your newsreader upon the mounting of said container. Just be aware that some applications like to leave temp files in the system drive (C:), but most should have an option to set such a directory (i.e. set it within the encrypted container itself). You will have to mount it to the same letter directory each time if you don't want to change it every session, however it makes it very handy to secure communications privately between you and someone else without the entire newsgroup seeing what you are saying or trading. There may be an instance where you spent a lot of money on a rare, vintage recording of an obscure album, and you don't want anyone else in the mp3 group trying to make money off it on eBay. Solution? Use Truecrypt to encrypt the mp3s. Rar them up with a password and upload to a newsgroup on Usenet.

If you are in a country that makes it difficult to engage in free discussion online, such as Iran, China and the like, make sure that you do not leave your encrypted images running with your Usenet newsreader/browser. Doing so leaves all the data open to any kind of government entity that decides to raid your place of residence. Thus, if you are a regular poster in the group "alt.discussion.tibetan-freedom" it would be wise to not leave your PC running unattended at all, especially with a Truecrypt image mounted and in operation.

PGP and Usenet

You can also use PGP to encrypt messages to newsgroup as well. PGP is a free encryption application similar (however more complex) to Truecrypt. You can encrypt messages from one newsgroup to another, to any recipient you like, and they can in turn decrypt your message. It is more efficient to use PGP for the purposes of covert Usenet communication than it is to use Truecrypt, as the applications are meant for different security scenarios. It should be said that the pgp manual is not an easy read. It will take you some measure of effort to get your head around encrypting/decrypting messages from Usenet, as it is not as straightforward and newbie-friendly as say, Truecrypt. It is worth your time in learning however if you want to exchange encrypted messages with other PGP members on Usenet.

PGP-related newsgroups:

alt.security.pgp

comp.security.pgp.announce

comp.security.pgp.discuss

comp.security.pgp.resources

comp.security.pgp.tech

Technical Sources on Cryptography, Security & Encryption

www.iacr.org – Intern. Association of Cryptologic Research – contains a wealth of data on crypto as well as miscellaneous related security programs www.pgpi.org – Homepage and Resource for PGP and its applications

www.nist.gov/aes – AES, or Advanced Encryption Standard used by Truecrypt, Drivecrypt, PGP

To moderate or not to moderate Usenet

It would be certainly short-sighted to suggest that Usenet should have total anarchy and no moderation at all. Newsgroups that employ the use of a moderator can have stark advantages over unmoderated groups, so much so that the group attracts far more attention from new users than it would without such moderation. The most glaring problems with a totally unmoderated setting can be seen quite clearly within discussion groups on Freenet, where moderation is not possible. Individual users can opt to "ignore" all posts from certain users on their own, or create their own Frost discussion group with a private encryption key (that is, unless said key is leaked, in which the spammers engage in a full frontal assault on the group). On Freenet, spam, personal attacks, racism and hatred abound, however the responsibility is placed upon the individual to self-censor/delete posts within the group. On Usenet, even moderators have been unsuccessful at completely eradicating spam and personal flame wars between members.

That is not to suggest that a moderator is the equivalent of a Big Brother-like censor, however it makes discussion in the newsgroup more honest and less prone to those who like to derail threads into off-topic discussions. An inherent downside to being a regular on a heavily moderated Usenet newsgroup is that tolerance becomes difficult to maintain.

After years and years of engaging in civil discourse in various groups, a user might find it a bit of a challenge to participate in a group that offers a more relaxed discussion topic structure. In one of the mp3 newsgroups (electronic), untold numbers of flame wars have erupted over the years concerning new users (as well as old) who would post collections of ambient/new-age artists. Now, there are other mp3 groups better suited for collections by, for instance, Michael Stearns. Few electronic music fans would find him suited for the electronic mp3 newsgroup, however every now and then a new Usenet user would show up and mistakenly post to the group his latest offering. He would be summarily crucified with curses, flames and threats to inform his Usenet provider that he was spamming the group. This type of intolerable attitude does more harm than good. There was also many uploads done of artist Steve Roach, whose music transcends several different genres: new-age, ambient, trance and electronic, yet the uploader of said music was similarly cursed and vehemently badgered by long-term users.

CHAPTER 5

Which VPN companies respect anonymity?

If you are a bit squeamish about accessing Usenet via your local ISP, you can always add an extra layer of privacy by subscribing to a vpn (virtual private network) service close to you. There are a plethora of good vpn providers that will route your internet connection through them and provide ssl (secure socket layer) encryption so that your isp cannot see what you do online. Most all of them use similar technology to achieve this, and have comparable speeds. A vpn service is much, much faster than using an onion-routing network like Tor, but not all of them will tolerate p2p usage. However, they will tolerate a Usenet account.

Unlike Tor, the vpn provider, which usually charges somewhere in the range of ten dollars per month for unlimited service (over and above what you pay your Usenet provider), WILL be able to see everything that you do through their connection, unless you route that connection through the Tor network. They are more tolerable to Usenet than they are P2P systems, as Usenet is less likely to incur a swarm of copyright lawyers sending them angry cease-and-desist letters. Bottom line: some vpns will log your IP, and some won't. If they know your real name and address, you can be sure that law enforcement will (and any other type of law agency) with a subpoena. It's a hit and miss game, and one which seems entirely dependent on whether the provider keeps online logs of the traffic that goes through their portal. One popular vpn provider, BlackVPN, said this in their FAQ:

"Although we do not monitor the traffic, incoming or outgoing connections of our users we may assign users to a unique IP address and log which user was assigned which IP address at a given time. If we receive a copyright violation notice from the appropriate copyright holder then we will forward the violation to the offending user and may terminate their account. We therefore ask our users not to distribute or transmit material which violates the copyright laws in either your country or the country in which our Service is hosted."

The above defeats the entire purpose of anonymity on the internet. A novice who didn't know the difference between privacy and anonymity might conclude from their website that they offered complete anonymity similar to what Tor offers, but that is clearly not the case at all. One has to be quite attentive to the fine details of the advertising on sites such as theirs to see if any logs are kept, and in many cases they will not reveal such information unless you explicitly email them and ask. Interestingly, in 2011 the website TorrentFreak initiated a rather close examination of all of the vpn provider's response to the question "Under what jurisdictions does your company operate and under what exact circumstances will you share the information you hold with a 3rd party?"

Some of the answers were expectantly evasive, and others were quite illuminating. One provider, CryptCloud, said

"We don't log anything on the customer usage side so there are no dots to connect period, we completely separate the payment information. Realistically, unless you operate out of one of the 'Axis of Evil

Countries" Law Enforcement will find a way to put the screws to you. I have read the nonsense that being in Europe will protect you from US Law Enforcement, worked well for HMA didn't it? Furthermore I am pretty sure the Swiss Banking veil was penetrated and historically that is more defend-able than individual privacy. The way to solve this is just not to log, period."

Two points to make. One, the HMA (Hide My Ass vpn) incident he refers to involved a member of the hacker group Lulzsec, in which one of their core members was arrested. Two, he cites the "Axis of Evil", but clearly they are not in one of those countries.

The above is not to suggest that their actual service is less than that which they advertise, but the distinction between privacy and anonymity often falls victim to the gnomes who work in the marketing department of said companies. CryptoCloud is located in...San Antonio, Texas, which has one of the most brutally unmerciful judiciary systems in the United States. If a federal judge (or Congress) wanted the identity of one of their customers, you can be sure that such information would be handed over in a heartbeat in order to avoid heavy day-to-day fines. If they are based in the US, they would *have* to have your personal identity information available in order to avoid bankruptcy by the federal government. To wit, this doesn't necessarily have to have anything to do with terrorism, cp, spam or counterfeiting. It could be as simple as running a file sharing server. The case involving Megaupload proves that true anonymity, at least that which is beyond the long arm of the law, is difficult to obtain, even if you reside in another country. Still, it is worth having a vpn account simply because it adds an extra layer of privacy to your sessions. If you are a habitual uploader, you could do a lot worse than to pay ten dollars a month for an extra peace of mind.

The solution? Sign up to a vpn provider anonymously. There are several providers who accept Bitcoins as payment.

http://www.thebitcoinlist.com/dp_internet/vps-vpn/

CHAPTER 6

The Cloud (the Enemy of Usenet and Anonymity)

It goes without saying that men are voracious collectors of many things obtained online: mp3 collections, digital wallpaper, pdf files and the like. The term "cloud" has been given flighty and unwieldy definitions from one blogger to the next, as if the "cloud" is actually some impenetrable fortress in the digital sky where no moth or thief can break in and corrupt or steal. However secure you feel that your files are "in the cloud", it is perhaps worth remembering that whoever owns the "cloud", owns your stuff. Thus, the cloud is nothing more than a server farm with hundreds of other people's hard drives & servers, all digitally categorizing... your stuff. No longer are your things flying under the banner of privacy in your own home, but rather you are subject to whatever litigious lawyer's terms and conditions contract he has drummed up for the cloud provider. Be wary of a future promised where your data is at the whims of some far away server operator who gets to dictate which of your purchased music, movies and games gets "streamed" to your pc.

The Windows 8 operating system has a feature called "Smart-

Screen" that is used for checking the validity and safety of files before they are executed. This type of feature was first implemented in Internet Explorer and Windows Live Messenger to thwart malicious sites from being able to exploit people's browsers. Thus, verification and authentication were at the forefront of the feature, as it sought to prevent spam, malware and adware from infecting people's computers. A good thing? Not for the majority of users, who found it rather annoying. It was a one-step-forward, two-steps-backward approach that actually hindered the internet experience for millions of users of Internet Explorer as they attempted to go to links that were not dangerous in the least. Enter Windows 8, in which the SmartScreen feature tries to verify whether applications are "safe" to download or run on the operating system. It checks a dynamic, ever-changing laundry list of exploitable URLs that Microsoft has identified as harmful for end-users on pc systems. An additional problem with this is that it is cumbersome to turn off, and once done, results in consistent nagging from the operating system to re-enable it. Where it will be three to five years down the road? Will you have to have every app or file on your pc "authorized" by Microsoft's servers before you can execute them? What about cloud content and streaming legally purchased items to your own pc?

For the uninitiated, Microsoft likes to assign "download reputation" points to digitally signed websites as well as programs. The problem with this is the same problem that manifests itself in anti-virus programs, namely that a lot of false-positives get thrown in the user's face, leading to frustration and annoyance. At times, downloads will get frozen in Internet Explorer 9 as the downloaded files get scanned. There is no option in Internet Explorer 9 to switch it off and let end-users decide what security setting to implement. Rare files constantly get falsely flagged as being somehow malicious for the pc. There is a further element of privacy intrusion for the Smart-Screen feature. It collects data on every program you install on your operating system, and checks to see if a valid certificate exists on Microsoft's "cloud" (i.e. their server) that verifies its "safety" for your operating system. It checks the hash of the program installer itself, and compares it to a list at Microsoft. Think about how many programs you have installed on your pc that are related to privacy: PGP, Truecrypt, BitLocker, the installer your vpn provider emailed you, and perhaps even encrypted keyfiles to your hard drive. It would be a gold mine of epic proportions for any hacker to get at such data.

Enter Usenet. As of 2012, it is relatively easy to hop on Usenet without having to jump through hoops to do so. When you download data from Usenet, it is typically decoded by your newsreader or NZB application and then saved to your hard drive. If you have an anti-virus installed, it most likely will have some element of checking each executable or installer that is downloaded to your pc, either by Usenet or some other variant of internet app. With the rush to maxi-mize the use of cloud computing, however, the responsibility of initializing these types of security settings is slowly being taken away from the end-user. What does this mean for Usenet? One of two things could happen.

1.) Eventually, users stream data off of usenet, which is then checked and "verified" through an intermediary cloud server, before being delivered to your hard drive (assuming you have one).

2.) Usenet SSL will be prohibitively expensive and/or reserved only for certain groups in society (think Government, Intelligence, etc). Secure, anonymous programs like PGP, Freenet, Truecrypt and the like will be stigmatized and shunned by cloud servers for their inability to unmask and decrypt their true contents.

In 2010, an article titled "The Death of the Hard Drive" explored Google's persistent momentum towards a hard-drive-less selection of flagship products, all citing the benefits of "cloud stor-age". In 2012, Microsoft is gearing Windows 8 towards such a platter-less scenario.

"Stop worrying about when the hard drive in your computer will die. Google wants to kill it permanently anyway.

The new Google Chrome operating system, which was unveiled Tuesday, as well as hints and suggestions from Apple and Microsoft, offers us a preview of the PC of the future. And it will come without that familiar whirring disk that has been the data heart of the PC for the past 25 years.

The Chrome OS will at first be available on all-black laptops from Samsung and Acer. And because the new platform stores everything — files, applications, data bits and bytes, literally everything — on online servers rather than on your home or office PC, those new PCs running it won't require gobs of storage. In fact, they won't require any storage at all."

Further reasons why you should never rely on the Cloud for your personal data backups.

1.) <u>You are completely at the mercy of your ISP's bandwidth cap.</u> They stand to make a fortune as you stream your own personal mp3s, games, video (which competes with their own brand) and the like to your personal devices. No hard drive means you'll be streaming quite regularly. Bandwidth caps will necessarily cause you to pay more for products that you have paid in full. Thus, true ownership becomes a misnomer. Instead, you will "rent" the products you buy from online digital sources. Usenet prices will go up, as customers will not be able to afford the massive price spikes in bandwidth costs. One of the hallmarks of Usenet premium providers is the "unlimited" package. However what good is "unlimited" when your ISP caps your connection? Many ISPs (especially those in Canada, such as Bell Sympatico) falsely advertise such unlimited options and speeds.

2.) <u>US jurisdiction.</u> Most of the server backbones related to cloud computing reside in the heart of the USA. That means your private data, while in the "cloud", is subject to laws dictated by the US Congress and US Legislature. What is quasi-legal in your own country in the Ukraine, or Timbuktu, might be dastardly illegal in the United States. Some government entities might insist that sites like Amazon not only cancel your account and delete your purchased files on their servers, but relay all personal subscriber information to them for proceedings in an American court. It has happened before. There is also the opportunity for said government agencies (or hackers) to intercept your data streaming down to you to verify its authenticity. For your own good, naturally. Google and Microsoft know what is best for you, right?

3.) <u>Encryption is allergic to Cloud Computing</u>. You can bet the ranch that almost every Cloud Computing server operator will demand to see what is inside encrypted files in order to minimize the risk of being fined by the FCC or investigated by other alphabet agencies like the IRS (taxes), and FBI (fraud/copyright). This is not necessarily the case today, in 2012, but you can be sure that if everyone has absolutely no choice but to upload their digital purchases to their servers, they will want to see the contents of every-thing since it resides on "their" server cloud. Google, Microsoft and Yahoo repeatedly scan personal emails in an attempt to better target their user's browsing habits with targeted ads. It would be no different for mp3s, videos or love letters contained in encrypted Truecrypt volumes.

4.) <u>It cheapens individuality</u>. The collective group-think that is inherent in the pursuit to herd all the digital sheep into one pen is the anti-thesis of not only privacy and human rights on an individual level, it makes everyone dependent on a single system. In August 2012, Steve Wozniak, co-founder of Apple said at a Washington expose said:

"I really worry about everything going to the cloud. I think it's going to be horrendous. I think there are going to be a lot of horrible problems in the next five years. With the cloud, you don't own anything. You already signed it away. I want to feel that I own things. A lot of people feel, 'Oh, everything is really on my computer,' but I say: the more we transfer everything onto the web, onto the cloud, the less we're going to have control over it."

And Steve would be correct. If Cloud computing takes off the way Google and Microsoft wants, you will find someone else in some other state, province, or country setting the times when you are allowed to access your own data, encrypted or not.

5.) <u>George Orwell's 1984</u>. Maybe it will never quite happen as it is alluded to in the book. Then again, no one could fathom that a Category 5 hurricane would wipe out New Orleans, or that 3000 people would die at the hands of 19 mangy terrorists on Sept. 11th, 2001. For several years now, the US has expressed the desire for an internet "kill switch" to deal with the less than desirable in our society. Today, it is terrorists, spammers and identity thieves. Tomorrow, it is people who obviously have something to hide if they implement SSL in their Usenet setups and upload Truecrypt volumes "to the cloud". It is this kind of slow erosion of private property that forced the hand of Revolution in the 17th and 18th centuries.

The above reasons are sufficient to put a shred of doubt insofar as Usenet usage is concerned. Usenet users rely on their physical hard drives for storage of their data acquired from Usenet, and regardless of what that data is, it would slowly kill the Usenet industry if users had to "stream" their files from their Usenet accounts with no place to securely store them. They also enjoy the privilege of not having their download logs kept by anyone. Such is certainly not true of most torrent trackers, where every seed participating in the swarm reveals their ip address to anyone connected, day or night, for days and weeks on end.

Disregard Authoritarians, Acquire Privacy

To reverse the heavy tide against groupthink and giving up private ownership of your own files (on Usenet, or elsewhere), a stand needs to be taken now, and with more than simply our wallets. There was once a time back in the 1990s where the purveyors of Usenet did not have to worry about their posts being chiseled in stone among the newsgroups which would last for generations. Even one year retention for textual newsgroups was not that common, and five year retention for binaries was but a dream. Many Usenet users weren't afraid to use their real names and real emails in messages. At the time, there was little reason to be. Now however, in addition to the ever-ominous threat of being stalked (and kidnapped/killed)

Every message posted to Usenet is archived by Google (Deja-News/Google Groups) in the same way that they are taking high resolution photos of every nook and cranny upon the earth via Google Earth. The aim of this digital push towards "the Cloud" seems to be to minimize individuality as well as putting an end to privacy. The technology is here that every move you make on the street will be recorded not by security cameras sitting atop state buildings and banks, but by each other. Google has not only recorded every single message posted to Usenet within the last five years, it wants to do something eerily similar with their Project Glass product, in which users will be sold a pair of glasses with a built-in webcam that monitors everything around it, giving immediate data about their surroundings: buildings, restaurants, museums and the like. Only it won't stop there. Eventually it will focus on people, as that is where the ad revenue streams lie. According to Google:

"We think Glass helps you share your life as you're living it; from life's big moments to everyday experiences. Today we're kicking off what we're calling Glass Sessions, where you can experience what it's like to use Glass while we build it, through the eyes of a real person, in real life. The first Glass Session follows Laetitia Gayno, the wife of a Googler, as she shares her story of welcoming a new baby, capturing every smile, and showing her entire family back in France every "first" through Hangouts."

True Security lies with the Individual, not the State

We may come to a point where it may be impossible to truly harbor any anonymity at all on Usenet or anywhere else. Users who don't have the latest "reality enhancer" (which just so conveniently carries every data imaginable about your birth, health, academic & employment history) would suffer severe ostracization from peers (i.e. Facebook defriending, etc)

As anyone with a RAID hard drive setup can attest, technology gets smaller with each generation, and holds infinitely more data the further into the future you progress. There will come a point where you will not need to wear glasses to record and upload your immediate surroundings to the internet. All of the surveillance will inevitably shrink in size to a state where your naked eye will not notice their presence at all. This is what happened with Usenet. No one knew back in the 1990s that everything we said or did online was going to be archived (archive.org) for anyone to peruse decades later.

Thus, we now censor ourselves on Usenet for fear of being reported to whatever authorities can punish us accordingly. Excessive data therefore, is actually the anti-thesis of freedom. Usenet SSL, VPNs, & Tor all provide a power to the end user that is slowly being shunned and minimized by those with the power to do so (i.e. Google, Facebook,). It is certainly not 100% integrated into society yet, but it is coming. To foster more privacy on Usenet, we need more anonymity. People need to be free to speak their minds and engage civil discussion without worrying about the powers that be (Google) pulling the strings of censorship. We will get to the point where we will be accused of "being up to no good" by refusing to play along. Have an encrypted volume and plan to cross the border? The border guard might ask you to decrypt. Refuse and they can confiscate your laptop for five days, making the trip fairly aggravating. Will it one day be considered a capital crime to erase some negative thing about your past history on the internet without some government entity's stamp of approval?

INVISIBILITY TOOLKIT

TABLE OF CONTENT

PREFACE

Winston Churchill once said, "If you find yourself in Hell... keep going."

I can relate to that as easily as you can. But these days Hell itself seems to have taken on an altogether foreign form that is wholly different than the medieval version. These days, many 'angels of light' profess to know what's good for us better than we do ourselves - which is sheer lunacy.

We're not sheep. We all see it. We're not blind. And some of us want to act as beacons of light in a sea of darkness rather than go "Baaaaa!" like sheep to the bloody slaughter. We want to lead others away from the slaughterhouse. But to do that requires a specific set of skills no college teaches.

Skills that will help us turn back the tide of Armageddon on individual sovereignty. Because let's face it, attacks on privacy have increased a thousand-fold. Every day new laws are passed that make privacy as rare as pink diamonds. In the future it just may come to be just as valued as pink diamonds. Do you want to hear your grandkids ask you what it was like in the old days when people weren't monitored 24/7.

Right. Didn't think so.

It's high-time we fought back and fought hard. If you've ever seen the Shawshank Redemption then you know what happens to weaklings - those that don't take action. They get raped again and again and again. Sooner or later you'll know what the meaning of this phrase is: "His judgment cometh and that right soon". It means war. Wouldn't you rather fight before the raping and pillaging starts? I would.

Judgment Day is already here. One cannot walk down the street without meeting a dozen street cams, and as an American/Canadian citizen there are times when I've wanted to disappear from society altogether. Vanish as though I'd slipped Frodo's elvish cloak over my neck and smoothed that runic ring right down my middle finger before flipping off the elites in power.

But first, a little story.

A story way back in 2001, ancient of days and land of vampires and hooded hoodrats wielding double-bladed axes.

Living in close proximity to the housing projects of New Orleans, most days driving back from the University of New Orleans were uneventful. For the most part. Only Mardi Gras seemed to break the monotony along with eating soggy beignets (powdered donuts) on Bourbon Street.

Except for one day in particular while sweating in Manila-like traffic. On that day something terrifying happened. I decided to take a shortcut which turned out to be a shortcut into trouble for no sooner that I sped towards home that a fourteen-year-old girl, black with ripped jeans, red sweatshirt and a nose that could put a bloodhound to shame ran in front of my beat-up Camaro while I drove 15MPH.

I slammed on the brakes and missed her hip by an inch. She slammed her fists on the hood of my car. Boom. Then she flipped me off real casual like this sort of thing happened every time it rained. I hopped out, furious, and proceeded to make sure she knew how damn close she'd come to a date with the grim reaper.

A cacophony of yelling ensued with every color of the rainbows.

Soft swearing, hard swearing, and sweating (mostly me) as she matched every curse word with one better, more deviant, and fueled with twice the rage as though she'd been bred for no other reason than to unleash it all upon me on that fiery summer day. A vampiric Lady Macbeth, this thuggette was. But none of that really mattered to the law. No sir, what mattered was when I grabbed her arm and stabbed a finger into her face as I shouted to be more careful. I began to walk away.

Only I wasn't going anywhere.

Her brother came running. A BIG brother wearing a dozen gold chains and carrying a chain big enough to tie a velociraptor. I swear the guy looked straight out of the A-Team. After that, her mother came screaming and what I presumed at the time was her grandmother, broom in hand (a witch?). I panicked as the big brother threw me to the ground as mama called the cops. I remember expecting a black cat to come along any minute to scratch my face to shreds. I was going down in flames though I was innocent of any abuse.

Fast-forward three weeks later and I'm having my ass handed to me by the most militant feminist judge I'd ever laid eyes on. A real manhater whose harpy-like claws seemed to grow the more I sweat. I had only one choice: Play along. So I kissed ass like I'd never in my whole miserable life. At the end of her screeching rant, I ended up getting off on a technicality. The police had screwed up somewhere, it seemed.

My record was as clean as a babe's arse. Clear as as crystal... or so I thought until later that year a detective came knocking. It seemed that the little girl had disappeared and to my horror, found he knew everything about me. Things that were not in the court transcript. Things I'd done were recorded by various cameras set up around the city. The entire city seemed to be turning a shade Orwellian.

"Talk to me," he said smiling with that shiny badge gleaming. I frowned. Talk to the cops? "Yeah," he replied. "Talk to me or get put on the sex offender's list for abusing that little girl."

Abuse?

I clammed up. Granted, I was native, but not stupid. He ended up letting me go after throwing down every threat imaginable. After that I wanted to vanish even more, and as I would later learn, I wasn't the first to go through such an ordeal.

Up until that point, I'd always trusted the police, or for that matter any kind of higher authority in government. I trusted the media. I trusted newspapers. I trusted juries. About the only thing I never trusted were the palm readers who always set up shop around the French Quarter.

Well, no longer.

From that point on, I swore to myself I'd learn how to be invisible, or die trying. True, I escaped the sex offender registry by keeping my mouth shut. Others have not been so lucky. I've heard another author (Wendy McElroy) relate a similar story:

"Last summer, an Illinois man lost an appeal on his conviction as a sex offender for grabbing the arm of a 14-year-old girl. She had stepped directly in front of his car, causing him to swerve in order to avoid hitting her.

The 28-year-old Fitzroy Barnaby jumped out his car, grabbed her arm and lectured her on how not to get killed. Nothing more occurred. Nevertheless, that one action made him guilty of "the unlawful restraint of a minor," which is a sexual offense in Illinois. Both the jury and judge believed him. Nevertheless, Barnaby went through years of legal proceedings that ended with his name on a sex offender registry, where his photograph and address are publicly available. He must report to authorities. His employment options are severely limited; he cannot live near schools or parks"

Here I was thinking I was the only guy that had experienced such a horrific day. The absurd part is not even that it happened. It's that it is never forgiven. It's never put in the past where mistakes are buried. They are broadcasted forever, branded over and over into our memories. Forgiveness (i.e. granting your past actions invisible to everyone but you and the Almighty) is outlawed.

Well. This book aims to reverse that trend. It aims to give you back your privacy and if you need it, **invisibility**.

You don't want newspaper reporters sticking mics in your face before you've had your day in court do you? That happened to me. I remember feeling like I'd killed everyone's favorite rock star though I'd never set foot anywhere near the concert.

Think on how your life would change if any of the following happened to you:

• Someone uses your unsecured WiFi to threaten the President.

• A hacker steals your credit card to purchase Russian child porn using proxies.

• You hear sirens just as your phone rings. You pick up to hear a news journalist asking for an interview since you were the last person to see the Governor alive at the Beau Chene Golf and Racquet Country Club (who was later found dead in a pool of blood in the restroom - the same you used!)

• The powers that be are coming after you for child support-- without allowing you to see your own children. You try to visit Canada to "get away from it all" for a while, when you are *arrested* at the border. Things get worse when they find a few "manga" comics in your back seat. Manga that is illegal in Canada but not the USA. Chaos ensues. They rip your reputation apart in the name of *the law*.

• Your ten year old brother jokes to his pals on the school yard that he has a shed full of Rambo-like grenades and a few barrels of gunpowder. A girl overhears. She snitches. The cops arrest him (not kidding) but later let him go. Years later, that report shows up when he tries to join the Marines. He is *rejected*. Yes, This really happened to a relative in Louisiana. And that's not to say Louisiana is any better or worse than any other state where hysteria can run amok and drag you along for the ride. The fact is, I'll show you how to prevent crap like this from happening **no matter which country you are in**.

If you are ever investigated, the authorities will likely tear your place apart looking for anything from which to build a solid case to hand to the prosecutor. Who knows what your situation might be at that time. You might need to go away for a while to strategize with attorneys, maintain your business, speak to family, move assets, etc. It is difficult to do that from a jail cell.

The USA now has a "guilty until proven innocent" legal system. You are not innocent, but I will teach you to gain that precious commodity called TIME which you can use to gather resources to defend yourself.

Resources that go well with becoming **invisible**.

You will learn:

1.) How to be anonymous *offline* as well as on.

2.) How to use your surroundings to lessen risk, special forces style.

3.) How to detect when you are being data-mined: How to hide where you went to school, where you've lived, whom you've loved, whom you did not. Your shopping habits, dating habits, political affiliations. You get the picture.

4.) How to look like a small fish and not a BIG FISH.

And that's just the beginning.

BURN NOTICE & SKIP TRACERS

Burn Notice is one of my favorite TV shows. I don't watch much TV but I do if that show is on. I'd stop to watch it even if a mugger came in and stuck me in the ribs before making off with my wallet. It's that grand. It's thrilling. It's top notch espionage and underground battle-of-the-wits style American James Bond. Sort of like True Lies, but with better looking agents.

The 'burn notice' itself usually comes from an intelligence agency, but can be from any alphabet agency really. It doesn't even need to be on paper. You can get 'The Call' while on a mission in Iran or Brazil or Eastern Europe. What happens is this: The CIA calls you up and at the most inopportune moment tells you they wish to 'wash their hands of you'.

You're done. You're cooked. You're career as an agent is finished.

They cut the umbilical quick and every connection to an agent is severed in true Mission: Impossible fashion. And all for what, you ask? Easy. So they can save face. Any agent has no idea what he did (well maybe a few might have an idea) but he knows he has no work history, no connections, no support and no cash. Poor guy is BURNED. For good.

Well, sort of. If some bigwig at the FBI wants info on him, he can get it from said agency if he has enough pull and the person is a high-value target.

As I watched this show for years I kept thinking: Wouldn't it be great to give yourself your own 'Burn Notice'? Disappear from society altogether? Get a fresh start with new name, new job, the works, in some country where pretty Filipinas fall out of coconut trees as you sit on a beach drinking margaritas?

Well okay, maybe not *that* extravagant. Perhaps it's more simple for you. You want to keep the collector's off your back while you grow a business to pay back your student loans. Start a new relationship. Get away from an abusive wife wielding a double-bladed axe.

It's all rather easy to speculate but difficult to implement. We like our safety nets. We like our 'safe jobs', and a lot of guys don't like losing money in online ventures. So they play it safe. They refuse to take risks. Then one day when they need to leave the country, they can't because they took no action.

Then there are skip tracers to worry about.

Skip tracers? What're those, they ask? From wiki.

Skip tracing tactics may be employed by debt collectors, process servers, bail bond enforcers (bounty hunters), repossession agents, private investigators, attorneys, police detectives, and journalists, or by any person attempting to locate a subject whose contact information is not immediately known. Similar techniques have also been utilized by investigators to locate witnesses in criminal trials.

Before we deal with skip tracers, a word of caution: NEVER fake your own death or disappearance since doing so will bring more heat on you than if you shot Dirty Harry in the ass. Even a simple disappearance can lead to a statewide manhunt, or womanhunt in the case of Leanne Bearden who after a 2-year globe-trotting vacation vanished one hot Texas day.

"I'm going for a walk. Be back in one hour!" were her last words. She hung herself from a tree in a wooded area close to her in-laws home. Police helicopters, dogs, and even state troopers spent hundreds of hours looking for her (no suicide note), fearing she'd been snatched and kidnapped. I sat stunned at all the Youtube comments calling for the husband's crucifixtion, and all without any evidence he'd done anything.

Don't do this.

Don't kill yourself over bad debts. Don't do it over unemployment (apparently why the woman hung herself). Don't do it over a failed marriage (taken the Red Pill, yet?). Don't fake your own death and try to buy fake IDs from Craigslist. If you try to cross the Canadian border with a fake passport (because we know how nice those border officers are on the Fourth of July with a thousand Canadian-made cars in line to shop), that **one guard** can ban you for **life**. Ask George Bush what happened when one tries to cross with a DUI record. He had to get a waiver. But more on this later.

Instead what we want to do is plant false leads that end in Nowhereville for any Skip Tracer hot on your trail. That's what the next few chapters are about. Getting somewhere while leading any skip tracer or other investigator to believe they're on a wild good chase.

A WORLD WIDE WEB OF DECEIT

Your most prized tool in seeking information is also your enemy's most prized tool for seeking your loss of freedom be it handcuffs, garnishments or even asset forfeiture, to which the ATF has turned into a profit-industry. Your neck is out there online as naked as the day you were born.

Being the smart cookie you are, you know it isn't rocket science to vanish online. Lots of guides explain how to cloak your identity using all kinds of tools. Tor for starters. Most computer literate people know of it. Then there's chatting on Freenet. That's not so easy. Then there are VPNs that hide your IP address. You can even chain proxies to post encrypted messages on Usenet with them if you know how to buy services anonymously.

But those guides rarely tell you what pops up when a seasoned skip tracer simply keys in your home phone number or alias into a search engine and starts calling every person you've ever known. That's the part even the encryption experts forget about: That which is right under their very noses. Tracers, like collections, will harass everyone on your city block about you. And boy do they lie. They lie with more skill than the Devil himself!

Let's talk about aliases. I'd bet good money that you or your kids use the same alias on Facebook and Twitter that you do on Usenet and The Pirate Bay, or some combination thereof. Maybe something cool like Windsong. You'll switch it up a bit on other sites, maybe go by Windsinger or some such. Oh there might be an extra number or two here and there, but we humans are creatures of habit. We don't like hard work and having multiple *different* aliases for every social media... well some of us just cannot be bothered because that's too much work for us to do. Mistake numero uno.

To prove a point to one of my beautiful nieces in Louisiana, I had her type in a nic she uses on Twitter and P2P. It wasn't just her P2P messages that popped up but those she'd typed on Usenet as well - messages from long dormant times when she was a wee pre-teen. As it turned out, Google indexes Usenet messages from decades ago. I almost felt bad for showing her Usenet at such a young age. And believe me, most of us Usenet guys back then never in a million years believed we'd have 7 year retention rates offered by Usenet farms.

But the real danger was using that same nic across the board on several social media sites.

One website allows you to look up people based on name alone. We found a dozen, yes... a dozen Americans in the south with the exact same name as her but not one with the same nic. Anywhere in social media.

The nic? LinuxGrl.

Any Skip Tracer worth their salt might think she has a nerd gene (she does). She loves coding C++, Java, too. She loves The Matrix and adores the little blonde hacker geek from Jurassic Park like a long lost sister. Any Skip Tracer would find her messages sprawled across the net on every tech forum known to man. She's quite open about her age, too.

When we looked at all the info, it lead a trail right to her bedroom. So many years and so many clues build quite the profile.

She freaked out as any red-headed teenager would but only because she feared they might find out which boy she has a crush on.

"Ye gods!" I snapped. "That's all you're worried about?" To which she replied, "What else could happen?"

We were even able to find out from these messages where she meets her fellow high school geeks for PvP Warcraft and Fallout marathons (the pen and paper game, not the PC RPG).

IP ADDRESS SEARCHES

Be cautious about skipping privacy protection if you have an online business. Skip Tracers can execute a simple online WHOIS search that often reveals who owns the domain, which would be *you*. They may even gain your address. If they cannot find the domain owner outright, they may be able to follow clues you've left in your posts. But you'd never be so careless as to leave your real name, right?

Right. But the problem isn't you. The problem is *your relatives. Your friends. Your business associates.* Your ex-lovers. A clever Skip Tracer will lie to fish the info out of them.

And they always sugar-coat it, appearing as someone who wants to help you - an angel of light and niceness and puffy clouds: A prospective employer. A lawyer looking to give away inheritance money (yeah, right). A movie director who wants to offer you the role of a lifetime.

You may hear a lot of affiliate marketers say that it doesn't matter if you have WHOIS protection or not, but I disagree. If you want to shield yourself, and by extension, your freedom (the secret to happiness btw), then you need to not leave a money trail to your front doorstep.

Got a speeding ticket recently? That will show up in a public court record. And those records are not difficult to get. Anything that happens on public, tax-funded roads is often available to any Joe Blow who wants it. That includes fender-benders, drug busts and well, anything that involves you pleading to a judge.

A big danger is privately owned property. That is, property that can be taken away from you by the IRS, the Dept of Education, your Uncle Frick who works for the EPA.

Loose lips sink ships. Who else knows about the land but you? Relatives? Friends? How easily can a Skip Tracer contact them about your land--which they so desperately want to buy for a million dollars (oil?)?

Worse, you might be tempted to put this land on a bank loan application as collateral. Don't do that either. Such things are available to the public eye. Not the account numbers mind you but your name and address. If you want to be invisible, don't go taking your elvish cloak off in Mordor where any green-skinned orc can sniff you out and ambush you.

KNOWLEDGE IS POWER

Knowledge is power. Or rather, knowledge is **potential** power. That's the crux of it alright as collectors and skip tracers must rely on your ignorance. In fact they prefer you not know your rights so as to better fuel whatever fear tactics they employ.

Let's say you see the writing on the wall and in six months you will default on a student loan. You feel helpless. You know the collectors will be coming. You know the phone will be ringing. You know they will be calling your employer to harass you and your friends, your family, so what can you do?

Allow me to sound like a broken record: Knowledge is power. They rely on your ignorance and assuming your lender won't work with you and your Ombudsman is fond of Houdini acts, there are a few steps you can take to minimize grief.

If your name/address is scattered over social media like pepper on eggs, then you need to remove it before the slime-skinned collectors get a hold of it.

- Study the FDCPA like your livelihood depends on it (which it does). Know what they can get away with and what they can't. Remember, knowledge is power. If you wield it, they will respect it

- Check your aliases. Are they the same on every social media website? Is your phone number visible? What about your email? Can a collector or any stranger for that matter view your private info on Facebok? How about Twitter? LinkedIn?

- This above all: ask for any debt or claim to be given in writing. Student loans? Ask for a copy of the promissory note. Often they will NOT have this information. They will give every deadbeat excuse in the world so as not to send it and believe me friend I have heard that ALL:

"We don't have to send that." (A lie)

"We'll send it next week." (Another lie. If that's true, ask her to send you a screenshot)

"You need to setup an automated payment plan first." (BIG LIE)

Always contest the debt and NEVER send a payment until you GET THAT promissory note or bank loan with your signature.

Also, look into these and know what they cannot do

Gramm-Leach Act - Legislation that limits the abuse they can leave on your message machine. Many collectors don't pay heed to this at all. Call them on it!

Fair Debt Collection Practices Act

Telephone Consumer Protection Act

The double-edged sword in all of this is that saying: "Please do not call me again!" This does not work. You must issue this in writing to the bank. It's called a no-contact order. Sometimes it works, sometimes not.

A close friend of mine happened to secure a lucrative deal (by her standards anyway) as an extra on a movie set in Los Angeles. He was an extra with a few speaking lines. Not much to brag about down at Igor's bar but it was a good amount for a day's work: $500. As luck would have it, her effort to pay down her student loan went awry. The collector called her mother and a few friends and managed to get the number of someone on the set. Snakes are clever!

You can imagine what happened.

The whole set had to stop filming to allow her to answer that stupid call. So never underestimate what those hucksters will do to your reputation, and prepare accordingly.

HOW TO CREATE AN ANONYMOUS BANK ACCOUNT

One wintery night when few were paying attention, the Canadian Parliament decided to pass a budget bill containing the single most wicked act of treason in western history.

It's name is FATCA (Short for FATCAT). Developed by Obama, Harry Reid and Nancy Pelosi in 2010 with a fully compliant Democratic Congress, it's workings are the kind of thing a superpower might enact in a sanctions bill against a terrorist state like Iran or North Korea, certainly not Canada. And when you get right down to it, it is an act of financial war - mandating every bank in Canada fork over the financial information of *any* Canadian with US citizenship. It's passed to the Canadian Tax Service, then to the IRS - the same who demand all Canadians with U.S. citizenship to file and/or pay taxes to the US despite not ever living there.

Things like this are a slippery slope to civil wars and revolutions. Worse, the Canadian Parliament did not resist in selling out it's own people. One politician in Parliament claimed "We had no choice as we had thirty days to decide or face a 30% penalty on all investments in the USA."

In other words, they were "just following orders."

Where've we heard that before?

At any rate it seems that Big Brother is alive and well and Judas himself could not have orchestrated a sharper backstab. A few Canadians have filed a federal lawsuit to be sure, claiming it to be unconstitutional (it is), but even if the suit is successful and the law overturned, banks will not be in a hurry to revert their systems as it is so expensive.

But make no mistake: If you are a US citizen, they want to know so as to rat you out to the IRS for not paying taxes in two countries. In essence, for not being a nice little lemming with wrists outstretched. This is a problem for those who love freedom, and by extension, happiness, to say nothing about those who love anonymity.

HIDING ASSETS

If you want to hide valuables from a spouse and do not mind **tangible** assets, look into opening an anonymous deposit box overseas. It is still technically an "account" but Das Safe, located in Vienna, does a good job of preserving your privacy and demand no ID from you. Bear in mind though that if you lose your key, it's tough to retrieve another one.

Also be aware that anything sitting in an overseas vault is not convenient. It is time-consuming to get it, sell it, convert it to gold or cash and retrieve it and all paying attention to leaving no financial trail. But then financial anonymity has never been cheap. You have to weigh the needs of an emergency to your need of invisibility.

Other Options:

Bitcoin

You can go the Bitcoin route and buy currency, but you will face stiff fees as Paypal is a high-risk method when the two are paired. And there is a tough learning curve if you're not good with computers. Nevertheless, there are guides that can walk you through it but Bitcoins are not anonymous by themselves.

Ptshamrock

Here you can buy an anonymous debit card and other items. They are legitimate and have been around for years, however are not cheap, nor are they perfect. Blackhat marketers sometimes use them.

Ocra

Ocra outfits offshore investments, trusts and foundations for, as they term it, "Wealth Protection" and "International Business". You may find they offer something you need.

As you can see, there are downsides to just about every facet of anonymous financial accounts. What we have not discussed is *accessing* any of those accounts online. This is dangerous and should be avoided. But (sigh) there are times when you simply must get access to an online account and be **secure** doing it. Here's how:

1. A VPN (Virtual Private Network). Trial versions abound. You need this to shield yourself from search engines, *not* the government. For that, use Tor. Buy the VPN, the price of which is usually under ten bucks, then install Tor.

2. Tails/Tor downloaded to a memory stick if you're truly paranoid. My Tor book gives details if you want lengthy examples but this above all: never reveal any personal data.

3. Anonymous Debit Card, Loadable. If you load the card with cash, you must not do so within your own town.

STUDENT LOANS

English majors, perhaps more than any other major (except Gender Studies), make up the bulk of criticism for student loan debt. It goes well beyond snide comments made at the office. Politicians have come out slandering liberal arts majors in general but you never hear them criticize STEM degrees, nor do they mention how brutal those programs are when Professor Punjab wants to shrink his incoming Biology class by 85% to free up some research time. We've all heard the usual questions.

"Why did you not study chemistry or engineering? Or go for an MBA? Maybe an M.D.?" they ask you.

Often, these stone-throwers neglect to do any research on these other STEM degrees. If they did, they'd realize that they take out just as much, if not more, debt than their liberal arts brethren. Automation coupled with outsourcing is making *every* degree irrelevant, some faster than others. Even medical students are graduating with $200,000 in student loan debt. That's debt that is neither dischargeable in bankruptcy nor easy to pay off as they:

- Garnish your wages (but not before slandering you to your work colleagues)

- Seize your assets
- Crucify your relationship with your employer

Now it is *everyone's* problem.

The main problem students face, and one we will eradicate, is this: how does one work off the debt without being terrorized? Better yet, how does one make a *fresh start* when they've absolutely exhausted all options save that of stringing themselves up from the nearest tree?

In short, how to disappear at least temporarily so you can grow a business that enables the paying off of said debt? Any businessman will tell you, debt will **kill any business**. You might be chuckling to hear this, wondering if such a thing is even *possible* for an English major.

"Pay off a student loan to the tune of a hundred grand by... writing, you say? Impossible!"

It most certainly is possible. I know this because my brother did it, but not before teaching him how to keep those baying bloodhounds at bay. Knowledge is 80% of the battle. That is, how to fight back. I showed him. He showed *them*. And I will show *you*.

TAX OFFSETS

Unless you live in Canada, any federally defaulted student loan will likely result in a tax offset by the IRS if it isn't dealt with. Cutting off communication works only if you've got leverage. If not, they take your tax return unless you happen to be self-employed (more on that later). Worse than this is when you are garnished *and* get a tax offset. Let's first discuss what legal options you have.

A few points:

- Your spouse can have her tax return taken as well even if she did not cosign the loan. She *can* however file an injured spouse form and send it to the IRS. Not the best option.

- You can **challenge** the offset using this link. It's difficult and for this to be successful you need to prove validity as to why the offset should not occur. Here are some valid reasons:

1.) You've already paid the debt prior to them kickstarting the offset

2.) You're disabled (not temporarily)

3.) You've recently claimed bankruptcy

4.) You view the debt as unenforceable

Real problems arise when people put off challenging it. They ignore all warning signs and only at the end realize how serious it is. Therefore, *prevention* is paramount if we want to avoid collection agencies.

Prevention: The Department of Education's Worst Enemy

Be aware that if you try to outsmart the Dept of Education, you will have a tough time of establishing a reputation for your business if you want to expand (i.e. borrow money). Anonymity will be your calling card, and you will always be looking over your shoulder in the USA. Problem is, creditors you ask for money don't like anonymity. It may get so difficult that you are tempted to leave for Canada, either to take up a student visa, work visa or to seek permanent residency there.

Other digital nomads have done this and succeeded. They're all over the place in every sense of the word. Some work for Odesk and eLance while others go the affiliate route, but not without jumping major hoops. That should be the last resort since you don't want something preventing you from using your passport.

That said, let's discuss how to prevent an offset so we don't get into that *very long* minefield of red tape.

Consolidation

Assuming you don't qualify for forgiveness, the Direct Loan program can be your ticket out of this mess if you're not too deep in the hole. One option is to group your loans together which would take your loan out of default and put it in good standing. The other is IBR, or Income Based Repayment. If you're making pennies working at 7-Eleven, then you will likely pay nothing. Nada. Zero. But the time to get approved can take one to three months. You can do the math at the link below:

http://www.ibrinfo.org/calculator.php

The other thing to remember about consolidation is that your interest rate must factor into any decisions you make. My advice is to wait until you are out of school before accruing additional loans by consolidation - when the interest rate is locked at a low amount.

Rehabilitation

Many students apply for rehabilitating their loans, which takes nine months. Talk with your lender to work out a payment plan. When the rehab process is complete, default status is changed to good standing. At issue is this: students are eligible for taking out massive student loans (again!) which does not help the situation.

Forbearance: This should be the last bullet in your holster. If all of the above fails, you can put your loan into forbearance. This helps stave off the vampiric collectors but with a terrible price: excessive interest! We're talking biblical revelatory interest here, called capitalized interest that will kill any business before it gets off the ground. Then there are fees the lender likes to tack on. Debt slavery is alive and well.

Those are the legal ways to deal with student loans.

The shady way is to just let them default. If you go this route, they will call and harass you dozens of times per day. They will hound your relatives and friends and colleagues. It will show up on a credit report for a potential employer to see. And that's not even the most absurd part. Want to know what it is?

Okay, here it is: They're not really interested in you paying them back. They're interested in you putting them back into deferral/forbearance so they can charge you insane *interest* (which they fleece the taxpayers to pay).

Bottom line: Pay something. Anything. Even fifty dollars a month. Heck even ten dollars a month by money order is something traceable you can show a judge, heaven forbid it should ever come to that.

SOCIAL SECURITY NUMBERS

If you've ever spent time googling your own name, you know how easy it is to find *other people* with the same name as you. I googled my own and found a pepper-bearded lawyer in Tennessee with the exact same name that I have. Same age. Same name. Different looks and different jobs. I write for a living. He sues people for a living.

But we have different social security numbers. He probably uses his for just about everything under the sun, including applying for work before he went lawyering up. I don't. Reason being is that I don't like where I sleep and fart being known by every red-headed harpy named Betty who works in HR. So to that I've used a fake address for as long as I remember. When I didn't have the luxury of using my own, I used my friend's address.

As any privacy-minded man should.

<u>Employment</u>

Back in 2008 when Obama took office and the economy nose-dived, I applied in person to some 600 jobs to supplement my income. I must have lost a hundred pounds hitting the pavement. The overwhelming response in 98% of the jobs I applied for?

Apply online.

It mattered not what establishment I went to. FedEx. Home Depot. Publishers. Newspapers. They all said the same thing: Apply online. Apply online. Apply online. I heard those two words so much that I began to see them in my digital alarm clock, blinking like some countdown on a thermonuclear device. Worse was the fact that many asked me for my social number *before* being hired. I found it all appalling and disrespectful of someone's privacy.

Never, ever give this out before you are hired. Doing so will set you in the crosshairs of any collectors/PIs out there looking to gun you down. The two jobs I did secure hired me despite that I'd given an obvious fake social number prior to hiring (1234-56-7890). The interviewer (a man) could have cared less though I did fork over my real one when they said, "Welcome aboard."

Things to Avoid

Universities

When I attended the University of New Orleans, the SSN was used for nearly everything. Checking out books. Scheduling classes. Asking for grade transcripts. I worked in the Financial Aid office and there, too, I found few students were referred to by name. You were just a number. I would call up to schedule an appointment and the first thing they'd say, before anything else:

"What's your social?"

Pathetic.

Even more pathetic was that anyone who worked in the UNO system had access to this number. It mattered not how secure the system was against identity theft because any schmuck who'd just transferred in could work in any department he wanted as long as the work-study money was there. Free money, they called it.

Taxpayer money.

Be careful about throwing this number around like monopoly money.

Class Rosters

This was another biggie.

On my way to the restroom, I happened to notice one professor had every student's SSN beside their name on the class roster. I began to wonder why this was, and if other professors did the same for all other classes. Sadly, there wasn't anything I could really do about this at the time.

Computer Labs

Back when we used a VAX system at UNO (around the time Netscape became popular), we had to use our SSN to login. This same login scheme was how one Harvard student was busted in 2014 when he used Tor to send a bomb threat... out of sheer boredom! Not too bright.

The other threat is that students walking by you in a lab setting can see you type it out. Heck they can even see you from behind since in many labs the chairs are fitted close together to accommodate a sea of new students every semester. Avoid this if you can by logging in from your own laptop.

Grades Listed Outside Class

I was a pre-med gunner before I got smart and quit. In my freshman chem class, grades were posted outside the classroom in the hall, listed with everyone else's social security number. I watched in disarray as many a student slid his finger down the list to see his grade. If I was the nefarious type, it would have been a no-brainer to match the kid with the social number and execute the beginnings of a clever identity theft scheme.

I scratched mine out with a Sharpie marker.

<u>Dorms</u>

My first semester of college had me and my brother lugging my few meager possessions up six floors of my dormitory. But prior to that, I had to check in. Only checking in was done *outdoors*, just outside the entryway.

I had to present my driver's license to show I wasn't some old cajun bum dropout from culinary school to shack up with the girls going to and fro. They checked my name on a paper roster to see which room I had been assigned (I requested a single room... they laughed). And there next to my name was my SSN. Wonderful, I thought. That number again.

There have been a few incidents with SS numbers being stolen over the years and used for all kinds of mischief overseas.

Now you might be thinking, why would someone go to all that trouble? Steal someone else's social security number so they can do... what exactly?

Well, I'll tell you. If you're a criminal, the best thing in the world is to steal someone else's identity. For this reason, you should never, ever use someone else's number. That other person can be on the FBI's Most Wanted list and the day you find that out will be too late without them charging you with identity theft *yourself*.

CHANGING YOUR NAME

<u>Changing Your Name Stateside</u>

Changing your name isn't difficult. It's getting a new SSN that's a pain. It isn't like reaching into a bag of Skittles. More often than not, it's done by a court order. The requirements are beyond strict, placing the burden of proof on you, the ever law-abiding citizen... One being that you must prove to a court of law that you are in danger of losing your life. And you need to *prove* it, not just say it. This might be an abusive spouse who tried to kill you or the FBI's Witness Protection Plan or some such, but the social security number will likely stay with you without this.

Here is what the government says about getting a new SSN.

We do not routinely assign different Social Security numbers. Generally, only the following circumstances are used to assign a different number:

Sequential numbers have been assigned to members of the same family and are causing problems; More than one person has been assigned, or is using, the same number;

An individual has religious or cultural objections to certain numbers or digits in the original number;

A victim of identity theft continues to be disadvantaged by using the original number; or

Situations of harassment, abuse, or life endangerment, including domestic violence, has occurred.

White Lies

Privacy advocates, no matter how careful, cannot get around the SSN requirements on FAFSA forms without risking them saying no. If you use a fake SSN, you can be charged with a felony. So what to do?

What you do is lie to *everyone else*. For instance:

There was a time when I was contacted by a collection agency. TransMediaCorp or some innocuous name. Usually when a collection agency calls, if you listen closely you can hear all the other script monkeys banging away on their keyboards in the background, chatting away (mostly lies). My answer was to lie right back to them.

"Is this Mr. X?" agent Betty asked.

"Mr. Who?" I shot back. (Always, always get them to repeat it!)

She repeated. I feigned deafness. "Say it once more?"

She did and at that point, I corrected her, saying she had the right first name but the wrong *last name*. It was misspelled and mispronounced. I feigned being insulted.

They had the wrong guy. Tough break. She then asked for my SSN. I gave her a false one for the simple reason that as soon as you **identify yourself** (it is after all the FIRST question they will ask), you paint a blood-red target on your back. They've matched the name with a legal address. From there, it will be one perpetual nightmare after another.

The amount in question was a $500 Perkins student loan I had paid off years earlier, and one that I'd taken on some 25 years ago. But I wasn't about to tell *her* that. God knows if I did, they might consider the debt paid after I faxed proof of payment, but not before they relayed my name to other collection agencies for *their* databases.

After this episode, I called up every service provider I could think of that held my SSN and had it changed to the fictitious one. Cable company. Electric. Internet Service Provider. It turned out that even the company that mows my lawn had it on file. Who knows how they got it, but only one company gave me grief over the change: the power company. So I handled it in writing, making sure to use plenty of CAPS and BOLD words filled with sound and fury (signifying nothing, now that I think about it). Some people can better sense a bluff over the phone than by mail.

By mail, you can sound like Tony Soprano and if you don't get some action you will send the boys over for a *polite little talk.*

Clone Home

One option you might employ is using a mail service that severs any connection to you. Examples abound of companies you can hire who ask very few questions. A few ask *zero* questions. I've had good experiences with earthclassmail.com, for instance, but there are others if you travel internationally.

Another idea is to check out abandoned houses where you live. Mostly this applies to city dwellers but I have found a few in rural settings, too. Use the address of the abandoned house to have any shipments/mail sent to you there. Just don't go using the same house over and over again.

It probably is a good time to repeat this: Never give out someone else's information on a credit card or loan application. Like, ever. This includes their address. In most first world countries this is a serious crime. Someone somewhere will get burned as one success will lead to another and it will become a habit that is as hard to get rid of as an alcoholic getting rid of margaritas in Maui. It can also destroy any chance you have if, at a later date, you want to legally get rid of debt via bankruptcy.

Lie, but lie responsibly!

PASSPORTS AND CANADA

This is an area I regret having personal experience in. Since 9/11, many systems have been built for inter-departmental communications yet airports *still* have lax security - especially the TSA. Border Stations are an interesting study and I dare say Canadian Border Officers are, fortunately, nothing like their lackluster TSA brethren. What gets flagged at one station gets flagged at them all. It's a little too Orwellian for my taste but I try to be respectful whenever I'm passing through.

If you drop attitude with the Canadian agent at the Niagara Falls crossing, the guard on the other side of the country can (notice I did not say *will*) know about it in minutes if he enters it into the system.

The SSN is tied to your name and employment but does not appear on the passport itself. But a border officer can ban you for LIFE if you lie about any criminal record entering Canada. They locked out George Bush from entering over a DUI he'd received in 1976. Not kidding. He had to get a waiver and that was just to *visit*, not actually move there.

Sneaking in carries risks too, unless you happen to be Nightcrawler from the X-Men and can teleport yourself in the blink of an eye across the Falls. As far as I know, I don't possess this ability.

What can we learn from this?

We can learn not to leave trails.

One option is to not use our passport since it leaves a trail just as visible as the sulfur did for Nightcrawler. But this is not very practical since it makes international travel problematic. Still, sneaking into Canada or into the USA does have its advantages if you have good reason to go off the grid. Many do. In fact, the U.S. border sees more sneak *into* Canada than the other way. From WinnipegPress:

"More people were caught trying to sneak into Canada at remote border points with the United States in 2008 than the other way around, a newly released intelligence report reveals.

It was the second straight year that continental human smuggling and other surreptitious crossings tilted in Canada's direction.

*The RCMP attributes the trend to factors including a U.S. crackdown on undocumented workers, more American agents along the border and the shaky state of the U.S. economy. The figures, the latest available, show 952 people were caught entering Canada between legitimate border crossings, while 819 were U.S.-bound. They work at strategic points between border crossings to thwart smugglers of everything from **people** and **drugs** to **currency** and **firearms**."*

Obviously, sneaking across is not a new trend. But let's assume you need to sneak into Canada and need to do it quietly, with no Orwellian tracking system sniffing at your heels. Let's also assume you are going it solo... with no assistance at all.

Without Assistance

Crossing outside of a checkpoint is very easy. Nothing to it in fact. But doing it anonymously, now that's *hard*. Harder in big towns. It's illegal to try and you might not get caught the first time. But most guys will keep doing what they think works the best and then rinse and repeat. If they succeeded on the first try, well dag nabbit they are ingenious! Rinse and repeat.

Bank robbers (usually) don't get caught the first time either. It's when they do it again and again using the same method that gets them caught. Their egos rocket into orbit. They get overconfident. They get cocky. In fact you could apply this trait to most low-level crimes, even non-violent ones like sneaking across.

The border itself looks like a typical power line cut, forests on each side, but the further you get from a town, the less guarded it is. But you should know the ecosystem of whatever area regardless if you plan to hike/drive/fly through because let's face it, it'd be quite a downer to make all that effort only to be the next contestant on Mr. Grizzly's 'You Bet Your Life'.

Most rural spots and undeveloped areas are heavily guarded by movement sensors. Trigger one of those and you'll alert the authorities.

Response time varies significantly, depending on population and distance to the nearest checkpoint and of course, **manpower**. All the technology in the world does the Borg no good if all of their Borg drones are overworked and stretched to the limit. This is in your favor.

It may be an hour or ten minutes before one arrives. If the latter, you'll walk a little ways before the border patrol drives up. After which you get to meet Officer Simon Sez who carries a semi-automatic rifle along with four of his buddies, one of whom will ask you point blank: "Do you realize where you are, sir?" To which you should

state with an innocent smile as you look around, feigning relief that
you happened upon this nice Canadian officer: "Hale no sir, I don't
believe I do. Can you please tell us?"

Politeness with a dash of respect (*always* saying sir) will win over
a Canadian border guard 80% of the time, assuming you're not
committing a crime, and you are if you're sneaking across!

But that's if you get lucky. If not, you'll be arrested and deported
if you don't have dual-citizenship. Not only will Canadian authorities
charge and fine you, so will American authorities. It's a $5000 US
fine and criminal record for circumventing a designated border
crossing.

With Assistance

Very much the easier of the two since it's not exactly rocket science to
get you across the border in either a privately owned plane or smaller-
than-usual boat or other watercraft. Better still if you're smuggled in
close to a Mohawk native reservation where cigarette smugglers get
picked up all the time (and overlooked) by Canadian border officials.

In the event you do try to cross, make sure it's not the 'easy path'
others take. It's all an illusion setup by the RCMP to catch you on a
well-worn trail. Most people caught do something stupid like crossing
at the Silver Lake Road area or farm land close to the Hunting-
don/Sumas crossing. Every time I hear of a bust, and the details that
come from that bust, I think of what T-Rex hunter Roland said in
Jurassic Park: Lost World when he tells Hammond's successor to
forget about setting base camp at their present location, a location
that's plagued with velociraptors.

"Listen, we're on a game trail and carnivores *hunt* on game trails!
Do you want to setup base camp or a buffet?"

Smuggling anything like contraband by way of car is foolish.
There are sensors at border crossings. Those include vehicle scanning
x-ray machines, chemical sniffers and sniffer dogs. So any attempt to
hide in a vehicle heading into Canada just won't work either. The

<u>GlobeandMail</u> ironically enough went into further detail on what not to do, even revealing that some hotels along the border are under surveillance for illegal crossers.

Bottom line: Don't ever go into velociraptor territory on the cheap!

ANONYMOUS PHONES

How the FBI Traces Calls

Not every average Joe who loathes the NSA has something illegal to hide, and I'm about as average Joe as you can get. I enjoy shrimp at Red Lobster. I love Mardi Gras in the French Quarter whenever I visit. I play video games with the kids down at the Fun Arcade. And sometimes I conduct business while they play on prepaid phones called **burners** while the kids play. Burners the NSA doesn't like. In fact they have a real hard time linking those phones to my real identity. It isn't impossible, mind you, only difficult. Since I am not a high-value target, they don't bother. At least, I *hope* they're not bothering.

Now then, you probably already know about MVNOs (Mobile Virtual Network Operators) that allow you to sign up pseudo-anonymously. They ask for no identifying info unless you want to give it to them - but that alone is not enough to thwart the NSA. Phone companies are now required to have the technology to work with law enforcement under the 1994 CALEA law.

Worse still is the fact that despite what appeals courts have said, we still have no real expectation of privacy. Most state law dictate that as long as one person knows about the recording, it is legal. Note I did not say one **other** person. Only one person... the one doing the recording. Wiretap laws are a maze of red tape that would make Stalin blush. The counter is this: not everyone uses the same phone.

That's in our favor.

The Cons of Using a Burner

You can pitch it in the trash after use and dissolve any trail to you. That's it, and even then.. as long as you took action to **conceal your activity**. The Craigslist killer was caught by the FBI visa cell triangulation--the GPS signals from his real phone and prepaid phone came from the same place. He even had it on him when he bought the burner phone. When he killed someone, both phones were easily traced since he had them on him when he committed the crime.

Not so smart, but then most criminals don't get caught the first or second time. They get caught on the *third, fourth* or *fifth* time (remember bank robbers?). The adrenaline rush addicts them to the point they're always looking for the next fix... often without upgrading their skillset.

The MAC address can kill anonymity as well. Like the IP address for computers tied to a network, it can lead right to your front door. There are apps like Macspoofer that aid in preventing this, but they are not perfect.

The Pros of Using a Burner Phone

Number one rule: Do not use it continually for any sensitive business or personal transactions. No more than a few days for something important. If you're on vacation in say, Singapore, and don't want the NSA spying on you and the kids, that's easy. Just switch the SIMs out upon arrival. Same for Philippines, Thailand, etc.

But for something like spying? That's a whole other discussion.

One might say, "Well, if I'm running a North Korean spy op, why not bypass any surveillance by having my entire team switch to newly bought phones at the same time?"

The problem with that is then you've created a clear pattern of a group of phones all activating at the same time. You might even get careless and give each operative the same phones. Further, if the police obtain the IMEI code off of the burner, then all SIM links previously attached to the phone are discovered. Good for them. Not for you.

You could even be outwitted if they visit the places they think you will buy the prepaid burners - obtain the IMEI numbers in advance so as to get a search warrant to eavesdrop on you. Boom. And you have to know that not all team members will dispose of the phones after every communiqué.

Problems, problems. So what to do?

Solution:

- Manage two persons responsible for managing all phones

- Buy phones from different locations, different days, different purchasers

- Swap phones out at different intervals from random locations (cell towers)

- Issue to operatives at different dates

- Operatives don't know when phones were activated

- Retire some phones unexpectedly, some sooner, after risky ops for example

- Each Op is given set of other Op's numbers, which changes daily

DISAPPEARING FROM SOCIAL MEDIA

Let's cut right to the chase. Social Media did nothing for me but make disappearing harder. With every passing year, Facebook wanted more data on me. More of my favorite childhood cereals (Chocolate Frosted Sugar Bombs, I told them - the favorite of Calvin and Hobbes). More of which movies made me cry. Which made me angry. Which made me cringe (the skeleton reveal in Psycho).

Employers love this about social media. They love that they can google your name and find all kinds of dirt on you from Ars Technica posts to Usenet flame wars you've participated in over the years. Once upon a time, Usenet was sacred. You didn't talk about Usenet. Now it's monitored by Chinese law enforcement. Yet things I wrote ten years back are visible to anyone. My inner child mutant came storming out, fists clenched, teeth gritted and spitting insults before the troll meme became fashionable.

While we can't exactly take a Delorean back to 1985 and start nuking old newsgroup posts, what you can do is take a flamethrower to the media giants who aren't doing your career any favors by allowing your ex to post photos of you so drunk in the French

Quarter that you performed mouth to mouth on a fainted carriage mule who you could swear winked at you as it went down.

Phase 1: Nuking the Sites From Orbit

I nuked my own Facebook account in May of 2010. Little did I know however that it wasn't truly gone. Instead, it went into a kind of hibernation state. Surprise, surprise. Facebook, like Google and LinkedIn and Twitter and YouTube all have this egregious habit of what I call vampire hoodwinking. They lull you into thinking your account is gone, when it really isn't. Nothing is really permanently gone with any of those behemoths. Not Google, Facebook or even LinkedIn. It'd take the fires of Mt. Doom to do to your account what it did to Frodo's ring.

But let's try anyway.

Facebook

Use this link to delete your account.
https://www.facebook.com/help/delete_account
This isn't like tossing out a batch of brownies when you're on a new diet. This effect is (supposedly) permanent. You're not going to get it back. You can't salvage anything for a new account. So contact lists, favorites, bookmarks, posts, pictures are all gone unless you saved them locally to your hard drive or dropbox. Now might be a good time to ask for some awkward pics to be taken down.

Twitter

Follow this link to deactivate your Twitter account. Like Facebook, once it's gone, it's GONE. But the process takes time. When I deleted one of my pen names, a horror pen that wasn't selling, it took *seven* days and a full moon. I never was good at writing omens.

Google+

For Google, go to the homepage here to deactivate. This will nuke your Gmail and Youtube accounts as well since they tie everything together, but you can be more selective <u>here</u> in what you wish to leave. They call it "Downgrading," but know that your identity might still pop up in search engines. Sucks, doesn't it?

I have personally found <u>AccountKiller</u> to be of high value here, as there were some accounts still active that I hadn't used in years, but a few that had stored my present phone number and address **publicly**. *Enhancements*, they claimed.

Phase 2: Nuking Criminal and Public Records

Now we come to the area where Skip Tracers love to dig, and dig DEEP. We're talking Gimli's drunken dwarf king deep who loves to delve in places he shouldn't (how'd that turn out for him?).

Without any background information, they will be chasing ghosts and wild geese to who knows where. Bad for them. Good for us. We'll nuke what remnants of our social selves are ripe for the taking -which in the end only hurt *us*, after all. As we go through these, realize this is a very short list and if there is one thing I love about Reddit, it's that they don't believe in short lists. The long version is <u>here</u>.

Here's the short version, i.e. the major players.

<u>Spokeo</u> - This is the big one. The one every Skip Tracer and collector uses by default. The amount of data they had on me made me want to retch my In n' Out burger! Former email addresses. Relationships. Marriages. Schools. For a few dollars more they'd probably tell a collector if I put ketchup on my fries or on the side. The kind of guys Agent Smith might call up to find where Neo was hiding.

<u>Intelius</u> - I was in this database too, but not for any criminal activity (whew!). Like Spokeo, they keep a lot of data on people

without their consent. Not Agent Smith's first choice, but if Spokeo is down... it is. They trawl social media sites as well as keep criminal data. Rumor has it mugshots are on the way. Are Christmas morning pictures next?

Zabasearch - I used this one once to find an old phone number I'd forgotten and didn't want to call up every friend to relay the new one. Later I found that this is THE site to use if you're a stalker since, after June 2014, emails containing personal info (not searchable by search engines) became publicly available. Ouch.

Going through every site that I'd given my data to over the last ten years was like trying to defect from a vampire clan. Easier said than done. They want something signed in blood. The worst however was hitting *paywalls* and *upsells*. You know, people who claim to save you *money* and *time*.

One site did seem to help shorten time taken to erase myself from the internet. That site is DeleteMe. At $129 bucks, it ain't cheap. But if you're strapped for time and don't mind the fee then it can be worth your while.

Staying Off The Radar

For the next two years you must be consistent with updates. Check those sites every few months for your compliance. Google your name. Your old phone numbers. Old addresses. Old flames. Your identity after all is more valuable to you than it is to them. To them, you're simply a number in a database, and if they had their way, wouldn't mind too terribly the thought of tattooing a number on the back of your neck.

From the moment of Armageddon, I've used Fake Name Generator for many things I do online. You can too. Yes, it does sound like some two-bit app on the Google Play Store that Babu wrote in Bombay one summer's day, but I assure you it isn't. It's quite effective.

If you want free, DISPOSABLE mail, try Mailinator (no relation to Arnold). No signup required. No passwords.

MOBILE APPS

Mobile phones and tablets that use WiFi are devious at hoarding every private detail of your life. Though it's nearly impossible to completely go off-grid with an online smart phone used for business, let's look at some options.

First up, there's Tor Browser

Bet you never knew this was available for Android. This app connects to the anonymous Tor network. Probably overkill for what we wish to do with social media, but helpful for anonymity nuts like me who like the ghost in the machine lifestyle. It spoofs the IP address you use and allows you to mask your own hardware.

Next, there's Spideroak.

If you like cloud-storage *and* privacy, check out Spideroak. It offers "zero-knowledge" security and has end-to-end encryption. The free plan gives you 2GB of storage. It's $10 otherwise for 100GB extra and goes up from there.

Next up is Red Phone. I like this app for it's ease of use whenever I'm in the USA. It secures every call with end-to-end encryption, allowing you privacy and peace of mind. As well it uses WiFi and offers neat upgrades if both callers have RedPhone installed.

It's not perfect, though, but at least it's not as expensive as say, TrustCall. There are convenience issues like lengthy connection times and dropped calls (ever Skype someone from Manila?) so it's not going to be as quick and easy as Jason Bourne does it in foreign locations.

But the pluses outweigh the minuses. I especially love the two-word passphrase as a security feature: If you fear Agent Boris is dead and has been killed by Agent Doris (who now has his phone), you can request she speak the second passphrase. Simple, yet effective.

Lookout - Lookout Security gives you the best protection against theft. Phone lost? You can login to the site at lookout.com to locate where a thief has taken your pone. Data backup is also a nice addition.

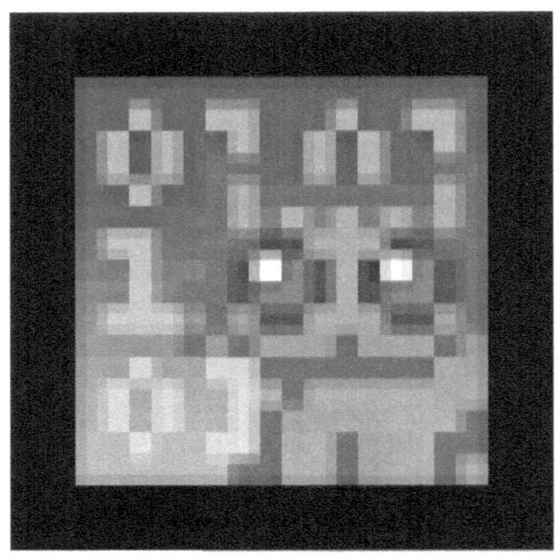

<u>CryptoCat</u> - Banned in Iran, Cryptocat is an open-source app that allows encrypted online chat. It employs end-to-end encryption so that you can trust your messages are private. Better still is that it can be used with Tor to *anonymize* your traffic. They also received top scoring in December 2014 on Electronic Frontier's security score benchmark with some stiff competition: ChatSecure, TextSecure, Silent Phone and Silent Text. Reason being is that all messages are not only encrypted, but that you can verify the other guy's identity without the company having access to it.

<u>BullGuard</u> - Bullguard offers anti-theft and backup similar to cryptocat but also offers SIM protections (auto-locks device if SIM is

removed), Call Management and Parental Controls (monitors your kids). Mobile security also lets you remotely manage your device.

Orbot - A free app that gives you anonymity with an Android device. I use it for my Galaxy Tab 4. Works well with Tor and wasn't hard to configure for my web browser, email client and Maps.Me app.

Wickr - An instant messenger for iOS & Android, it offers end to end encrypted messages that... self-destruct. Includes file attachments/photos, too. PC Magazine named Wickr an "Editors' Choice for Android secure messaging."

Titanium for PC and Android - Without a doubt my favorite app on my Android tablet for backups.

STALKERS

For some reason stalkers tend to be overwhelmingly male when Hollywood spits them out. I can count the number of female stalker flicks on one hand: Fatal Attraction. Misery. The Crush. Those're the ones I've seen. And they make the male ones look pale by comparison. Stick the knife into poor Jimmy and laugh in his face.

Not exactly realistic, though since they're always a thousand times worse on the silver screen than up close. Most stalkers are your next-door neighbor types. But sometimes, well... sometimes there's an exception. An anomaly if you will that slices to bits any preconceived notion of what a stalker looks and acts like. They break the rules.

What follows is my own story. It's one memory I can't quite seem to delete from my memory banks no matter how hard I try. And lordy, who knows why. Perhaps it's the dark element... the unknown. What COULD have happened. What she could have done had I not taken it as seriously as I did. Even now my fingers hurt from the constant flexing, cracked-knuckle strain I exert as I contemplate the telling of it all.

But I'll leave out the truly disgusting parts in case you've just eaten lunch.

The Bayou Grandma Stalker

The new house I'd rented was as good as any I guessed. Way out there, too, out near the bayou and close to La Place and juuust outside Kenner, Louisiana but far enough from the traffic and airport that it squashed any worries about jet engines overhead. But the mosquitoes, sweet Jesus were they big. Winged vampires with probos so damn big you'd swear you'd been shot in the buttocks with a poison dart like one of them pigmy tribes make.

My father had rented the place to parolees - mostly thieves from what I'd heard. Big time, small time, bank robbers, shoplifters, pimps. Didn't matter what kind. It'd been far enough out of town so as to limit temptation, he'd said, but a couple months passed with no takers. Enter yours truly on a 3-month dry spell in book sales and just generally unemployable for eons.

I still remember his words as he handed me the keys: "Don't turn the place into a dirty whorehouse. Sheriff don't like that." "Whore? What're those?" I asked. He smiled back. That toothless grin of his never put me at ease like it did when I was five, but now I knew how much of a hard ass he was.

I only paid a quarter rent in exchange for repairing the place, but lordy how I loathed crawling under the house to fix *anything*. It wasn't the tarantulas I feared. It was that dadgum Daddy-long-leg spiders that spooked me the most. Mobs! I'd bang out 1000 new words daily (my self-imposed quota at the time) and they'd bang out 10000 baby spiders as I typed the last word. On some dark nights I could swear I heard em popping out under the floorboards like popcorn in a microwave.

Pop-pop-pop-pop-pop-pop.

Then things got louder in July. Peeper frogs amid every god-forsaken bog noise in the universe kept me up. You'd think I'd have gotten use to em, but no. Afternoons were only slightly better. I made a promise to keep busy. I'd survey the property, check mail, repair pipes, try not to sweat too much as it killed my writing mood, when one day I noticed something off.

Some of my mail looked opened. In fact it looked *read*. That feeling, you know? Smudges. Strange scents. Like the kind church ladies wear on Sunday. Letters were out of order, too. Bills were upside down like someone'd repacked them after sticking a cherry bomb into the mailbox.

Humidity. Maybe.

I walked down the lonely road to meet the neighbor I'd put off meeting. A neighbor who lived in a house that *leaned* toward the airport, like the wood wanted to fly off and forever be rid of this frog-infested shithole. Spooky branches prevented this, of course. "You're staying here," the wood seemed to say.

Anyway I knocked and knocked. No answer. Went around back, knocked some more, ridged my forehead and looked around as I wiped away sweat and scratched. The bog seemed far quieter here despite La Place more than living up to its reputation as the Saharan desert of marshes.

I left a note, an invitation for the neighbor to come by and share a beer with me, the new guy (or an iced tea and a Bigfoot flick if a lady). A guy could hope, right?

After heading home I banged out 1500 more words and popped in The Thing as I kicked back a couple of Buds. "Where's Blair?" a voice said into the gloom. Ah, I'd forgotten the electricity had cut out midway the previous Saturday. I ignored the creaky boards under my feet and sank into the couch. Dusty as hell, it was like sinking into a puffy mushroom. The kind some British kids like to play soccer with.

Just when the movie got to the gross "Let's see who's The Thing" blood-test-by-self-inflicted-razor, I heard a noise. I sat up just as, once again, the electricity shut off.

Shit.

Then came a catty sound. Mauling. A yawning slow kind of sound. What the hell?

...scratch....scratch....scraaaaatch.

The door, I thought. I crept to the door over-thinking it as usual. A cat? Not a chance - too slow to be a cat. This was more like a *taunt*. A set of nails being dragged across a chalkboard to grate someone's nerves kind of taunt. My nerves.

I looked out the window. Darkness looked back at me and I started flexing my fingers and cracking my knuckle one-handedly. Think rational. Think logically. But the darkness was so thick it seemed stitched into the clothing of whomever had disturbed me. Intense camouflage. *Whoever* it was standing out there. I could swear I saw *something*. Something frozen so stuff and absolute it was as though dark matter had enveloped it. Despite this, I hated the thought of showing fear by running to get my revolver in the bedroom. No, I thought, and frowned chewing on my bottom lip. I'd face this punky prankster head on.

I swung the screen door open so hard it flew off the hinges.

The monolithic figure was gone. Not a soul stood there, nothing at all but boggy air. I stepped out and as I did waved the fog away. Nothing, absolutely nothing, made a sound. Not even peeper frogs.

A few days later I walked next door once more, determined as ever to find out if my neighbor knew of any rascally kids making mischief in these mossy parts. God knew they had nothing better to do.

This time I met her: a sweet old lady that could never harm a fly. She invited me in. She even made tea and biscuits. A British lady with a midnight cat straight out of Sleepy Hollow. Herself? Liverpool from the sound of it. Who knew but what I did know was that she had a class and a grace I couldn't quite match due to my swampbilly upbringing. I let her prattle on and simply nodded and hmm'ed and smiled rather than allow my lips to leak my ignorance.

French-Acadian lineages was the topic, her *spessscialty* apparently. Not my cup of tea but I listened anyway as she did most of the talking and I just sat there like a bump on a log soaking it all in. And that she did with a vengeance! Talked my ear clean off as frogs croaked outside.

Ten minutes into it, my mind wandered and I noticed a faint lisp. I stared at her wrinkled lips as they quivered and bounced from topic to topic and saw an oddity. No, not her lips. Her *tongue*. Her tongue looked cut. A small one to be sure, right at the tip that affected her speech. Was I seeing things? The day was hot and hazy.

A paper cut? I wondered.

The only time I'd ever done that myself was when I licked an envelope a little too fast.

Lightning struck.

She'd half-assed the licking of my envelopes somehow. When this light bulb bloomed in my head, I noticed her eyes widen and her speech crawl. I coulda sworn I heard her heart speed up as a dark narrative began to unroll in my thoughts. She knew I knew. She had to! It was written right there in her liquid-green eyes.

I excused myself to the restroom and on the way back cut through the kitchen and out of the corner of my eye saw a familiar name next to a Home Sweet Home frame with a few scattered nails. It was an open envelope with my name on it.

I grit my teeth so hard my loose tooth almost popped out. That crinkly old thief!

I paused to rub my chin, my neck, both my eyes. Maybe I was just imagining things, I told myself. Working too hard. Worrying too much. Swamp fever possibly... or perhaps the mailman simply slipped one into the wrong box. I'd done that myself a few times working campus mail back in the day.

But I just couldn't stomach the thought of that old bat, smart as she was, scraping through my mail. Scraping *my* things. Stabbing *my* privacy in the back. Stalking me. And for what reason? So I called her on it in as polite a way as I could fathom yet fully expecting a sincere apology, to which I'd apologize right back.

I was wrong.

Her face *changed* right before my eyes. I thought I was hallucinating at first. That maybe the old witch had poisoned my tea with some dart frog resin. Those sweet, elderly church fingers clenched as she stared at the floor coldly, the paleness of her jaw becoming steely, a kind of veil of jaundice sliding over her face. She seemed to be turning to stone! It was a look I had never seen even in a hardened criminal. A faraway, ancient look, like she'd just celebrated her 2000th birthday and here I was spoiling her party by not outstretching my own wrists. And when she fixed her cataract eyes on me, I nearly bolted for the door right then and there. She noticed this and said,

"Well now, dearie. It seems that you've c--"

Before she could finish, I tipped my old Port Authority cap and exited before she could finish. That was it. I was outta there, permanently.

Later when I asked my father to look into her past, it turned out she was anything but the nice, country granny I'd believed. She'd done time for murder, theft and chronic shoplifting. Oh, and slapping a judge as he sat in Preservation Hall just inside the French Quarter. Just walked right up to him. Brilliant. This on top of the sweet, sugar-coated lies she told me, smiling like a Cheshire cat right into my face.

I was forced to move three days later due to further circus-monkey antics.

The old crone stole my mail as though each and every one of them were sealed with liquid gold.

But there was more. She broke into my house while I vacationed way up in Thunder Bay, Ontario. I'd set up a hidden cam to silence my naysaying father hoping to catch her in the act and send her to the Big House once again with all the other harpies. Only I failed.

She'd spent hours simply rocking back and forth in my living room with her black cat (who kindly relieved himself behind my couch). My father laughed. Pointed, and laughed. But I was determined. I did some more digging.

It turned out she had a son that died a year prior running from police after a robbery. A son with a history of crime with a face *remarkably* like mine. I could sense some residue of reason behind her madness.

Only now I cannot watch John Carpenter's The Thing without smelling that darn cat.

So what did I learn from this? What can *you* learn?

I learned that stalkers come in all sizes and flavors of the rainbow and in all likelihood, will not be a stranger to you. You will know this person personally. They may even be in a relationship with you. Celebrities have the cash to deal with them: Catherine Zeta-Hones and Dave Letterman come to mind. Guys like you and me must use our wits since we're not winning the lottery anytime soon.

The Hitchhiker

In the 1990s I picked up a hitchhiker on my way from New Orleans to a local Mississippi college to inquire about teaching for a semester. It was a long ride. My radio was broken. I could use some nice conversation, I thought. Besides that, he looked like a clean-cut, Leave-It-To-Beaver type. You've seen them: Sharp dresser. Smooth talker. Great big smile with a perfect row of teeth. The perfect guy to sell a Porsche to someone with eight of them already. The kind of guy you'd trust with your daughter in your weekend cabin for the weekend but who'd later break her heart in half, lickety-split. When he got into the car, he smelled like Georgio cologne and cigarettes.

Well we got to talking about everything under the sun. Politics. The weather. The cool new age music on the Weather Channel that he wanted to badly to identify (Pat Metheny, I said). We even talked about Mississippi girls compared to Canadian girls - a world of differ-ence, actually. I asked him what he was studying. His reply?

"I want to be a sorcerer just like my daddy."

I nearly hit a fire hydrant just as a dog was doing his business. By god, I had a male wiccan in my car dressed like Bill Gates.

Before I could laugh at this obvious joke he was playing on me, he proceeded to lay out his whole philosophy of life, real slow and methodical like, waving his fingers around like a magician. I began to ask him questions about this so-called "career." As it turned out, I had to give him personal info about me for every question I asked. Sort of like bartering for dummies. A power thing to him. Personal validation was everything, *as was his image*. I went along with it just as my hands became sweat-filled on the steering wheel and by the time I dropped him off at his destination, I said a little prayer of thanks to the Almighty that the guy never pulled a gun on me.

Would he have? I dunno, maybe. Maybe not.

Bottom line? Appearances are deceptive. That includes: Scents. Visuals. Touch. Audio. Strangers can get into your head and stay there unless you say one word at the outset:

"NO."

Say no to clinginess and control-freaks who'd rather you hang out with them then visit your dying mother in the retirement home.

Now, I was beyond polite with him. A lot of guys I know in Mississippi wouldn't. They'd boot his butt right out as soon as he prattled on about his plans to conquer the world with "Dark Energy." But if you do THAT, you're gonna risk trouble. Be firm, but polite. Don't say, "Get the hell outta my truck, Bozo, before I pump yer gut fulla lead!"

Say, "That's interesting," which I did, to which his reply was: "So do you accept my philosophy, brother?"

(he called me brother the entire trip and it always coincided with him touching my knee)

I feigned ignorance, explaining I needed him to tell me more... more... more... all the way to the college. It worked. But he did demand my phone number and address at the end. Fake, of course.

Violence ensues if you take the wrong road, and that certainly might have happened if I'd brought his whole self-image crumbling to the ground. Leave the "tough-love" talk for someone else. A judge, maybe.

DISAPPEARING DIFFICULTIES

You might be wondering what it truly takes to do a Houdini-style disappearing act. The answer is this: it depends on how invisible you want to be. There are different levels to it that require different mind-sets and experience. You might be invisible one day but goof the next, and now people can see a sliver of an outline as you walk down the street. They may come closer to investigate since invisibility is a power few people wield effectively. Power draws attention. Most people want that attention, if they aren't running like you are.

Another thing it takes, is balls. Fortitude and courage too, but mostly balls because you're not only evading a stalker but his family too since he can call any one of them at any time to aid in the pursuit. That's what law enforcement does with prison escapees - they call for help (unless they're New Yorkers in which case they like to solve the case all by themselves and take all the credit - kinda like Patton).

"The quicker we clean up this goddamned mess, the quicker we can take a little jaunt against the purple pissing Japs and clean out their nest, too... before the goddamned Marines get all of the credit!"

Anyway, stalkers take all kinds of forms. Even Stalin was a stalker, lurking in the shadows and waiting to pounce and rip out the heart of anyone rebuking him for slitting throats on the way to the top.

So let's say you are on the run from someone who wants to take your life. Someone far less powerful than Stalin was. Someone you thought was Mr. or Ms. Romantic, before they turned to the Dark Side. The short of it is that you must have a battle plan IN PLACE long before you run. Turning invisible is the easy part. Staying invisible is the hard part.

Actually now that I think about it, let's up the threat a little bit. Forget romance stalkers. Let's say you're on the run from the **authorities**. If you can master that, you can master anything else since it becomes a hundred times harder if you now have not one, but *dozens* of stalkers who are trained to find people on the run. They don't master pathfinding and detective work in any federal training program, by the way, not even in the ATF which has one of the longest programs for agents. They master it by doing it for years and years and learning from not only their *own* mistakes, but their comrades in other State departments and Federal agencies with which they share strategies of capturing prey.

It's not all gloomy, however. Knowing what the authorities greatest strengths and weaknesses are can help immensely since many get cocky and overconfident after years of success. Can they monitor every train station? Bus depots? Can they shut them down with a court order on the fly? A few can post-9/11. How about gas stations - how many have cameras? Which ones don't? Underground tunnels - can they seal you tight by closing off both ends? You must know all of this before running.

And forget about using even a small airport to jet away.

ID

The other pain the neck is your identity. There's a world of difference between showing a fake ID to a bank to open an account and one that will get you past airport security. So you'll need a fake passport which is expensive (more than a grand in most cities, and you have to know whom to contact).

Do you plan on hoofing it by foot or hitchhiking? This brings a whole new level of risk since you'll stick out even more than you're already sticking out. A stick in the mud with one of those twirly caps.

Think about it. How many hitchhikers did you see last week? If you live near Yosemite or the Appalachian trailer, I'll grant maybe thirty or so. Anywhere else, not so many. Better to rent a car, but you should be picky about it and find a rental outlet that accepts cash deposits. Know that whatever identification you use will be used to run a credit check. More risk.

Sanctuary: Go someplace where American tourists/expats are few and far between. You need not go to Yemen, but consider South America which is filled with nice little getaways to let the heat simmer down. Mexico is a bit too close for comfort (though Yucatan is a nice spot). Many go to Venezuela, but you don't want to stay there forever. Can your parents visit you? Should they, if the evil wizard Foozle is watching them like hawks?

Funds

You run out of money quickly being on the run. So you needs lots of it. Enough to bankroll your hotels as well as gasoline for travel and, let's face it, you don't want to eat Thai food 24/7/365 days a year. I'd say save at least five years worth as this will buy more than you can imagine. This brings up our next topic: Friends.

Friends

There's a saying in Hong Kong about money:

"When money is stolen you can only beat the dog."

Put another way, if you have money - you have *friends*. It's rather Nietzschian to my aged eyes but it is what it is. Sad fact of life, isn't it? About as anti-virtue as you can get. Money indeed does buy friends. And those same friends can help you out in a jam and believe me that jam will come sooner or later. The difference could be whether you sleep in a house or sleep in a cell with mice running over your ankles at night next to Soapy the Bum.

There is a lot to be said about humility and shunning the love of money, but when all is said and done the Almighty might not help you out in this regard if you don't prepare for winter. So get it then, don't procrastinate. Save! Again, you need five years worth if for no other reason than to sleep at night with peace of mind. Worries that stack tend to cloud judgment and contribute to mistakes we wouldn't otherwise have had made if we had green in the bank. You'll also need it to buy intel, but careful about buying intelligence on your enemies since merely *looking* can tip them off if the guy you hired is sloppy.

SECURING YOUR COMPUTER

When I relayed to my grandmother last Christmas that I write books on anonymity and how to become invisible, she nearly gagged on her macadamia nut cookie. I got dead air. I thought maybe I'd given her a heart attack. Then came the lecture. I was going to get arrested by the FBI and every other alphabet agency. I'd be waterboarded. Chipped. Brainwashed. I'd be the next Edward Snowden (though I'm not nearly as handsome).

People, old people especially, tend to group the word anonymity under a pretty big umbrella that includes hackers, spies and contract killers. If you've got an encrypted hard drive, then you've got something to hide, perhaps the location to where you buried Jimmy Hoffa.

"Encryption?" she asked, "I hope you're not hanging around one of those Goodfella guys. Besides, isn't that illegal, dearie? Hm?"

"Not on your life, and thank heavens for small miracles. But I can tell you this: " I reassured, "Even if it were, I'd *still* teach people how to secure their data somehow. Keep it away from snoops."

"But we're all snoops, dear."

"True, but some are more snoopy than others."

"But dearest, I don't want you getting into trouble with the government. They're are friend y'know and they know best (a silent groan from me at this point)."

As we've mentioned before, the last thing you want is for a stalker to grab your laptop while you're in the restroom in a public place. This happened to me on a cold, foggy morning at Wendy's close to the New Orleans French Quarter. Patrons were few and pigeons were still perched on the wires as early as it was. Seemed safe enough. No harm in just leaving my laptop running since all I'd intended was to get in and out of the john, right? My bookbag as well was right beside it. You know what happened next.

Next thing I saw when I walked out of the restroom was a ten year old black kid in grey sweatpants gunning it for the streetcar that went round to the projects; the *worst* place to chase a thief with a car.

But I was determined to get back, 1.) my laptop and 2.) my bookbag that contained the new shrinkwrapped Elder Scrolls game I'd bought from Babbages. Later I recalled being more concerned with the game, such were my hobbled priorities.

So I used my feet and dashed like the wind, chasing him down Canal St. all the way to St. Charles Ave. When I finally caught up with him, the kid swung and slipped from my grasp like one of those kids in the Philippines who can shimmy up a palm tree in 3 seconds flat to avoid a big cat's teeth. Thankfully I was the faster one, at least horizontally. He ended up dropping it. My laptop shattered as it hit the concrete. My grip tightened like a vice around his arm. He snapped at me like I was in the wrong.

"Get the hell offa me 'fore I bust yer face!"

He got off lucky, as did I. As he ran down the street flipping me off, I realized that if he'd been a stalker, an ex-flame, and if my laptop had been unencrypted I'd have been toast. He'd have access to:

- My credit cards
- Login passwords for every tech forum under the sun
- Emails
- Amazon, eBay, Google+, Facebook, etc.

The same can happen to you. Worse case scenario: he steals your laptop then leaves it on your doorstep the next morning with an anonymous sticky note. Something about "feeling guilty." Which is a load of bull since your Alienware laptop is now accursed with a keylogger. The kid wants bank account access. Greedy access.

And that's just identity theft. There are other risks, like getting caught trying to preserve invisibility. Some people just like to stay out of the spotlight for whatever reason. By encrypting your laptop you not only defeat identity thieves, you defeat anyone and everyone that has an interest in seeing you burn.

<u>Tor</u>

I hate to insert a bit of overlap here as some of my other books delve quite deep into Tor territory, but you just can't write a book on invisibility without at least mentioning it. So here goes.

Tor hides the IP address that websites identify you with. No matter where you go on the internet, if you're not using Tor, you're being tracked somehow by someone, somewhere. Usually the big name companies like Coke and Dell and Google. The good news is that it's free. As in, really free. No upselling at all as it's not a commercial product. It is *the* app for anonymity enthusiasts and beginners alike. So much so that the NSA targeted it specifically along with Truecrypt because they were so powerful. So powerful, in fact, that when used together they grant you *complete invisibility* online.

The NSA failed to defeat it. Though that did not stop the FBI from taking a stab at it. They hacked a few websites on the Deep Web by way of browser exploits (or NIT - Network Investigative Technique) that manipulated Javascript to reveal IP addresses. Addresses that lead to your front door. These exploits that have been fixed and it's important to note that you don't need Javascript for the internet to work. Some websites, however, won't work (porn!).

Still, after downloading it from the Tor <u>homepage</u>, you need to ensure via the NoScript addon that Javascript is turned off. This will break some websites that use it heavily like CNN and sites with tons of flash videos. But then if a site is running a dozen scripts it is likely those scripts are tracking you in some way to as to better target you with ads.

Benefits of Tor

1. Immune to Ad Tracking. What you'll see is ads targeted to some guy in Germany or Japan, since the IP will be that of a Tor user's exit relay (Tor users can volunteer as exit nodes if they wish, but it's not mandatory to use Tor).

2. You can surf the Deep Web, aka .onion sites that are not reachable via the regular internet. The downside is little to no moderation. If you remember how 'Wild West' Usenet was back in the 1990s, you'll have a good idea of what it's like. Freenet is also like that, though it does not connect to the Deep Web in the same way Tor does. In fact, it's a whole different Wild West show, which we will go over shortly.

3. Communicate Anonymously. Using Tor, you can say whatever you want in a forum and not have it traced back to the real You. But don't expect all moderators to not take action to ban your account if you step over the line. Yes, I realize I just contradicted myself here. Perhaps it's better to state that there is little moderation rather than no moderation on the Deep Web. But what there is, is moderated by lords of the sith in one flavor or another.

4. Upload to file-sharing sites Anonymously. Sites like those owned by the former Megaupload founder. If you need to get something to someone without leaving a trace (even if the zip file is encrypted), such is possible with Tor as long as the website does not block it.

Tails

Tails allows you to use Tor and avoid tracking and censorship and in just about any location you could want. It houses its own operating system and is designed for those who don't wish to use their main rig to connect to Tor (though you still can, however if you wish).

You've got several choices at your disposal: You can run it via USB stick, SD or even a DVD. This is pretty handy as strengthens your resistance to viruses. It's also beneficial if you don't want your hard drive to leave remnants of your browsing session. The best part is that it's free and based on Linux *and* comes with chat client, email, office, and browser. Everything the anonymity enthusiast needs to wear Frodo's cloak online.

The downside to using a DVD though, is that you must burn it again each time you update Tails. Not very convenient. So let's install it to USB stick instead.

1.) Download tails installer here. You must first install it somewhere, like a DVD, and THEN clone it the USB stick or SD card.

2.) Click Applications --> Tails --> Tails install to begin the installation.

3.) Choose Clone & Install to install to SD card or USB Memory Stick

4.) Plug in your device, then scan for the device in the Target-Device drop down menu. You'll get a warning about it overwriting anything on the device, blah-blah. Choose yes to confirm the installation.

Tails by itself is quite a powerful tool to use to cloak yourself online. But when combined with an air-tight and secure operating system like Linux, it is virtually *unstoppable*. If you have the luxury of choosing vanilla Tor browser in Windows or using Tails, always go with Tails. Windows has always been the favorite whipping boy of the FBI as well as hackers in general since the number of security holes far outnumber those in Linux.

But Linux doesn't have nearly the amount of supported games.

Few supported games = fewer families using it = fewer hackers interested in exploiting it for personal or financial reasons. Them's the breaks.

VPNs

VPN stands for Virtual Private Network. Great for privacy, lousy for anonymity unless you use it in **conjunction with Tor**. If you want rock-solid privacy and anonymity (they're not the same thing), then double-wrap.

When I signed up for my first VPN, I was surprised how easy it was. Almost as easy as signing up with my Usenet provider, Astraweb. Only instead of paying $10/month for newsgroups, you pay $10 for a private connection that masks your IP address. You install the app from the service like CloudVPN and connect through that. The VPN can be from any country but if you want subpoena-resistant VPN service that approaches anonymity, you better pick a VPN that resides in a country that isn't known for cooperating with U.S. authorities. No, not Iran. Think France, China or Venezuela. It's not 100% subpoena-proof, but luck favors the prepared.

Freenet

The Big Brother of Tor, Freenet doesn't really hide your IP address. It hides *what you're downloading with your IP address*. Say you want to download a blu-ray movie (not many of those on Freenet, but let's say for argument that you had one you wanted to share). You'd install Freenet. Then the Frost frontend addon (discussed below). Then you'd click the upload button which would give you the Chk address you need to share it with others. Then you'd paste said Chk address to one of the hundreds of Freenet groups available.

Benefits of Using Freenet

Chat anonymously. Freenet is known for it's "Darknet" functions that allow complete anonymous communication between two people or even a group. Upon installtion, you choose the security level. Low security, in which it is easy for others (with sufficient resources) to find your identity, or high security, in which you only connect to darknet peers - friends you absolutely trust. Your files are still encrypted end to end so that no one knows who uploaded or downloaded what.

Download Anonymously. As stated, anything you downloaded, provided you chose normal security levels at installation, will not be viewable by anyone else because of the end-to-end encryption.

<h3 align="center">Downsides to Using Freenet</h3>

1.) Freenet is SLOW. It is not nearly as fast as Bittorrent or eMule. It takes hours to days to download files a gigabyte in size or higher. Plus, if you've an older PC, it is a bit on the resource-intensive side of things, though anything with an i3 cpu and up will be much faster. That's faster resource-wise. Not download speed.

2.) Freenet is complicated. It's not that hard to install and use. It's just hard to find darknet peers you can trust if you want Full Anonymity. The "average" security level is fine for most people, but if you're the leader of a resistance movement in Iran, by all means go perfect dark. Just be certain your darknet peers are 100% trustworthy - a hard feat in this day and age when you've never actually met any of those peers!

3.) Freenet is buggy. It's insanely good at giving you anonymity. Even better than Tor, many say, but you need Java installed for it to work. Because of the sheer complexity of it all, it's not perfect. Yes, Freenet checks whether you have Java on install but even then it occasionally spits out an error if you try to connect. It's usually wrapper-related if on Windows. If this happens, keep trying! Even now, in 2015, I get errors on occasion. I just ignore them and keep hitting 'Connect' until it 'locks on'. Three times is usually enough.

Oh and by the way, never give your Freenet ID to anyone on Freenet. It breaks your anonymity.

Frost

Freenet on its own is unbearably complex to my old eyes. So I was elated when Frost came around. It's a good front end to make reading groups (and downloading CHK files) easier.

Rest assured, there are far more groups then what you see in the above image. This is just the ones available after install - a few I cherry pick just to get things going. You'll have to click the "globe" icon at the top to get a full list, and it will take some time, anywhere from an hour to a day to reveal every single group available.

But first, let's download and install it. It's available at:

http://jtcfrost.sourceforge.net/

Extract the contents into wherever you want to run the application from. If an encrypted container, then you need to have that encrypted container mounted first, then unzip it there.

e.g. Z:\Freenet\Frost

Next create a shortcut to the 'frost.bat' file within. I like to then drag the shortcut to my accessories menu in Windows. Then I disable the annoying splash screen within the Frost options screen.

After that Frost will ask you for an identity nic, something you can use to post messages. This has nothing to do with your IP address, so fear not. It's just a nickname like you'd use for a Usenet posting in a discussion group.

Options

What I do is go into the News2 section in the options page and check to see if "Hide Messages with Trust States" has "Bad" checked.

Then I look at the other option: "Don't add boards to known boards list from users with trust states"... I check off Check, Bad, Observe and None (unsigned) so that I don't end up with boards I don't want in the known boards list. Easy, peasy.

Now then. Look in the News1 section and set the "number of days to display." If you want to see what you missed for the last few months, adjust this number accordingly, to say 300 or however far back you want to download. This is wholly different than Usenet, where a group will go as far back as five years automatically.

Trust

You can control what Frost displays and what it does not. Believe me, this is a godsend when you want to ignore or vet certain users. This is done by way of the trust settings coded into Frost itself.

The options are: Trust, Observe, Check, or Bad. If you mark a user to "Trust," then that person can send you encrypted messages and vice-versa in addition to providing missing blocks of data you might happen to need that this person has. The Observe and Check options are simple: Observe means that I will observe that person's behavior until I can make up my mind on whether to trust him or not. Check is the normal state of trust, meaning no decision's been made on their trust state.

Setting a user's trust to BAD will nuke any posts that person makes on any Frost board. That doesn't mean it's nuked from Freenet, as there is no censorship. It's still there, just invisible to my own eyes. I simply won't see his racist rants (of which there are many on Freenet).

Now then. It could be that we've had conversations on Freenet that we don't want the wife to know about, or the police. I spoke with an attorney on here once and I remember thinking that if ever the police were privy to what went on in that conversation, the jig was up. And over a lousy ticket! They'd know my defense before I could even mount it.

Well. Speaking of mounting, that's something we need to implement: We need to encrypt our operating system, or at least at a minimum, our conversation and preferably our Freenet and Frost installation. We do this by way of encrypted containers. If we're trying to disappear and we need to cross the border for example, what we don't want happening is Mr. Groucho the Canadian Border Guard getting angry about wanting to see what we were talking about in that darknet room. Loose lips and all.

I've been back and forth across the Canadian border more times than I can count and if there is one thing I've learned, it's that the personality of border guards are notoriously inconsistent across the board. On Monday you'll get someone with the personality of Super-Grover. That smiley guy could be asked to wear a red cape and he'd salute his supervisors and thank them for the great idea. Then on Tuesday you'll get the border guard no one likes to get: a cross between Animal and those two grumpy old farts in the nosebleed seats of the Muppet Show. He's the kid who was scarred for life when his mint ice cream cone fell over at Disneyland. And now he takes that trauma out on you!

So with that horrid image out of the way, let's discuss encrypted *containers*.

Counter-Forensics
____

Encrypted containers are easy to store files in. What isn't so easy is learning the application that enables it. But fear not. Truecrypt took me but a mere weekend to figure out and when I did, I kicked myself for not installing it sooner. My earliest thought was that one needed to be an advanced coder of some sort to use it. Maybe one of those so-called NSA superhackers we hear so much about. I was so wrong.

If you can install Windows, you can install Truecrypt. Or Veracrypt or Drivecrypt or Diskcryptor or any variation thereof. They all encrypt your files but have different ways of doing it, and many, many apps are available as you will see. But let's go with the free ones first: Truecrypt and Veracrypt, two excellent choices for us that give a lot of bang for less than a buck.

Truecrypt is first up since the GUI of Veracrypt is practically the same as it's digital brother.

"Hold on a second," you say. "Isn't the NSA involved in undermining Truecrypt?"

Yes and no. It's true from NSA slides leaked that we can see Truecrypt and Tor were in their crosshairs for a long time, but then so is everything else that's tough to crack.

Here's what Veracrypt developers had to say about it. You can interpret it however you wish.

"I am sure the people involved in TrueCrypt couldn't have stayed anonymous and the security agencies knew who they were," he said. "But when you look at the code, you get the idea that these people must have been in their 40s back in 1995. So now they are in their 60s, and they are probably tired or retired."

Truecrypt

There's something else about Truecrypt you might not have heard. It's been discontinued as of 2015, but all the major encryption apps work similarly and it is still secure according to many reliable sources. Once you learn how to use Truecrypt, Veracrypt is a peace of cake. Or you can go ahead and start with Veracrypt in the next section. Your choice.

If you choose Truecrypt, you need to know the basics of creating container files. Once you do that, encrypting the OS is simpler. So let's create a container file.

Download the app from here and install. Create a container file. Think of it as a treasure chest for which you will create a magic password to open it. Being magic, you wouldn't share that password, right? Right. So never share that password.

Here's the quick rundown:

1. After installation, ensure you have enough free space for your

container. How big is the data you're putting inside? Blu-Ray size? Set it accordingly.

2. Select "Create new Volume" from the drop-down menu.

3. Now you've two choices: go the standard route or the double-encrypted treasure chest route (Hidden volume), also called **plausible deniability**. For a beginner, let's go with a simple file container since hidden volumes require two passwords and can get a little tricky if you want to store files larger than 4 gigs therein.

4. You'll soon get to a screen where you have to 'Select File'. Click it. Browse to where you want to store this encrypted container soon to be full of treasure. Don't click on any files yet. Just type in a name in the filename box and choose Save-- We'll add our treasure later.

5. Choose AES for an encryption algorithm. Either is fine but AES has never failed to foil an attacker as it's super strong. The others get hit with performance penalties on slower systems.

6. Choose the size. Don't select a size too small if you're storing your honeymoon HD videos inside.

7. Now comes the password. The longer it is, and more random with letters and numbers and symbols, the stronger the entropy and thus the stronger the pass. Write it down if you must but never forget it. There's no retrieving it if you do.

8. Use your mouse to create a random key, which changes the more you move it. You don't have to do it more than a few seconds. The NSA could spend years and years trying to figure out which direction you moved it first.

9. Now pick a file system, but realize if you're storing big files (4gig and up), you'll need NTFS.

10. You're done! Now just click on the file you initially created. Input the pass, and pick the letter drive you want it to mount to. Then paste in your videos/documents/treasure. You won't be able to delete this container unless you *unmount* it, which can be done on the Truecrypt screen.

Passwords

At this juncture I should probably answer a question I get quite frequently, which is:

"Help me! I forgot my password but... I know 15 out of the 20 or so character string and in order so... uh... what are my chances of hacking it?"

The answer is: Slim to none unless you have access to NSA resources, and even that is a long shot for a long password. Encrypted passwords are stored as "hash" files. When you hash a file, even if you change but ONE character in that string, the hash changes. The same is true of jpegs. Throw a picture into Gimp and apply a cool effect or tweak something small and... voila. It's changed. Completely different hash set. Same with encryption.

Evil Maid Attack

Truecrypt, like many other encryption apps, stores your encryption keys in memory ram. A cold boot attack can possibly siphon this if the ram is dumped in the event of a raid or our Jamaican laptop thief gets access to your running operating system. If the former, they can cart off your PC *still running* and freeze the ram sticks *and* dump your keys - which contain your password! The thief, probably not. But an FBI team with a black van parked out front? You can bet the ranch on it. They're used to all kinds of lowlifes using encryption. Tax evaders. Counterfeit operations. Drug runners. Hells Angels gang members using PGP to communicate where the meth lab is.

The takeaway lesson is this: Don't leave your computer running with any encrypted containers mounted, as it will be dead simple to sniff your passwords from your ram. Unless of course, you break them in half - which in and of itself might be a obstruction of justice charge. Ten years ago this might not have been the case but the world we now live in is radically different. It demands vigilance on the part of would-be patriots. Always have a plan B.

Drivecrypt - Drivecrypt brings back fond memories. It was my first foray into proprietary encryption apps and seemed to offer nothing but good things in those early days.

These days though, there are a few downsides as technology has progressed about the same rate as exploits in the wild. One is that it's closed source and at over $100, it's not cheap. But it's got a great front end and extra goodies if you don't mind paying through the nose. It wasn't for me at the time. For me the bigger issue was if the NSA greased Securstar's palms enough (or threatened) to code in a backdoor for the government. If you visit their homepage, you'll see them swear up and down that that's not the case. In the end you'll have to decide for yourself whether or not they can be trusted. For what it's worth, they're based in Germany, not the USA. But if there were a conspiracy then it wouldn't matter which country they operated in.

If you choose yes, know that the demo they offer does not offer strong encryption - only a weak AES key that gets upgraded to full strength if you buy it. I can't recommend Drivecrypt for these reasons:

1. Closed source

2. Pricey

3. Bruce Schneier, a respected authority on all things security, mentioned in passing after the Snowden leaks that most commercial applications in the USA "...probably have back doors coded into them." Probably, he said, which sounds suspiciously like *certainly* to me. He probably has no more proof of that than I do, but then you don't need to see the code to know using closed-source is a risky endeavor after the NSA (and GCHQ) got caught with their pants down.

Veracrypt - Veracrypt is probably your best bet if Truecrypt has you worried about backdoors. To that, even I have to admit that the account of the strange falling out by the development team had me worried for a time. Rest assured Truecrypt **is** still secure, it's just not **as** secure as other apps, depending wholly on what your security needs are. Plus, later volumes allow you to mount Truecrypt volumes.

So what's so great about it? Well, the developers of Veracrypt emulated the TrueCrypt 7.x code and made it stronger for one thing. Brute forcing is now much more difficult because of the iterations and enhancements added to it. Whenever you encrypt a hard drive partition using Truecrypt, it uses 1000 iterations and 2000 for your containers. But Veracrypt uses a whopping 327,661 of the RIPEMD160 algorithm, which keeps your password and safe contents, well, safe. For encrypted containers? Almost double, at 655,331 iterations of SHA-2 encryption. The only performance penalty comes in at a somewhat slower time to unlock encrypted partitions, a fair tradeoff since it now makes it over three hundred times harder for a hacker to crack by brute force alone.

All of that, plus the user interface looks very similar to Truecrypt, so if you're familiar with that GUI, there's not much of a learning curve at all.

Diskcryptor - With DiskCryptor you can encrypt any disk partitions or even your main system partition. Being open-source, it was intended as a replacement for Drivecrypt Plus Pack (a commercial closed-source app) and PGP full disk encryption. It supports AES-256, Serpent & Twofish algorithms with the encryption key being stores in the first sector of a volume.

Benefits to using DiskCryptor when I compared two different systems:

- SHA-512 hash algorithm in Windows partitions

- Quicker boot than Truecrypt or Drivecrypt Plus Pack

- No mandatory "Create Rescue Disk" like Truecrypt (see workaround)

- Compiles easier than TC.

Cons to Using Truecrypt

1.) Discontinued. Probably the best reason to use Veracrypt, though it did pass a security audit which you can read about here. DiskCryptor as well does not use the same GUI like Truecrypt does, so you'll have to get used to learning a new one. Not a problem for most but I tend to be stubborn about learning new any new GUI.

2.) Limited to RIPEMD-160 hash algorithm for Windows

3.) No support, no future security holes fixed

4.) A few motherboards (Gigabyte's Black Edition line) don't like it.

UPDATE: I must have spent a month trying to figure out why the Linux-like BIOS of my Z97X-UD3H failed to boot after I'd input my TC password. Customer Support laughed as they knew about as much of Truecrypt as they did nuclear waste management (beyond it looking like green radioactive goo leaking from a rusty barrel). In the end I chalked it up to a bad hard drive. THEN a month later, after further investigation, figured it due to having installed Drivecrypt on said hard drive at some point in the past (the demo). So use multiple encryption schemes on the same hard drive with caution.

LibreCrypt - LibreCrypt is open-source disk encryption for Windows and unlike the above, is LUKS compatible (formerly DoxBox). That's a big plus if you like to dual-boot. Even better is that it supports the same plausible deniability that Truecrypt does. It's listed on the features page as "Deniable encryption that protects you from 'rubber hose cryptography' (snicker!). If you don't know what that is, it's something like this...

Other features include:

- Easy to use, with a 'wizard' for creating new 'containers'.

- Full transparent encryption, containers appear as removable disks in Windows Explorer.

- Explorer mode lets you access containers when you don't have administrator permissions.

- Compatible with Linux encryption, Cryptoloop "losetup", dm-crypt, and LUKS. Linux shell scripts support deniable encryption on Linux.

- Supports smartcards and security tokens.

- Encrypted containers can be a file, a partition, or a whole disk.

- Opens legacy volumes created with FreeOTFE

BORDER OFFICERS AND ENCRYPTED LAPTOPS

Bringing any kind of guns or even knives across the Canadian border is a serious offense - at both ends. Marines have been arrested in Mexico with shotguns in the back of their pickup trucks and northward, cops have been arrested (yes, cops!) for failing to check in handguns. Ever since Marc Lépine shot up a school in Montreal way back in 1989 over what he perceived as feminists ruining his life, Canada has made it 1000 times more difficult to own a firearm.

Not that you'd want to smuggle one in. Canadians are notorious for being friendly to outsiders. It's what lies in the likes of Banff Park or out in the Yukon that demands gun ownership the most: Polar bears. Grizzlies. A few smugglers here and there but they probably will leave you alone if you leave them alone.

And on that topic, smuggling anything into Canada requires cunning unheard of, the likes of which Jabba the Hutt himself was never privy to. It's serious business.

And there's no end to crazy ideas, believe me. Stories in which officers have relayed to their families probably number in the thousands.

One involved a Canadian teenager who, at the border, sobbed

like a little baby when the officer asked him if he had any weapons. Like that 'Father, I confess!' scene from The Godfather, the kid admitted how he'd gotten into some trouble down south at a bachelor party and found himself stuck with a handgun he'd never laid eyes on before. When sent to secondary checkpoint it turned out his gun was a BB gun. His 'friends' had played a delicious joke on him, telling him he'd killed a hooker. HA, good ol' Southern Comfort.

Anyway. Let's discuss bringing laptops across the border and other electronic devices in which said device could easily make or break your attempt at becoming invisible. Namely, what tips them off.

Contrary to popular belief, Border Officers on the Canadian side do not know your entire life history when they scan your passport. When you drive through a Canadian checkpoint, here is what happens:

Your passport is scanned (the part that has all the '<' left arrow symbols) using an international-standard that's easily readable by a CBSA language named IPIL. This searches through law enforcement records such as outstanding warrants, both present and past. Beyond this, there's no time to go through every database with the lineup these guys deal with. It simply takes way too much time as planes land every other day with 1000 Canadians who are eager to get home to some nice Timbits and Poutine.

Therefore, the shortcut to seeing if you're a criminal or not isn't by searching databases, as useful as they are (a seasoned criminal will know how to secure false passports anyway). The way to tell deception is by studying your behavior - Tics. Facial changes. Visual cues (where are you looking? DEA agents study where you look to see if you'll give up the drug location after a raid). Tone. Hesitation. Fidgeting. Sometimes a smuggler will, when pressed with questions by a Sam Elliot lookalike, they get nervous.

If *you* act nervous, the jig is up. And they know the difference between fatigue and nervousness. But for what it's worth, being an absolute jerk to the officer will not put you on any blacklist. They have to let you in as a Canadian since that is what the Canadian Charter dictates. What they don't have to let in is *your stuff*. So what *will* put you on the nasty list? These:

- Shipping drugs by mail
- Refusing to report to secondary inspection
- Lying (aka 'Making a False Declaration' which is admittedly a broad topic, and lies always travel faster than truths: If you lie to one officer in Vancouver, the one at Niagara Falls will know about it)
- Having *any* bad history at the border

So what else might tip off a BDO?

Not giving up your password. As stated, they'll let *you* through but not your beloved laptop. They do not need a warrant at all to search your phone/Galaxy Tab/Ipad.

So then, encrypt? Yes! By all means but you should have a hidden operating system because you absolutely, unequivocably want to give them *something* that makes you *look like you have nothing to hide*. You don't have to make yourself look like a schmuck. You simply have to look like a professional who values your privacy. They won't sit down and fine-comb your files, since they have programs built to search for signature IDs to microniche porn videos (you know the kind) and a few banned anime.

Solution

You need to lock down your data prior to your border arrival. Designate a section of your hard drive so that it's encrypted out of an officer's plain sight and with a second encryption key. There you will store your private files. Do this even if you have full disk encryption! Diskcryptor offers this as well as most older encryption applications like PGP and Drivecrypt.

Border officers aren't forensics experts. They can't go through your Windows or Linux directory to see you've got one encrypted file that's fifty gigs in size, nor that you've got a shortcut to it via menu that says 'Calculator' which even has the stock Windows icon. If they want to "image" your hard drive, that's no sweat off your back as long as your password is good.

Speaking of which, try to drop a symbol in the middle of your password. Mix it up with upper/lowercase with a number. Yes, these are harder to remember. To counter this you can use PasswordSafe.

If you're on the way to the border station from the airport, say from Buffalo, NY to the Canadian Border Station at Niagara Falls, it might be too late to encrypt anything. So do it **before** you get on the plane. You need to have that decoy ready to show, with *recent* activity in case they want to boot up the OS. It will look suspicious if the decoy OS has not been used in a month. Perhaps not to every customs agent, but there may be one smart cookie in the batch who knows you can have a fake OS.

Store nothing incriminating on that decoy OS. What's illegal in Canada might not illegal in the USA. So don't put freaky underage catgirl anime of any kind no matter how much your Japanese girlfriend likes it. Vanilla bookmarks (no social media!). A nice backdrop, not the stock install wallpaper that comes with Windows or Linux. Maybe a picture you took on vacation of all the Latina lovelies with you, smiling while refilling your frosty margarita on a white sandy beach in Rio.

Once, while coming back from Manila to Canada (a backbreaking 22 hour flight!), I stored my encrypted container in my camera, one that the border agent asked for directions to flip through the pics. He saw some beach pics I'd shot in Dumaguete but not the encrypted container on the SD card. They're not going to remove it with 20 cars behind you.

HIDING VALUABLES UNDERGROUND

Things may get to the point where you must hide valuables underground. There's nothing particularly unethical about this, so long as it isn't dead bodies or something like enriched uranium leaking out of barrels. Regardless of what you store, know that anything can happen. You could get get mauled by Rottweilers in a junkyard. Who knows why you'd be there. Maybe looking for spare parts. Maybe to pay Uncle Spanky who runs the place a visit. And then what happens to your cache when you get buried six feet under? Right.

We can avoid a few problems if we follow a few self-imposed rules.

Avoid X Marks the Spot - This is a big one. Never mark the treasure cache spot with anything unnatural. No arrows in trees or painted rocks with bright and yellow smiley faces or mini "Stonehenges." These attract fraternity idiots. Idiots will damage the site - they will move things around when they call up other idiots to come and have a hot dog cookout... just before one of those drunken fools drops his cig near the base of the tree.

Google Earth - Use Google Earth to locate the exact coordinates. Memorize them but do not save it in Google Earth unless your drive is encrypted. And forget about using that Garmen, too. Some models save your history. Obviously this should not be on your property if what you're burying is illegal (or if the IRS can take it). Always assume that someone will find it. Someone with a shiny badge and lots of time to kill.

Insulation! - Take a hard drive apart, say an external one that's dead. See how dry it is? Now re-screw it and fasten. Then freeze it for awhile. After, put it out on the porch and then throw it in the freezer again. Open it a few hours later. Yeah, condensation. Lots of it. This happens to motherboards and ammo alike so bury beneath the frost line since moisture will kill any electrical component.

No Water, No Problems! - Try not to bury valuables near streams, rivers or heaven forbid, swamps. Think "Up" when you think Underground. Escarpments and hills tend to make great spots but only at night unless it's out in the boonies. So do cemeteries (if you own one!). Bury it in a non-populated area with elevation enough that discourages daily visitors.

Bury It Naked - Avoid toting internet items with you whenever you visit your sacred spot. That means: Tablets. Phones. Cameras. Laptops. Ipads. Watches that have WiFi (Apple). That also means ditching your car with the fancy-pants navigation system (one the cops will have fun tearing apart to see where you visited). Bike it if necessary. Silence is golden. To this, what works for me is to think "Zombies!" since the undead are attracted to loud noises like Camaro engines and big trucks, too. If in doubt, watch Walking Dead, Season 1 where one of the group steals a sport's car and the alarm goes off as he travels up to the hideaway camp. When morning comes, so does the zombie hoarde.

GOING TO EXTREMES

One day, your financial situation just might drive you to this:

Looks tranquil, doesn't it?

Almost like someplace a Bond villain might set up base camp, far away from the eyes of any intelligence agency. I sometimes meditate and dream of what I missed when I was walking along beaches like this not too long ago. Know where it is? I'll give you a hint. It isn't Bora Bora, though the turquoise water certainly does look it. It's the Philippines, and if pictures could relay the Venus-like temps, the salty wind of the sea and the feel of a waif's sticky finger slipping into your pocket to filch your passport, you might think twice about defecting there. A week-long vacation is one thing, but to live there is a whole other world filled to the brim with it's own set of unique challenges.

You could want to leave for any number of reasons, and they're probably all justified. Your student loans might be preventing you from securing employment or getting married. Perhaps you're divorce didn't go quite as stress-free as planned and now you're required to "maintain" your spouse's lifestyle. Or it could be you're just tired of driving down Main Street, USA and always looking over your shoulder for fear of being thrown in the can over a lousy expired brake tag.

There's something I need to tell you about exotic places like this. Something I learned that was ingrained into my very soul.

And it is this: Your problems follow you around like a stray puppy.

No I don't mean your *financial* problems. Over there your student loans won't mean jack. I mean your *personal* issues. Anger management. Jealousy. Wanton vandalism. Piracy. Alcoholism. Cat hoarder/herder. Whatever your ethics, whatever your spiritual weakness, it will not magically change overnight when you leave the West. Don't hightail it to escape a bad habit, be it gambling or drinking or cockfighting. You'll just run in a circle until you tackle the problem headon.

But you might find that you need to get away to an exotic place to heal yourself as you restart your life. That's darn near impossible to do if Betsy from SallieMae loans is constantly harassing your family every hour on the hour and Uncle Frick is threatening to kick you to the curb if they don't stop. That's no way to heal. That's a way to the grim reaper's front door. Now, we all meet death at some point, but there's no reason Betsy needs to accelerate it by giving you a heart attack.

Let's look at some destinations that might give you some time to reset your dreams without the usual distractions.

Philippines

It wasn't the sticker shock of the trip to Philippines that almost had me in tears ($1400) or even the insanely long flight (18 hours). It was the *sweltering* heat I had to deal with. I sweat like a stuck pig and burned like a roasted turkey on a spit under that Manila sun. Being raised in New Orleans was no peace of cake mind you, but even our July heat was nothing compared to this. I began to think some of them only went to Mass to escape it. Who could blame them? Certainly not the Almighty.

But I could see myself adapting, as I know you can, if you don't panic. Keep your wits about you. Think rationally about problems (something that seems lacking in Filipino culture and you'll see this if you use Google Earth to view their city grid layouts.

Life is slower there. Relationships are faster, much faster. By the fourth date your sweetie will be proposing. No lie. If you meet the parents, you're not getting out of her sight, ever, because she knows every filipina will be approaching you en masse.

There are other issues, too. You cannot own a gun. If you're a white single male you will stick out like Marvin Martian in Bunkie, Louisiana. No country is more networked than the Philippines. Gossip reigns supreme because of the social nature of the entire country.

And it really is a third world country in some parts. Lack of electricity. Lack of clean water, with Manila being the worst. But the women, heavens. You'll think you'd time-traveled to Hawaii in 1955. The level of attention I got was insane, and I'm no George Clooney either. I'm about as average Joe as they come. Walking through SM mall (as long as you don't resemble an ogre), you'll have massive numbers of women approaching you. If you are in Davao, Cebu, Dumaguete, or pretty much anywhere except Manila (crime-ridden) and Zamboanga (terrorist central), this is a fact of life.

Unfortunately this brings unexpected attention where the sweet, endearing Filipinas take lovely selfies of you eating by yourself and post it on Facebook and Twitter and Instagram before joining you. Your stalker may take notice if you use your real name with them. They may even do an image search and start some carnage there.

Solution?

A fake profile and persona if you go this route--different interests that go along with that shiny fake ID and fake last name, fake Facebook. Everything to use with the locals but **never** the government. A lockbox is useful for this.

Canada

Running to Canada to escape student loan debt is one thing. Running for a crime like "kidnapping" your son is another.

If you want to run to Canada to escape a crime, forget it. It's the last place you want to be unless you happen to be Jeremiah "liver eating" Johnson and know how to trap beaver, scale a mountain and survive in sub-zero freezing temperatures.

That Canadian friendliness we see in John Candy's movies comes at a high price: They will hand you over with a side of Canadian bacon if U.S. authorities demand it. I've lived here for over twelve years and though the Canadian police (Toronto excluded) were far more polite and professional than any of my Cajun brethren down in Louisiana, I've never heard of any cases where they hand out asylum benefits like Willy Wonka bars. In fact, they don't grant asylum to Americans, *period*.

There's a funny scene in the film *Escape From New York* where Van Cleef's character, a real "hang em high" supercop kind of guy, threatens Snake Plisskan with death if he so much as thinks of turning his loaned police glider around and flying off to Canada instead of saving the President of the U.S.A

I nearly cracked a rib laughing as I thought, "How stupid does he think Snake is?"

Canada would dropship poor Snake no matter what crime he'd committed. Oh they'd be nice about it, I'll grant you that. Maybe they'd send him back handcuffed in a coffin filled with a hundred bottles of delicious Canadian maple syrup Han Solo-style. After that, they'd throw in some Tim Horton's donuts. Ol' Van Cleef would've loved that, I'm sure.

So heed this advice: Canada is a no-fly zone if ever you're in serious, deep trouble. They turned over Mark Emery, eminent marijuana activist and he was one of their own. Canadian judges have extradited other, more serious criminals, one of whom was a young Canadian who'd never set foot in the States. The crime? He emailed child porn (38 pics) to an undercover Homeland Security agent. He was sentenced to 8 and a half years. Foolish doesn't begin to describe it.

But I don't believe the U.S. taxpayers should be the one footing the bill.

Remember, just because a country does not have an extradition treaty with the USA does not mean they will not extradite you.

Below is an interesting list, where you will stand a good chance of "disappearing," and in the case of a country like Syria, disappearance can be a whole other world of hurt if you don't have **connections**.

Afghanistan, Algeria, Andorra, Angola, Armenia, Bahrain, Bangladesh, Belarus, Bosnia, Herzegovina, Brunei, Burkina Faso, Burma, Burundi, Cambodia, Cameroon, Cape Verde, the Central African Republic, Chad, China, Comoros, Congo, Djibouti, Equatorial Guinea, Eritrea, Ethiopia, Gabon, Guinea, Guinea-Bissau, Indonesia, Ivory Coast, Kazakhstan, Kosovo, Kuwait, Laos, Lebanon, Libya, Macedonia, Madagascar, Maldives, Mali, Marshall Islands, Mauritania, Micronesia, Moldova, Mongolia, Montenegro, Morocco, Mozambique, Namibia, Nepal, Niger, Oman, Qatar, Russia, Rwanda, Samoa, São Tomé & Príncipe, Saudi Arabia, Senegal, Serbia, Somalia, Sudan, Syria, Togo, Tunisia, Uganda, Ukraine, United Arab Emirates, Uzbekistan, Vanuatu, Vatican, and Vietnam.

In the case of Cambodia, we saw they quite willingly handed over Pirate Bay founder Gottfrid Svartholm to Sweden (though why he would want to live in Cambodia when Sweden prisons are this posh is another discussion).

We saw Edward Snowden run to Russia when the heat was on, catching a flight from Hong Kong and later requesting (and being granted) temporary asylum. We'll see if that pans out in the long term.

Fredrik 'Pirate Bay' Neij's country of choice was Laos, after being sentenced to a whopping one year in a Swedish prison and ordered to pay (gasp) $905,000 in "damages." Laos refused to hand him over. Later in November 2014, Neij was arrested on an Interpol warrant as he attempted to cross into Thailand.

Costa Rica may be another option. There have been a few high-profile cases of runners making it there but do your research beforehand. Know the differences in culture. Know the history of extraditions to your native country. Know how to get out fast if revolution starts. Everything safe costs money so you need to have a substantial savings and a portfolio that is diversified. This is so that no one bank can close your accounts over something like student loans and wipe you out.

Thailand

We left out Thailand in the above list. It's a nice place to run to escape problems. Just not *criminal* problems. Putting aside their extradition treaty with the U.S., for one you need to speak Thai to stay there long term. Forget about what you heard on an expat forum that you can "get by" with English. No matter where you are - Bangkok, Chiang Mai, Phukut, you need the language to get around because it's hard enough being a stranger in a strange land without expecting everyone to know sign language. This is the most glaring difference between Thailand and Philippines, with clothing being somewhat high priced.

Thailand Expenses

Rent is dirt cheap, with some places like Chiang Mai being cheaper than others. Bangkok is where most of the tourists hang out and for good reason. Better food than out in the provincial areas and far more reliable Internet. You can go to the website Numbeo.com to see a breakdown of just what you'd spend if you lived there. For 2015, this is what you'd likely be looking at:

Restaurants (average)
 Meal, Inexpensive Restaurant $1.48
 Meal for 2, Mid-range Restaurant, Three-course $17.81
 McMeal at McDonalds$4.45

Utilities (Monthly)
 Basic (Electricity, Heating, Water, Garbage) for Apartment $107.10
 1 min. of Prepaid Mobile (No Discounts or Plans) 0.04
 Internet (6 Mbps, Unlimited Data, Cable/ADSL) $18.82

Clothing
 1 Pair of Jeans (Levis 501) $84.48
 1 Summer Dress in a Chain Store (Zara, H&M, ...) $53.56
 1 Pair of Nike Running Shoes (Mid-Range) $102.00

Rent Per Month
 Apartment (1 bedroom) in City Center $589.57
 Apartment (1 bedroom) Outside of Center $318.34
 Apartment (3 bedrooms) in City Center $1,746.38

Two things jump out at me when viewing the costs. One is the price for a nice restaurant, obviously targeting out-of-towners. The other is clothing. Clothing there is similar to what you pay in Philippines for electronics. Very expensive for the average Thai, but there are ways around this since you don't have to buy name brands.

All in all, it's possible to live there on $600 USD per month, just not in style.

<u>Religion</u>

This is also in stark contrast to the West, as most Thais are Buddhist. Not only that, the King is considered a kind of sacred entity, a sort of messianic figure, the kind you don't want to cross. If you are in a theater and the king is visible, you'll be required to stand like we do when we salute the flag at a baseball game. Only in America this is totally optional. You can even burn the flag in the States. This confuses the average Thai like no other.

In 2008, a <u>woman</u> visiting Thailand refused to stand in respect to the king's image in a theater just before the film (The Other Boleyn Girl) began. Police had stated she appeared to be quite insane (Naturally only an insane person wouldn't bow or stand to a foreign king, right?)

That's not to say the Thais don't have a sense of humor, for in 2012, Thailand police introduced <u>Hello Kitty</u> armbands as a way to shame certain officers for showing up late or getting too many parking tickets. They discontinued this practice though when the world began to laugh (perhaps this was the whole point?)

That's just two examples of major differences that can cause problems if you don't know the culture. So immerse yourself in a few travel books or forums before you even think of going. You may inadvertently face a prison sentence for the crime of ignorance.

<u>China</u>

China is pretty big and easy to get lost in. Fortunately if you're dead set on running here, you won't have to worry about extradition treaties since mainland China has none with the U.S. This comes in handy for whistleblowers like Snowden who leak classified documents. <u>Hong Kong</u>, however is another matter.

For what it's worth, China can veto any extradition if it interferes with defense or public policy. It's all a bit murky to be honest. On a technical level, yes, Hong Kong has an extradition treaty with the U.S. but that was before Great Britain gave control of Hong Kong over to the mainland. In interviews, it's been crystal clear even Snowden felt this was just too much of a grey area to risk staying in the country long term. Not that he wanted to stay in Moscow since that was where he was when the passport got yanked (no pun).

Disappearing in China - The Good, The Bad, & The Ugly

This is easier said than done. It's easy to flee there, sure, but hard to disappear. Very hard. Americans abroad tend to acquire an affliction there ten times quicker than even in the Philippines. It's called "Rock Star" affliction. And once you've got it, it's brutally hard to get rid of since the celebrity factor alone hits your ego first. Any thoughts on being a humble little shepherd go out the window after a day or so off the plane.

Ethnic diversity isn't really as widespread in China as some westerners think. You will stick out like Big Bird if you are not Chinese, and if you are of the Dutch blonde hair/blue eyes variety of westerner, you'll be as visible as Big Bird would be traveling with those little green aliens from Toy Story. Believe it.

The picture taking is the most obvious. Cute at first, it will quickly grate on your nerves as many Chinese will ask you, "Take picture of my baby?" many times when you go out and about. Only after three or four of these in a week, you'll begin to suspect a conspiracy. Well, it sort of is. They like your *white skin*, for starters. You'll even get special attention by teenage schoolgirls who will try and spy on you while hoping their giggling girlfriends don't give them away as they twirl their Hello Kitty purses. More conservative areas will yield less obvious giggling (behind curtains instead of telephone poles), but the effect is the same: It's impossible to blend in without actually speaking Chinese and knowing Chinese culture.

Then come the questions. From everyone. In Japan they call them "Gaijin lovers" (foreigner lovers) and these nice yet quirky and strange beings will come up to you in Tokyo (or anywhere else in Japan) and launch wave after wave of data mining questions. In China this happens as regularly as the sun coming up. Again, cute at first but it quickly becomes an annoyance after the twentieth stranger comes up to you and asks:

- Is true all Americans own Glock like John Wayne?

- Is Texas like Seinfeld?

- You have beautiful wife yet? Our city offer you many pretty wives!

- Are alien UFO really in Nevada? (hint: Don't tell them it's in New Mexico)

- You has rose tattoo like all Americans, yes? I can see? (eyes your crotch)

- You has Hells Angels in family? Show photos! (begs you to take out wallet)

<u>Rudeness</u>

Now for some of the bad and the ugly.

This mainly applies to Hong Kong and other metro areas where the ancient god Mammon rules with an iron fist. Bare in mind that not every one is like this. Only a few rotten eggs that spoil it for everyone else. But like I said, when discussing rudeness and the Chinese with an Indian, Pakistani, African or Filipino, they in all likelihood will think of Hong Kong as number one on the list.

Deep breath.

The horking and spitting and public flatulence was bad enough, but worse than this was that few trash cans could be seen anywhere. If there were, I didn't see any (or maybe they're just too expensive). This is in stark contrast to Japan, where throwing your Coke can on the ground is seen as slapping the Prime Minister's face. Japanese love foreigners and they want as many visitors as possible. So for this reason their streets are sparkling clean.

In fact, you'd be hard pressed to even see garbage in a subway or even a busy city street in metro Tokyo.

But in China? Friend you don't know rudeness until you've been down a busy HongKong street at rush hour. Think New York is bad?

It's not. Hong Kong is like Seinfeld's "Bizarro World" where up is down and down is up and Superman is evil. And believe me when I say I'm no neat freak. But even I had expectations that had to be adjusted accordingly.

As you may have guessed at this point, rudeness make disappearing problematic. Americans, myself included, tend to go Wyatt Earp when confronted with rudeness overseas. This causes problems for anyone wanting to disappear because it draws massive attention to yourself. Thus, if there is one thing I learned, it's that when in HongKong, turn the cheek if at all possible.

A friend of mine relayed what he'd seen once on a weeknight at a high-end restaurant whereby the waiter, who was obviously nursing a hangover as he applied every other ice cold drink to his forehead in between taking orders, suddenly horked his lunch all over the floor. After cleaning it up, this waiter doesn't bother to go to the restroom to wash up! He simply took a mop to the floor, pushed the bucket back into the corner of the place and resumed taking orders with the same filthy hands he'd horked with. That's pretty tame, though next to other incidents I've heard.

In Hong Kong, the mad rush to earn money there is, well, maddening. Far more than even Wall Street exhibits. People ram right into you in Hong Kong in the middle of the street without blinking. They seem allergic to apologizing. They don't even blink if you slip and fall. They merely continue as if they were a couple of medics getting shot at on the beaches of Normandy and you're in the way. Foreigners have been almost run over by cabs that would've stopped or at least honked had it been New York.

Again, mostly in Hong Kong. Provincial areas are far more hospitable but even there you may find a woman saying you "are too fat" if you've been on a date with her. This isn't rudeness to them. It's just honesty.

COUNTERFEITING

Counterfeit items are everywhere in China. The Philippines unfortunately gets a lot of it sent to them because it's cheaper. Cheap shirts that rip in two weeks. Cheap Chinese electronics (phones, tablets, etc) that break within two months. Iphones that aren't Iphones. Hard drives that seem to have been made from twigs and fish bones that croak after a week of use.

Souvenirs as well are hit and miss. You'll see items sold in antique stores that cost far below what they'd really sell for if they were even 10% authentic. Statuettes fall into this category and it is easy to get suckered. They know how to replicate the look and feel of something old. Something dusty and archaic and webby. They may charge you $100 for something like a vase that they claim is from 8th century China. If that were the case, the price would be closer to ten grand. Not kidding. This goes on all over China, where counterfeit goods fool naive visitors every year. If you're going drop major cash on a statue, ensure it is appraised by someone you trust implicitly *before* laying your cash across the counter.

<u>The Disappearing Act</u>

As you can imagine, the cameras everywhere being pointed in your direction is catastrophic to anonymity. A disguise might prove embarrasing (and possibly attract the attention of law enforcement) if your mustache falls off in front of a crowd of gawking Chinese. They may whisper,

"Is he a spy?"

"Why did he dye his hair?"

"Why she feel need to wear a wig?"

"Should I tell someone?"

This in addition to the fact most of those photos may end up online somewhere. Nevertheless, here are some things you might consider. They've helped me whenever that 'Stranger in a Strange Land' feeling came over me.

I.) <u>Learn a basic level of Chinese</u> and they will forgive just about anything you do short of stealing nuclear launch codes. You can't travel incognito well without it anyway, so learn the basics of how to get around - how to rent cars, hotels, how to read maps, open a savings account, check into a B&B, order a steak at a restaurant... And try to be compassionate with Chinese culture. It is not rude for them to say "You're getting fat!" like it is in America. It's like saying, "You're a little sunburned" to someone Stateside. But it is *very* rude for a Chinese woman on a subway to mutter "hei gue" (black devil) to you if you're black. It's quite the catch-22 if you know Chinese and want to call her out publicly on it. If you do, chances are good her eyes will well up with tears and beg for your forgiveness.

II.) <u>Rock Star Status</u> gets old believe it or not. Read any interview with Steven Tyler or Garth Brooks and you'll see that even those heavyweights grow weary of it after awhile, as will you. To that, don't assume that since everyone is taking *your* picture that it's okay to take everyone *else's* picture. Keeping a low profile is okay but not to the extreme, which may arouse suspicion as well.

III.) <u>Talk With Your Hands</u> - If you don't speak Chinese, don't shoot a pic of a local Chinese guy without doing some sign language to ask first (point to him, then to the camera, then smile).

IV.) <u>Be assertive and say NO</u> when necessary. Learn how to say it in Mandarin and learn not to worry about hurting their feelings. Some Chinese students once asked to snap a picture of me because I am 6'2 and have vampire-white skin (this was just outside the French Quarter near the St. Louis Cathedral). I calmly told them my vampire clan would be upset if they ever found out I was walking around in the daytime since it was against the clan's rules, and likely come after who shot the picture. Their eyes grew as big as dinner plates.

"Vampires?! Ooh!"

Snap. Snap. Snap. Snap.

CIA MANIPULATION AND DISAPPEARING

Jason Bourne and James Bond are a bit of a joke to CIA agents. Unrealitsic is being too kind. If agents had half of the gadgets Bond uses, their offices would be filled with resumes from every city in the U.S. But to the rest of us normal guys, there's nothing funny about Bond being sliced in half by a laser or Brosnan resurrecting his heart-beat (Die Another Day).

Well, maybe the latter. A little.

They're spies we want to emulate, fair enough, but sadly a lot of methods of disappearing into thin air don't translate well from the silver screen to reality. In fact, the real deal is often quite different.

What you see in True Lies and the Bourne movies that gets the bad guys usually ends up with a CIA agent shaking his head in the theater. It's just not done that way. Not usually. In the past, CIA techniques relied on deception - deceiving the target's mind with psychology - false trails, leads, and lies, lies, lies, but that's less common today. These days it is about intense networking and analyzing and tracing and focusing, getting as much data as you can and all while being as quiet as a church mouse. Boring stuff for James Cameron and Michael Bay.

Yes, you do learn a lot of survival techniques that, for a few moments, might resemble something Bond did on a bad hair day in Madrid, but it's rare. And if it comes down to you chasing a terrorist mastermind through traffic while riding a horse that leads you to the top of the Marriott, well, forget it. You're beyond sloppy. The visibility factor alone would make world headlines. Attention whoring x 1000 = Mission Failed.

Manipulation Tactics

Back when I ran online ad campaigns (my first business failure), I manipulated people left and right without even realizing it. Every day.

I'd fire up CPV Lab on my server and spend (and lose) thousands running ads for affiliate companies like Neverblue and Clickbank while buying traffic from TrafficVance and LeadImpact. Not cheap, but once I split-tested two ads enough to see my sales skyrocket, I was *hooked*. This was effective manipulation. Giving people what (they think) they need in exchange for something I *wanted*: a nice income stream.

Corporations do this all the time. Sears. Target. Wal-Mart. Best Buy. They're artists at it. But what you find works in the USA might not work in Canada. Just ask Target.

Point being? Don't hesitate to manipulate if it's required to keep you invisible. A good CIA agent will have zero problems with manipulation if it means it will push the mission objective *forward* - that is, one step closer to completion. Best Buy does this, and they have pretty atrocious pricing on many items, not the least of which is the worthless extended warranty they pressure you into buying.

So why do more people shop there instead of a smaller PC repair shop? The answer is manipulation, and it isn't that different than what the secretive CIA does. This doesn't mean you have to be a brown-noser. Just know how to manipulate without giving valuable intel about your past away.

<u>Forging Allies</u>

The CIA does not like to make pure enemies. They like to make *allies*. They like to forge alliances. To this end, they spend tons of money on operations that find common ground with pseudo-enemies and accelerate common goals. Suppress the bad and elevate the good, which they hope will turn into a nice, flowery friendship.

Then they send in spies.

The Soviets liked to do it this way, only they employed far more evilness in the implementation of it all. Subversion was the name of their game. Specifically, subversion tactics to undermine the *stability* of a country. The moral fabric if you will. You know, kill patriotism or any kind of idealism that could unify a country against outside enemies. It really mattered little what it was that got under people's skin as long as it drove them to fight each other, and that was good enough.

The KGB defector <u>Yuri Bezmenov</u> relayed this expertly and perhaps as ominously as Jonah did to the inhabitants of Ninevah, but with compassion and a dire warning to the West. Manipulation and deceit are the tools of darkness. Devastatingly effective yet as dangerous to deploy as a suitcase nuke. Eventually, things start falling apart.

He laid it out like a strategic battle plan at Midway in his "Love Letter to America," how everything the KGB did to undermine western democracy and freedom as you know it was put above all else. The interview (from 1983) is quite telling and even shocking in some parts of the telling of it, how the Russians would invite every diplomat to mother Russia, get them drunk, plastered, pickled and primed for a lie, then paint a rosy picture of how pretty and flowery Russia was, both the people and her politicians.

Only it wasn't.

Prisons were turned into nurseries overnight. Spies and liars tricked every reporter that came around shooting for LIFE and Time. Magazine spreads portrayed the entire country as victims of the evil

U.S. capitalistic empire, yet Russia bore it all like a messiah wearing a crown of thorns, with smiling faces and vigorous "happy" handshakes living under the benevolent Soviet government.

And we know how that story ended. The Soviet Union broke up. The lesson, I believe, for anyone contemplating disappearing in a free country, is this:

Have Ethics. Have a moral base and keep your manipulation tactics sane so that, Heaven forbid you are caught red-handed, you won't be strung up from the nearest tree by your compatriots. Not to sound too preachy here but, God is watching, after all, and sees what lies in a man's heart. Things that cannot be legislated. Sew your relationships to your advantage, certainly, but don't sacrifice your soul to do so.

HOW THE NSA FINDS ANYONE

Your physical location is easy to track if you're predictable. To that, most of us are. Maybe 90% of us.

Think about it. We wake up at the same hour and place most days. Wear the same style of clothes every season. Shop at the same retail outlets. Visit the same places come Memorial Day. Date the same type of people even if they aren't our dream dates (for me, redhead librarians with glasses). Married people? Forget it. You're not getting off the NSA radar without good security.

Cell Towers

Cell phone grids are a bit like computers in that they need to know *where you are* in order to "talk" to you. Networked computers, too, need IP addresses. Without 'em, there's *zero* communication since it has nowhere to send the data packets. Same with cell networks. Cell geolocation is required to send you your stuff; Skype, emails, Warcraft pings. Doesn't really matter what kind it is, but know this: The NSA prefers you favor convenience over security since breaching security is harder for them. If massive numbers of people put convenience above security, well that's all the more power in their hands. They win, you lose.

But triangulation is really nothing new. It's just that now they've refined it, looped it, hacked it and mangled it in such a way that it's now intertwined with emergency services. Case in point: you're a hiker whose dog gets stuck in a cliff crevice with no way back up. Remember what Ben Franklin said about liberty and security?

"Those who sacrifice a little liberty for security deserve neither."

And no two ways about it. It's easy-peasy for the NSA to tap your private data either by listening in or CEO-inked backroom deals (Verizon). At any rate it's pretty darn easy for them to narrow their scope to a particular GSM phone given the number of towers everywhere. From their lips to your eyes:

"GSM Cell Towers can be used as a physical-geolocation point in relation to a GSM handset of interest."

They also use drones.

DRONES (AND HOW TO DEFEAT THEM)

Above, a U.S. Customs Patrol Drone.

If you're trekking across the border and wondering whether or not you'll see a drone 20,000 feet up, chances are you won't. It isn't just the sheer height of the blasted things that are the problem. It's how easily Mother Nature tends to obscure their flight patterns with clouds, fog, and thunderstorms, making any anti-drone technology an exercise in frustration. This in addition that they fly soundless. Silent killers in the night sky. How would you know a twinkling star from one flying overhead?

But fear not, there are a few measures we can deploy, er *employ*.

1.) <u>Sensor Disruption</u> - Any technology with sensors needs to see the target it's trying to capture. So give it a dose of it's own medicine: lasers. Ever wonder why a kid with a laser-pointer gets a visit from the FBI when he points it at the cockpit of a 747 flying overhead? Right - the laser disrupts not only the instruments onboard but the visibility of the pilots. Blind pilots cannot fly straight nor can they read their navigation systems. Same with drones, and though pilotless, have cameras that relay images to a set of human eyeballs. The downside of course is that you make it all too obvious that you're not some kid with the kitty's laser-pointer.

2.) <u>Hacking</u> - This is far easier said than done. It used to be that drones could be hacked just as flight navigation systems on a 747 can be hacked, but it's harder to do now with encryption. The movie Interstellar goofed. Matthew McConaughey's character (with his daughter's help) hack into a drone flying overhead from years ago. Only it looks all too easy because there is no encryption to hack past. Years prior to the film's release, <u>North Korea and Iran</u> both claimed to have downed drones using hacking techniques whereby they "spoof" the GPS signal and, as irony would have it, send it on a suicidal death spiral.

3.) <u>EMP Pulse</u> - The problem with this is that even if you could create this by yourself, the pulse cares not a whit about your own electronic equipment or grid. So it'd be like shooting yourself in the foot. Actually, worse. Recall the MAD tactic (mutually assured destruction) Trinity used in The Matrix just as the A.I machines were drilling into the Morpheus' ship: The Nebuchadnezzar, with Neo and Morpheus still jacked in. She hit the switch and fried every bot but left her ship defenseless. They all lived, however, an in the end it may just come to that for us.

4.) <u>Counter-Drones</u> - This requires downed drones, of course, unless you manufacture your own. Set these drones to survey the skies for unfriendlies and scan and identify via encryption keys the same way that PGP users do over the internet. The issue of course is that the enemy can see these just as you can see theirs... unless you've got decoys set up to give off fake heat signatures.

5.) <u>Occupy The High Ground</u> - For this to work you'd need teams specially trained and camouflaged to lookout for drones all day, all night, armed with microwave-type weaponry. The microwave itself

You'd also need powerful scopes to distinguish a drone from a plane which is not discernable to the naked eye even from high up. As well, noise-sensors would be required that detect the low-hum engine noise from a drone, assuming of course you knew the make/model of said drone.

6.) <u>Camouflage</u> - No I don't mean like the Ghillie suit used in Call of Duty 4, but rather the natural camouflage given by large structures. Shadows, bridges covered in vines, that sort of thing. Just remember that traveling at night is risky no matter what you're wearing since the drone will detect your heat signature anyway. Better to stick to tunnels, under bridges, railroad tracks and moving building to building, cover to cover as a disguise had other uses. This is of course assuming you know how to travel incognito as you might be in enemy territory. If you can blend in with what the drone considers 'non-adversaries', then it will not be able to distinguish between you and Vladmir. The downside is if that drone is using facial recognition tech, whereby they can match your face with what they have on file. If you're a wanted man, better wear a hood, makeup, beard or whatever you need to look thinner or fatter than you really are. That also goes for your voice. Learn accents because advanced Voice DNA technology is willing and able to turn you in.

7.) <u>Radar</u> - This is the expensive option. But at thirty thousand feet, you're not going to see a drone without expensive equipment and if you're dropping money like Ebenezer Scrooge, well you might as well go all the way.

Even if you were to step outdoors and see a trail from a jet liner, it will be as a tiny sliver even on a clear, sunny day. Rain and fog? Forget it. So you need radar installations that are secret enough to evade enemy detection but close enough to see the enemy. Quite the catch-22. Detecting the drone is easier than detecting it anonymously. There are CO_2 infrared lasers you can buy from various internet outlets.

8.) <u>Civilian Patriots</u> - Obvious perhaps, as there are over a million gun owners in North America, but it is unlikely that drones will be turned against the populace en masse anytime soon since they must be rearmed and refueled, and a patriotic force would seize this opportunity to string the pilots up from the nearest tree. And believe me, they would find them *quickly*.

But drone *spying* is different than a drone *firing*. And in the end, perhaps that is really all they want - to launch a hundred thousand drones to spy on everyone without ever firing a shot, because when you know where someone is 24/7, what restaurant they eat at, what ballgames they attend and whether they put their ketchup on top of their fries or on the side, well, they don't really need to fire from the skies, do they?

ONLINE FOOTPRINTS

The NSA collects IP addresses like ants collect food. It's a nice analogy, isn't it? They store whatever they can get, usually from apps that bypass security and provide you with convenience. Apple and Samsung made their fortunes this way - convenience above all. Thus many phone apps not only send your IP address which is correlated with Facebook and Skype, but your login **locations**--cafes, libraries, etc., with the times you did. Thus everyone's digital fingerprint is stored. Well, most people's. If you're one of the ones that are tracked, read on, because we're about to put a stop to that nonsense.

Fortunately, an IP address is not a person *yet*. On that topic, ask yourself this: how might their power be enhanced if everyone did have their own unique number, say like those in Germany, 1938? To login? To send email? To play online games?

I walked into a free WiFi on a trip to California a few years back. A few kids had managed to play World of Warcraft despite the posted rules of NO GAMING during school hours. Well, the NSA certainly knows which games their playing, and who played them at which hour if they decide to go the subpoena route. This is how the NSA finds people who want to disappear.

People on the run forget the digital trail they've already established for years. The NSA hasn't. Sites you've visited. Calls you've made. Friends you've unfriended. They know about them all. So if you want to put an end to this, you must forge a **new identity** that muddles up the former digital *you*.

And no, turning off the cell won't help. Neither will popping out the SIM because the NSA already has the network map for that WiFi area. The only exception to this would be if you were in Syria. Here is <u>animation</u> that shows how the NSA accomplishes this. Just bear in mind it's quite old by NSA standards so they've no doubt refined it by now.

Perhaps it's too axiomatic these days that I, like my colleagues, love free stuff. And also how we love *free services!* The price we pay, however, is our freedom and our privacy. Avoid them like the Black Plague if you require anonymity.

Bin Laden's Courier

Sheikh Abu Ahmed was not an easy man to find. The CIA spent a year tracking him down, and Bin Laden's rule of no calls or laptops made it all the more difficult. So difficult in fact, that they had to rely on getting intel out of prisoners.

The big break, however, came in 2010 when Ahmed broke Bin Laden's rule by talking about him on, you guessed it, a *cell phone*. Intelligence agencies were already monitoring who he was talking to. When Bin Laden's name came up, the call led them straight to the Pakistani town called Abbottabad.

You probably know the rest.

Soon thereafter, Navy SEALs stormed the compound with 18 foot walls and barbed wire. They were in and out in under 40 minutes and met little resistance. There were no guards or schedules. No guard dogs. No field of tripmines and no Barrett .50 caliber guns to worry about. Not much in the way of fortification that couldn't be easily defeated with a moderately trained infantry. Or a sledgehammer in the case of one SEAL.

The takeaway here is that you don't want to draw attention to yourself by being loud. If you want to truly disappear, don't be a bar braggart. Bin Laden, for all his demonic activity, had this part right. C4 is loud. Mines are suicidal. Tripwires can kill your own and sentry guards are visible from the sky. They're also notoriously loose-lipped as they gossip to kill time.

Despite knowing all this, I watched Zero Dark Thirty expecting the worst. I facepalmed several times due to how loud the actors playing the Navy SEALs were.

"Shut up you fools or someone'll hear! Stop chattering!"

Bin laden was smart. Prime evil, but smart.

Chatter breaks anonymity faster than a maggot spoils rotten meat, and sometimes Hollywood gets it wrong. Those SEALS (the real ones) knew how to be silent. In fact it's the very thing they do best. They'd prefer to get in and out and *then* blow the place sky high... as they're running to the beach.

If there is one thing that will put a silver bullet in your disappearing act, it's blabbing about your old life.

"I sure showed the IRS! Those turkeys won't bother me ever again!" you say just a little too loudly in Bangkok, piquing the interest of a former IRS tax agent a few stools down.

Bottom line: You should value your new identity as though it were your life, because, well, it is. Treat it as such. Loose lips and all.

Restrict Physical Access

Never trust anyone with your laptop overseas. If you loan it out, ensure you're there as they use it.

Inside your laptop lies the heart and soul of your business. Break it off with a vengeful Thai girl and she can do a lot more than just the battery-acid-to-the-face on the other girl. She can **ruin** you. Thus, you must encrypt your operating system. You needn't go as far as Bin Laden did and avoid laptops altogether, but you need to be aware that comfort breeds mistakes, and costly ones at that.

If you're a freelancer, an author, or just have an online side hustle, guard your passwords and pen names like they were the keys to Heaven itself. Never give too many details, especially to strangers. Last thing you want is a string of bad (fake) reviews from every one of her Thai brothers calling you a white hot ball of canine terror who plagiarizes and eats freckled pigtailed girls.

Want to stay invisible? Don't give out your last name.

Preserve Your Reputation

Ever watch Game of Thrones? I did, right up until they offed poor Ned at the end of Season 1. But a line from Tyrell stuck with me: A Lannister always pays his debts. So should you. And no I don't mean your student loans. I mean debts to friends and family and other alliances, other businesses. Local, unpaid debts make enemies *fast*. Enemies can poor a can of puke-yellow paint all over your invisibility act. Imagine poor Bilbo standing there in front of all those guests covered in yellow goop.

Cut Them Loose

This means cutting loose someone who is unstable and detrimental to your stability - the same stability you worked hard to obtain. Financially unstable people tend to borrow without asking. Mentally unstable people tend to embarrass and stalk until you until your house is burning down to the riff of Ozzy.

This requires saying no. In some cases it requires *firing* someone in your life who makes a lot of noise flapping their gums (remember Bin Laden's courier?). A maid with sticky fingers, too, can be catastrophic, but still easier to fire than your live-in girlfriend. Better to suffer a bruised ego for a day than lose a business... and clients.

When I dated a filipina in Dumaguete, it was expected of me to bring a gift to her brother's birthday party. She wanted me to buy him an Ipad. I nearly choked to death on my cashews.

"Can't you afford it?" she slyly asked. "Sure can. But I'm not your white ATM," I sternly replied.

I hurt her feelings, true enough, but spared myself the expense of buying all her relatives electronic gadgets that cost $300-400 per item on all future social engagements. Later I found this to be common no matter where one is in the Philippines. They all think you're rich if you are there since a plane ticket costs an arm and a leg.

Yep, if you can pay a grand for a ticket to Asia, you're rich buddy. Bill Gates rich.

Risky Friendships

When you are a stranger in a strange land, it can be tempting to accept any and all friendships that fall into your lap. You've got a shiny new identity. You feel more alive than ever before. No debts. No criminal past. No angry ex looking to string you up from the nearest tree if you don't fork over two grand by the end of the month.

Then you meet someone at a convention and offer a beer after you forge a connection. He smiles with a row of perfect teeth. Nods and hmms and offers expert marketing advice. You think, "Gee, this guy appears to be intelligent and business-minded. I like him. Could make for a decent business partner."

After all, you could always use more clients as a digital nomad, right? Only later you find out he runs a tranny dating website for Thais and wants you to "meet someone to discuss better ways to attract clientele."

I'm sure you know the risks of such a scenario.

SNOWDEN'S MISTAKES

Edward Snowden. He's an interesting character study as to how far a single man will go on ethics alone. Here was a guy who gave up a six-figure salary, his U.S. citizenship, and stoked the fury of the very powerful U.S. elite in leaking classified NSA documents. Whether you agree or disagree with the traitor label John Boehner spat his way on CNN and FoxNews, I believe we can agree on one thing:

It took brass balls to do what Snowden did.

He had insisted from the very beginning that he believed the NSA's surveillance programs to be in violation of the U.S. Constitution, and that the people who founded that Constitution ought to know about them. Nothing good, he said, ever came from keeping tax-funded programs in the dark from the taxpayers themselves. They needed to *know*, one way or another, what their money was funding and who was responsible.

No one knows, me included, what a future Congress is capable of, and the fact that future Congresses can *change* laws at will is an immense power that needs balance. Simple concept, right? Only nothing is simple when our congress critters are in session, and I've no doubt that the Weimar Republic had their own data collecting scheme in place long before Hitler came on the scene.

There exists a lot of risk in trusting the future to government. Blackmail. Selling our data to foreign enemies in exchange for prisoners. Becoming lax with security to the point that hackers can infiltrate systems that we were assured were secure (Obamacare, the IRS, etc.).

Moscow was never a co-conspirator with Snowden, nor were they part of his plan. He first flew to Hong Kong, then to Cuba, but by the time he was in layover Russia his U.S. passport had been nuked by, well, who knows what person gave that first order but I'd bet it was someone very high in the chain of command in Washington D.C.

He said,

"I did this to give the American people a chance to decide for themselves what type of government they want to have. That is a conversation that I think the American people deserve to decide."

Putting reasoning aside, what can we learn about what to NOT do when we decide to disappear?

Mistake #1: Moscow

It was WikiLeaks founder Julian Assange that provided for Snowden's stay in Hong Kong, even recommending that he not go to South America on account of the physical danger to himself. Not that the place is paradise since the general instability of the area makes for a miserable experience in a lot of cities, cartels included.

So as luck would have it, he ended up in Russia when his passport was yanked.

And it isn't even what Snowden *said* that is most appealing to the Russians. Rather, it's what he did not say - those unwritten, unspoken matrix of secrets that are a veritable *gold mine* for Russian Intelligence. It's a good bet that if Washington ever offers him a plea deal and allows him back on American soil, we will see the same stalling behavior we saw with Putin's decision. They'll not give him up so easily. Quite the catch-22.

Mistake #2: One Passport

With the kind of security clearance Edward had, getting a second passport in a country friendly to the United States should have been easy peasy. Yes, said country would certainly have handed him over, but not without at least a delay that might have granted him more time. The U.S. government will know it if you do, but it is not a foregone conclusion that they would be revoked simultaneously. If that were the case, we'd all be living under One Government by now (Thank Heaven for small miracles).

Mistake 3: Facetime

Facetime kills anonymity quicker than anything else. This nail in the coffin had a two prong effect: The first being that of honesty. Snowden could address the American public without there being any doubt to the validity of his identity. If he'd stayed anonymous, he'd have always struggled with proving who he was and that his words rung true.

The mistake of course comes in on that second effect: The FBI now knew his face. Eventually the NSA would have nailed him even if he hadn't gone public, but it might have given him more time since Snowden's appeal could very well have dragged out any extradition request.

Takeaway: Don't flee to a country that will do you more harm than the country you are fleeing *from*. True, we see Edward as living a somewhat normal, if modest life in that sprawling ex-Soviet country... but that life may one day be short lived.

When the dust settles, and the interviews by comedians cease, and we no longer hear of Snowden or WikiLeaks, we might just have missed the disappearing act of Putin deciding to be a little more forceful in gaining access to that vault of secrets between Edward's ears. Don't let that be you.

DEFEATING FACIAL RECOGNITION TECHNOLOGY

I'm not Spiderman, and I'd wager you're not Quicksilver from the X-Men (mutant kid who can run 200mph and push bullets around like Skittles).

Let's be honest for a moment. I don't care for the government using much of any kind of facial-scan technology to measure how many steps it takes me to go to the gym or if I'm whistling a copyrighted tune out of my backside after eating a bowl of Chocolate Frosted Sugar Bombs.

Nor can I (legally, anyway) take a double-bladed axe to all of the traffic cams in the city where I live. So what *can* I do? What can *you* do?

First off, let's not panic since we have some credible legal options. Let's also discuss what it is and what it is not and where it is going to be a decade out.

Facial recognition is not Star Trek technology, nor is it a perfect way to spot a kidnapper or merely spy on Uncle Frick. And rest assured that for the rest of us, there are flaws that can be exploited. When you hear about facial recognition technology such as that used by social networks, what they really refer to is the techniques used to identify a photo or a moving face in a reel of film. The algorithms target spacial differences and anomalies along your face: how far the chin protrudes, how far the eyes are apart, the biometrics of the ears and so forth. Does she have Asian features? Russian cheekbones and nose? Indonesian lips? There are almost a hundred nodes along a human face for an algorithm to work with. That doesn't sound so bad.

Only the bad news is that it only takes 20 or so nodes relative to a man or woman's face to be identified. If a satellite can identify a person's brand of shoe from low orbit, you can imagine how easy it would be to size up a person's face and match that with a database.

The good news is that even mathematical algorithms can be tricked. Take Google for example. Google spends billions on its algorithms and much less on its programmers, which coincidentally happen to be some of the best on Earth, yet it is often simple techniques blackhat marketers use to fool the engine into thinking data is relevant when it really isn't. A false positive, to say. Google coders adapt the code. The blackhatters catch on. Word spreads around the hive mind and they adapt as well.

<u>Look At Your Feet</u>

Alex Kilpatrick is a facial-recognition expert and research leader at the TIS (Tactical Info Systems) in Texas. He did an <u>interview</u> for the BBC where he talked about simple ways to defeat these systems. One being: Look at your feet. This obscures your identity in ways the cameras can't account for. And yes, you guessed right if you said the homeless have the advantage here.

When I was a student at Loyola University in New Orleans, donating my plasma kept my belly full on a few hard months as I awaited the arrival of my student loan check. Lots of students did this. Selling plasma was like selling gold when you were starving and I could think of a lot of other bodily fluids that might prove embarrassing to sell.

Well as fate would have it, I had to bus it down to the plasma center once when my car engine went kaput. Buses in New Orleans were something I absolutely *dreaded.* I had to walk a block or so down Canal Street, aka Bum Central. It was an educational walk.

But it was no short walk. And I recall bringing my psychology book along on the RTA route to kill time. I'd occasionally look up, grinning at how in sync the bums and winos walks would be: Jazzy yet almost in tune with each other.

You've seen it no doubt... Head down over a long beard, shotglass of bourbon and swaggering. I came to admire them for their stealthy way of blending into the trashy panoramic atmosphere. The entire street had several theaters back then and I'd see them hawk and hork and spit and panhandle and all the while barely raising their eyes to speak to honest Johns. Some of them even wore sunglasses.

Sunglasses Don't Work

Perhaps a few bums wanted to be trendy bums. But the problem with wearing shades in order to fool surveillance cams is that the algorithm will simply ignore that section of your face and focus more intensely on other parts of it. In fact I'd say judging from the research done by the Chinese on facial recognition systems, it doesn't matter how big the glasses are, either.

Obnoxious Clothing DOES Work

If you've got a few articles of clothing with pictures of other people's faces on it, that will disrupt the algorithm in the same way billboards disrupt Google Earth's Street View algorithm that tries to smear real people's faces on the street for privacy.

Clothing like this:

Or this:

You don't necessarily need to go with a "face shirt" either, but the image below is probably a stretch for society to accept:

Helmets

Speaking of what society tolerates and what it doesn't, a beard and hat disguise is probably better than wearing a helmet for too long. A friend of mine remarked that he wears a full-face helmet whenever he rides a Ninja. Keeps the bugs out of his hair, he says, but when he tries to pump gasoline while wearing it, the gas attendant won't turn on the pumps until he takes it *off*.

Well, no wet-behind-the-ears teenager is going to tell him what to do, so off he goes to another gas station. An Exxon this time. The end result: Same thing. He found out that the owners of these gas stations like to have a biker's face on the camera in case the police come by asking about a kidnapped little girl.

IR LEDs

Remember that what facial recognition systems zero-in on is *relative triangles*, such as the tip of your nose to the bottom of your chin and over to your ears, or from your chin to your forehead and over to your eyes. You're unique in this way just as your fingerprints are unique. No two people are the same.

But an IR LEDs will disrupt this greatly. We discussed laser pointers disrupting instruments on jets. Well the same principle applies here, and I predict this will find its way into our clothing styles in the coming years whether we like it or not, depending on how invasive Big Brother's systems become in the next decade.

The downside is that it doesn't work unless everyone is doing it since by using this you will clearly stand out on a monitor. Some celebrities used to wear/use these to discourage the paparazzi whenever they'd come sniffing. It was set off by a camera flash and the results were not quite what they'd hoped.

Then again, the antivirus company AVG is reportedly working on so-called "invisibility glasses" that thwart facial software altogether. It uses LEDs that move around the eyes and nose which distort any images the system takes for the purpose of recognizing you.

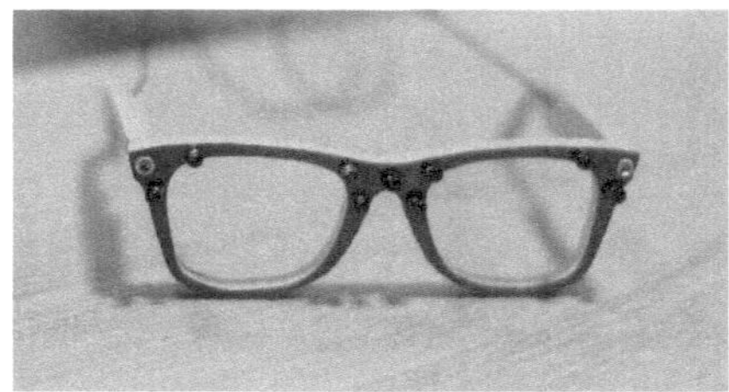

Unfortunately it's only in the beginning stages at this point, but I believe this is only the tip of the iceberg. Can Frodo's elvish cloak be far behind?

College Dorms

These are the absolute *worst* for privacy. At Loyola University during my junior year, I as well as every other resident of the Cabra Hall residence had to show our IDs every single time we entered to the desk attendant. It didn't matter if we'd spoken to said attendant a thousand times that day or (heaven forbid) we were related to her. Neither did it matter if we swiped the card without an error.

Nope. Every single time we walked through the front double-steel doors to that fortress of doom, we got the "Papers please!" spiel.

Only one time the grad student behind the dusty counter caught me on a bad day after a hard rain and a failed calculus test, and I refused. For a nanosecond I even considered flipping her off. But no, that'd too rude even for me as well as granting her that power of attention she craved. So I just walked right by her as though I'd swallowed an invisibility potion.

She didn't like that, and the next time I came around at dinnertime about 7 o'clock, she lashed out at me with a few insults she'd brewed in my absence. Not only that, her face changed right before my eyes, going from conservative librarian girl with glasses and cinnamon latte to a gorgon's daughter looking for fresh meat.

That was it. I got pretty steamed myself and so I frisbeed the ID at her like that feral kid with the boomerang in Road Warrior - so fast I thought it'd put her eye out. It struck her forehead dead center before flipping away, over her desk and down her arm and into her bookbag. Next thing I knew I'm in the resident manager's office justifying my terrorist-like actions. But more shocking than this was that he had my midterm grades on a Matrix-green computer screen in front of him.

I didn't enjoy sitting it out a semester.

CHARTING A NEW COURSE

It could be that you want to disappear for non-criminal reasons. You don't have any debt. You simply want to get away to start a new chapter in life. Wipe the soul-draining high school slate clean and build anew. Become a French artist. Maybe a trainer of wind surfers in Bora Bora, watching fire dancers twirl flame every night as the sun sinks down while three filipinas you've never met are eying you up and down from the water.

Maybe you want to be a boat tour guide in the Philippines that brings all the newly minted expats out to see the whale feedings while exotic filipinas coo over your white skin (I saw with my own eyes how obsessed filipinas are with with this - entire aisles in pharmacies filled with skin-whitening products.)

Or maybe something more daredevilish... An acrobat (the net alone would kill me).

Memories often make the man, but if you get rid of the things, that is, the settings, the people, the jobs, the polluted air, that miserable dragon-breathing boss named Winona who works in HR, well you just have no idea *what* gifts await you on the other side. Just do it.

It's not the things we did in life that we regret on our death beds, but the things we never took up. Those procrastinations that we kept waving back into the horizon, over and over, never **taking action**. Forever leaving it to *some other guy* to step out of the safe zone.

When I lived in a small town in Louisiana many years ago, I kept running into old girlfriends. Old high school chums. Old sluts. Old memories that dragged me down like the girl I'd never asked out who was now the woman in the red dress, a wall survivor now hitched to the mayor.

Life's little moments like these made a habit of creeping up on me like a flow of lava does a small sleepy town in Hawaii. Moments that I never thought I'd be reminded of day in, day out, slowly devouring me like lava embers do straw huts. Slow at first, warm before the embrace, but when the hit, well... They melt any sense of adventure.

So I made a break for a clean slate. First to Canada, then to SE Asia.

Don't just *dream* about the clean slate. **Take action**. Meditating on your dreams, as I've discovered, can actually prevent them from becoming reality. It's suboptimal to meditate on the end results - You sipping margaritas in Bora Bora. That only works if you meditate on taking active steps towards making the dream happen in the first place. So don't meditate on the end-result...You must visualize yourself *working toward the dream*, mixing the reagents that, when all is said and done, is powerful enough to give you wings.

Are you a writer? Visualize yourself writing at the keyboard, banging out five thrilling novels per year, or making six figures by building an insanely good client base as a copywriter.

AFTERWORD

A tough question I repeatedly asked myself when I was overseas was this: Am I still the same person in Dumaguete that I was in New Orleans? What about Toronto, Canada?

I mean I acted the same, very laid back and easy to approach, almost too easy now that I think about it. I ate the same - a good Mexican restaurant with cheese enchiladas and salsa with a side of guacamole with Blue Bell Homemade Vanilla ice cream for dessert. I even smelled the same - Midnight and Noir cologne since the day they arrived.

Though no Mardi Gras or beignets were anywhere to be found in the Phils, I still believed in the same God. I'd not really disappeared so much as just teleported, I feared, just as Nightcrawler did in so many comics, escaping doom.

Truly becoming invisible, I found, involved throwing out old grudges, grudges that rot the spirit and the mind. Grudges, I later found, that not only cause ulcers but rot any sense of risk or adventure. We're explorers and we don't like being anchored too far from shore without a rowboat. We like safety. We like security. But sometimes you must throw caution to the wind and swim for it completely naked... yes, even with sharks lurking about. And it is this unknown (How many sharks? What kind? Meat-o-sauruses?) that keeps so many would-be explorers at bay.

The key to overcoming your fear is courage. Well, that and a little imagination.

Envision yourself as someone else, say, a storyteller like Bilbo Baggins, tired of the retched relatives squawking like harpies over who gets what if he croaks one midsummer night. Bilbo the wanderer. Bilbo the *explorer*.

You have sufficient gold to navigate every hillside, every culture, every dragon's den. You can visit South Korea and meet the most beautiful people on Earth and all with a clean slate since no one knows of your mistakes. Where every moment is now, where you are invisible, yet visible. Tokyo, Thailand, Philippines, it's all yours for the taking. Your new face will go a long way in those parts of the world.

So go and take action to make it real!

CONCLUSION

First off, I owe you a big thanks for downloading this book. You could have picked any one of dozens of great books on this topic and you took a chance with mine. So thank you for that. Reading to the end of any technical book takes prowess and due diligence - and a strong mind.

You can now stay cloaked, go dark and tell the elites to get stuffed in your sleep!

But that's not all. You now possess digital clairvoyance, that sixth sense called a gut-check and an enhanced one at that. Whereas before was little more than a rusty sword, it is now a double-bladed lightsaber. You'll spot others looking to fill tyranny's place when they come calling and call they will because no galaxy ever tolerates a vacuum. You'll spot those taffers a mile away.

If you enjoyed this book, please let others know by writing a good review. I'm but a indie church mouse lighting the path for others in these dark times and it would help me a lot if you could spread the word. It really does make a difference!

God Bless and Keep You Safe on Your Journey!

Coming Soon:
Burners & Black Markets 2
Superhackers
Dark Linux